W9-BWL-817

Discover
Glacier National Park

Glacier National Park is the undisputed "Crown of the Continent." Its glaciers accent steep arêtes where mountain goats walk like acrobats. Acres of lush green parklands plunge down jagged red pinnacles, exposing some of the world's oldest stones. Waterfalls roar, ice cracks, and rockfall echoes in scenery still under the paintbrush of change.

In this rugged one million acres, indigenous grizzly bears and wolves top the food chain. Wolverines romp in high glacial cirques. Bighorn sheep graze in alpine meadows while pikas shriek nearby. Only two animals present in Lewis and Clark's day are missing: woodland caribou and bison.

The Continental Divide splits Glacier into a west and east side — both different in character, yet wrought from the same geologic building blocks that scratch the sky. Two Wild and Scenic Rivers splash along park boundaries, converging at 3,150 feet while six peaks top 10,000 feet. Mount Cleveland stretches the highest, its north face one of the tallest vertical walls in the United States.

Slicing through the park's heart, the historic Going-to-the-Sun Road twists and turns on a narrow cliff climb. Tunnels, arches, and bridges lead sightseers over precipices where no road seemingly could go. Views of ice abraded, glacially scooped valleys; thundering cascades; mammoth lakes; and serrated peaks make uttering "wow" never enough.

Glacier snakes more than 700 trail miles through remote wilderness.

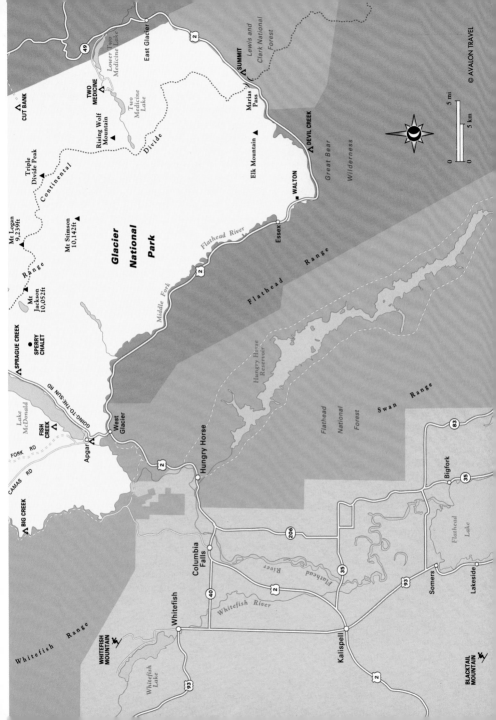

Contents

Hikers prance up verdant valleys, shimmy beneath frigid waterfalls, and crawl over high passes. Peak panoramas and blue-green lakes string like pearls along trails in places of solitude.

Designated a Biosphere Reserve and World Heritage Site, Glacier corrals a rich diversity of wildlife and a wealth of natural attributes. The park not only holds ancient geological secrets, but for centuries provided sacred lands for Native Americans. Combined with Waterton Lakes National Park in Canada, Glacier is the world's first International Peace Park.

As the Crown of the Continent, the park's glaciers fuel North America's major rivers, with water tumbling to Hudson Bay, the Atlantic, and the Pacific. But as the park celebrated its centennial in 2010, ecologists bumped the predicted death of the park's namesake glaciers to 2020 – a change that will repaint the scenery once again.

Glacier preserves some of the nation's wildest country. Welcome to this rugged slice of nature's best.

Planning Your Trip

▶ WHERE TO GO

West Glacier and Apgar

Together, West Glacier and Apgar form the park's western portal. Divided by a nationally declared Wild and Scenic River, the pair whip into a summer frenzy with white-water rafting, trail riding, fishing, kayaking, boating, hiking, and backpacking. Apgar houses the largest campgrounds on the park's largest lake—Lake McDonald.

North Fork

For those looking to escape crowds, the remote North Fork on Glacier's west side has real rusticity—not just the look of it. Without electricity, Polebridge Mercantile and Home Ranch Store attract travelers who relish bumpy dirt roads, solitude at Bowman and Kintla Lakes, and wolf serenades.

Going-to-the-Sun Road

As the park's biggest attraction and the only road bisecting the park, Going-to-the-Sun Road leads drivers on a skinny cliff shimmy into the craggy alpine. The National Historic Landmark crosses the Continental Divide at Logan Pass, a wildflower wonderland dancing with glaciers, waterfalls, mountain goats, and trails with top-of-the-world vistas.

St. Mary and Many Glacier

Small, seasonal St. Mary bustles as a hub of campgrounds, lodges, cabins, cafés, shops, and Going-to-the-Sun Road's eastern portal. North in prime bear country, hikers find heaven in Many Glacier with glimmering sapphire lakes and the historic Many Glacier Hotel roosting idyllically below jagged peaks.

IF YOU HAVE . . .

- **ONE DAY:** Drive over Going-to-the-Sun Road.

- **THREE DAYS:** Add on Many Glacier.

- **ONE WEEK:** Explore West Glacier, Waterton, and Two Medicine.

- **TWO WEEKS:** Add the North Fork, Highway 2, and Flathead Valley.

Going-to-the-Sun Road

Two Medicine and East Glacier

In Glacier's southeast corner, the park's historic headliner hotel, Glacier Park Lodge, greets travelers with its flowered walkway and huge lobby. It buzzes with golfers, swimmers, and trail riders. But Two Medicine Lake yields a quiet contrast for hikers, boaters,

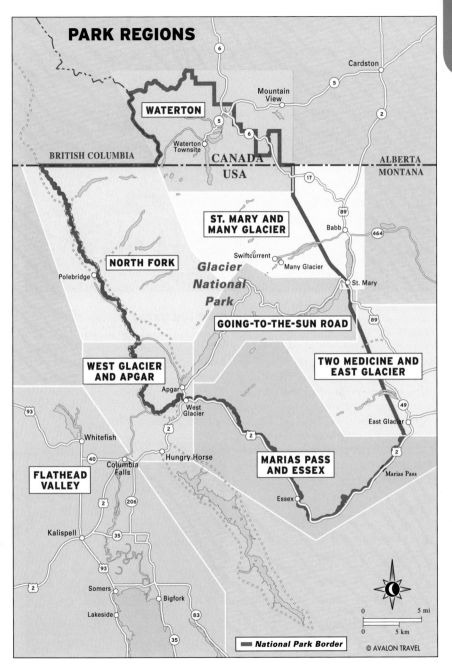

historic Many Glacier Hotel

anglers, wildlife-watchers, and campers under Rising Wolf.

Marias Pass and Essex

Pale next to Going-to-the-Sun Road's drama, Highway 2 crosses mile-high Marias Pass in the fastest route over the Continental Divide along Glacier's southern end. The scenic drive squeezes between Glacier and the Bob Marshall Wilderness, passing the Goat Lick, historic Izaak Walton Inn, and a Wild and Scenic River.

Waterton

In Canada, Waterton Lakes National Park, a sister park over the border, provides access to Glacier's remote north end. Visitors on Waterton Lake travel by boat to cross the international boundary to Goat Haunt, U.S.A., and walk to the International Peace Park Pavilion. Presided over by the historic Prince of Wales Hotel, Waterton Townsite is a nucleus for boat tours, hiking, shopping, bicycling, dining, and camping.

Flathead Valley

More than Glacier's western gateway, Flathead Valley is an attraction in itself, with Kalispell, Whitefish, Bigfork, and Columbia Falls drawing visitors for their unique personalities. The valley lives up to its outdoor reputation with boating, fishing, rafting, camping, biking, golf, swimming, hiking, and skiing.

Binoculars aid wildlife watching.

▶ WHEN TO GO

Summer attracts hordes when lodges, campgrounds, and trails are open. Barring deep snows, Going-to-the-Sun Road opens mid-June–mid-September, with peak visitation crammed into four weeks during midsummer. Snow buries some trails into July, when moderate weather rides in. Mosquitoes descend with a vengeance in early summer, wildflowers peak in late July, and huckleberries ripen in August.

Although saddled with unpredictable weather, off-seasons offer less-hectic visits. Low-elevation trails are usually snow free, but few commercial services are open. While Going-to-the-Sun Road is closed to vehicles, bikers and hikers tour it sans cars. In spring, May and June rains intersperse with cobalt blue skies. In fall, warm, bug-free days

wild huckleberries

and cool nights usher in peak-top snows by September's end. Often, early October sees a blue-sky spell, when larch and aspen turn gold. In winter, snow closes most park roads, which become snowshoeing and cross-country ski trails.

▶ BEFORE YOU GO

Nondriving travelers usually fly into Flathead Valley—the closest airport—or hop the Seattle–Chicago train that stops in East and West Glacier. Once at Glacier, shuttles aid travel, but only in summer and only to certain locations. Summer travelers should reserve rental cars in advance. Visitors heading to Waterton will need appropriate documentation to cross the international border.

grizzly bear cub in Waterton

Northwest Montanans have a saying: "Wait five minutes…the weather will change." Because snows fall even in August, dress in layers—lightweight wicking synthetics, fleeces, and breathable waterproof or water-resistant fabrics. Bring gloves, a warm hat, and rain gear for cold snaps and a hat, sunscreen, and sunglasses for sun. Sturdy walking shoes or hiking boots work best on Glacier's rugged trails.

Dressing for dinner here means putting on a clean shirt. Casual attire is the restaurant norm, as are hiking boots and river sandals. Cool weather brings out fleece rather than cashmere. Despite the Wild West heritage, cowboy hats and boots garb only wranglers.

For hiking, bring a pack and a water bottle; you can buy pepper spray for bears here. Bring binoculars for wildlife-watching. Don't forget the camera, for Glacier's scenery creates foolproof photo opportunities.

Explore
Glacier National Park

► THE BEST OF GLACIER

Glacier offers rugged country to explore—several-thousand-foot cliffs, sapphire lakes, forested valleys, parapets, and ice-scoured basins. This six-day active tour experiences the best in outdoor fun with plenty of hiking. Arrange this tour to coordinate with staying in lodges or at campgrounds.

Day 1

Begin on Glacier's west side, camping or lodging in West Glacier, Apgar, or at Lake McDonald Lodge for two nights. In the afternoon, get acquainted with Lake McDonald via a boat tour or rent a kayak to paddle the shoreline.

Day 2

In the morning, take a trail ride on horseback followed by a white-water raft trip on the Middle Fork of the Flathead River. Smile when you splash through Bonecrusher Rapid as a photographer captures the fun.

Day 3

Pack a lunch for a long day of exploring Going-to-the-Sun Road. Pull over on the National Historic Landmark highway to snap photos as you climb the west side. Stop at Logan Pass to hike 3.5 miles to Haystack Saddle on the Highline Trail. Continue driving to St. Mary, stopping at Sun Point and

the Highline Trail

GLACIERS: UP CLOSE AND PERSONAL

Sadly, the park's namesake ice fields are melting. See them up close while you still can. Trails lead to the edge of several glaciers, but without proper gear and safety training, stay off the ice. Crevasses, ice bridges, and underground streams make them deadly.

SPERRY GLACIER

Hike or ride horseback six miles from **Lake McDonald** to **Sperry Chalet**. Spend two nights among mountain goats at the backcountry campsite or the chalet and climb four miles up through the rock-hewn stairway at **Comeau Pass** into the scoured basin that houses Sperry Glacier. Follow rock cairns to the overlook of the ice – now reduced one-third of a square mile.

PIEGAN AND SEXTON GLACIERS

Catch a morning shuttle to Siyeh Bend to hike the 10.3-mile **Siyeh Pass Trail**. The route offers views of the 62-acre Piegan Glacier while climbing to the pass and Sexton Glacier while descending to Sunrift Gorge. A spur trail leads closer to the 68-acre glacier hugging Going-to-the-Sun Mountain.

GRINNELL GLACIER

From **Many Glacier Hotel**, hop the early hiker shuttle across **Swiftcurrent and Josephine Lakes**; then climb four miles to Grinnell Glacier. Sit on the shore of the 152-acre glacier that is melting into a frigid iceberg-filled lake. The 42-acre **Salamander Glacier** clings in the cliffs above the lake while **Gem Glacier**, a mound perched on Mount Gould, no longer has the required size to qualify as a glacier.

BLACKFOOT AND JACKSON GLACIERS

You can see these glaciers from Going-to-the-Sun Road at **Jackson Overlook** and the next two pullouts east, but they are about six air miles away. Use binoculars to scope out the 688 acres of Blackfoot and Jackson Glaciers.

fast-melting Grinnell Glacier

Two Medicine Lake

Wild Goose Island for a postcard picture of the park. When you reach St. Mary, do as the locals do and hit Park Café for fresh-baked pie before camping or lodging in Many Glacier or St. Mary for three nights.

Day 4

In Many Glacier, hike 4.5 miles to turquoise Iceberg Lake, floating with icebergs even in August. Go for a frigid swim or at least dip your toes into the icy water. While in Many Glacier, be sure to waltz through the historic Many Glacier Hotel if you're not staying there. Bask on the hotel's deck with binoculars in hand to spot grizzly and black bears foraging on Altyn Peak's hillside.

Day 5

Drive Chief Mountain Highway to Waterton Lakes National Park for the day. Book an early cruise on the historic *MV International* to Goat Haunt, U.S.A. and walk to the International Peace Park Pavilion. After returning, peruse a few Townsite shops. For grand views of Waterton Lake, stop at the Prince of Wales Hotel or climb the short, steep 45-minute trail to Bear's Hump for the biggest view.

Day 6

Drive to Two Medicine to spend the day enjoy high-elevation lake fishing. If fishing's not your thing, rent a kayak, or take a boat tour and walk to Twin Falls. Those with enough energy left to hike some more will gain the best views by climbing 2.9 miles to Scenic Point. Finish with a night camping in the quiet at Two Medicine or lounging in the historic ambience at Glacier Park Lodge in East Glacier.

▶ NATIVE AMERICAN ROOTS

Native American tribes called Glacier home long before Lewis and Clark reached the Rockies. The Blackfeet, Salish, Kootenai, and Flathead Indians held sacred ceremonies along the park's lakes. They relied on berries for pemmican and bison that proliferated on its eastern prairies. Peaks, such as Chief Mountain, offered lofty aeries for vision quests. While you can tour Glacier all summer long with this trip, those visiting the second week in July can add on the sixth day. Plan to lodge in East Glacier or camp at Two Medicine for the first two days and then move to St. Mary or Many Glacier to overnight starting on Day 4.

PHOTOGRAPHER'S PILGRIMAGE

Both amateur and professional photographers find countless photo ops in Glacier. They hit **Going-to-the-Sun Road** at dawn to set up tripods for morning light. They haul out the giant telephoto lenses for wildlife photography at **Logan Pass** and macros for shooting delicate wildflowers. The Sun Road's top sunrise photo op spots include **Heaven's Peak** from the **West Side Tunnel** and **The Loop, Logan Pass, Sun Point,** and **Wild Goose Island Overlook. The Garden Wall** lights up best in the late afternoon or evening.

Day 1

Start in Browning on the Blackfeet Reservation at the Museum of the Plains Indians for a background on the Blackfeet people. A block east, find the works of more than 500 Native American artists at the Blackfeet Heritage Center and Art Gallery. Head to East Glacier for a horseback trail ride on the reservation. In the evening at Two Medicine Campground Amphitheater, learn about the culture of the park's early peoples through the Native America Speaks program.

Day 2

Hike Scenic Point in the morning. From the summit, you'll look out on the prairies of the Blackfeet Reservation—a view that has changed little from a century ago. In the afternoon, hop on *Sinopah* at Two Medicine

hiking Scenic Point trail above Two Medicine Lake

WILDFLOWER WANDERS

When Glacier's spring hits Lake McDonald and St. Mary, Logan Pass still cowers under winter snows. Lower-elevation flowers bloom first, and as summer progresses, like a mist lifting, buds pop open in higher and higher habitats. Wildflowers do not bloom parkwide at once but aim for late July to hit the big high meadow displays. To identify wildflowers, pick up a field guide from **Glacier Natural History Association** (406/888-5756, www.glacier association.org).

FORESTS

Tiny and pale cream-colored forest wildflowers choose to live under fir, hemlock, and cedars for shade-producing canopies that protect fragile plants from drying sun rays. Queen's cup, fairybell, and pipsissewa scatter no more than boot high. Most trails in the **North Fork** and **McDonald** valleys bloom with these gems, especially **Trail of the Cedars** at Avalanche. Rich forest duff also sprouts diminutive orchids. Find fairy slipper orchids growing along the **Quartz Lakes** loop.

PRAIRIES

Except for the **North Fork** prairies, most prairie grasslands amass on the east side at **Two Dog Flats,** along **Many Glacier Road,** and in **Waterton Lakes National Park,** which preserves 13 square miles of prairie. Minus trees for shade, wildflowers adapt to dry conditions: hot temperatures, wind, and less rain. Look for the sunflower-like arrowleaf balsamroot and dusty pink prairie smoke.

ASPEN PARKLANDS

Many flowers proliferate in a rich mix of meadows and aspen groves. Mountain death camas, paintbrush, pasque flower, lupine, stonecrop, and horse mint span the color rainbow. Along **Two Medicine Road,** blue camas blooms hardily. Beside **Many Glacier Road,** pink sticky geranium makes a show. Along **Chief Mountain International Highway,** wild roses and tiger lilies line the road.

SUBALPINE

A drive on **Going-to-the-Sun Road** climbs to

pink monkeyflower

high meadows – a rough place for wildflowers. Long winters, high winds, little shade, and a short growing season mean that flowers must do their business fast. At **Logan Pass,** walk toward Hidden Lake Overlook or out along the Garden Wall to see colors Monet would envy in pink shooting stars, yellow arnica, deep blue gentians, and fuchsia monkeyflowers. Yellow glacier lilies – the harbingers of summer – force their blooms up, even through snow. Some years, three-foot-tall beargrass grows so thick that slopes appear to be snow covered. For one of the best midsummer flower displays, hike from Siyeh Bend to **Preston Park** for fields of color.

ALPINE

Alpine wildflowers struggle against high winds, drying altitude, and rocky soils lacking organic matter. But the diminutive wildflowers that survive by hugging the ground bloom with a show during their short few-week season. In Two Medicine, hike short, steep **Scenic Point** to see several-hundred-year-old mats of pink moss campion, small bluebells, and the red tops of king's crown. To see blue Jones columbine and creamy mountain avens, grunt up to 8,000-foot-high **Siyeh Pass.**

for a narrated boat tour. You'll learn how the legendary name "Two Medicine" came about as well as the stories behind peaks named for Blackfeet.

Day 3

Hire Blackfeet historian Darrell Norman for a private tour of ancient tepee rings and buffalo jump sites on the Blackfeet Reservation. Spend the night west of Browning curled around your fire in a tepee at Lodgepole Gallery and Tipi Village after dining on a traditional Southern Blackfeet meal of bison, elk, or fish.

Day 4

In the morning, visit the new exhibits in St. Mary Visitors Center, a tribute to the many native tribes whose lives intertwined with the park. Catch an evening performance of the Two Medicine Singers and Dancers, who perform fancy, jingle, traditional, and grass dance demonstrations.

Day 5

Departing from St. Mary, tour the Going-to-the-Sun Road with Sun Tours. Your Blackfeet guides will give you insights into the cultural past of Glacier with legends from buffalo days and stories from today. In the evening, drive to Many Glacier for Jack Gladstone's Native Anthropology

North American Indian Days features four days of dancing.

program, a unique series of tribal stories and animal legends in song.

Day 6

Cap off your explorations with a visit to North American Indian Days in Browning. The family-friendly four-day powwow during the second week of July features traditional regalia, dance competitions, drum contests, a rodeo, and a parade.

▶ ON THE TRAIL: KID-FRIENDLY HIKING

Glacier offers trails suited to introduce children to hiking. (An added bonus when hiking with kids is that they typically make loads of noise on the trail, so you'll avoid surprising any bears.) This itinerary is aimed at getting 6- to 12-year-olds out on the trail, but tots can do some of the shorter excursions. The seven-day tour can be geared toward staying in lodges and cabins or camping. After spending the first night in East Glacier or Two Medicine, base the next three nights in Many Glacier or St. Mary, and then shift to the west side for one night. To make hiking successful with kids, outfit them in sturdy shoes and take along plenty of bug spray, extra clothes for changeable weather, snacks, and water.

GLACIER ON TWO WHEELS

bicycling Going-to-the-Sun Road

BY BIKE

Bicycling Going-to-the-Sun Road stands in the annals of lifetime routes for many riders. While you can bike it from either east or west, most cyclists opt for starting in **West Glacier** for the dramatic 3,500-foot thigh-burning climb up the west side. Timing, however, is crucial with uphill road restrictions. Plan to leave West Glacier at 6 A.M. to reach **Logan Pass** by 11 A.M.

The best road tour loops 142 miles over the Sun Road and Highways 89, 49, and 2. Road racers ride the loop in one day; tourers do it in two days, overnighting in **East Glacier,** or in three days, staying one night in **St. Mary** and one in **East Glacier.** Enjoyable side trip rides from St. Mary can extend the length by includ-ing a day trip to **Many Glacier** or an overnight to **Waterton Lakes National Park.** Most park campgrounds have shared biker-hiker camp-sites available.

BY MOTORCYCLE

While motorcyclists can tour the park like any other vehicle, many bikers are attracted to riding **Going-to-the-Sun Road** with the wind blowing through their hair! Montana requires no helmets for motorcyclists over 18 years old, hence the feel of freedom amid an alpine won-derland. The park attracts scads of decked-out Harleys and Goldwings, as well as motorcycle clubs who come specifically to tour Going-to-the-Sun Road.

Children enjoy swimming in Lake McDonald.

Day 1

Drive to Two Medicine Lake to catch the tour boat across the lake. Hike 1.8 miles to Twin Falls and Upper Two Medicine Lake. Bring binoculars to spot mountain goats on the cliffs above the lake and fishing rods to cast the lake for trout.

Day 2

Take the kids on a choice of waterfall trails. In Many Glacier, walk the Swiftcurrent Trail one mile west to Red Rocks Falls and continue two more miles over the swinging bridge to Bullhead Lake. Fish either lake, too. From St. Mary, drive west on Going-to-the-Sun Road to hike 1.8 miles to St. Mary Falls and mist-spewing Virginia Falls.

Day 3

Catch the morning boat from Many Glacier Hotel across Swiftcurrent Lake and Josephine Lake. Younger hikers will enjoy the swinging bridge en route to turquoise Grinnell Lake, a two-mile round-trip flat walk. Stronger

kids can climb 7.8 miles round-trip to see Grinnell Glacier, the most accessible glacier in the park.

Day 4

Drive to Waterton Lakes National Park for a north of the border adventure. Go for the big views, climbing 45 minutes up Bear's Hump

11-year-old backpacker at Red Eagle Lake near St. Mary

WILDLIFE-WATCHING HOTSPOTS

With 57 animals and over 210 varieties of birds, wildlife watchers have plenty to spot. Bring binoculars and scopes, for your own safety as well as the animal's well being. Die-hard birders will want to hit early summer as migrations prompt some birds to head south as early as August.

Both Glacier and Waterton Parks have wildlife and bird checklists. Ask for them at visitors centers or check park websites. Look for Watchable Wildlife programs in Glacier. Interpretive rangers set up spotting scopes for public viewing and can answer questions.

three bighorn sheep ewes

GOAT LICK
Located on Highway 2, the Goat Lick is a natural mineral lick that attracts **mountain goats** in late spring and early summer.

INSIDE NORTH FORK ROAD
While **gray wolves** are elusive, you may have a chance of spotting one on the Inside North Fork Road near dawn or dusk.

MCGEE MEADOWS
For birders, the North Fork Valley holds over 196 species of **birds,** 57 percent of which are nesters. Fens, like McGee Meadows, bustle with red-winged blackbirds, snipes, and soras. Woodpeckers drum; songbirds chatter.

LOGAN PASS
Mountain goats and **bighorn sheep** wander through the parking lot at Logan Pass and frequent the Hidden Lake Overlook trail. **Blue grouse** and **ptarmigan** strut in open meadows.

AVALANCHE CHUTES
In early spring, **grizzly bears** prowl avalanche slopes on Mount Cannon and the Glacier Wall between Avalanche and The Loop on Going-to-the-Sun Road in hopes of finding carcasses.

FALLS
St. Mary and Virginia Falls create perfect habitat for **American dippers.** Recognize these small dark birds by their bobbing.

HENKEL AND ALTYN
Grizzly and black bears congregate on these two peaks in Many Glacier mid-July through September – looking for bulbs, ground squirrels, and huckleberries. Spot them from Many Glacier Hotel's deck, or stop by the park service viewing scope in Swiftcurrent parking lot.

SWIFTCURRENT VALLEY
A short, gentle hike tours through good **moose** country to Red Rocks and Bullhead Lakes. The valley also teems with **birds:** white-crowned sparrows, loons, finches, Townsend's solitaires, hummingbirds, kinglets, and Clark's nutcrackers. Look for **golden eagles** soaring high along cliffs.

TWO DOG FLATS
Early morning in spring and late fall, herds of **elk** drop out of the high country to feed at Two Dog Flats along Going-to-the-Sun Road near Rising Sun. The surrounding aspens attract **woodpeckers, flickers, sapsuckers, mountain bluebirds,** and several species of **owls.**

BISON PADDOCK
In Waterton, stop at the **bison** paddock to see the small herd of monster shaggy bovines that once roamed wild.

WATERTON LAKES
In Waterton, the wetlands around Maskinonge and Linnet Lakes abound with **waterfowl, osprey, swans, and kingfishers.** Over 250 avian species pass through here on two major migratory flyways because of the rich wetlands and varied habitats.

KOOTENAI LAKES
Accessed via the Waterton tour boat, Glacier's Kootenai Lakes harbors **moose** and sometimes **trumpeter swans.**

to look down on the Townsite. Stronger hikers can catch the water shuttle to hike 11.2 miles round-trip to Crypt Lake, crawling through its tunnel en route.

Day 5

Get an early start to drive up Going-to-the-Sun Road to Logan Pass. Hike 1.5 miles up to Hidden Lake Overlook. Look for baby and nanny mountain goats along the trail. Strong hikers can add on another 1.5 miles to swim in Hidden Lake, but only with the stamina to climb the steep trail back over the saddle on the return trip.

Day 6

Hike to Avalanche Lake. Start on Trail of the Cedars, where fallen cedars look like an imaginary gnome world. Turn up the trail to the lake, taking at look at Avalanche Gorge. Climb to the lake to wade in its shallow north end or continue to its south end for fishing.

Day 7

Finish off the hiking week with a bang with a hike-raft combo day on the Middle Fork

playing in the lake near Essex

of the Flathead River with Glacier Guides. You'll hike upriver to Lincoln Creek, perusing the rapids that will later drench you. After lunch on the beach, you'll raft the white water back downstream.

▶ ON THE WATER: CANOEING AND KAYAKING

Leave Glacier's roads behind and launch a canoe or sea kayak for adventures on clear lakes and streams. Winds crop up fast around the Continental Divide; for safety's sake, stay close to shore. Only those comfortable with Class II flowing water should tackle floating the North Fork of the Flathead River.

Day 1

Head toward Two Medicine to grab a campsite for one night. Launch from Pray Lake to paddle upstream onto Two Medicine Lake, watching for bears on Rising Wolf and mountain goats on Sinopah. With late season

water levels, drive instead to the boat ramp for launching.

Day 2

Drive north to Many Glacier Campground. After nabbing a campsite, launch from the boat ramp east of Swiftcurrent Picnic Area to paddle one mile south across Swiftcurrent Lake. Continue 0.5 mile up Cataract Creek beneath the footbridge. In late season, the creek may be low, requiring a few portages. At the head of Cataract Creek, tour Josephine Lake to Oastler Shelter one mile across at the southwest corner, watching for bear on the slopes of Grinnell Point and moose at the head of the lake.

Day 3

Pack up early to drive over Going-to-the-Sun Road to Lake McDonald, snagging a campsite at Sprague Creek. In the afternoon, paddle 4–6 miles around the east shoreline to the north shore, picnicking for dinner on one of the gravel beaches and paddling back to catch the sunset on the return trip.

Day 4

Drive two miles to Glacier Raft Company in West Glacier to arrange for the vehicle shuttle on the North Fork of the Flathead River if you have only one vehicle in your party. Drive north to the Polebridge River Access. (If you have two vehicles in the party, setting up the shuttle to Big Creek River Access will take about 90 minutes.) From Polebridge, launch onto the Class II Wild and Scenic North Fork of the Flathead River and float

West Glacier is the rafting capital of Glacier.

downstream. No permit is needed, but camping is only allowed on the west shore.

Day 5

Paddle downstream to Big Creek to take out 18 miles south of Polebridge and before the

Kintla Lake offers one of the park's most remote paddles.

TOP 10 DAY HIKES

Hikers explore Glacier's trails.

Glacier is a hiker's park. With over 700 miles of trails, it's a place to explore on foot, June–September, to sample the top trails. Shuttles running from July through Labor Day help accommodate point-to-point hiking over Going-to-the-Sun Road.

APGAR LOOKOUT
Located at Lake McDonald's foot, the lookout requires a little more than three-mile climb to attain a far-reaching panoramic view of Glacier's peaks that stretches from Canada to the Bob Marshall Wilderness. It's a short hike with big view rewards.

AVALANCHE LAKE
A two-mile trail leaves the McDonald Creek Valley, heading up a red rock side canyon to the idyllic lake. It's the most easily accessed subalpine lake – hence the crowds. Fed by Sperry Glacier above, waterfalls spew thousands of feet down the cliffs surrounding the lake below the Little Matterhorn.

HIGHLINE TRAIL
Beginning at Logan Pass, the stunning 11.6-mile point-to-point goatwalk tiptoes through high wildflower meadows along the Garden Wall arête to historic Granite Park Chalet before dropping to The Loop. Acrophobes may clench their stomachs as the trail prances along cliffs looking down at Going-to-the-Sun Road.

SIYEH PASS
Just east of Logan Pass at Siyeh Bend, this point-to-point trail climbs 10.5 miles over a high elevation saddle with views of sparkling glaciers. The trail wanders through Preston Park ablaze with purple wildflowers and alongside bighorn sheep, as it circumnavigates Going-to-the-Sun Mountain.

SCENIC POINT
High above Two Medicine Lake, this short three-mile climb lets you look far out across the plains and then turn around to stare at rugged peaks as you stand atop a promontory of the Lewis Overthrust Fault.

DAWSON-PITAMAKIN LOOP
In a hike that includes a boat ride across Two Medicine Lake, the 16-mile loop actually crosses three passes: Dawson, Cutbank, and Pitamakin. You'll feel like you're walking on top of the world as the narrow path hangs dizzyingly thousands of feet above the valley floor.

ICEBERG LAKE
For the rarity of seeing icebergs in August, a 4.5-mile gentle ascent in Many Glacier leads to a glacial remnant lake where chunks of white ice float in its deep blue waters. Tradition dictates a quick dive in, but be ready for cold like you've never felt before.

GRINNELL GLACIER
In Many Glacier, the Grinnell trail provides the quickest path in the park to reach a glacier. In its scenic climb, its 5.5-mile path delights en route with wildflowers, bighorn sheep, grizzly bears, waterfalls, and stunning views of turquoise Grinnell Lake.

CARTHEW-ALDERSON
Beginning at Cameron Lake in Waterton, the nearly 12-mile Carthew-Alderson trail climbs high into windswept alpine tundra with panoramic views extending in to Glacier. Then it drops past gleaming tarns set against giant stone walls to the Waterton Townsite.

CRYPT LAKE
Requiring boat access across Waterton Lake, the trail throws a unique twist at you with a ladder, tunnel, and cliff walk in its five miles to reach the lake set in a hanging valley. But be prepared for hiking with hordes – everyone begins the hike together from the boat dock and races at the end of the day to catch the return boat.

curious bighorn sheep rams

white-water section. Watch for river otters, moose, and kingfishers. Camp overnight at Big Creek. Drive Camas Road to the Apgar Backcountry Permit Office to pick up a permit for backcountry camping at Kintla Lake Head for Days 6 and 7.

Day 6

Get an early start for the nearly two-hour dirt road drive to Kintla Lake. At the lake, load gear into the canoe or kayak and paddle six miles along the north shore of Kintla Lake to the Kintla Head backcountry campsite.

Day 7

Pack a lunch and hike to Upper Kintla Lake for a swim. After returning to the campsite, take a short paddle for wildlife-watching in the evening and grab photos of the sun setting across the lake.

Day 8

In the morning after breakfast, load the gear into the boats for the last day of paddling. Follow the south shoreline, which burned in the 2003 Wedge Fire, back to Kintla Lake Campground.

WEST GLACIER AND APGAR

Sitting just two miles apart, West Glacier and Apgar span Glacier Park's southwestern boundary—the Middle Fork of the Flathead River. While West Glacier sprouted up outside the park along Great Northern Railway's line, early trapper and logger homesteads dug in a foothold at Apgar on Lake McDonald—the port to the park's wild interior before Going-to-the-Sun Road was built. Connected by the "new bridge," the park entrance road, and a two-mile paved bicycling and walking pathway, the pair are doorways for exploring Glacier's western wilderness. As such, they throng with cars and visitors in summer; 60 percent of visitors access the park via this west entrance. The pair also launch sightseers in two disparate directions: to the untrammeled North Fork Valley and to Glacier's crowning highway, Going-to-the-Sun Road.

Today, many concessionaires headquarter themselves in West Glacier, just outside national park boundaries. The tiny town evolved into the seasonal mecca for rafting, guided hiking and backpacking, guided fishing trips, trail rides, and helicopter tours. Along with the train station, campgrounds, restaurants, motels, shops, and even an espresso stand, West Glacier is a place to gas up the car one last time before seeking Glacier's interior. On Lake McDonald's shores and inside the park, Apgar resounds with calm in comparison. Although its restaurant, lodging, camping, shopping, boat ramp, and petite west-side visitors center swarm in high season, miles of lake sprawl with blue waters and lakeshore enough to find a niche for solitude.

© BECKY LOMAX

HIGHLIGHTS

◖ Belton Chalet: Enjoy a tribute to a by-gone era of tourism in a chalet as old as the park. On chillier days, enjoy the ambience by its stone fireplace; on warmer days, lounge at sunset on its deck with a local brew (page 34).

◖ Robert Fire: See a forest renewing itself after the 2003 fire on Apgar Mountain and Howe Ridge. The fire forced the evacuation of West Glacier, Apgar, and the McDonald Valley (page 36).

◖ Lake McDonald: Leap into the park's largest lake for a refreshing swim, or paddle its shoreline in a kayak or canoe. Its clear waters lure boaters, anglers, scuba divers, photographers, and rock skippers (page 36).

◖ Apgar Lookout: Climb to where you can look down Lake McDonald, West Glacier, and the North Fork. You'll see a huge panorama of peaks from Canada to Glacier's southern tip (page 38).

◖ Huckleberry Lookout: Traipse along a top-of-the-world ridge walk where views stretch from Flathead Lake to Canada on this 12-mile round-trip hike (page 39).

◖ Middle Fork of the Flathead: Crash through white water on a raft. The Wild and Scenic River drops through rapids such as Screaming Right Turn, Bonecrusher, Jaws, and Could Be Trouble (page 43).

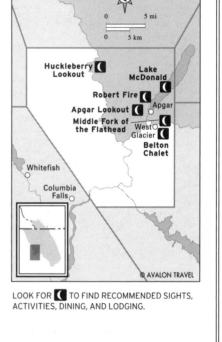

LOOK FOR ◖ TO FIND RECOMMENDED SIGHTS, ACTIVITIES, DINING, AND LODGING.

HISTORY
Native Americans
For the Ksanka or Standing Arrow people (known today as the Salish and Kootenai, whose tribal lands are at Flathead Lake's south end), Glacier's Lake McDonald area held special significance. Ten thousand generations ago, as legend says, the Ksanka were first given a ceremonial dance by the spirits at their winter camp near Apgar. Originally called the Blacktail Deer Dance, the ceremony became an annual event for the tribe, and the area became known as "the place where people dance." Today, the annual dance—now called the Jump Dance—takes place on the Flathead Reservation, but rapids on McDonald Creek still hold the original name, Sacred Dancing Cascade.

Early Tourism
When Great Northern Railway completed its westbound track in 1891, early tourists jumped off the train in Belton (West Glacier) to see Glacier. With no bridge across the Middle Fork of the Flathead, visitors rowed across the river and then saddled up for a horseback ride to Apgar. Finally, in 1895 a rough dirt road eased the two-mile journey, followed two years later by a bridge across the river.

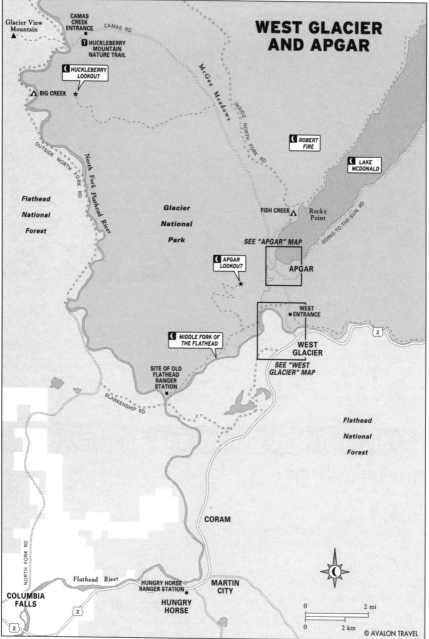

WEST GLACIER AND APGAR

Glacier View Mountain ▲

CAMAS CREEK ENTRANCE

CAMAS RD

T HUCKLEBERRY MOUNTAIN NATURE TRAIL

Mc-Gee Meadows

☾ HUCKLEBERRY LOOKOUT

△ BIG CREEK ★

INSIDE NORTH FORK RD

OUTSIDE NORTH FORK RD

North Fork Flathead River

☾ ROBERT FIRE

☾ LAKE MCDONALD

FISH CREEK △   Rocky Point

Flathead

National

Forest

GOING-TO-THE-SUN RD

Glacier

National

Park

SEE "APGAR" MAP

☾ APGAR LOOKOUT ★

APGAR

WEST ENTRANCE

☾ MIDDLE FORK OF THE FLATHEAD

2

WEST GLACIER

SEE "WEST GLACIER" MAP

SITE OF OLD FLATHEAD RANGER STATION ■

BLANKENSHIP RD

Flathead

National

Forest

CORAM

NORTH FORK RD

Flathead River

COLUMBIA FALLS

2

2

HUNGRY HORSE RANGER STATION ■

HUNGRY HORSE

MARTIN CITY

0   2 mi

0   2 km

© AVALON TRAVEL

Belton Chalet turned 100 along with Glacier Park in 2010.

As the railroad dumped visitors in Belton, Lake McDonald homesteaders leaped into the tourism business, offering cabins, meals, pack trips, boat rides, and guided tours. After Glacier became a national park in 1910, local landowners along the lake retained their property as inholdings. While private summer homes still exist here within the park boundaries (to the envy of everyone), when sellers are ready, the National Park Service purchases these properties at fair market value.

To coincide with Glacier's first summer as a national park, Great Northern Railway opened Belton Chalet in 1910 across from the depot.

Exploring West Glacier and Apgar

ENTRANCE STATION

Crossing the Middle Fork of the Flathead River on the West Glacier Bridge officially escorts you into Glacier National Park. There's even a pullout before the park entrance sign for those who photo-document their travels by park signs. The park entrance is usually staffed during daylight hours all summer long and off-season on weekends. If you miss someone in the station, you can use the self-pay cash-only kiosk to purchase a pass. If you don't have an annual pass, seven-day passes cost $25 per vehicle or $12 for individuals on foot, bicycles, or motorcycles. (Rates drop to $15 and $10 Nov.–Apr.) Also, pick up a map and the summer or winter edition of the *Waterton-Glacier Guide,* the park's newspaper.

You can also enter Apgar via the Camas Entrance from the rough dirt North Fork Road. At its northwest end, an entrance station sits unstaffed along with a self-pay cash-only kiosk.

VISITORS CENTERS
Apgar Visitor Center
The tiny Apgar Visitor Center (on Apgar

© BECKY LOMAX

Get info and park books at Apgar Visitor Center.

Loop Rd. 0.2 mile from Camas Rd. or 0.9 mile from Going-to-the-Sun Rd., 406/888-7800, 9 A.M.–5 P.M. daily May–late June and after Labor Day–Sept., 8 A.M.–7 P.M. daily late June–Labor Day, 9 A.M.–4:30 P.M. winter weekends) seems crowded with 15 people, but it sees 190,000 visitors annually. In the small shell of what was once a two-room house, the visitors center houses a few displays, an information desk, and a small Glacier Natural History Association bookstore. The backcountry permit office (May–Nov. 406/888-7859, winter 406/888-7800) sits a few doors west opposite the old red schoolhouse. In spite of the visitors center's diminutive size, park personnel are big on information. Pick up maps, naturalist activity guides, and Junior Ranger Activity Guides. You can also get the latest updates on trails, roads, campgrounds, fishing, and boating. Restrooms sit around the side of the building. The park service hopes to build a new larger visitors center eventually near the Apgar Transit Center.

For some free, fun, hands-on activities for kids, stop by the **Discovery Cabin** in the woods across the street from the Apgar Visitor Center. With the help of interpretive rangers, learning stations teach about wildlife, geology, and natural history. Limited hours change; consult the visitors center for the current schedule and walking directions to the cabin.

Apgar Transit Center

A new $4.3 million transit center constructed in 2007 houses the unstaffed **Discovery Center,** loaded with park information in visual displays and electronic kiosks. It's open 24 hours a day. By car, find its parking lot northeast of the Camas and Going-to-the-Sun Road junction, or walk by trail from the Apgar Visitor Center. The center reflects the highest green building standards: restrooms with low-flow toilets, automatic lights, and indigenous flora landscaping. Outdoor signage highlights interpretive information for all major park regions. Shuttles depart to go up Going-to-the-Sun Road.

Alberta Visitor Information Center

Located in West Glacier, the Alberta Visitor

© BECKY LOMAX

Catch free Going-to-the-Sun Road shuttles at Apgar Transit Center.

Information Center (125 Going-to-the-Sun Rd., 800/252-3782, www.travelalberta.com, 8 A.M.–7 P.M. daily late May–early Sept., closes around 5 P.M. during late Sept.) is a building-size advertisement for Canada, complete with dinosaur bones. For those heading over the border to Waterton, the center is worth a stop to help with travel planning. The staff has plenty of brochures and maps to give away. You'll also find big, clean public restrooms.

SHUTTLES AND TOURS
Shuttles
Free shuttles link Apgar Campground, Apgar Village, and Apgar Transit Center with stops on Going-to-the-Sun Road. Shuttles circulate every 15–30 minutes 7 A.M.–7 P.M. July 1–Labor Day. Look for obvious interpretive signs marking the shuttle stops. From the transit center, you can catch shuttles heading up Going-to-the-Sun Road toward McDonald Lodge, Avalanche, several trailheads, and Logan Pass, where you can transfer to the St. Mary shuttle. The no-reservations, no-tickets-needed shuttles are popular, so

you may have to wait for a seat during the peak season. Designed as hiker shuttles, the shuttles do not come with interpretive guides. If you are heading toward Logan Pass, be sure to take a day pack with water, snacks, and extra layers for fast-changing weather.

Running late May–late September, **Glacier Park, Inc.** (406/892-2525, www.glacier-parkinc.com) shuttles train passengers between West Glacier's Belton Depot and Apgar Village Inn ($6) or Lake McDonald Lodge ($10). Reservations are mandatory; kids cost half price. The shuttle does not stop at campgrounds, but campgrounds sit within a 10-minute walk of the inn or lodge.

Flathead-Glacier Transportation (406/892-3390 or 800/829-7039) runs shuttles by reservation between Glacier International Airport and West Glacier ($40 one-way) or Apgar ($45 one-way). Rates are for the first person, with each additional person costing $3.

Bus Tours
For those with oversized vehicles not permitted

on Going-to-the-Sun Road, two tour companies offer the easiest way to tour Logan Pass when it is open.

Glacier Park's fleet of **Red Buses** (406/892-2525, www.glacierparkinc.com, late May–Sept., adults $40–85, kids half price) are the best way to tour in historic style, with roll-back tops allowing for uninhibited peak views and au natural air-conditioning. Make reservations a day in advance, especially midsummer. Half-, full-day, and evening tours are based out of Lake McDonald Lodge but have pickups at West Glacier KOA and Apgar Transit Center. When the pass is closed (before mid-June and after mid-September), the red buses tour around Huckleberry Mountain. Rates do not include park entrance fees, meals, or driver tips.

With a pickup at the Alberta Visitor Information Center, **Sun Tours** (406/226-9220 or 800/786-9220, www.glaciersuntours.com, June–Sept., adults $40, kids ages 12 and under $15, meals and park entrance fees not included) departs at 9 A.M. daily from West Glacier for four-hour tours to Logan Pass and back. The air-conditioned 25-passenger coaches are extremely comfortable, with extra-big windows enhancing views. Native American guides give insight into the park's rich native peoples heritage—from buffalo days to modern spirituality.

Helicopter

Two helicopter tour companies—both within one mile west of the train depot—fly half-hour and one-hour tours over Glacier Park daily mid-May–September. Per person rates vary $110–875, based on the number of passengers and flight duration. Even though tours are weather dependent, make reservations from home, especially if you want to be able to keep the cost down by sharing the ride with other passengers. You may have to adjust your schedule when you're here, but you'll still have your reservations. **Glacier Heli Tours** (11950 Hwy. 2 E., 406/387-4141 or 800/879-9310) flies three helicopters, seating four or six guests. **Kruger Helicop-Tours** (11892 Hwy. 2 E., 406/387-

4565 or 800/220-6565, www.krugerhelicopters.com) carries four passengers per flight.

SERVICES

Gas services are *not* available inside the park, on Going-to-the-Sun Road, up the North Fork Valley, or on Highway 2 until East Glacier. The last chance for gasoline is West Glacier: **Glacier Highland** (gas available year-round with a credit card), across from the train depot, or **West Glacier MRC Gasoline** (mid-May–Sept.), across from the Mercantile.

The **West Glacier Laundromat** (8 A.M.–10 P.M. daily mid-May–mid-Sept.) sits behind the Alberta Visitor Information Center. If it is packed, both the West Glacier KOA and West Glacier Campground have launderettes. You can also get a hot shower ($3–5) at both campgrounds.

The post office sits in West Glacier opposite the Alberta Visitor Center. ATM machines are located in Apgar at Eddie's and in West Glacier near the MRC gas station.

Glacier Highland Resort (12555 Hwy. 2 E., 406/888-5427 or 800/766-0811, www.glacierhighlandresort.com), across from the West Glacier train depot, rents cars.

The owners of Great Northern Raft Company (800/735-7897) applied for a permit in 2010 to run a dog day care in West Glacier since pets are not allowed on park trails. Call for location and rate information.

Cell Phones and Internet

Cell service is available in West Glacier and Apgar, but intermittent in adjacent canyons. Only a few hotels and private campgrounds between West Glacier and Hungry Horse have Internet.

Shopping

West Glacier and Apgar each have several small gift shops with souvenirs, T-shirts, and books. In Apgar, stop by **Montana House of Gifts** (on Apgar Rd. next to the visitors center, 406/888-5393, 9 A.M.–8:30 P.M. daily in summer, until 5 P.M. in winter) for its locally made pottery, weaving, jewelry, crafts, and arts—some by Native

© BECKY LOMAX

Montana House celebrated its 50th year in 2010.

Americans. In West Glacier, **Glacier Outdoor Center** (11957 Hwy. 2 E., 406/888-5454 or 800/235-6781, open daily year-round) carries outdoor gear for hiking, rafting, and fishing.

Located in the historic Belton Railway Station in West Glacier, the **Glacier Natural History Association** (GNHA, 406/888-5756, www.glacierassociation.com) headquarters sells books, posters, and maps of Glacier. This is the place to go for all park books—reference, natural history, centennial, hiking, and picture books. GNHA also runs a small bookstore in the Apgar Visitor Center and six other park locations. You can also order products from the GNHA website.

Newspapers and Magazines

Look for three daily newspapers: Kalispell's *Daily Interlake, The Missoulian* from Missoula, and the *Great Falls Tribune.* For the scoop on park news, the weekly *Hungry Horse News* gives a good inside look. You can also find the free weekly *Flathead Beacon* (www.flatheadbeacon.com), covering Flathead Valley and park news.

Emergencies

For emergencies within park boundaries, contact a ranger or call 406/888-7800. Outside park boundaries, call 911. The nearest hospitals are in the Flathead Valley: Kalispell Regional Hospital (406/752-5111) and North Valley Hospital in Whitefish (406/863-3500 or 888/815-5528). An urgent care clinic has opened some summers at the West Glacier Fire Hall.

The nearest ranger station inside the park is **Glacier National Park Headquarters** (406/888-7800), on Going-to-the-Sun Road just west of the park entrance station. Turn onto the well-signed side road and take the first right into the parking lot for the headquarters building. You can also get assistance at the Apgar Visitor Center.

Outside the park, the nearest U.S. Forest Service ranger station for Flathead National Forest is in Hungry Horse on Highway 2 at milepost 143.1. Call **Hungry Horse Ranger Station** (10 Hungry Horse Dr., 406/387-3800, www.fs.fed.us/r1/flathead) for any emergencies on the Flathead River system or in Flathead National Forest.

DRIVING TOUR
Camas Road

Outside Apgar, the 11.3-mile summer-only Camas Road heads north across Lower McDonald Creek toward the North Fork of the Flathead River. Climbing along the base of the Apgar Range, the road traverses through the **2003 Robert Fire** and the **2001 Moose Fire,** which offer a contrast in forest succession after burns. Several pullouts en route are worth a stop: If you can stand the mosquitoes, grab binoculars to peruse **McGee Meadows** (at 5.5 miles) for moose, deer, and bear. Just west of the Camas entrance station at 11.1 miles, a turnoff leads to **Huckleberry Mountain Nature Trail,** a 0.9-mile self-guided loop and views of the remote Livingston Range. After crossing the park boundary—the North Fork River—the Camas Road terminates at North Fork Road. When bears frequent the Camas Road, you may see rangers hazing them away from the roadway. They are trying to condition the bears to steer clear of trafficked areas for their own safety.

SIGHTS

While most visitors head straight to Lake McDonald, the biggest attraction in the area, there's plenty more to see in West Glacier and Apgar.

West Glacier

The town of West Glacier (originally known as Belton) centered historically around the Belton Train Depot and Belton Chalet. Today, Highway 2 divides the pair, and West Glacier now harbors recreational concessions such as rafting, backpacking, hiking, helitours, and fishing. To leave the highway bustle, drive through the railroad tunnel and enter a historic world preserved by the Lundgren family, operators for over 50 years of the West Glacier Mercantile Company. The vintage brown 1938 buildings house a bar, restaurant, gift shops, grocery, and motel. Fall finds lazy birch leaves covering the ground as shops board their windows, leaving the town's 224 year-round residents to themselves.

© BECKY LOMAX

Historic Belton Bridge provided the first west side entrance to Glacier.

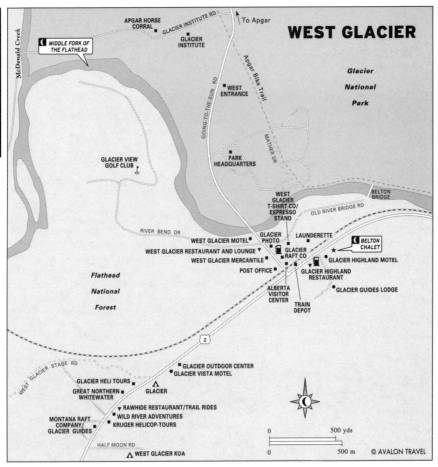

Belton Chalet

In 1910, Glacier became a park, and the Belton Chalet opened its doors to guests arriving via Great Northern Railway. The first in a series of railroad company Swiss-themed chalets built throughout the park, the Belton served as the park gateway. Milkmaid-attired hostesses and flowered walkways greeted guests. (In the Taproom, you can see its original look in the photo that includes the trellised walkway from the train depot to the chalet.) Over the years, the chalet changed hands, serving as housing

for Civilian Conservation Corps crews building Going-to-the-Sun Road as well as a pizza parlor and bakery. After heavy snows destroyed roofs and floors in the late 1990s, owners from Bigfork restored the lodge and cabins to the tune of $1 million. In 2000, Belton Chalet was recognized on the National Register of Historic Places.

Historic Belton Bridge

The Belton Bridge opened in 1920; park visitors could drive across the Middle Fork of the Flathead River without rowing. Ironically, this

WILDFIRES

In an average summer, 13 wildfires burn in Glacier, altering the forest landscape on 5,000 acres. Most are lightning caused, with over 80 percent of strikes touching down in the park's heavily timbered west side. Some are small and unseen while others send huge smoke plumes thousands of feet in the air.

Two large fire seasons ripped through Glacier in the past decade. In 2001, the Moose Fire burned almost 30,000 acres in the North Fork area. In 2003, an onslaught of lightning strikes burned 150,000 acres in several locations around Glacier in one of the largest fire seasons in the park's history. (You can see the evidence from Going-to-the-Sun Road across Lake McDonald and at The Loop.) In 2006, the Red Eagle fire ate up 32,000 acres outside St. Mary. But even in these recent fire zones, plants and forests are already regenerating.

As flames eat up wood, ash falls to the ground, releasing nutrients. Similar to putting a good fertilizer on a garden, the ash fosters energetic plant growth, especially with the open tree canopy permitting more sunlight. As a natural succession of greenery takes over, wildlife dependent on plant foraging finds improved habitat. In short, fires help maintain a natural balance. They also remove deadfall and infested insects, such as pine bark beetles

that kill trees, turning their needles to rust. Fires reduce the power of future fires and create forests more resistant to drought and nonnative plant invasions. Fire isn't the end of a forest, but an ongoing process of succession in an ever-changing landscape.

Larch and ponderosa, with thick resinless bark and minimal low branches, survive fires. Some species even rely on fires for reproduction: The lodgepole's serotinous cones require high heat to release its fast-growing seeds from the sticky resin. Ceanothus, hollyhock, and morel mushrooms flourish after fires.

Until 1968, federal policy suppressed all fires – resulting in excessive fuel buildup, bug infestations, and elimination of some floral species. Today, the Park Service manages each fire individually. If fires threaten human life or structures, they will be suppressed, along with most human-caused fires, but lightning fires ranging in the wilds will often be monitored, allowing for a natural cycle. Sometimes, park crews set intentional fires to reduce fuel buildup or protect a resource, such as a prairie, from invasion by other species.

Glacier's wildfires used to be monitored from 17 different lookouts. Today, satellite and airplane surveys have reduced the need for staffed lookouts to Huckleberry, Scalplock, Numa, and Swiftcurrent.

---

wood and cement bridge remained standing during the 1964 flood while torrents of water destroyed the new bridge downstream. For a time, this bridge served again as the new bridge was repaired. The park service recently fixed up the "Old Bridge," as locals call it, open now for foot traffic only. It accesses the Boundary Trail, Middle Fork fishing spots, and calm but deep chilly pools for swimming. To find it, turn right in West Glacier on Old Bridge Road, driving to the end.

Middle Fork of the Flathead
The Middle Fork of the Flathead collects its waters from deep within the Bob Marshall

Wilderness Complex and Glacier National Park. Its north shore high-water mark denotes the national park boundary. Designated a Wild and Scenic River, the Middle Fork—the shortened moniker most people use for the river—vacillates between raging rapids and mesmerizing meanders. Anglers and swimmers gravitate to its blue-green pools. Rafters and kayakers splash through rapids known as Bonecrusher and Jaws. Hikers tootle along its Boundary Trail.

Apgar
Two miles from West Glacier, Apgar sits on the shore of the park's largest body of water—Lake

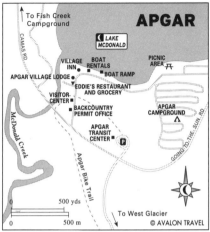

flames in Glacier Park's history. Raging winds shoved the Robert Fire over Apgar Mountain, gobbling 7,000 acres in four hours. Campers, motel guests, and park headquarters personnel evacuated from West Glacier and Apgar while helicopters doused the fire with water scooped from Lake McDonald. The fire's 39,000 acres comprised 29 percent of the park's aflame forests that summer. See post-fire forest regeneration on the Camas Road, the Lake McDonald Trail starting at Fish Creek Campground, or from Apgar Lookout. Fast-growing new vegetation thriving on the fire's ash and nutrient-rich soils prompted prolific flower blooms, like pink fireweed, and some tree species requiring fire to sprout are growing again.

McDonald. With Apgar Campground within walking distance and Fish Creek Campground a couple of miles away, Apgar is crowded in high season but still quiet compared to the West Glacier highway hubbub. It's the quintessential national park community. The tiny west-side visitors center, a restaurant, a camp store, two inns, Lake McDonald's only boat ramp, swimming beaches, and picnic areas all cluster here at Lake McDonald's foot. One local gift shop is in Apgar's historic red schoolhouse. Like West Glacier, most of Apgar shuts down by October and opens again in May.

(Robert Fire

Summer 2003 unleashed some of the biggest

(Lake McDonald

Catching waters from Glacier's longest river, Lake McDonald is 10 miles long by 1.5 miles wide—the largest lake in Glacier National Park. Squeezed between Mount Brown and Stanton Peak at its head, the lake plummets to depths of 472 feet—the deepest waters in the park. Resting in an ice-scoured trough, the 6,823-acre lake is buffered by larch forests that turn gold in fall. On it, visitors fish, boat, and swim in its quiet, cold blue (no Jet Skis are allowed). Even waterskiing attracts a few wet-suited diehards. Access the lake's shores via Fish Creek or Apgar Picnic Area, the Apgar boat ramp, or the many pullouts along Going-to-the-Sun Road.

Recreation

If Glacier has a recreation center, it's West Glacier and Apgar. The pair offer hiking, biking, rafting, horseback riding, kayaking, boating, fishing, swimming, and golfing. West Glacier is the unofficial park headquarters for white-water rafting with two Wild and Scenic Rivers (nationally designated rivers protected for their wilderness and beauty) a short step from the back door.

HIKING

Hiking in Apgar improved substantially with the 2003 Robert Fire. Flames opened up views amid once thick dark forests, and nutrient-enriched ash soils sprouted lush growth. Wildflowers now run amok on slopes that once had meager color. This also is the only park area where a trail permits dogs: The two-mile paved Apgar Bike Trail connecting West

HIKING ESSENTIALS

Hiking in Glacier demands preparedness. Unpredictable, fast-changing weather can mutate a warm summer day into wintry conditions in hours. Different elevations vary in temperatures, winds, and visibility: Sun on the shore of Two Medicine Lake may hide knock-over winds barreling over Dawson Pass six miles away. Hot valley temperatures may give way at Grinnell Lake to chilly breezes blowing down from the Continental Divide and across the ice. To be prepared in Glacier's backcountry, take the following:

- **Extra clothing:** Rain pants and jackets can double as wind protection, while gloves and a lightweight warm hat will save fingers and ears. Carry at least one extra water-wicking layer for warmth. Avoid cotton fabrics that stay soggy and fail to retain body heat.

- **Extra food and water:** Depending on the hike's length, take a lunch and snacks, like compact high-energy food bars. Low-odor foods will not attract animals. Always carry extra water: Heat, wind, and elevation lead quickly to dehydration, and most visitors find they drink more than they do at home. Avoid drinking directly from streams or lakes. Due to possible giardia and other bacteria, always filter (with a one-micron filter) or treat water sources before drinking.

- **Map and compass or GPS device:** Although Glacier's trails are extremely well signed, a map can be handy for ascertaining distance traveled and location. A compass or GPS device will also help, but only if you know how to use it. In deep heavily forested valleys, a GPS may not pick up satellites.

- **Flashlight:** Carry a small flashlight or headlamp. In an after-dark emergency, the light becomes invaluable. Take extra batteries, too.

- **First-aid kit:** Two bandages may not be enough! Carry a fully equipped standard first-aid kit with blister remedies. Many outdoor stores sell suitably prepared kits for hiking. Don't forget to add personal items like bee-sting kits and allergy medications.

- **Sun protection:** Altitude, snow, ice, and lakes all increase ultraviolet radiation. Protect yourself with 30 SPF sunscreen, sunglasses, and a sun hat or baseball cap.

- **Emergency bathroom supplies:** Not every hike conveniently places a pit toilet at its destination. To accommodate an alfresco bathroom, carry a small trowel, plastic baggies, and toilet paper, and move at least 200 feet away from water sources. For urinating, aim for a durable surface, such as rocks, logs, gravel, or snow. "Watering" fragile plants, campsites, or trails attracts mineral-starved animals that dig up the area. Bury feces 6-8 inches deep in soil. Do not bury toilet paper; use a baggie to pack it out.

- **Feminine hygiene:** Carry heavy-duty zippered baggies and pack tampons, pads, and everything out.

- **Insect repellent:** Summer can be abuzz at any elevation with mosquitoes and black-flies. Insect repellents containing 50 percent DEET tend to work best. Purchase applications that rub or spray in a close range rather than aerosols that become airborne onto other people, plants, and animals.

- **Pepper spray:** If you want to carry pepper spray, purchase an 8-ounce can, as nothing smaller will be effective; however, do not bother unless you know how to use it and what influences its effectiveness. It is not to be used like bug repellent.

- **Miscellaneous:** A knife may come in handy, as can a few feet of nylon cord and a bit of duct tape (wrap a few feet around something small like a flashlight handle or water bottle). Many hikers have repaired boots and packs with duct tape and a little ingenuity.

Glacier and Apgar is open to walkers, leashed dogs, and bicyclists.

Rocky Point

- Distance: 2 miles round-trip
- Duration: 1 hour
- Elevation gain: none
- Effort: easy
- Trailhead: Fish Creek Campground by Apgar

Rocky Point is a short interpretive romp along Lake McDonald through the 2003 Robert Fire and looping around a promontory on Lake McDonald's north shore. Places of heavy burn with slow regrowth alternate with lighter burn clogged now with lush greenery. Don't forget your camera: The view from Rocky Point looks up the lake toward the Continental Divide and grabs grand shots of Mounts Jackson and Edwards to the south. If the lake is calm, you'll nab some stunning reflection photos. Snow leaves early and comes late to this trail, making

it good for spring and fall hiking. The loop trail connects to the Lake McDonald Trail.

◖ Apgar Lookout

- Distance: 6.6 miles round-trip
- Duration: 3.5 hours
- Elevation gain: 1,850 feet
- Effort: moderate
- Trailhead: end of Glacier Institute Road, 1.9 miles from Going-to-the-Sun Road
- Directions: Take the first left after the West Entrance Station at the Glacier Institute sign. At the first fork, follow the sign to the horse barn and veer left, crossing over Quarter Circle Bridge. Drive to the road's terminus at the trailhead.

Beginning with a gentle walk along an old dirt road, Apgar Lookout Trail soon climbs steeply uphill toward the first of three long switchbacks. As the trail ascends, large burned sentinels stand as relics from the 2003 Robert Fire. In 2010, more than 300 of the burned

Rocky Point is a kid-friendly destination.

trees blew down, opening up the views of the Middle Fork drainage, Rubideau Basin, the railway line, and West Glacier. Following the third switchback, the trail traverses the ridge—which holds snow in June—to the rebuilt lookout. A panoramic view unfolds from Canada to the park's southern sector, and you can see all six park peaks over 10,000 feet.

From this 5,236-foot aerie, you can see the path of the Robert Fire, where it burned 7,000 acres in four hours. Prior to the fire, heavy timber and brush occluded views, but Apgar Lookout now ranks as one of the park's most scenic hikes. While fire and blowdowns improved the views, trees no longer shade the southwest-facing slope; hike in the morning on hot days. Park communication radio antennas clutter the summit, but at least they are clustered in one location at the lookout instead of spread out.

◖ Huckleberry Lookout

- Distance: 12 miles round-trip
- Duration: 5–6 hours
- Elevation gain: 3,403 feet
- Effort: strenuous
- Trailhead: six miles up Camas Road from Apgar just past McGee Meadows

Huckleberry Lookout trail is aptly named, for huckleberries do abound in this area. During certain times of the season, usually late summer to early fall, the trail closes due to bear activity. The heavy concentration of huckleberries attracts a significant bruin population looking to bulk up for the winter. Check with the park service for current status. When the trail is closed, the trailhead posts obvious closure signage.

The trail begins with a gentle walk through lodgepole forest. Shortly, the path climbs, steadily gaining elevation among larch until it emerges on steep-sloped meadows and reaches a saddle at 4.5 miles. In a short reprieve from the climb, the trail traverses a wide bowl until it crests the Apgar Range for the final ascent to the lookout at 6,593 feet. A spectacular

© BECKY LOMAX

Huckleberry Lookout's final ridge walk gives top-of-the-world views.

view of the North Fork Valley and the park's Livingston Range unfolds. During fire season, the lookout is staffed. Evidence of the 2001 Moose Fire clings to Huckleberry Mountain as well as Demers Ridge below and the North Fork Valley. Snow often packs the upper trail until mid-July.

Lake McDonald West Shore Trail

- Distance: 7 miles one-way
- Duration: 3 hours
- Elevation gain: none
- Effort: easy
- Trailhead: Fish Creek Campground or North McDonald Road

This year-round trail (use skis or snowshoes in winter) follows the north shore of Lake McDonald, wandering back in the trees, then close to the shoreline. While views of peak-flanked Lake McDonald are dramatic, more remarkable is the study of postfire forest succession along the trail. Burned by the 2003 Robert Fire, the trail passes through lush new growth spurred by nitrogen-rich ash returned to the soil. With a car shuttle, hikers can walk this point to point, but most opt to saunter out for a few miles from either direction, perhaps drop a fishing line into the lake, and turn around again.

South Boundary Trail

- Distance: 10.6 miles round-trip to Lincoln Creek
- Duration: 5 hours
- Elevation gain: minimal
- Effort: easy
- Trailhead: behind park headquarters on Mather Drive's south end or the old bridge in West Glacier

After parking at headquarters, walk through the headquarters housing area to the trailhead. Follow the old Glacier Park Entrance Road to the historic Belton Bridge, where a trail continues upstream. You can also access this trail via the Belton Bridge, but the trailhead here does not have as much parking. With gentle ascents and descents, the path hugs the north-shore hillside above the Wild and Scenic Middle Fork of the Flathead River.

This year-round trail won't feel like wilderness: Noise from the railroad and highway competes with the river's roaring white water. But it's a great place to watch rafters shoot rapids, swim in deep pools, or fish. The trail descends to a fine rocky beach at Lincoln Creek, a stopping point for rafters before they hit the white water. From here, backpackers can opt to continue another 15 miles upriver to Coal Creek or turn 9.4 miles up Lincoln Creek to Lincoln Lake.

Guided Hikes

National Park Service naturalists guide hikes and walks around Apgar mid-June–mid-September. Days and times vary, as do the hikes—easy to strenuous. In winter, the park service offers guided snowshoe trips to look for animal tracks. Grab a current copy of *Ranger-Led Activities* at visitors centers to check the schedule. These guided hikes are the best price of all: free!

Glacier Guides (11970 Hwy. 2 E., West Glacier, 406/387-5555 or 800/521-7238, www.glacierguides.com) leads day hikes, but most destinations are outside the West Glacier–Apgar area. Solo travelers can hook up with their Tuesday Hikes ($75 per person, July–Aug.). Group Day Hikes costing $375 for 1–5 people (June–Sept.) depart from the West Glacier office at 8:30 A.M. Custom Day Hikes ($450, up to five people) depart from your lodge or campground. Hikes require reservations and include guide service, deli lunch, and transportation to the trailhead. The guide service also leads backcountry chalet hikes (three or six days, $697 or $1,805) and three-, four-, and six-day backpacking trips ($435–840, June–mid-Sept.) departing weekly.

Rentals

Two companies in West Glacier offer rental gear for hikers, backpackers, and campers.

Glacier Outdoor Center (11957 Hwy. 2 E., 406/888-5454 or 800/235-6781, www.glacierraftco.com) carries the most extensive line of rental gear: day packs ($10), backpacks ($20), trekking poles ($5), and child carrier packs ($20). They also rent a full car camping setup for four people for $125 per day and individual gear from ice axes to sleeping bags, tents, cook stoves, coolers, camp chairs, lanterns, and water purifiers. Rates reduce for additional days. **Glacier Guides** (11970 Hwy. 2 E., 406/387-5555 or 800/521-7238, www.glacierguides.com) rents tents, backpacks, or sleeping bags and pads at $8–10 per item or the complete set for $20.

BIKING
Bicycling Glacier National Park is not for everyone. Narrow, shoulderless roads are packed with curves, and most trails prohibit bikes. However, West Glacier–Apgar is one area in the park that does provide two off-road biking options.

Bike Trails
A level, paved bicycle trail connects West Glacier with Apgar. Approximately 2.6 miles long, the **Apgar Bike Trail** begins on the north side of the West Glacier Bridge. After dropping through the woods, it crosses through the park service employee housing area before entering the forest again, where it continues on to Apgar, connecting finally with the campground. Be cautious at two road crossings en route. The short dirt **Fish Creek** bike trail provides a shortcut between Apgar and Fish Creek. Bike trails permit dogs on leashes, and they're good flat riding for kids.

The 10-mile round-trip **Old Flathead Ranger Station** ride tours a combo of dirt road and trail that was once a road. It terminates at the confluence of Flathead River's North and Middle Forks. Access the route from midway between West Glacier and Apgar on the Apgar Bike Trail, turning west on the dirt Glacier Institute Road. At the first junction, follow the sign to the horse barn; at the second, hang a left toward Quarter Circle Bridge. About 0.5 mile past the bridge, the Old Flathead Ranger Station Trail begins. Turn left, biking 3.7 miles to the confluence.

Road Biking
Many bicyclists enjoy short road rides from Apgar up Camas Road, the dirt Inside Road (see the *North Fork* chapter for details), or just to Fish Creek Picnic Area.

For a longer mountain-bike tour (approximately 37 miles, four hours) on a mix of dirt and paved roads, the **Apgar Mountain Loop** takes off from West Glacier heading west over Belton Stage and Blankenship Roads to connect with North Fork Road. From here, ride north, parallel with the North Fork River to the Camas Road entrance and back into the park. Follow paved rolling Camas Road back to the Apgar Bike Trail. The scenic loop is well worth a ride, especially in late spring before Going-to-the-Sun Road is open, but be prepared to suck serious dust on the dirt sections during dry spells and battle bears and mosquitoes along Camas Road.

Apgar is also the launch point for those bicycling Going-to-the-Sun Road. For details, see the *Going-to-the-Sun Road* chapter.

Rentals
No bicycle rentals are available in West Glacier or Apgar. You can rent bikes in Flathead Valley (see the *Flathead Valley* chapter).

TRAIL RIDING
Catch the horseback experience in Apgar or West Glacier. For trail riding, be sure to wear long pants; you'll be a lot less sore afterward. For safety, wear sturdy shoes or hiking boots—not sandals.

For guided trail rides in Apgar, make reservations with **Swan Mountain Outfitters** (mid-Sept.–mid-May 800/919-4416, summer 877/888-5557, www.swanmountainoutfitters.com). Their **Apgar Corral** (406/888-5010, late May–early Sept.), located on the Glacier Institute Road, leads three daily trail rides ($40–107). A one-hour easy saunter to McDonald Meadows and a popular two-hour

© BECKY LOMAX

Swan Mountain Outfitters runs daily trail rides in Glacier.

ride along the C. M. Russell Trail depart several times each day. The half-day ride to Apgar Lookout, which requires four people minimum, departs at 7:45 A.M. The company does not take children under seven nor riders weighing over 250 pounds.

In West Glacier, **Rawhide Trail Rides** (12000 Hwy. 2 E., 406/387-5555 or 800/388-5727, www.glacierrawhide.com, mid-May–mid-Oct.) leads horseback tours through the lodgepole foothills of Flathead National Forest. One-, two-, three-hour, or half-day rides begin daily at 8 A.M. ($28–67 per person); tours depart multiple times throughout the day, with the last ride leaving at 4 P.M. You can just show up for these, but if you want to guarantee a time, make reservations. Rawhide can accommodate kids 4–7 years old with small saddles. You can also do a full-day ride with a minimum of four people ($120 per person, including lunch; reservations required) or an overnight trip ($215 per person). The company also works in tandem with a raft company to offer ride and raft combo trips, day trips or overnights ($99–675).

RAFTING

Two rivers designated Wild and Scenic form the boundary of Glacier's west and southwest. The Middle Fork and North Fork of the Flathead River offer scenery, wilderness, float sections, and white water. Together, the rivers provide 219 miles of recreation. The rafting season runs May–September, with high water usually peaking in late May. Rafters should purchase the *Three Forks of the Flathead Float Guide,* available through Glacier Natural History Association (406/888-5756, www.glacierassociation.org, $12.95) for location of rapids and public land for camping. Flathead National Forest manages both rivers; consult the Hungry Horse Ranger Station (10 Hungry Horse Dr., 406/387-5243) in Hungry Horse, nine miles west of West Glacier, for assistance in planning a self-guided overnight trip. Toilet systems are required for overnights, and fire pans are recommended to prevent scarring.

◀ Middle Fork of the Flathead

Bordering Glacier's southern boundary, the Middle Fork of the Flathead interrupts scenic float sections with raging white water. The river draws its headwaters from deep within the Bob Marshall Wilderness Complex and drains Glacier's immense southern valleys.

While the white water cannot compete with the Grand Canyon's monster waves, the Middle Fork is a fun, splashy place with rapids such as Screaming Right Turn, Jaws, and Pinball. It's easy enough for kids and good introductory fun for a first-time river trip. White-water trips begin at Moccasin Creek and end in West Glacier; scenic float trips begin in West Glacier and end at Blankenship.

The Middle Fork River offers several put-ins and take-outs easily accessed along Highway 2. Different sections are appropriate for overnights, day trips, fishing, and short floats. While a few rapids at certain water levels are rated Class IV, the river along Glacier's boundary is primarily Class II and III. No permits are required. However, all camping must be done on the south shore; no camping is permitted on Glacier's shoreline. Since private property abuts some of the south shore, you'll need to be knowledgeable about where you can camp. Find more detailed floating info in the *Marias Pass and Essex* chapter.

North Fork of the Flathead

From Canada, the North Fork of the Flathead flows 59 miles through the remote North Fork Valley. As the river enters the United States, it forms the western boundary of Glacier. Accessed via the bumpy, dirt Outside North Fork Road, the Class II–III river provides multiday float trips, day rafting, and fishing. Those looking for tamer water can take out at Big Creek before the Upper Fool Hen Rapids. Put-ins and take-outs range up and down North Fork Road. No permits are required, but campsites must all be set up on the western shore; no camping is permitted on Glacier's bank except for Round Prairie. The river ends at the confluence with the Middle Fork at the Blankenship River Access, 10 minutes west of

© BECKY LOMAX

Small thrill-seeker boats give splashier rides on the Middle Fork of the Flathead.

West Glacier. Find more detailed floating info in the *North Fork* chapter.

Guides

The commercial rafting season runs May–September, with high water usually peaking in late May. Four West Glacier rafting companies lead half-day and full-day float trips on the Middle Fork River as well as scenic floats, dinner, barbecue, or evening floats. Each company also launches four to five half-day raft trips daily through the white-water section and guides overnight and multiday trips. Children should be at least six years old for white water.

If you're comparing rates between companies (they're all very similar in cost), be sure to ask if the 7 percent service fee is included in the rate or added on. Also, ask about the size of the raft and the number of people it carries. Smaller rafts will have a more exciting ride. Expect to pay (not including service fees) around $48 per person for an adult half-day raft trip or $82 for full day; kids run about $10 cheaper. For more fun, tackle the white water in a small sport raft with more kick (available at three companies) or an inflatable kayak, otherwise known as a rubber ducky (available at all four companies). Both run around $15–20 more per person; rates include helmets. Paddles and life jackets are included in all rates, but some companies charge additional fees for wetsuits and/or booties. Clarify fees when you make your reservation. Plan on tipping the guide $7 per person for half-day trips.

Overnight rafting trips range 2–5 days; longer ones are usually paired up with hiking, horseback riding, or backpacking. Expect to pay $160–170 per person per day for an overnight rafting trip and $30 less per day for children. Specialty trips with cabin stays, horseback riding, or flights will cost more. Plan to tip 15 percent for overnights. When making reservations, clarify what you'll need to bring for your overnight. The companies can provide tents, sleeping bags, and pads. Dry bags are supplied for your gear.

Glacier Raft Company (6 Going-to-the-Sun Rd., 406/888-5454 or 800/235-6781,

www.glacierraftco.com) sits right in West Glacier village adjacent to the river—close enough to the take-out that white-water rafters debark at the Middle Fork Bridge to walk two blocks back to the office. Sport rafts for 4–6 people are available. A cast and raft package combines a half day of fly-fishing with a half day of white-water rafting. The company offers two-, three-, and four-day overnights and is the only local company permitted to guide trips on the Class III–IV Upper Middle Fork of the Flathead River in the Great Bear Wilderness. Their four-day excursion ($1,495) requires flight access to a remote put-in near the headwaters; their five-day trip ($2,000) reaches the put-in via two and a half days of horseback riding.

Located one mile west of downtown West Glacier, **Great Northern Whitewater** (12127 Hwy. 2 E., 406/387-5340 or 800/735-7897, www.gnwhitewater.com) sold to new owners in 2010. In addition to daily trips, the company specializes in saddle-paddles ($108), two- to three-day floats on the Middle Fork River ($335–455), and one- to six-day river school programs for those who want to master their own skills.

Just off the highway 1.5 miles west of West Glacier, **Montana Raft Company** (11970 Hwy. 2 E., 406/387-5555 or 800/521-7238, www.glacierguides.com) is the only company that can combine hiking in the park and raft trips, as sister Glacier Guides runs the park's sole hiking concession. An extensive menu of hike-raft or backpack-raft combos can fill a day or week. Sport rafts are available in their arsenal of day trips. Overnight trips float the Middle Fork or the North Fork of the Flathead River. One family-friendly trip puts together a three-day North Fork float with staying in rustic cabins (adults $652, kids $552).

Also located 1.5 miles west of West Glacier, **Wild River Adventures** (11900 Hwy. 2 E., 406/387-9453 or 800/700-7056, www.riverwild.com) offers 12-foot sport rafts on their daily menu. The company also specializes in full-day to four-day horse-raft combo trips ($95–670). Overnight trips tour the Middle Fork River for three days (adults $440, youth $365).

Rentals and Shuttles

Got the river savvy to guide yourself? If so, you can rent a raft ($100–140) or inflatable kayak ($45–75) from two of the West Glacier raft companies. Both companies also rent dry bags, wetsuits, booties, throw bags, fire pans, toilet systems, and camping gear for overnights. Packages from **Glacier Outdoor Center** (11957 Hwy. 2 E., 406/888-5454 or 800/235-6781, www.glacierraftco.com) include paddles, helmets, life jackets, pump, and repair kits. The company will also shuttle your vehicle from the put-in to take-out for $30–275, depending on distance up the Middle Fork or the North Fork. A shuttle in their rigs costs $85–355. **Montana Raft Company** (11970 Hwy. 2 E., 406/387-5555 or 800/521-7238, www.glacierguides.com) rentals include life jackets and paddles.

BOATING

With its vast acreage of water, Lake McDonald attracts boaters, but it's never crowded—usually just a few quiet anglers in the early morning followed by a couple die-hard water-skiers, sightseers, and kayakers touring the shoreline. Because the frigid waters inhibit most water-skiers and Jet Skis are not permitted, the lake never has a frenzied hubbub of noise. In fact, national park regulations enforce a maximum noise level of 82 decibels. Similar to many of the park's lakes, you'll rarely see a sailboat or sailboard: unpredictable, swirly winds on Lake McDonald make other lakes outside the park more appealing. Located adjacent to Village Inn, Apgar's boat ramp provides the lake's only public ramp access.

Boaters must get free permits and show that their boats have been cleaned, drained, and dried to avoid bringing Aquatic Invasive Species into park lakes. Permits for up to 14 days are available at the **Apgar Backcountry Permit Office** (406/888-7859, May-Oct.), two buildings west of the Apgar Visitor Center.

Rentals

For boating and fishing on Lake McDonald, **Glacier Park Boat Company** (406/257-2426,

© BECKY LOMAX

paddling Lake McDonald

FISHING IN GLACIER

With 27,023 acres of lakes, 563 streams, and 22 species of fish, Glacier is a place where no angler should sit with a slack line. Although only a scant 10 percent of park visitors fish, those who do typically enjoy calm vistas and a few native trout. While weather and skill variables influence success, a few tips for Glacier's waters can help.

FISHING TIPS

- Avoid a long hike to a remote lake to fish... unless you want to go for the sake of the journey. While many anglers find more success angling in waters away from roads, remoteness doesn't mean good fishing. Waterfalls prevent fish from reaching some streams and lakes.

- Since arrival at a high mountain lake will most likely be at midday when fishing is not the best, stay overnight in the backcountry or at a lodge nearby. This way, you can fish in the morning or evening, when fish feed, for best results. Overcast days also tend to be better than sunny days.

- During early summer runoff when river waters cloud with sediments, fish hang out on the bottom to feed. Try lures that mimic insect larvae. Or fish lakes instead.

- When streams run clear, fly-fishing is the most productive. Try to match a prominent hatch, but traditional high-floating attractor patterns will also move fish.

- At lakes, look for inlets and outlets to fish, but be considerate of heavily trafficked areas.

- Trolling from a motorboat (where allowed) or canoe is the most effective way to fish for lake trout.

FISHING AND BEARS

- Fishing in bear country poses special considerations. Since smells attract bears that travel along waterways, minimize your chances of a bear encounter by keeping fishy smells away from your clothing. In general, catch-and-release fishing minimizes the chances of attracting a bear.

- For cleaning fish in the front country, dispose of fish entrails in bear-resistant garbage cans. In the backcountry, do not bury

---

www.glacierparkboats.com) rents rowboats, canoes, kayaks, and eight-horsepower motorboats for $18–24 per hour from the Apgar boat dock next to Village Inn. Paddles, life jackets, and fishing regulations are included in the rates. Its tiny boat dock office takes cash only.

Regulations

Two shoreline closures affect boaters: from the Apgar boat ramp north to the lake's outlet, and between the Apgar Amphitheater and Going-to-the-Sun Road. To protect swimmers, boaters must stay 300 feet off the shoreline and are not permitted to beach. Watch for additional temporary wildlife closures marked with buoys, especially where bald eagles nest at the lake's east end.

While any craft over 12 feet must be registered in Montana, temporary use of out-of-state boats is permitted without registration. On Glacier's waters, federal boating regulations and water travel etiquette apply. For a complete list of boating regulations, check with visitors centers or Glacier's website: www.nps.gov/glac.

WHITE-WATER KAYAKING

White-water kayakers drop into the **Middle Fork of the Flathead,** which churns up Class II–III rapids. Kayakers play in the froth between Moccasin Creek put-in and the West Glacier take-out, surfing the waves on Tunnel Rapid. Some eliminate the flat water before and after the rapids by using railroad accesses. To or burn the innards, as that may attract bears. Instead, be at least 200 feet away from a campsite or trail, puncture the air bladder, and throw the entrails into deep water. If you plan to eat your fish, keep only what you can eat, and eat as soon as you can.

NATIVE SPECIES

Glacier Park's fishing regulations enforce protection of native species through selected area closures and limits on the taking of native species. The park service no longer stocks fish, as many of the introduced species took a toll on native fish through competition for food and predation. Until 1972, an estimated 45-55 million fish and eggs were planted in Glacier's waters, introducing **arctic grayling, rainbow trout, kokanee salmon, brook trout,** and **Yellowstone cutthroat trout. Lake trout** and **lake whitefish** also invaded the park's west-side water systems through stocking in Flathead Lake, although lake trout are native to park waters east of the Continental Divide and **mountain whitefish** are native throughout the park.

Of Glacier's 10 sport and 12 non-sport fish, the **bull trout** is the one listed as a threatened species under the Endangered Species Act. In Montana, this predatory fish, which can grow to two feet long, now inhabits less than half of its original streams, due to a number of factors, including habitat degradation. No fishing for bull trout is allowed; any incidentally caught must be immediately released. Look on the dorsal fin: no black, put it back.

Glacier is also one of the few remaining strongholds for **westslope cutthroat trout,** which now inhabit only 2.5 percent of their original range. Mostly threatened by interbreeding with rainbow trout, genetically pure populations of cutthroat remain in 15-19 park lakes.

While bull trout are protected by law, other native fish need conscientious anglers to help preserve the native fishery. Learn to identify native and nonnative species and follow park guidelines for which fish to harvest and which native fish to release. But in general, release native fish; keep only your limit of nonnative species.

For the best fishing recommendations, grab a copy of Russ Schneider's *Fishing Glacier National Park.*

locate rapids and difficulty, consult *Three Forks of the Flathead Float Guide,* available through Glacier Natural History Association (406/888-5756, www.glacierassociation.org, $12.95).

Great Northern Whitewater (12127 Hwy. 2 E., West Glacier, 406/387-5340 or 800/735-7897, www.gnwhitewater.com, $100–625, all equipment included) leads half-, full-, multiday, and overnight kayak trips on the Middle Fork rapids in their **kayak school.** One- to six-day river school courses are available. Instructors, who are all ACA White-Water Certified, walk beginners through the basics or teach playboating skills to the experienced. You can even take a special roll clinic. None of the West Glacier raft companies rent white-water kayaks; you have to go to Flathead Valley.

SEA KAYAKING AND CANOEING

With its monstrous shoreline, **Lake McDonald** is a treat for canoeing and sea kayaking, but watch for winds whipping up large whitecaps. When glassy, calm waters prevail, you'd be hard-pressed to beat it at sunrise or sunset. Touring the shoreline, you may encounter wildlife closures, especially for nesting bald eagles at the lake's head.

Two rivers offer options for flat-water paddlers. The **Middle Fork of the Flathead** is gentle enough for canoeing and sea kayaking from West Glacier downriver to Blankenship. But the section includes one challenging rapid that has been known to flip lazy paddlers. A 90-minute paddle, the scenic **Lower McDonald**

Creek starts north of the Apgar boat launch on Lake McDonald and floats past beaver dams to Quarter Circle Bridge.

At the Apgar boat dock next to Village Inn, **Glacier Park Boat Company** (406/257-2426, www.glacierparkboats.com) rents canoes and double plastic kayaks for $18 per hour. Boats come with paddles and life jackets. Bring cash; the company does not take credit cards. For sea-kayak rentals, go to Flathead Valley.

FISHING

While **Lake McDonald** may be the biggest body of water in Glacier, expert anglers head to other lakes. Boats work best to troll for lake trout. For catch-and-release fly-fishing, **Lower McDonald Creek** from the lake to Quarter Circle Bridge works, but it's also heavily fished because of its easy access. For several miles in both directions from West Glacier, the **Middle Fork of the Flathead** presents good fishing, but be ready to contend with rafters and fishing outfitters. Because of the concentration of visitors in the West Glacier–Apgar area during high season, you may not feel like you're off in the wilderness when you toss in a line, but you just might pull in native trout.

Park Regulations

Fishing inside Glacier Park does not require a license, but waters here have some restrictions. Lake McDonald has no limit on lake trout or whitefish, but westslope cutthroat are catch-and-release only. Lower McDonald Creek from the lake outlet to Quarter Circle Bridge has been catch-and-release only, but check with the park service as nonnative species rules may change. Despite its name, Fish Creek is closed to fishing.

Licenses and Gear Rental

Fishing outside Glacier on Flathead River drainages requires a Montana fishing license. You can pick one up at **Glacier Outdoor Center** (11957 Hwy. 2 E., West Glacier, 406/888-5454 or 800/235-6781, www.glacierraftco.com). A two-day license costs $25; a seasonal license is $70. The center, which is also a fly shop, rents fishing gear ($5–60): rods, waders, and float tubes.

Guides

Four fly-fishing companies in West Glacier guide half-, full-, and multiday trips in drift boats on Glacier's boundary waters in the Middle Fork or North Fork of the Flathead River, but none guide fishing adventures inside Glacier Park. For beginners, they offer fly-fishing schools to teach the basics of casting, mending, and catch-and-release. Reservations are mandatory.

For a half-day guided fishing trip for one or two people, expect to pay around $325, and add on about $100 more for full days. Overnights run around $400 per person per day with two people minimum or $750 for one person per day. Plan on tipping the guides about 15 percent, or more if you catch lots of fish. It's pricey, but the guides usually get you to the good fishing holes. Rates include all equipment, such as life jackets, rods, and flies. As with rafting trips, a 7 percent service fee is added to all fishing trips, but some companies include it in the price. You'll also need to buy your own fishing license.

Glacier Anglers (Glacier Outdoor Center, 11957 Hwy. 2 E., 406/888-5454 or 800/235-6781, www.glacierraftco.com) leads fishing trips on the Middle Fork and North Fork of the Flathead mid-April–mid-October. Their specialty four- to seven-day Great Bear Wilderness fishing trips cost around $695 per person per day. The half-day pond fishing for families costs $236, and a one-hour casting clinic runs $30. **Glacier Guides** (11970 Hwy. 2 E., 406/387-5555 or 800/521-7238, www.glacier-guides.com) has half- and full-day fly-fishing trips on the Middle Fork of the Flathead River and overnights on the North Fork River July–mid-September. **Montana Fly-fishing Guides** (Great Northern Whitewater, 12127 Hwy. 2 E., 406/387-5340 or 800/735-7897, www.gn-whitewater.com) leads half- and full-day trips on the Middle Fork River late June–October. **Wild River Adventures** (11900 Hwy. 2 E., 406/387-9453 or 800/700-7056, www.riverwild.com) provides anglers with half- and full-day trips on the Middle Fork of the Flathead and overnight trips on the North Fork late June–September.

GOLF

Glacier View Golf Club (640 River Bend Dr., West Glacier, 406/888-5471 or 800/843-5777) may tax your concentration as you tee off. Moose, elk, bears, and deer wander across the fairways, and the mountain views are hard to ignore. The 18-hole course has a pro shop, restaurant, practice green, driving range, lessons, cart rentals ($26) and club rentals ($12). Open daily to the public April–October (snow permitting), the course charges $29 for 18 holes. To locate the golf course in West Glacier, turn west onto River Bend Drive and follow signs to the clubhouse. The club has RV hookups for $20 per night.

CROSS-COUNTRY SKIING AND SNOWSHOEING

Between late November and April, winter converts the roads and trails around Apgar into easy cross-country ski and snowshoe paths. Quiet and scenic, road skiing makes for easy route finding with little avalanche danger in lower elevations. Roads are plowed into Apgar and up Lake McDonald's south shore. Beyond plowing, popular ski tours follow roads and trails to **Fish Creek Campground, Rocky Point, McGee Meadows,** and the **Old Flathead Ranger Station** near the Middle Fork and North Fork confluence. Those with stamina and skiing expertise climb to **Apgar Lookout.** For route descriptions, pick up *Skiing and Snowshoeing* in visitors centers or online: www.nps.gov/glac. Skiers and snowshoers should be well equipped and versed in winter travel safety before venturing out even on snow-covered roads.

Glacier Outdoor Center (11957 Hwy. 2 E., 406/888-5454 or 800/235-6781, www.glacierraftco.com) daily grooms a delightful 10 kilometers of trails for both skate and classic skiing. Trail fees are $8 per day. Until noon, the trails are for skiers only, but after noon, dogs are permitted ($2 each). You can even rent

© BECKY LOMAX

The Middle Fork of the Flathead River winds around Glacier View Golf Club.

Glacier Outdoor Center grooms trails for cross-country skiing in winter.

skijoring gear ($10 for half day) to be pulled around the course by Fido. The center rents skate skis, waxless touring skis, pulk to pull tots ($18), and snowshoes for $15–22 daily; weekly rates are available, too.

Guides

The park service guides free weekend snowshoe tours from Apgar Visitor Center (406/888-7939) January–mid-March. Call for departure times for the two-hour walks. Interpretive rangers point out how flora and fauna adapt to harsh winters, and look for tracks. Hikers should wear winter footwear, dress in layers, and bring water. Snowshoes rent for $2.

November–April, as snows permit, guided snowshoe and ski tours are available through two companies. Expect to pay $185–200 per day for one person for a full-day tour. The more people, the less the per-person rate. A full-day trip for four people will run about $310. Plan on tipping the guide 15 percent. **Glacier Outdoor Center** (11957 Hwy. 2 E., West Glacier, 406/888-5454 or 800/235-6781, www.glacierraftco.com) leads half- and full-day snowshoe or cross-country ski trips. **Glacier Adventure Guides** (406/892-2173, www.glacieradventureguides.com) guides

full-day and multiday tours—road cross-country skiing and snowshoeing to backcountry telemark and alpine touring skiing. If you're a solo traveler, it's the best way to get accompanied into the backcountry with avalanche-certified guides to find pristine powder stashes. Lunch, snacks, and equipment are included.

ENTERTAINMENT

Most park visitors take advantage of long daylight hours (dark doesn't descend until almost 11 P.M. in June) to explore everything they can instead of seeking nightlife. If you're looking to party, you can hang at the West Glacier bar shooting pool with the river rats.

Park Naturalist
Evening Programs

Fish Creek Campground Amphitheater and **Apgar Campground Amphitheater** host free park naturalist evening programs on wildlife, fires, and natural phenomena. Check a current copy of *Ranger-Led Activities* for subjects, times, and dates for these 45-minute programs (usually mid-June–mid-September). Schedules are posted in campgrounds, hotels, and visitors centers, too.

Accommodations

On Lake McDonald's shore, the limited lodging at Apgar is extremely popular, so West Glacier options often serve as backup. But given that the communities are only two miles apart and connected by a bike path, they are equally convenient to each other and their outdoor activities. Additional lodging is found on the nine miles between West Glacier and Hungry Horse. Montana tacks on a 7 percent bed tax, so your bill will be higher than the quoted room rate.

APGAR

Reservations are a must at the two adjacent nonsmoking lodges in Apgar at Lake McDonald's foot, where their locations, rather than their amenities, make them top picks. To preserve their get-away-from-it-all ambience, neither have air-conditioning, Internet, in-room phones, or televisions. Pay phones are outside the lobbies. Both share a block with Eddie's Restaurant and Grocery, the visitors center, the boat dock, several gift shops, free shuttles, and the beginning of the Apgar Bike Trail. They sit adjacent to McDonald Creek for fishing or canoeing. The Apgar Campground Amphitheater for naturalist talks is a seven-minute walk away or quick shuttle ride. Although the area is a busy hive during the day, at night it's quiet.

Set back in huge old-growth cedars on McDonald Creek, **(C Apgar Village Lodge** (on Apgar Loop Rd. 0.3 mile from Camas Rd. or 0.8 mile from Going-to-the-Sun Rd., 406/888-5484, www.westglacier.com, late May–Sept., $105–275 per night) clusters 20 motel rooms and 28 rustic cabins—most with kitchens—within a few steps of the lake. The creek cabins (6, 7, 8) are particularly serene—mixed with a wonderful ambience of wildlife and the sound of the stream. Although older, the cabins have all been upgraded since the mid-1990s, with the bathrooms containing shower stalls. Some cabins require a two-night minimum stay. Ask about early season discounts.

Village Inn rooms overlook Lake McDonald.

© BECKY LOMAX

On Lake McDonald's beach, every one of the 36 rooms in the **(C Village Inn** (on Apgar Loop Rd. 0.3 mile from Camas Rd. or 0.8 mile from Going-to-the-Sun Rd., 406/892-2525, www.glacierparkinc.com, late May–mid-Sept., $136–215 per night) wakes up to a striking view uplake toward the Continental Divide. Some rooms include kitchenettes and can sleep up to six people. No elevator is available for the second floor. Although the inn has been redecorated, not much else has changed since the inn was built in 1956. Despite nondescript rooms, the views are stunning.

WEST GLACIER

Lodging in West Glacier is convenient for hopping the train, going river rafting or fishing, and heading off on guided backpacking trips. It's also such a quick jaunt to Lake McDonald that if park lodging is full, West Glacier options work as an easy backup. Be prepared, however, for nightly noise—not from people (they're crashed from packing in so much activity during the long days), but from almost 30 trains that ride the Burlington Northern Santa Fe rail daily. Bring earplugs if you're a light sleeper. During midsummer, most West Glacier lodging options fill nightly with bookings; reservations are wise.

Lodges

Located across from Belton Train Depot, the National Historic Landmark **Belton Chalet** (12575 Hwy. 2 E., 406/888-5000 or 888/235-8665, www.beltonchalet.com) saw a $1 million restoration in 2000. Centered around a large stone fireplace, the cozy lobby contains a piano, stuffed rockers, and a table displaying the owners' soap collection. Stay in the main lodge rooms (late May–early Oct., $125–180) or private year-round cottages ($230–325 summer, $99–230 winter), both of which are discounted in spring and fall. Simple rooms are a slice of history: original wainscoting and wood floors, push-button lights, twig tables,

and historic photos, but no phones, Internet, televisions, or alarm clocks. Original closets were converted into in-room bathrooms with showers. Stay in one of the nine balcony rooms to sit in wicker rockers with a glass of wine as the sun sets over the Apgar Range. Remedies Day Spa massages are available on-site. The chalet's restaurant serves outstanding dinners. A five-minute walk leads to gift shops, rafting, and other restaurants.

Glacier Guides Lodge (turn left 400 feet up Highline Blvd., 406/387-5555 or 800/521-7238, June–Sept., $161 double occupancy, plus $7 each additional person), owned by Glacier Guides/Montana Raft Company, is the newest lodging in West Glacier. The LEED-certified lodge, which opened in 2010, offers 12 rooms with two queen beds in each. Continental breakfast is included with stay, and two lounge areas give places to relax outside rooms that have decks, wireless Internet, TVs, and air-conditioning. Its location back in the woods tucked under mossy cliffs makes it one of the quietest places in the area.

Glacier Guides Lodge, which emulates historic park lodges, opened in 2010.

Cabins

Two nonsmoking cabin complexes open year-round sit less than one mile west of West Glacier's shops and restaurants. Both come with fully equipped kitchens, wireless Internet, televisions, and gas grills. **Glacier Outdoor Center** (11957 Hwy. 2 E., 406/888-5454 or 800/235-6781, www.glacierraftco.com, $299–499 per night) has one-, two- and three-bedroom log cabins that sleep 6–14 people. Set back from the highway amid birch trees around a trout pond or groomed ski trails in winter, the cabins include log furniture, decks, and gas fireplaces. The deluxe cabin has a washer, dryer, and hot tub. The center rents gear for hiking, skiing, snowshoeing, and fishing. Multinight stays chop off $10–24 per night, and rates drop by 30 percent early June and September. Winter rates run $119–269.

Part of the Great Northern Whitewater complex, with the rafting, fishing, and kayaking company located on-site, **Great Northern Chalets** (12127 Hwy. 2 E., 406/387-5340 or 800/735-7897, www.gnwhitewater.com, $260–295 summer and late Dec.) rents two small six-person and three large eight-person log chalets. Set around a landscaped garden pond, the cozy two-story chalets are decorated in Glacier outdoor themes, and several have sweeping views of Glacier's peaks. New owners in 2010 remodeled several chalets and plan to reopen a restaurant in their the caboose. A three-night minimum stay is required July–mid-September. Outside of high season, June and September rates run cheaper, and off-season discounts cut rates in half or more.

Motels

For basic rooms, motels in West Glacier give sheer convenience to shopping, rafting, restaurants, and park entrance. All are nonsmoking and lack in-room phones. Early and late season discounts are available. Located on the Middle Fork River, **West Glacier Motel** (200 Going-to-the-Sun Rd., 406/888-5662, www.westglacier.com, late May–mid-Sept.) has 32 motel units ($85–140) and three cabins ($150–270,

two-night minimum). None have televisions, air-conditioning, or Internet.

Sitting across from the Belton Train Depot, the **Glacier Highland** (12555 Hwy. 2 E., 406/888-5427 or 800/766-0811, www.glacierhighlandresort.com, year-round, $95–130) has 33 rooms with satellite television, but no Internet.

A half mile west of the Belton Train Depot, **Glacier Vista Motel** (milepost 152.5 on Hwy. 2 E., 406/888-5311, www.glaciervistamotel.com, mid-May–mid-Oct., $90–140) sits perched on a hill with Glacier views. The family-run, 1950s motel, with wireless Internet and light continental breakfast but no television, has the only outdoor heated swimming pool in town.

OUTSIDE WEST GLACIER

Lodging facilities in West Glacier and Apgar book up before summer for high season. However, plenty of motels and cabins line the nine miles of Highway 2 from West Glacier to Hungry Horse—good alternatives, just a short drive to reach the park entrance, but be ready to hear trains rumble nearby. Hungry Horse has several less-expensive motels.

Cabins

Two complexes of modern cabins have log furniture, wireless Internet, and satellite televisions. Neither permits pets or smoking. **Glaciers Mountain Resort** (1385 Old Hwy. 2 E., 406/387-5712 or 877/213-8001, www.glaciersmountainresort.com, year-round, $220) has five air-conditioned one-bedroom knotty pine cabins with distant Glacier views. Sleeping four, the cabins come with fully equipped kitchens and gas grills. Off-season rates drop 25–50 percent, and a two-night minimum stay is required. **Silverwolf Log Chalet Resort** (Gladys Glenn Rd. and Hwy. 2 E., 406/387-4448, www.silverwolfchalets.com, mid-May–mid-Oct., $168) rents 10 two-person log chalets set on a landscaped lawn under lodgepoles behind a privacy fence. Chalets include gas fireplaces, microwave, coffeemaker, and minirefrigerator. The resort is an adults-only place; kids are taboo. Multinight stays reduce per-night rates, and discounts are available in spring and fall.

Check into the **Evergreen Motel** (10159 US Hwy. 2, Coram, 406/387-5365, www.evergreenmotelglacier.com, May–Oct.) for budget lodging at $75–95 per night in small cabins or rooms located seven miles west of the park.

Bed-and-Breakfasts

The **Glacier Park Inn** (9128 Hwy. 2 E., 406/387-5099, www.glacierparkinn.com, year-round, $100–150) tucks five rooms in its remodeled, octagonal, nonsmoking home with a giant wraparound deck overlooking the Apgar Mountains and Flathead River—the perfect place to unwind with a view. The inn, which has wireless Internet, gets rave reviews for its location, breakfast, and the owners—avid hikers who can recommend trails for appropriate seasons.

Built in 1907, the **Tamarack Lodge** (9549 Hwy. 2 E., 406/387-4420 or 877/387-4420, www.historictamaracklodge.com, year-round, $104–131) offers one renovated log-beam room in the historic lodge and eight knotty pine cabins. Rooms include satellite TV, wireless Internet, and continental breakfast.

CAMPING
Apgar

In Apgar, two park-service-operated campgrounds sit amid thick forests with easy access to Lake McDonald. Rustic and without hookups, both have flush toilets, fire rings with grills, disposal stations, shared hiker-biker sites ($5 Apgar, $8 Fish Creek), amphitheaters for evening naturalist talks, and sites that accommodate large RVs. Due to the location inside the park, away from highway and railroad noise, they are popular. Bring your own firewood, as collecting is prohibited.

Fish Creek (end of Fish Creek Rd., 406/888-7800, June–early Sept., $23 per night), one of two campgrounds in the park that can be reserved through the National Park Reservation System (877/444-6777, www.reservations.gov), is one of the larger park campgrounds, with

178 sites tucked under cedars, lodgepoles, and larch. Loops C and D have the best sites adjacent to the lake. Eighteen campsites accommodate RVs up to 35 feet long; 62 sites fit RVs up to 27 feet. To find Fish Creek, drive from Apgar 1.25 miles north on Camas Road and turn right, dropping one mile down to the campground. Lake McDonald Trail departs from the campground.

Apgar Campground (on Apgar Loop Rd. 0.4 mile from Going-to-the-Sun Rd., 406/888-7800, early May–mid-Oct., $20 per night) is within short walking distance to Apgar Village and Lake McDonald. The 194-site campground on the shuttle stop is the park's largest, with group campsites and 25 sites accommodating RVs up to 40 feet. A paved trail connects to the Apgar Transit Center, Apgar Bike Trail, and Apgar Village, which includes a restaurant, gift shops, visitors center, and boat dock. Primitive camping ($10, Apr. and mid-Oct.–Nov.) has pit toilets available but no running water. In winter, you can camp free at the Apgar Picnic Area, but it's just a plowed lot with a pit toilet.

West Glacier

Commercial campgrounds in the West Glacier vicinity are convenient for rafting, fishing, biking, and trail rides but are located outside the park. If you require hookups, this is where you'll need to be. Standard amenities in these campgrounds include flush toilets, laundries, hot showers, camp stores, picnic tables, fire rings with grills, firewood, propane, disposal stations, playgrounds, and wireless Internet or modem dataports. Also, these campgrounds can handle the big RV rigs. If you're a light sleeper, bring earplugs, for many of the campgrounds hear the rumble and screech from trains.

Although most commercial campgrounds lean toward servicing RVers and car campers, bikers and backpackers should ask about special rates in shared area sites, which often run $6–10 per person. Many of the campgrounds offer rustic camping cabins or yurts, which have no kitchens or bathrooms; bring your own sleeping bags or pay extra for clean linens, blankets, and towels ($9–15 per person). Commercial campgrounds tack on a 7 percent Montana bed tax to their rates. When you make your reservations, check for deals; many give discounts for Internet registration, seniors, early and late season, and Good Sam, AAA, or military members. Make reservations for July and August, especially for big rigs requiring large sites.

On 40 timbered acres a half mile from West Glacier, **Glacier Campground** (12070 Hwy. 2 E., 406/387-5689 or 888/387-5689, www. glaciercampground.com, May–Sept., $20–30) sits one mile west of the park entrance. Lush undergrowth surrounds private sites separated by birch and fir trees. Several cabins ($40–50) share a covered outdoor cooking area with gas burners and barbecue. Leashed pets are welcome. With the campground set back from the road, trees reduce highway and railroad sounds. For evening entertainment, the campground sponsors Forest Service presentations.

Removed one mile from Highway 2 and 2.5 miles west of the park entrance, **West Glacier KOA** (355 Half Moon Flats Rd., 406/387-5341 or 800/562-3313, www.westglacierkoa.com, mid-May–Sept., $28–58) is the only campground with a heated swimming pool (June–mid-Sept.) and a couple of hot tubs that are open all season. It also has evening programs, cabins ($62–90), horseshoes, and summer barbecue dinners and pancake breakfasts. Due to its location away from the highway and railroad, this is one of the quieter campgrounds.

Outside West Glacier

Seven more commercial campgrounds sprawl along Highway 2 in the nine miles between West Glacier and Hungry Horse, with rates running $25–40. Some offer distinctive features. **San-Suz-Ed RV Park** (11505 Hwy. 2 E., 406/387-5280 or 800/630-2623, www.san-suzedrvpark.com, May–Oct.) runs a nightly community campfire pit: BYOM (bring your own marshmallows) or BYOHD (bring your own hot dogs). For those needing open space for clear satellite reception, **North American RV Park and Campground** (10784 Hwy. 2 E., 406/387-5800 or 800/704-4266, www. northamericanrvpark.com, mid-Apr.–Oct) sits in a big grassy area with shorter trees. **Canyon RV and Campground** (9540 Hwy. 2 E., 406/387-9393) is the only one bordering the Flathead River, accessible by trail. One of the quietest campgrounds, **Mountain Meadows RV Park** (9125 Hwy. 2 E., 406/387-9125, www.mmrvpark.com, May–Sept.) spans 77 acres of forested hillside with a stocked catch-and-release rainbow trout pond.

Food

Glacier is a place for good down-home cooking, where tasty, fresh-baked fruit pies are still the rage, rather than upscale or ethnic delicacies. Seasonal restaurants cater to summer visitors, but few remain open October–May. Many of the restaurants pack lunches to go for travelers.

RESTAURANTS
Apgar

Under the same ownership now as Izaak Walton Inn, **Eddie's Restaurant** (on Apgar Loop Rd. 0.3 mile from Camas Rd. or 0.8 mile from Going-to-the-Sun Rd., 406/888-5361, 7 A.M.–9:30 P.M. daily late May–mid-Sept.) is the only game in town, but it has good family-friendly breakfasts and lunches ($6–11), including hiker lunches to go. Dinner ($11–20) features entrée salads, grilled trout, broasted chicken, and buffalo meat loaf or burger. With large waiting lines midsummer, takeout can be quicker; walk a few steps away to Lake McDonald's shore to picnic. Montana microbrews and wine are available. Leave room for the signature chocolate Bear Paw pie ($6). Hours may shorten in shoulder seasons.

West Glacier

At the historic ◖ **Belton Chalet** (12575 Hwy. 2 E., 406/888-5000 or 888/235-8665, www.beltonchalet.com, Taproom 3 P.M.–midnight, dining room 5–10 P.M., daily late May–early Oct.) you can dine in the intimate Belton Grill, by the fireplace in the Taproom, or on the deck watching trains and the sunset over Apgar Mountain. The Belton is a treat—not just for its ambience, restored to its 1910 grandeur, but for its fine-dining flavors made with fresh local ingredients. The lodge's old boiler was converted into the kitchen's outdoor grill. Entrées ($27–34) like the flavorful Montana meat loaf—buffalo wrapped in hickory-smoked bacon with roasted tomato gravy—pair well with Taproom wines and Montana microbrews. The dessert tray changes nightly, but if available, try the huckleberry crisp or cheesecake with sauce made of cherries from the owners' Bigfork orchard. Lighter Taproom meals ($8–19) feature hors d'oeuvres, sandwiches, and salads. Box lunches to go are available. In winter (December–March), the Belton opens on Friday and Saturday (3–9 P.M.), serving sandwiches and entrées such as a German plate to hungry skiers and Sunday brunch (11 A.M.–3 P.M.).

◖ **West Glacier Restaurant and Lounge** (200 Going-to-the-Sun Rd., 406/888-5359, 7 A.M.–10 P.M. daily mid-May–late Sept.) serves up tasty café fare. Located between the park entrance bridge and the railroad tunnel, the restaurant packs out with lines midsummer. Breakfast and lunches run $7–11, with blueberry pancakes as a specialty. Dinners ($9–18) span fish, pasta, steaks, sandwiches, or salads. Ironically, the best thing to sate a hungry hiker stomach—the Glacier Monster Cheeseburger—is listed under "Lighter Appetites," but it's huge with bacon and cheese atop a half-pound hamburger, with fries. The burger-and-beer crowd heads to the adjacent bar—locally known as Frieda's—to order off the restaurant menu.

Across from the Belton Train Depot, the **Glacier Highland** (12555 Hwy. 2 E., 406/888-5427, www.glacierhighland.com, 7 A.M.–10 P.M. daily mid-Apr.–mid-Oct.) bakes large huckleberry muffins, cinnamon rolls, and fruit pies. Their breakfasts, lunches, and dinners cover typical café fare—sandwiches and burgers ($6–9) or steaks and trout (up to $19). Beer and wine are served, too. The restaurant closes at 8 or 9 P.M. in shoulder seasons.

Convenient following trail rides, the **Rawhide Trading Post Restaurant and Steakhouse** (12000 Hwy. 2 E., 406/387-5999 or 800/388-5727, www.glacierrawhide.com, 11 A.M.–10 P.M. daily mid-May–mid-Oct.) serves a fast lunchtime pulled barbecue brisket on a hoagie ($10). For dinner ($14–23), you can dive into the house specialty of mesquite-grilled prime rib—a 10-ounce cowgirl, 12-ounce cowboy, or the 14-ounce Wayne's cut. The restaurant also does kids' meals and takeout for easy campfire dinners. Until mid-June and after Labor Day, the Rawhide opens only from 4–8 P.M.

Outside West Glacier

In Coram, 5.5 miles west of West Glacier, **Glacier Grill and Pizza** (10026 Hwy. 2 E., 406/387-4223, 11 A.M.–11 P.M. daily) serves café fare ($7–12) year-round, but the main reason to go here is the pizza ($12–19). The loaded all-meat pizza is packed with sausage, Canadian bacon, and pepperoni; the Mediterranean special with feta cheese is baked with a delightful twist on spices.

CAFFEINE

Several summer-only espresso stands attend to the caffeine fix. Hours vary at each, depending on the season. **Eddie's Snack Bar** in Apgar offers espresso drinks, ice cream, and giant cinnamon rolls. **Glacier Espresso** near the Alberta Visitor Information Center in West Glacier carries a few baked goodies to go with your latte. If temps climb, you can get an Italian soda or granita instead.

GROCERIES

Groceries (food, beer, wine) and camping items (ice, firewood, stove gas) may be purchased in both West Glacier and Apgar. In Apgar, get supplies at **Eddie's Campstore** (on Apgar Loop Rd. 0.8 mile from Going-to-the-Sun Rd. or 0.3 mile from Camas Rd., 8 A.M.–10 P.M. daily midsummer, closes at 6 P.M. in shoulder seasons, open June–mid-Sept.). In West Glacier, the **West Glacier Mercantile** (0.1 mile west of Hwy. 2 junction on Going-to-the-Sun Rd., 8 A.M.–10 P.M. daily in midsummer, early and late season closure at 5 P.M., open May–Sept.) has the bigger selection of meats, fresh veggies, and fruits. Convenience store items are also available at **Glacier Highland** (across from the Belton Train Depot on Hwy. 2, 7 A.M.–9 P.M. daily mid-Apr.–Oct., may close earlier in shoulder seasons), with cheaper beer and wine prices. In summer, the farmers market comes to West Glacier, adjacent to the mercantile in late afternoon on Friday.

The nearest year-round grocery store is in Hungry Horse, on Highway 2 nine miles west of the park entrance. Look for the Supermarket sign. You'll have to drive 30 minutes into Flathead Valley to hit the megastores that carry huge brand selections.

PICNIC AREAS

Two picnic areas, both with beach access, rim Lake McDonald's western shores. **Apgar Picnic Area** is just off Going-to-the-Sun Road on the lake's southwest corner, with a beautiful uplake view to the Continental Divide. **Fish Creek Picnic Area** sits next to Fish Creek Campground, where a one-mile hike leads out to Rocky Point for more views. Both have picnic tables, flush toilets, and fire rings with grills, but firewood is not provided and gathering it is prohibited; purchase firewood in Apgar or West Glacier.

NORTH FORK

It's remote. It's wild. It's not for everyone. The North Fork Valley defines rustic. Not rustic as in cute, comfortable rustic, but real rustic as in you nearly have to fend for yourself. No flush toilets, no electricity, and mostly no phones. But for those who want to get away from the mayhem, it's the place to go. A visit to the North Fork transports you back in time. The pace of life slows with the ambience of the Polebridge Mercantile.

For the average traveler, the North Fork's nasty dirt roads alone deter interest. Brutal potholes, jarring washboards, and clouds of dust launch vehement debates about paving the North Fork Road, but pavement into this remote enclave would alter its nature forever.

The North Fork Valley spans diverse habitats from grassland prairies to alpine glaciers. It's home to an immense range of wildlife—huge grizzly bears to tiny pygmy shrews. Spruce trees 300 years old root the valley in deep history. Surrounded by thick subalpine fir forests, Bowman and Kintla Lakes have miles of empty shoreline dotted with only a boat of anglers or a few kayaks. Trails from the North Fork see only a few people, even in high season. For those who have patience to sit with binoculars, wildlife-watching and birding are the best. Nothing chills the soul quite like the wild call of wolves in the dead of night.

HISTORY

In the late 1800s, handfuls of homesteaders, loggers, hunters, and trappers eked out a living in the North Fork Valley, connected to each other only by a network of trails. In 1900, a

© BECKY LOMAX

HIGHLIGHTS

◖ Inside Road: Survive this rough road! This scenic byway presents a real challenge for both vehicles and mountain bikes. Drive or ride its 28 miles for a close encounter with its wildlife and potholes (page 64).

◖ Polebridge Mercantile: Smell fresh-baked cookies and breads when you walk in this historic hub of the North Fork Valley. It has no electricity; an old-fashioned cash register clangs up your groceries (page 65).

◖ Northern Lights Saloon: Order a microbrew and sit outside to enjoy the view or just soak up the chatter from locals inside. In spite of its remote location, the saloon attracts diners for its tiny log cabin historic charm (page 65).

◖ North Fork of the Flathead River: Throw your watch away to let river time take over as you float this scenic river. Forming the park's western boundary, the river courses through prairie and forests where grizzly bears and wolves hunt prey (page 65).

◖ Bowman Lake: Look down the lake; you're looking straight into wild country. Rainbow Peak juts straight up 4,500 feet from the lakeshore, while Thunderbird Mountain scrapes the sky behind nesting bald eagles (page 66).

◖ Kintla Lake: Get far away from civilization at this remote lake. Although it may have been the site for oil drilling a century ago, today it's a mean 42 miles from pavement and launches into some of the park's most isolated backpacking terrain (page 66).

◖ Quartz Lakes: Hike to three lakes lined up like pearls on a necklace. The lakes lure anglers for native westslope cutthroat trout – but pack the bug spray, for they're mosquito havens as well (page 67).

◖ Glacier View: Climb up a short grunt with scenery galore. The route may tax the lungs, but you'll smell wild roses, and your eyes will relish Glacier's panorama at the top (page 70).

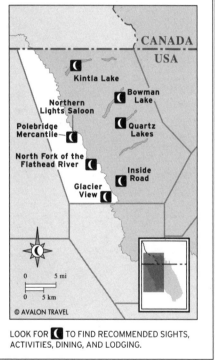

LOOK FOR ◖ TO FIND RECOMMENDED SIGHTS, ACTIVITIES, DINING, AND LODGING.

Butte business, on a quest for oil at Kintla Lake, built the Inside North Fork Road—a 65-mile wagon track riddled with ruts, bogs, and stumps. It was sufficient, however, for hauling drilling equipment from Belton (West Glacier) to Kintla Lake, where sleds skidded supplies across the frozen lake to drill Montana's first oil well in 1901. The road attracted more homesteaders, but talk of Glacier becoming a national park was already afoot—a change the homesteaders disliked because parkhood meant an end to their hunting and timber livelihoods.

When Glacier achieved national park status in 1910, construction of the rough Outside North Fork Road two years later prompted

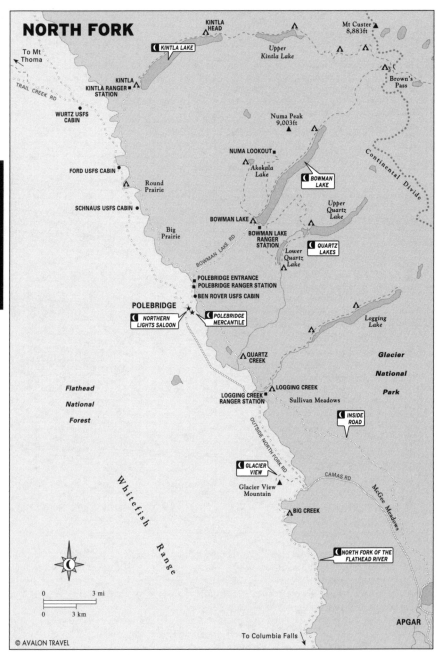

NORTH FORK

KINTLA
HEAD

☾ KINTLA LAKE

To Mt
Thoma

Upper
Kintla Lake

Mt Custer ▲
8,883ft

Brown's
Pass

TRAIL CREEK RD

KINTLA
KINTLA RANGER ■
STATION

WURTZ USFS
CABIN

Numa Peak
9,003ft
▲

Continental Divide

NUMA LOOKOUT ■

FORD USFS CABIN ●

Akokala
Lake

☾ BOWMAN
LAKE

Round
Prairie

Upper
Quartz
Lake

SCHNAUS USFS CABIN ●

BOWMAN LAKE

Big
Prairie

BOWMAN LAKE RD

BOWMAN LAKE
RANGER
STATION

Lower
Quartz
Lake

☾ QUARTZ
LAKES

POLEBRIDGE ENTRANCE ■
POLEBRIDGE RANGER STATION ■
● BEN ROVER USFS CABIN

POLEBRIDGE

☾ NORTHERN
LIGHTS SALOON

☾ POLEBRIDGE
MERCANTILE

Logging
Lake

Glacier

△ QUARTZ
CREEK

National

LOGGING CREEK
RANGER STATION

● LOGGING CREEK

Sullivan Meadows

Park

☾ INSIDE
ROAD

Flathead

OUTSIDE NORTH FORK RD

National

Forest

☾ GLACIER
VIEW

CAMAS RD

McGee Meadows

Glacier View
Mountain ▲

W h i t e f i s h   R a n g e

● BIG CREEK

☾ NORTH FORK OF THE
FLATHEAD RIVER

0   3 mi

0   3 km

APGAR

To Columbia Falls

© AVALON TRAVEL

many of the 35 homesteading families within the park boundaries to move across the North Fork of the Flathead River, outside the park boundary. One resident, Bill Adair, built a new mercantile in 1914 near Hay Creek—a two-story plank building. The "Merc," as locals call it, is now listed on the National Register of Historic Places. The area today is known as Polebridge—named for the funky North Fork River bridge, a one-lane lodgepole affair that burnt in the 1988 Red Bench Fire.

CULTURE

The North Fork is unique. It's a small, intimate community that prides itself on its rustic nature. Not L.L.Bean squeaky-clean cookie-cutter rustic, but real bucolic earthiness with no electricity and few phone lines. Generators and propane tanks provide lights and power, along with some solar energy. The population of the four-mile-wide floodplain comprises year-round residents living off the grid and summer cabins. Most residents roll their eyes at visitors who complain about the North Fork Road's dust and potholes; talk of paving raises the hackles of many, who don't want to see the North Fork changed. The state launched a study in 2010, which could result in paving.

The year-round hub of valley life is the Polebridge Mercantile, where residents catch up on news, sometimes not much differentiated from gossip. The town's dogs run amok and lounge on the front porch. However, visiting canines must be leashed. Hand-painted signs will tell you so: "Local dogs at large." One of the warning signs on the Northern Lights Saloon claims, "Unleashed dogs will be eaten."

ECOLOGICAL SIGNIFICANCE

The North Fork area contains all five of Glacier's ecosystems: grassland prairies, aspen parklands, montane forests, subalpine, and alpine tundra. Rich floodplains teem with wildflowers, berries, shrubs, and trees. Fens abound with orchids, bladderworts, sundews, mosses, sedges, ferns, and bulrushes. McGee Meadows, which is actually a fen, houses at least 50 species of flora. The valley is rife with grizzly and black bears, moose, coyotes, mountain lions, and elk—all manner of wildlife down to its tiniest occupant, the pygmy shrew, which preys on 25 species of bugs, insects, and snails. Birders have documented 196 species of woodpeckers, owls, raptors, waterfowl, and songbirds, over half of which nest here.

With the natural migration of wolves from Canada in the 1980s, Glacier saw its first wolf pack in 50 years, with its first litter of pups in 1986. Numbers have since rebounded. Now wolf packs range across Montana, which has prompted controversy over their status as an endangered species. But don't expect to see a wolf around every tree; their numbers vary year to year, they roam up to 300 square miles, and they are elusive. But you may hear them—especially at night. High deer and elk concentrations make the North Fork Valley prime habitat; to maintain its health, a wolf must eat 10 percent of its body weight in meat every day.

FIRES

Rich timberlands of the North Fork are prime fire lands due to years of fire suppression policies that led to thick lodgepole stands and bug infestations. The 38,000-acre Red Bench Fire in 1988 saw fire policy change with letting the fire run its natural course. Silver sentinels stand as a reminder that Polebridge was nearly wiped off the map. In 2001, the Moose Fire shot over Demers Ridge, burning 71,000 acres, over one third inside Glacier. In 2003, the Wedge Canyon Fire burned 53,315 acres, jumping the North Fork River into the park and traveling up the side of Parke Peak, while the Robert Fire burned the valley's south end. Evidence of each of these fires is obvious, but swift new growth is building a new forest blooming with fireweed, arrowleaf balsamroot, and lupine.

NORTH FORK WONDERS

TINY FAUNA

The North Fork Valley is home to the rare **northern bog lemming,** a small, brown-backed, gray-underbellied rodent that seeks mats of thick, wet sphagnum moss for habitat. Weighing only one ounce (the same as one heaping tablespoon of sugar) but growing up to six inches long, the tiny cousin of the Arctic lemming is a relic of the Pleistocene ice age, which began two million years ago. Although it's rarely seen, look for small, neat piles of clipped grass along the mossy thoroughfares en route to underground nests. One study found that bog lemmings make up 2 percent of the pine marten's diet.

Glacier's smallest predator, the **pygmy shrew,** inhabits floodplains in the North Fork Valley. This tiny carnivore is one of North America's rarest mammals. Less than 2.5 inches in size and weighing less than a quarter ounce, this shrew's voracious appetite for insects, slugs, snails, and carrion can put larger shrews to shame. One study watched a female eat three times her own body weight daily for 10 days. Their high metabolism echoes their respiration rate – 25 times more than humans – and their hearts beat up to 1,320 times per minute when excited. To feed their high metabolic rates, pygmy shrews eat every couple hours 24/7 year-round.

PLANTS

Carnivorous plants inhabit North Fork fens. The **sundew** attracts insects to its sparkling droplets like morning dew on leaves. Sitting atop hairs lining its leaves, the sticky droplets, like wet cement, entrap unsuspecting visitors. Slowly, the leaves curl around the victim as digestive juices work their magic. The **bladderwort** also refined trapping. Buoyant bladders trap anything that swims by – mosquito larvae to fish fry. When the prey passes, it brushes hairs, opening a trapdoor that sucks water in along with the naive prey. Digestive enzymes make short work of the meal, with the trap reset in 15 minutes to two hours.

BIRDS

Birders find a feast for their eyes and ears in the North Fork. With 196 species of birds documented – at least 112 nesters – the valley teems with avian activity. Migratory birds stop on their flight highways to wintering ranges or summer nesting. To help with identification of Glacier's birds, pick up a bird list from visitors centers or on the park's website.

Raptors: Birds of prey find abundant food in the North Fork Valley. Numerous rodents, ground squirrels, songbirds, and carrion feed their appetites. The valley's forests attract sharp-shinned and Cooper's hawks. Bald eagles nest on Kintla and Bowman Lakes. Northern harriers, red-tailed hawks, goshawks, and American kestrels prowl above the prairies. At night, the hoots of large great-horned and pygmy owls haunt the air.

Waterfowl: With the Flathead River, many large lakes, swamps, and wetlands, waterfowl have no shortage of suitable habitat. Herons, ducks, grebes, geese, loons, and swans migrate through or nest in the plentiful waters.

Songbirds: The North Fork could be considered downright noisy at times – not from traffic, but from the scads of songbirds flitting among its trees and cattails. American redstarts, warbling vireos, kinglets, nuthatches, crossbills, sparrows, and warblers are just a few of the neotropical songbirds that migrate annually into the valley. In winter, you'll spot tree sparrows and redpolls.

Woodpeckers: After fires, dead standing timber attracted the three-toed woodpecker, picking away for bugs. Watch also for the large, red-headed pileated woodpecker looking for a favorite food – carpenter ants.

Exploring North Fork

ENTRANCE STATION

The North Fork River is the boundary between national forest and national park. From the North Fork Valley, two roads cross the river into the park. On the south end, the paved **Camas Road** enters from the dirt North Fork Road, with an unstaffed entrance station and a self-pay cash-only kiosk. A mile northeast of Polebridge, the **Polebridge entrance station** is staffed during summer only, but a self-pay cash-only kiosk is available, too.

TOURS AND SHUTTLES

The closest thing to guided tours in the North Fork is guided outdoor recreation: river rafting or backpacking. However, the companies that guide these trips are based in West Glacier (see the *West Glacier and Apgar* chapter for contact info and pricing). You can also hook up with a **Glacier Institute** course that might be wildlife-watching in the area (see the *Background* chapter).

The North Fork does not see any routine bus service; however, **Flathead-Glacier Transportation** (406/892-3390 or 800/829-7039) provides a shuttle between Polebridge and Glacier International Airport ($90 one-way for one person, $3 for each additional person). Reservations are required.

SERVICES

You won't find strip malls nor services up the North Fork. You can get gas at the Polebridge Mercantile or Home Ranch Store, but it's pricey. Forget the ATMs, post office, television, visitors centers, and shopping. You'll find only outhouses and vault toilets—no flushers. Phone lines run only as far as Polebridge. The **Polebridge Mercantile** (265 Polebridge Loop, 406/888-5105) has a pay phone on its front deck. **Home Ranch Bottoms** (8855 North Fork Rd., 406/888-5572, www.homeranchbottoms.com, 9 A.M.–9 P.M. daily, late May–early Sept.) has hot showers ($7). It's pricey due to the power source—a generator.

Cell Phone and Internet

Cell reception is spotty to nonexistent. Those who can't cut the technological umbilical cord head to Home Ranch Bottoms. When the store is open, you can get Verizon cell service and dial-up modem Internet or watch television.

Emergencies

For emergencies within park boundaries, contact a ranger or call 406/888-7800. Outside park boundaries, call 911. The nearest hospitals are in the Flathead Valley: Kalispell Regional Medical Center (310 Sunny View Ln., 406/752-5111) and North Valley Hospital in Whitefish (1600 Hospital Way, 406/863-3500).

The **Polebridge Ranger Station** (staffed year-round, 406/888-7800) sits one mile from Polebridge across the North Fork River at the park entrance; backcountry camping permits are available here when someone is available to write one. During summer, Logging Creek Ranger Station on the Inside North Fork Road is staffed, as are stations at Bowman and Kintla Lakes; however, these seasonal rangers may be out patrolling miles of backcountry trails.

DRIVING TOURS
Outside North Fork Road

Open year-round, the Outside North Fork Road is the easier drive of the two dirt and gravel access roads. Although the road running from Columbia Falls to Canada is wide enough for two cars to pass, be prepared for washboards, potholes, ruts, dust in summer, slush in fall or spring, and ice in winter. Locals refer to this road as simply the North Fork, dropping the "Outside," for it is the valley's main gateway. Every few years, clamor arises about paving the North Fork, which many locals oppose because pavement would change the valley's nature. Montana launched a study of the road in 2010, which could result in paving portions. The North Fork Road is intermittently plowed in winter to the Canadian border, but do not attempt it without good snow tires and four-wheel drive. Carry chains and emergency supplies in the car.

From Columbia Falls, the North Fork Road leaves pavement just past Blankenship Road and follows the North Fork River for 13 miles. After a junction with the paved Camas Road, an alternate access from Apgar, the road passes a few small bucolic ranches whose pastures provide browse for cows and wild elk herds. You'll hit six miles of rough pavement again at Home Ranch Bottoms, where cattle walk the road; drive with caution. At 32 miles and a little over one hour's drive, the road meets Polebridge Loop—the cutoff to the Merc, the Inside North Fork Road, and **Bowman** and **Kintla Lakes.** Hand-painted signs used to warn drivers entering town: "Slow Down, People Breathing." Respect residents here; speed kicks up a tremendous amount of dust in summer.

From the Polebridge junction, the road continues 22 more miles north toward Canada—another hour's drive. It accesses the upper Whitefish Range, the North Fork River, and Forest Service cabins. Although drivers used to cross into Canada, the Trail Creek port of entry is closed due to a road washout on the Canadian side.

【 Inside Road

Not for everyone, the summer-only (May–October), dirt Inside North Fork Road throws precipitous drops, curves, and climbs at drivers. Monster potholes and washboards are commonplace; spaces wide enough for two vehicles to pass are rare. You're definitely off the beaten path on this bumpy trek where speeds top out at 20 mph. Marked as Glacier Route 7 on some maps and known as simply the "Inside Road" to locals, the road is the rougher of the two choices and requires high-clearance vehicles. Big RV rigs have trouble, and it's a rough ride for a trailer. Although only 29 miles to Polebridge, the drive will take two hours. Many link it up with Outside North Fork and Camas Roads for a 53-mile scenic loop drive.

From the south, the Inside Road begins at Fish Creek Campground and climbs through the 2003 Robert Fire. Atop the ridge, look for peek-a-boo views of **McGee Meadows,** good wildlife-watching spots if you can squeeze your vehicle off the road and tolerate swarms of mosquitoes. Then compare fire reqrowth as you drive through the 2001 Moose Fire. After dropping down steep Anaconda Hill (12.5 miles from Fish Creek) and crossing the creek, the road bisects Sullivan Meadows, famous for Glacier's wolves, before passing two small campgrounds—Logging Creek (17.5 miles) and Quartz Creek (20 miles). At 28 miles, the road intersects with the Polebridge park entrance. From here, cross the North Fork River, drive one mile to **Polebridge,** and connect with Outside North Fork Road.

You can also continue up the Inside Road to **Bowman** and **Kintla Lakes.** A few minutes north of the Polebridge Ranger Station, the curvy Bowman Lake road turns off, a six-mile (25-minute) snakelike drive eastward up the valley. Continuing northward toward Kintla,

Bowman Lake is one of the North Fork's remote lakes.

the Inside Road crosses **Big Prairie,** the largest of the North Fork's unique grasslands. **Round Prairie** follows at one third the size. The road reenters the forest and passes through the 2003 Wedge Canyon Fire zone before dead-ending at Kintla Lake, 14 miles north of the North Fork entrance station.

SIGHTS
(Polebridge Mercantile

Located 25 miles north of Apgar, the hub of the North Fork community is the red-planked "Merc." The Polebridge Mercantile, listed on the National Register of Historic Places, was built in 1914. It is more than a place to buy that forgotten can of pork and beans for camping. It sells local handmade jewelry and not-to-be-missed bakery goods fresh from the oven. While the smell of cookies and pastries fills the small room, an old-fashioned cash register clangs up sales. New owners in 2009 are keeping the Merc's flavor but upgraded from a diesel generator to solar power.

(Northern Lights Saloon

Next door to the Merc, the tiny Northern Lights Saloon looks like a ramshackle log cabin but packs in diners, extras spilling outside onto picnic tables. Hikers celebrate their adventures here with whatever Montana microbrew is currently on tap and lounge outside, staring at Rainbow Peak. Open for dinner nightly in summer.

(North Fork of the Flathead River

Forming the western boundary of Glacier National Park, the North Fork of the Flathead River draws its headwaters from Canada and ends near West Glacier at its confluence with the Middle Fork. Fifty-nine miles of waters flow through private, state, and federal lands while descending the North Fork Valley's diverse habitats. Designated as a Wild and Scenic River, the Class II river with six accesses is great for multiday float trips, day rafting, fishing, and scenic floating.

NORTH FORK

© BECKY LOMAX

Polebridge Mercantile, a bakery and camping supply store

The North Fork of the Flathead River winds along Glacier's western boundary.

McGee Meadows

McGee Meadows is a wildlife-watching spot, but during much of the spring and early summer, the fen is too wet to walk due to its soggy nature. It is also a mosquito haven. As a fen, its low-oxygen waters build up dead plant matter, but nutrients feed it via precipitation and ground water, making it fertile ground for diverse vegetation. The meadow is home to rare plants and over 50 species of flora—bulrushes, bladderworts, sphagnum moss, sundews, and orchids. Potential wildlife sightings can include bears, moose, deer, and a host of birds. Access McGee Meadows from the Camas Road (6 miles from Apgar) or from the Inside Road (4 miles from Fish Creek). You can cross-country ski the meadows in winter.

◖ Bowman Lake

The closest of Glacier's northwestern lakes to reach, Bowman Lake sits in a narrow glacier-scoured trough seven miles northeast of Polebridge on a dirt road with a bouncing ride. The lake's six miles sprawl toward nesting bald eagles and Thunderbird Peak; its half-mile width squeezes in between the hulks of Numa Peak and Rainbow Peak, the latter rising 4,500 feet straight up from the south lakeshore. In summer, lake waters offer solitude: Drop in a canoe to tour its shoreline. In winter, the icy expanse and snow-laden crags call to cross-country skiers, who ski in on the road pockmarked with wolf and elk tracks.

Big Prairie

Located 30 miles up the Inside North Fork Road, just two miles past the Bowman Lake turnoff and three miles from Polebridge, Big Prairie is the largest of four Palouse prairies in the North Fork. At one mile wide and four miles long, the prairie is a grassland with wheatgrass, fescues, oatgrass, and sagebrush. Because the Whitefish Range causes a rain shadow, the North Fork receives only 20 inches of precipitation per year, which fosters this drier flora.

◖ Kintla Lake

Kintla Lake is a place to go only on purpose. Fifteen miles of washboarded, rutted road links Polebridge with the remote lake. Its tiny campground tucked deep in the trees offers quiet, a place to decompress. Cowering between Starvation and Parke Ridges, the half-mile-wide lake curves a little over five miles up valley, a prelude to Upper Kintla Lake. Only one trail takes off along the north shore toward the isolated Kintla-Kinnerly peak complex and Boulder Pass. Haul a canoe or kayak to Kintla Lake for unbeatable secluded paddling.

Recreation

HIKING

Hiking in the North Fork leads to stunning vistas, but be prepared for tromping through long, mosquito-ridden, thick-forested valleys to earn your views. While day hikers trek to lakes and lookouts, backpackers gain altitude into rugged glaciated alpine bowls above the tree line. In this undeveloped area, you're on your own to get to trailheads; no shuttle service runs up the North Fork. On both sides of the valley, hikes depart into Glacier and the Whitefish Range in Flathead National Forest. Those looking for hikes for the pooch should head to the latter.

While trails in Glacier Park are well signed, Flathead National Forest trails are less so. Trail signs may consist of just a number with no distances, destinations, or directions. For that reason alone, always hike with a topographical map in Flathead National Forest, and know how to read it. National forest trails are maintained less frequently: Expect to encounter deadfall and downed trees as well as brushy routes. For hiking maps of Flathead National Forest, contact the Glacier View Ranger District in Hungry Horse (406/387-3800). Topographical quads of the Whitefish Range can be purchased at outdoor sporting-goods stores in Flathead Valley. For hiking Glacier's trails, take along a topographical map, available through Glacier Natural History Association (406/888-5756, www.glacierassociation.org).

◖ Quartz Lakes

- Distance: 12.4-mile loop
- Duration: 6 hours
- Elevation gain: 1,470 feet to Upper Quartz, 1,000 feet on return over ridge
- Effort: moderate
- Trailhead: backcountry parking area at Bowman Lake in Glacier Park

In June, early parts of the trail burst with calypso orchids while the path crossing Cerulean Ridge is still buried under snow. Within a half mile up the trail, the path splits. You'll return to this junction at the end of the loop. Take the left fork, heading to Quartz Lake. With peek-a-boo views of Numa Peak, the trail climbs through thick spruce and fir forests until it crests Cerulean ridge. As the trail drops 1,000 feet to Quartz Lake, it enters the 1988 Red Bench burn, where open meadows afford views of Vulture Peak's steep north face and the lake.

At Quartz Lake, the trail cuts through the backcountry campsite and rounds the lake through boardwalk bogs, passing Middle Quartz Lake. Even as the trail moves away from water, mosquitoes pester hikers. The trail drops to a backcountry campsite at Lower Quartz Lake's outlet. From here, it climbs 1.5 miles with good views to the top of Cerulean Ridge before dropping back to the junction. For families with kids, an out-and-back excursion just to Lower Quartz Lake may be easier at seven miles round-trip.

Numa Lookout

- Distance: 11.2 miles round-trip
- Duration: 5.5 hours
- Elevation gain: 2,930 feet
- Effort: moderately strenuous
- Trailhead: from Bowman Lake Campground in Glacier National Park

Although the bulk of the trail crawls through deep forest, the view from Numa Lookout is well worth the climb. Following the northwest shore of Bowman Lake, the trail winds 0.7 mile through damp cedars to a junction. Take the left fork. The trail climbs steadily uphill to a saddle with a small boggy pond. During mosquito season, hike fast to get by the swarms.

After the trail switchbacks up the final climb within eyesight of the lookout, the treed slope breaks into dry open meadows. At 6,960 feet high, the lookout, which is staffed during fire

Not all creeks have bridges.

© BECKY LOMAX

season, stares across Bowman Lake at the steep massif of Square, Rainbow, and Carter Peaks.

Bowman Lake

- Distance: 14.2 miles round-trip to head of lake
- Duration: 6 hours
- Elevation gain: none
- Effort: easy, but lengthy
- Trailhead: from Bowman Lake Campground in Glacier National Park

This easy-walking trail wanders the forested northeast shoreline of Bowman Lake. For a stroll, walk it as far as you want, and then turn around. The trail nears the shore close enough for beach access only a couple times where June water levels flood beaches. Intermittent views of the Square, Rainbow, and Carter massif poke out from the trees.

At the head of the lake, a backcountry campground with a marvelous pebble beach is a great place to lunch, but do so by the community cooking site rather than in or near backcountry sleeping sites. Bring binoculars, because bald eagles nest at the lake's head. For backpackers, the trail continues on, climbing to Brown's Pass atop the Continental Divide, where it splits, either dropping east to Goat Haunt on Waterton Lake (23 miles total) or climbing around Hole-in-the-Wall and over Boulder Pass to Kintla Lake (37 miles total).

Kintla Lake

- Distance: 12.4 miles round-trip
- Duration: 6 hours
- Elevation gain: none
- Effort: easy, but lengthy
- Trailhead: from Kintla Lake Campground in Glacier National Park

The gentle trail cruises along Kintla Lake's north shore with an expanding view up the lake before its midsection tours deep back in the trees. Look for woodland flowers: trilliums, twisted stalk, queen's cup, fairybells,

© BECKY LOMAX

head of Kintla Lake: a place for remote quiet

bunchberry, and bog orchids. Toward the head of the lake, the trail returns to a shoreline tour.

At 6.3 miles, the trail reaches the Kintla Lake backcountry campground. Pull out the binoculars, for you might see moose, bear, or bald eagles from its shoreline. When eating lunch, do so by the community cooking site rather than in or near backcountry sleeping sites. The trail continues on through the 2003 Wedge Fire growing with prolific pink fireweed and past the dramatic Long Knife Waterfall to Upper Kintla Lake, 2.9 miles from Kintla Head Backcountry Campsites. At the head of Upper Kintla, it begins a substantial climb to Boulder Pass, where it drops through Hole-in-the-Wall cirque to Brown's Pass on the Continental Divide and then splits, either dropping east to Goat Haunt on Waterton Lake (32 miles total) or down to Bowman Lake (37 miles total).

Logging Lake

• Distance: 8.8 miles round-trip

• Duration: 4 hours

• Elevation gain: 477 feet

• Effort: easy

• Trailhead: Logging Creek Campground on the Inside North Fork Road in Glacier National Park

With large views en route, the trail attracts mostly anglers fishing for cutthroat, some with gumption enough to haul in float tubes to get away from the brushy shoreline. Above Logging Creek, the trail climbs quickly at the start but then levels out across a timbered ridgeline that offers a glimpse or two of the creek canyon. At the lake, far beyond its opposite shoreline eight miles away, you can spot Mount Geduhn and Anaconda Mountain.

Mount Thoma

• Distance: 10 miles round-trip

• Duration: 5 hours

• Elevation gain: 2,917 feet

• Effort: strenuous

• Trailhead: on north side 3 miles up Trail Creek Road in Flathead National Forest

• Directions: Drive north of Polebridge on the Outside North Fork Road approximately 13 miles to Trail Creek, 6 miles from the Canadian border. Turn left and drive 3 miles to the trailhead.

The forested trail starts off gently but soon pitches into an uphill grunt. Brushy and rarely maintained, the trail frequently has downed trees barring the path, requiring climbing and worming through branches. But soon it breaks out into a high ridgeline meadow with bluebells. At the end of the ridge, it climbs a series of switchbacks to the summit.

The summit is well worth the hike. Glacier's peaks sprawl southeasterly. The border swath between Canada and the United States slices an unnaturally straight line across the valley. In Canada, a mosaic of clearcuts leads up to Akamina-Kishinena Provincial Park bordering Waterton National Park. To the south, the Whitefish Range layers off peak after peak as far as the eye can see.

Hornet Lookout

- Distance: 2 miles round-trip
- Duration: 1 hour
- Elevation gain: 498 feet
- Effort: easy
- Trailhead: at Hornet Road's terminus in Flathead National Forest
- Directions: 10 miles north of Polebridge, turn west on Whale Creek Road #318 for 4 miles, then turn north, climbing on narrow Hornet Road #9805 for 5.2 miles.

A short climb uphill through huckleberry, fireweed, and beargrass slopes leads to a small lookout with great views of Glacier's skyline and the North Fork Valley. Silvered trees remain from the 2003 Wedge Fire; you'll get a good look at the full scope of the burn. While the drive may take longer than the hike, the lookout makes a great kid destination with an eyeful of view rewards for adults. Two people can rent the USFS lookout to spend the night.

◖ Glacier View

- Distance: 4.5 miles round-trip
- Duration: 4.5 hours
- Elevation gain: 2,687 feet
- Effort: strenuous
- Trailhead: at the junction of Camas and North Fork Roads in Flathead National Forest (trail sign says Demers Ridge)

A steep climb up the side of Demers Ridge leads to Glacier View. Its name says it all: Views from the top span the park's peaks. You'll even see Flathead Lake in the distance. The trail passes right through the 2001 Moose Fire zone, with charred stumps and silver toothpick trees. In the valley below, you can see the fire's mosaic as it burned with different intensities and leaped tree glades. In June, wild roses scent the air amid a botanical dream of wildflower species.

Right from the start, the trail makes no bones about going uphill: no flats to catch your breath, no warm-up for the legs. But with a

A steep climb leads to Glacier View, a full panorama of park peaks.

© BECKY LOMAX

decent pair of lungs, the steep ascent is not bad. Just adopt a slow, steady plod, and you'll reach the top, where meadows afford a scenic top-of-the-world place to lunch, with Glacier's peaks from its southern border to Canada spread across the skyline. The fire removed shade from the slopes, so the trail is a baker in hot August heat. In winter, snowshoers trek up.

Guides

Glacier Guides (406/387-5555 or 800/521-7238, www.glacierguides.com), in West Glacier, has the sole guiding concession for Glacier Park. Most of their day-hiking trips head elsewhere; however, many of their multiday backpacking trips begin or finish at Bowman and Kintla trailheads. See the *West Glacier and Apgar* chapter for details. No

companies have guiding services for hiking in the Whitefish Range of Flathead National Forest.

BIKING

With the North Fork's rough gravel roads, mountain biking is the only way to go; road bikes won't cut it here. Bike rentals are not available in the North Fork—only in Flathead Valley.

Many mountain bikers ride a 54-mile loop from Apgar up the Inside North Fork Road, overnighting in Polebridge and cycling down the Outside North Fork and Camas Roads. Because the Inside Road packs in serious elevation gain as it climbs and drops through five creek drainages, the loop is a good two-day ride, but it requires carrying only minimal

TIPS FOR WILDLIFE-WATCHING

- Safety is important when watching wildlife – safety for you and safety for the wildlife. For spying wildlife up close, use a good pair of binoculars.

- Do not approach wildlife. Although our inclinations tell us to scoot in for a closer look, crowding wildlife puts you at risk and endangers the animal, often scaring it off. Sometimes simply the presence of people can habituate an animal to hanging around people; with bears, this can lead to more aggressive behavior.

- Let the animal's or bird's behavior guide your behavior. If the animal appears twitchy, nervous, or points eyes and ears directly at you, back off: You're too close. The goal is to watch wildlife go about their normal business, rather than seeing how they react to disruption. If you behave like a predator stalking an animal, the creature will assume you are one. Use binoculars and telephoto lenses for moving in close rather than approaching an animal.

- Most animals tend to be more active in morning and evening. These are also op-

timum times for photographing animals in better lighting.

- Blend in with your surroundings. Rather than wearing loud colors, wear muted clothing that matches the environment.

- Relax. Animals sense excitement. Move slowly around them because abrupt, jerky movements can startle them. Look down, rather than staring animals directly in the eye.

- Don't get carried away watching big, showy megafauna like bears and moose only to miss a small carnivore like a short-tailed weasel.

- Use field guides to help with identification and understanding the animal's behavior.

- If you see wildlife along a road, use pullouts or broad shoulders to drive completely off the road. Do not jam the middle of the road. Use the car as a blind to watch wildlife, but keep pets inside. If you see a bear, you're better off just driving by slowly. Bear jams tend to condition the bruin to become accustomed to vehicles, one step toward getting into more trouble.

supplies. (Some do the trip in one long day without exploring much en route.) By staying at the North Fork Hostel and renting linens, you can leave the tent and sleeping bag home. Plan for dinner at the Northern Lights Saloon and breakfast on baked goodies at the Merc. Just carry your lunch, the day's water, emergency supplies, and, of course, bug juice. In June, while moisture still clings to the gravel, the ride is less dusty, but you'll eat your share of mosquitoes on the Inside Road. By late July, you might need a dust mask to survive the ride back south on the Outside North Fork Road.

RIVER RAFTING AND KAYAKING

Floating the Wild and Scenic **North Fork of the Flathead** decompresses you to river pace on its Class II waters. Upper Fool Hen is the only Class III rapid. Six river put-ins stagger down the river's 59 miles from the Canadian border to its confluence with the Middle Fork: the border, Ford, Polebridge, Big Creek, Glacier Rim, and Blankenship. Flows peak in late May,

with low water in August. In July, the average float time from the border to Blankenship is 16 hours, which most floaters tend to break into three days. The section between Big Creek and Glacier Rim contains rapids. *Three Forks of the Flathead Float Guide,* available through Glacier Natural History Association (406/888-5756, www.glacierassociation.org, $12.95), provides details on camping, rapids, and navigation. Solid human waste containment is required; take a toilet system, groover, or disposable biodegradable waste bags. Fire pans to prevent fire scarring are recommended.

Overnight Permits

No permits are required for floating, but all camps must be set up on the western shore rather than Glacier's eastern shoreline. Camping—first-come, first-served only—is free in Flathead National Forest and on state lands. Round Prairie is the one exception on Glacier's bank; it requires a permit ($5 per person per night, kids 8–15 years half price, kids 7 years and younger are free). Permits are

The North Fork of the Flathead offers Class II-III rafting.

© BECKY LOMAX

available by advance reservation ($30 per trip for mid-June–September) and must use the official Backcountry Camping application (www. nps.gov/glac). You can pick up permits at the Polebridge Ranger Station the day before your departure, but call ahead to be sure someone is available to write the permit (406/888-7742). Otherwise, head to the Apgar Backcountry Permit Center (406/888-7859).

Respect the rights of private-property owners along the river. Signage at river accesses identifies land ownership en route. For questions regarding rafting on the North Fork, call Glacier View Ranger District (406/387-3800).

Guides

Several river rafting companies lead overnight trips down the North Fork; however, none base their operations in the North Fork Valley. All commercial outfitters begin their trips in West Glacier. (See descriptions in the *West Glacier and Apgar* chapter for options.) Due to the Class II nature of the river, most trips are float trips appropriate for families and kids. **Glacier Guides** (406/387-5555 or 800/521-7238, www.glacierguides.com) runs unique three-day North Fork float trips that combine rafting with overnight cabin stays rather than camping ($652 adults, $552 kids, add 7 percent user fee).

Rentals and Shuttles

No raft, inflatable kayak, or kayak rentals are available in the North Fork; however, in West Glacier, you can rent rafts, frames, oars, inflatable kayaks, paddles, PFDs, toilet systems, fire pans, and camping gear from **Glacier Guides/ Montana Raft Company** (406/387-5555 or 800/521-7238) or **Glacier Outdoor Center** (406/888-5454 or 800/235-6781). The latter also offers vehicle shuttle services in your rig ($60–275) or theirs ($85–355). If you're accessing the North Fork via Columbia Falls, plan to rent a raft from a Flathead Valley location.

BOATING

All types of rowed boats and sail craft are allowed on both **Bowman** and **Kintla Lakes;** however, the constrictive mountains create swirly winds that make sailing and sailboarding almost impossible. While Kintla does not permit any motorboats, Bowman allows motors of 10 horsepower or less. Both lakes are closed to Jet Skis and waterskiing. No boat rentals are available in the North Fork Valley; plan ahead for rentals in Flathead Valley.

Park boating regulations require that motorized vehicles have free permits. Boaters must show that their boats have been cleaned, drained, and dried to avoid bringing Aquatic Invasive Species into park lakes. Permits for up to 14 days are available at the Apgar Backcountry Permit Office and Polebridge Entrance Station.

Be aware of wildlife closures on the lakes. Both lakes harbor nesting bald eagles at their heads; seasonal closures marked with orange buoys protect the areas.

SEA KAYAKING AND CANOEING

Skilled canoers can float the Wild and Scenic **North Fork of the Flathead** via six river access sites run by Flathead National Forest. Floaters must be able to handle Class II ripples; those looking to avoid the Class III Fool Hen Rapids should take out at Big Creek. See *River Rafting and Kayaking* for details on permits, camping, and regulations.

The larger quiet waters of **Bowman** and **Kintla Lakes** appeal to sea kayakers and canoers, with backcountry campsites at the head of each lake. Backcountry permits are required for overnight camping at both lakes. Kintla is a paddling paradise due to its ban on motorized watercraft. While both lakes on calm days make for stellar paddling, their waters kick up with lusty winds in minutes. Wildlife closures are marked with orange buoys at the head of each lake, where bald eagles nest. The nearest rental shops for kayaks, canoes, and camping gear are in West Glacier and Flathead Valley.

FISHING

Anglers are attracted to the North Fork for its native fish: westslope cutthroat and bull trout.

No motors are allowed on Kintla Lake.

Be able to identify each, as they are catch-and-release only. Bull trout have spots on their sides that are pink or orange, and they lack black on their backs; cutthroats have a red slash under their jaw.

Kintla and **Bowman Lakes** are the main lakes accessible by car for fishing. Shorelines near their campgrounds are rimmed with trails. For those willing to hike, the three **Quartz Lakes** hop with native trout and whitefish. Along the Inside North Fork Road, most of the western creek drainages provide some fishing, with various degrees of accessibility. Fishing closures in the area include Upper Kintla Lake and Kintla Creek between the two Kintla Lakes, Bowman Creek above the lake, and Logging Creek between Logging and Grace Lakes.

The most popular North Fork Valley fishing is on the **North Fork River** itself, where six river accesses (Canadian border, Ford, Polebridge, Big Creek, Glacier Rim, and Blankenship) allow for raft or boat launching and fishing. Anglers also fish around the Camas Bridge.

Several commercial outfitters guide overnight fishing trips on the North Fork River; all fishing outfitters base their operations out of West Glacier.

Licenses and Regulations

The North Fork River's high water line on the eastern shore provides Glacier's western boundary. Inside the park, fishing licenses or permits are not required, but outside the park, anglers must possess a Montana State Fishing License. When fishing the North Fork River from the east bank, park regulations apply; when fishing from the west bank, state regulations apply. Purchase one before you come up the North Fork; none are sold in Polebridge. Find license information in the *Background* chapter.

HUNTING

Hunting is illegal in Glacier National Park. But in the North Fork, Flathead National Forest holds popular deer, elk, and bird hunting grounds. Get hunting regulations, seasons, and license info from Montana Fish, Wildlife, and Parks (406/444-2535, www.fwp.mt.gov).

CROSS-COUNTRY SKIING

Roads in the North Fork convert to easy avalanche-free cross-country ski and snowshoe trails in winter. But don't expect pristine smooth snows: The North Fork thrives as a winter habitat for moose, wolves, deer, elk, snowshoe hares, coyotes, and bobcats. Their tracks pockmark roads easy for animal travel, too. Grab a track identification book to help in deciphering the footprints. If you need rental gear, pick it up in West Glacier or the Flathead Valley before coming up the North Fork; no skis are available in Polebridge.

Park at the Polebridge entrance station to ski to **Bowman Lake,** touring less than a half mile north on the Inside Road before climbing six miles up to Bowman Lake's frozen shores. Be cautious about continuing out onto the ice in shoulder seasons. Stick close to shore if you want to ski the lake. **Big Prairie, the Inside Road,** and **Hidden Meadows** all provide other routes starting from the same point. Pick up a free brochure on *Skiing and Snowshoeing* online or from visitors centers or ranger stations for route descriptions.

For an overnight, skiers traverse 12 miles up Whale Creek Road to stay in one of the Forest Service cabins—Ninko—on the flanks of Thompson-Seton Mountain. For information on this trip, call Glacier View Ranger Station (406/387-3800).

SNOWMOBILING

While snowmobiles are not permitted in Glacier, they are allowed in Flathead National Forest in the Whitefish Range, where snowfall piles up 6–12 feet. December–April, unplowed roads heading west off the North Fork Road are used by snowmobilers, and a few are groomed by Flathead Snowmobile Association. Contact Montana Snowmobile Association (406/788-2399, www.snowtana.com) for current information on the local association and maps. Glacier View Ranger Station (406/387-3800) regulates snowmobile use, season, and closures; check for current conditions and restrictions. The nearest rentals are in Flathead Valley.

ENTERTAINMENT

Instead of red, white, and blue marching bands, witness cross-dressers, beer-can draggers, bicycles, the 1956 Polebridge fire truck, and rafts in Polebridge's annual **Fourth of July Parade**—the more slightly off-kilter, the better. Hundreds of people line the dirt main street for the noon parade-that's-really-not-a-parade. Parking is a nightmare, and it's a two-for-one show as the parade goes up the street and then back down the same street. Enter for free; watch for free. Who's in charge? No one knows.

Accommodations and Food

North Fork lodging is off the grid. With no electricity, generators or solar panels provide power, lights are most often propane, woodstoves provide heat, and phone lines only reach Polebridge. However, despite the rusticity, the state of Montana still charges its 7 percent bed tax.

IN POLEBRIDGE

Located a quarter mile south of the Merc and Northern Lights Saloon, the **North Fork Hostel** (80 Beaver Dr., 406/888-5241, www.nfhostel.com) may be off the electric grid, but you don't "rough it" here. A huge storage battery powers phone, fax, and wireless Internet access. You can even recharge your digital camera batteries from it. Propane powers lights, a cooking stove, and a refrigerator, with a few kerosene lights added in. Wood heats up the cedar hot tub. The hostel has a shared living room, fully equipped kitchen, outhouses, and washrooms with hot showers. Lodging options include mixed dorm bunks ($20 per person), private rooms ($45), tepees ($40), and two small cabins and a 1950s trailer called the Green Zucchini ($45). Bring food, towels, and sleeping bags, or rent linens for $5. The hostel has a few mountain bikes, canoes, cross-country skis, and snowshoes for guests to rent. Some facilities are open year-round, but make reservations to be sure.

Nearby at **Square Peg Ranch,** the hostel also rents two log homes ($80 per night)—one a 1918 homestead. Propane lights, refrigerator, and cooking ranges stock the equipped kitchens, and wood heats the buildings. Cold running water, solar showers, and outhouses complete the rustic stay. Bring sleeping bags or sheets, food, towels, and containers to haul fresh drinking water from the hostel. Each home sleeps four adults and two children.

Cabins

Open year-round, the **Polebridge Cabins** (265 Polebridge Loop, 406/888-5105, $45 per night double occupancy) are stark. Be ready for smoky woodstoves and an out-house. Adjacent to the Merc and Northern Lights Saloon, the tiny cabins have beds, tables, chairs, and propane refrigerators. Bring your sleeping bag, pillow, cooking utensils, a water jug, and a flashlight for middle-of-the-night trips to the outhouse. Ask if you need to bring firewood.

OUTSIDE POLEBRIDGE

For those looking to get away from it all, **The Way Less Traveled Bed and Breakfast** (16485 North Fork Rd., 406/261-5880, www.thewaylesstraveled.com, open year-round) is about as far away as you can get and still have the comforts of civilization. Proprietors Paul and Nancy Winkler encourage guests to forget about the world. Located 17 miles north of Polebridge near the Canadian border, the smoke-free, alcohol-free bed-and-breakfast has three themed rooms. Two of the rooms ($90) share a bathroom, but the Lewis and Clark room ($110) has a private bath and deck. The dining room, where the full breakfast features goodies like cinnamon-raisin-vanilla French toast, is surrounded by wildlife-watching windows; in summer, breakfast on the deck is accompanied by loons singing on a nearby lake. A generator powers lights, hot water, a satellite television for those who just cannot live without it, and wireless Internet. While phone lines don't reach this far, you can make Internet calls.

Cabins

Flathead National Forest (Glacier View Ranger District in Hungry Horse, 406/387-3800, www.fs.fed.us/r1/flathead) maintains six cabins for rent scattered throughout the North Fork. With a three-night maximum stay, the cabins ($20–65 per night) have beds, outdoor vault toilets, equipped kitchens with propane cook stoves, outdoor fire pits, and firewood. Bring water, bedding, and food. The nonsmoking cabins do not permit pets, tents, or RVs. Reservations are mandatory (877/444-6777, www.recreation.gov). After confirmation, you'll get the cabin combination. You must

clean up at the end of your stay and pack garbage out with you.

Four cabins are available year-round. In a rather drafty tiny 1922 building perched atop a mountain, **Hornet Lookout,** which sleeps two, has a one-mile hike in summer or 11-mile ski or snowmobile trek in winter. The lookout has a small cupola with spectacular views of Glacier. The deck at **Schnaus** yields sweeping views of Glacier's Livingston Range, making it a local favorite for its sunrises and sunset alpenglow. The cabin, which sleeps 12, has vehicle access right up to the front door and sits less than one mile from the North Fork River. Located on the North Fork River, **Ben Rover,** which sleeps eight and has drive-up access, is popular for skiing to Bowman Lake in winter, walking to Polebridge in summer, and fishing right out the front door. Located the farthest north, **Wurtz,** which sleeps 12, is an old 1913 homestead with a large yard on the west side of the North Fork Road. The river sits within a 15-minute walk.

Two small cabins offer seasonal lodging. Open December–March, **Ninko,** which sleeps seven, requires a 12-mile ski or snowmobile trek to reach its remote forested setting. Open late May–mid-March, **Ford,** which was built in 1922 as part of the ranger station, sleeps eight. It has drive-up access and sits adjacent to a river access site.

CAMPING

Don't expect large commercial campgrounds. Rustic national park or national forest campgrounds—all first come, first serve—are the norm, with a sprinkling of private options. If you require hookups and disposal stations, the nearest options are West Glacier and Columbia Falls.

Glacier National Park Campgrounds

Glacier's seasonal North Fork campgrounds (406/888-7800) are only accessible via rough dirt roads. Between rugged roads and smaller sites, these campgrounds don't accommodate huge RVs or trailer combinations. But that's precisely their attraction: Fewer people equals solitude and quiet. They have pit toilets, fire rings, and picnic tables. While the park prohibits firewood collecting in most places, including the campgrounds, you can collect dry, downed firewood on the Bowman Lake Road and the Inside Road from one mile north of Fish Creek Campground to Kintla Lake. Cutting live timber is not permitted. After fall closures, Bowman and Kintla campgrounds permit primitive camping ($10). You can haul cooking water from lakes and streams to boil or purify. The four campgrounds are buggy in June, serene in August, and closed in winter when the roads are buried in snow.

At the foot of Kintla Lake, **◖ Kintla Lake Campground** (late May–mid-Sept., $15 per night) sits 15 miles north of Polebridge. Even by park standards, the tiny 13-site campground set within large trees is rough, with hand-pumped water and small sites. One hiking trail leads uplake and beyond to Upper Kintla Lake and Boulder Pass. If you don't have reservations, plan to arrive early enough that if

all campsites are full, you can still drive back toward Bowman Lake.

At the foot of Bowman Lake, **◖ Bowman Lake Campground** (late May–mid-Sept., $15 per night) sits seven miles from Polebridge. Its 48 sites, which make up the largest of the North Fork's campgrounds, are sprinkled under a mixed conifer forest. It has running water, and a short five-minute walk leads to the lakeshore and the boat ramp. Trails connect to Quartz Lakes, Numa Lookout, Akokala Lake, and up Bowman Lake to Brown's Pass.

Two tiny campgrounds sit on the Inside Road—both set in the woods midway between Apgar and Polebridge and best for tent campers who can drive the rugged road. No running water is available, so bring your own or plan to purify stream water. Arrive by midafternoon, which should allow plenty of time to go elsewhere if the campground is full. **Quartz Creek Campground** (July–Nov., $10 per night), a tiny seven-site campground six miles southeast from Polebridge, is adjacent to Quartz Creek. From the campground, a 6.8-mile rough trail with infrequent maintenance follows the creek up to Lower Quartz Lake. Located 8.3 miles southeast from Polebridge, **Logging Creek Campground** (July–Sept., $10 per night), adjacent to Logging Creek Ranger Station, has only seven sites. This is a popular site for anglers heading to Logging Lake.

Glacier Backcountry Camping

North Fork trails lead to some of the park's most coveted backcountry campsites in the high country between Bowman and Kintla Lakes. Spectacular **Boulder Pass, Brown's Pass,** and **Hole-in-the-Wall** campsites are snow free late July–early September. Low-elevation campsites are snow-free at the heads of **Bowman** and **Kintla Lakes** May–October, providing prized canoe and sea-kayak destinations. Anglers head to **Quartz Lakes** and **Logging Lake.** Pick up permits 24 hours in advance ($5 per person per night; kids 8–15 $2.50; kids 7 and younger free) in person at the Polebridge Ranger Station by calling ahead or the Apgar Backcountry Permit Office

camping at Upper Kintla Lake

© BECKY LOMAX

NORTH FORK

(406/888-7900). Reservations for mid-June–September trips are available ($30) via the Backcountry Camping Application available online: www.nps.gov/glac.

National Forest Campgrounds

Located 20 miles north of Columbia Falls and 13 miles from Apgar on North Fork Road, **Big Creek Campground** (Glacier View Ranger District, 406/387-3800, mid-May–mid-Oct., $12 per night) sits in Flathead National Forest. It can be accessed via a five-minute gravel road drive from the Camas Road park entrance. Several of the campground's 22 sites can accommodate 40-foot RVs and trailers among its large cottonwoods and doghair firs. Drinking water is available, along with vault toilets. Prime campsites line up along North Fork of the Flathead River with easy fishing access. You can collect firewood here, but by late season the surrounding woods are scoured.

Private Campgrounds

Camping is also available at two North Fork businesses. The **North Fork Hostel** (80 Beaver Dr., 406/888-5241, www.nfhostel.com) accommodates tenters at $10 per night. **Home Ranch Bottoms** (8855 North Fork Rd., 406/888-5572, www.homeranchbottoms.com) charges $35 per night for two people, which includes shower use.

FOOD

A rustic off-the-grid restaurant in a tiny, funky old log cabin, the **(Northern Lights Saloon** (255 Polebridge Loop, 406/888-9963, 4–9 P.M. nightly late May–Sept., entrées $6–18) was purchased by new owners in 2010, who regained the license for beer, wine, and liquor. The ever-changing menu bent towards homemade goodies features seasonal specialties, vegetarian dishes, chili burgers, and steaks. Friday nights pack the building for pizza night. The new owners overhauled the restaurant interior and equipment, and waiting lines attest to its unique backwoods ambience. Some people even drive up the North Fork just to go to the historic restaurant.

Open year-round, the **(Polebridge Mercantile** (265 Polebridge Loop, 406/888-5105, 8 A.M.–6 P.M. daily, until 9 P.M. weekends, closed Mon.–Thurs. Thanksgiving–Apr.) stocks limited groceries, white gas, propane, fishing tackle, and beer. You can pick up forgotten camping items, but don't expect a broad selection of choices. New owners took over in 2009, but it still maintains a reputation for yummy baked goodies yanked fresh from the oven—pastries, cookies, lunch breads, snacks, and sandwiches to go.

Closed for several years after a grizzly ripped apart the building, **Home Ranch Bottoms** (8855 North Fork Rd., 406/888-5572, www.homeranchbottoms.com, 9 A.M.–9 P.M. late May–early Sept.) opened again in 2005 after Beth and Greg Puckett rebuilt the cabin. It's worth a stop just to see the preserved grizzly-clawed floor and photos of the ripped-up wall. Well signed with hand-painted advertising, the small store sells convenience-type groceries, beer, coffee, pop, T-shirts, firewood, and ice. In 2006, the Pucketts added a large log bar—**The Bottoms Tavern.** The tavern serves pizza, burgers, cold beer, and a daily $2 beer special. Try one of their signature drink specials: The Moose Dropping (Montana version of an Irish Car Bomb) or North Fork Margarita. They fire up the woodstove on chilly days, and folks lounge on the deck when it's warm. Music jams happen here, with a guitar and banjo kept on hand. If there's a crowd, they'll stay open later than 9 P.M.

GOING-TO-THE-SUN ROAD

Historic Going-to-the-Sun Road is a testament to human ingenuity and nature's wonders. Tunnels, switchbacks, arches, and a narrow two-lane highway cutting across precipitous slopes nod to engineering feats—marvels in themselves. Yet in the road's 52 miles, an incomparable diversity unfolds, with surprises around each corner. Cedar rainforests give way to windblown subalpine firs, broad lake valleys lead into glacial corridors, thousand-foot cliff walls abut wildflower gardens, and waterfalls spew from every pore. Defying gravity, ragged peaks rake the sky, crowning all.

This National Historic Landmark is a highway to savor every nook and cranny. "Ooohs" and "aaahs" punctuate every sweep in the road as stunning scenery unfolds. Stopping at myriad pullouts along the road, many sightseers burn through their digital pixels only halfway up the alpine section. The sheer immensity of the glacier-chewed landscape leaves visitors gasping, "I can't fit it all in my camera!"

To stretch the legs, well-signed short paths guide hikers through a dripping rainforest, along a glacial moraine, amid mountain goats, and beside a roaring waterfall. Those ready to put miles on their boots should tackle at least one of the longer high alpine trails, where you'll feel you've reached the apex of the world to send the human spirit soaring.

The Sun Road, as locals call it, is one place you won't want to miss. Its rugged beauty leaves a lasting impression.

HISTORY
Early Development
By 1895, Lake McDonald boomed with

HIGHLIGHTS

(Red Bus Tour: Ride over Logan Pass in historic style. The 1937 vintage touring sedans, designed especially for national parks, roll their canvas tops back for superb views and perhaps dousing from the Weeping Wall (page 86).

(Boat Tours: Hop aboard *Little Chief* for the best way to see St. Mary, or aboard the *DeSmet* to see Lake McDonald – the park's two largest lakes (page 86).

(Lake McDonald: Stop to see Glacier's largest lake, which fills a monstrous valley gouged by an ancient ice age glacier. Rent a boat to fish, or swim from any of the pullouts on Going-to-the-Sun Road (page 90).

(Lake McDonald Lodge: Sit on the back porch of the historic lodge gracing Lake McDonald. The lodge's rustic hunting motif harkens back to a pre-national park era when the area served as a hunting preserve (page 90).

(Logan Pass: Touch the Continental Divide, where waters stream toward both the Pacific and the Atlantic. The apex of Going-to-the-Sun Road sprawls with broad alpine meadows teeming with wildflowers and mountain goats (page 94).

(Wild Goose Island Overlook: Bring the camera! Hands down the most photographed spot in the park, tiny Wild Goose Island cowers in St. Mary Lake below the Continental Divide's rugged skyline (page 96).

(Trail of the Cedars: Walk through the easternmost rainforest in the United States. The trail follows a boardwalk and paved pathway under a tree canopy that keeps temperatures cool, even in midsummer (page 98).

(Highline Trail and Granite Park Chalet: Hike a wildflower-packed trail clinging high on cliffs along the Garden Wall to a historic backcountry chalet where bear-watching is a worthy pastime (page 99).

(Siyeh Pass: Climb over one of the most scenic and diverse trails in Glacier. The path wanders wildflower parks and descends colorful sedimentary strata – perhaps touching on every color in the rainbow (page 100).

(Swan Mountain Outfitters: Saddle up for the best trail ride in the park. Join the Swan Mountain Outfitters for a ride to Sperry Chalet, where you can lunch in the historic dining room and smack your lips on fresh-baked pie (page 104).

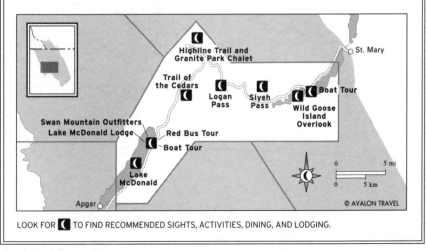

LOOK FOR **(** TO FIND RECOMMENDED SIGHTS, ACTIVITIES, DINING, AND LODGING.

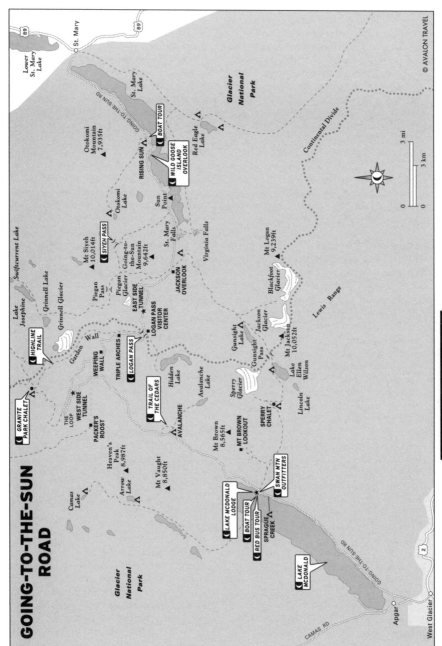

GOING-TO-THE-SUN ROAD

© AVALON TRAVEL

St. Mary

Lower St. Mary Lake

Glacier National Park

Continental Divide

89

GOING-TO-THE-SUN RD

St. Mary Lake

BOAT TOUR

Red Eagle Lake

Otokomi Mountain 7,935ft

RISING SUN

WILD GOOSE ISLAND OVERLOOK

Otokomi Lake

Sun Point

St. Mary Falls

Virginia Falls

Mt Logan 9,239ft

Mt Siyeh 10,014ft

SIYEH PASS

Going-to-the-Sun Mountain 9,642ft

JACKSON OVERLOOK

Blackfoot Glacier

Swiftcurrent Lake

Lake Josephine

Grinnell Lake

Grinnell Glacier

Piegan Pass

Piegan Glacier

EAST SIDE TUNNEL

LOGAN PASS VISITOR CENTER

Jackson Glacier

Mt Jackson 10,052ft

Lewis Range

HIGHLINE TRAIL

Garden Wall

TRIPLE ARCHES

WEEPING WALL

LOGAN PASS

Gunsight Lake

Gunsight Pass

Lake Ellen Wilson

GRANITE PARK CHALET

THE LOOP

WEST SIDE TUNNEL

PACKER'S ROOST

TRAIL OF THE CEDARS

Hidden Lake

Avalanche Lake

AVALANCHE

Sperry Glacier

Lincoln Lake

Heaven's Peak 8,987ft

Mt Vaught 8,850ft

Mt Brown 8,565ft

MT BROWN LOOKOUT

SPERRY CHALET

Camas Lake

Arrow Lake

LAKE McDONALD LODGE

BOAT TOUR

SWAN MTN OUTFITTERS

Glacier National Park

RED BUS TOUR

SPRAGUE CREEK

LAKE McDONALD

GOING-TO-THE-SUN RD

CAMAS RD

Apgar

West Glacier

2

N

0   3 mi

0   3 km

89

tourism brought on by the railroad's arrival in West Glacier. Hauling a 40-foot steamboat up from Flathead Lake, George Snyder shuttled guests from Apgar to his 12-room hotel, where Lake McDonald Lodge currently sits. With Sperry Glacier's discovery in 1896, Snyder's guests had a popular horse trip destination above his lodge. Funded by Great Northern Railway, Dr. Lyman Sperry and 15 of his students built the Gunsight Pass and Sperry spur trail to accommodate travel between St. Mary and Lake McDonald. While the west side surged with turn-of-the-20th-century tourism, on the east side, Roes Creek (Rose Creek at Rising Sun) boomed as a short-lived mining town—vacated with the Alaska gold rush.

Lodges and Chalets

Under dubious circumstances—perhaps a poker game—ownership of Snyder's hotel went to John and Olive Lewis in 1906, who moved the old hotel and built a cedar and stone lodge facing Lake McDonald. Opening in 1914, Lewis's Glacier Hotel imitated the Swiss theme of Great Northern Railway's hotels and chalets springing up parkwide. Lewis promoted Going-to-the-Sun Road, spending his own money to cut part of the route along the lake, grade the road, and build bridges. From West Glacier, the road reached his hotel in 1922, increasing the hotel's visitors with automobile popularity.

Because of Lewis's foothold in McDonald Valley, Great Northern Railway ignored the area around the park's largest lake—instead frenetically erecting chalets between 1912 and 1914 at Sun Point, Gunsight Lake, and Sperry, and using Sperry's trail over Gunsight Pass to link the three. A year later and quite behind schedule, Granite Park Chalet was finally completed—a destination from Many Glacier Hotel and Sun Point. With packed bunk-bed dorms and canvas tents outside, Granite and Sperry could house 144 and 152 guests, nearly four times the number each sleep today. Their popularity increased in the 1920s as wealthy easterners spent an average of 21 days in the park touring on horseback with Park Saddle

Company. However, Gunsight Chalet lasted only five years, wiped out by an avalanche.

In 1930, Great Northern Railway purchased Lewis's hotel, adding it to its lodge arsenal. When ownership changed, so did the name— to Lake McDonald Lodge. Two years later, the lodge was sold to the National Park Service.

Ironically, along with the Depression and increased auto travel, Going-to-the-Sun Road, which was completed in 1932, hastened the demise of the chalets. Horse-trip visitation dropped from 26 to 3 percent. Natty automobile drivers sought more affordable places to stay. In 1940, the railroad company built East Glacier Auto Cabins (now Rising Sun Motor Inn), where two people could rent a cabin without a shower for $1.75. Finally, World War II park closures, deteriorating buildings, and increased costs of supplying the chalets taxed the railway company to the point where it razed Going-to-the-Sun Chalets and sold Sperry and Granite Park to the National Park Service for a dollar.

Building the Road

Nearly 20 years of planning and construction went into building Going-to-the-Sun Road, fueled by burgeoning excitement over the automobile. While proponents proposed various passes for the "Transmountain Highway," its original name, in 1918 Logan Pass won the park service selection. However, the plan called for 15 switchbacks up the west side, replaced later with one long switchback. Over several years, Congress appropriated $2 million for its construction.

Surveying the route required tenacity to hang by ropes over cliffs and tiptoe along skinny ledges—perhaps causing the 300 percent crew turnover in three months. Over six seasons, three companies excavated rock using only small blast explosives and minimal power tools to create tunnels, bridges, Triple Arches, and guard walls. With power equipment unable to reach the East Side Tunnel, crews cleared its 405-foot length by hand boring 5.33 feet per day.

In 1932, during late fall, the first automobile chugged over Logan Pass. The following July, over 4,000 people attended dedication ceremonies at the pass, celebrating the road's completion and ending with a peace ceremony for the Blackfeet, Kootenai, and Flathead tribes.

Although guardrails, surfacing, and grading were not completed until 1935, nearly 40,000 visitors in its first year flocked to the road despite its rough tread and the Depression. Until the late 1930s, crushed rock covered its surface. Finally, in 1938, the park service embarked on a 14-year project to pave the scenic highway—at last completed in 1952.

Exploring Going-to-the-Sun Road

Going-to-the-Sun Road connects West Glacier and St. Mary by 52 miles of one of the most scenic highways in America. The road links two immense glacier-carved valleys—McDonald and St. Mary—via Logan Pass. It crosses the Continental Divide at 6,646 feet. From Lake McDonald, the road ascends up 3,400 feet to the pass; from St. Mary, it rises about 2,200 feet. Given the road's extremes in elevation, it takes rash punishment from brutal weather.

ENTRANCE STATIONS
Both ends of Going-to-the-Sun Road have entrance stations: one at West Glacier, the other at St. Mary. Staffed during daylight hours all summer long and on weekends only in the off-season, the stations have national park maps and the *Waterton-Glacier Guide,* the park's newspaper, which is updated twice annually. If you miss working hours, you can use the self-pay cash-only kiosks on the right just beyond the booths. If you don't have an annual pass, seven-day passes cost $25 per vehicle or $12 for individuals on foot, bicycles, or motorcycles. (Rates drop to $15 and $10 November–April.)

VISITORS CENTER
The one place everyone wants to go is Logan Pass, but its visitors center is small and the

GOING-TO-THE-SUN ROAD

© BECKY LOMAX

Logan Pass features a visitors center and trailheads.

parking lot cramped on sunny days. We all put up with the hassle, for no one wants more pavement and a larger building impinging the meadows. Unprepared visitors arrive expecting a resort atmosphere at **Logan Pass Visitor Center** (406/888-7800, 9 A.M.–7 P.M. daily mid-June–Labor Day, 9:30 A.M.–4:30 P.M. daily Labor Day–Sept.). It's a seasonal outpost with a tiny Glacier Natural History Bookstore (406/888-5756, www.glacierassociation.org), an information desk, and a few displays. Set your hand in the grizzly paw cast to marvel at the size difference!

While a fireplace crackles upstairs on cold days, one bench allows only a few to snuggle up to its heat. Restrooms downstairs have the coldest running water you'll ever dip your fingers into. In shoulder seasons when the water is turned off, port-a-potties line the parking lot. No food or beverages are sold here, not even coffee and candy bars. Due to the elevation, expect harsher weather—wind, rain, and snow even in August. Don't be surprised if you left the lowlands in sunny summer only to arrive at Logan Pass in winter.

SHUTTLES AND TOURS
Shuttles
To avoid Logan Pass parking lot hassles, shuttles are the way to go. Better yet, shuttles enable point-to-point hiking on some of Glacier's most spectacular trails. In 2007, Glacier added a free shuttle service (406/888-7800, www.nps.gov/glac) to eliminate congestion on Going-to-the-Sun Road during construction. These shuttles are extremely popular: Midsummer, you may find yourself waiting in lines to get on or see full shuttles bypass a stop. But going car free to trailheads is still worth it, compared to not finding a parking spot.

The park service runs **free shuttles** over Going-to-the-Sun Road, July 1–Labor Day, stopping at 17 locations. Get on or off at any of the stops denoted by interpretive signs—each one featuring a different animal print. No tickets are needed; no reservations are taken. Both east- and west-side shuttles begin running up the road at 7 A.M.; the last shuttles depart Logan Pass at 7 P.M.

On the west side, shuttles depart every 15–30

Free shuttles make 17 stops along Going-to-the-Sun Road, including Logan Pass.

RED BUSES

© BECKY LOMAX

Tops roll back on red buses for unlimited peak views.

Red buses are a Glacier icon. Built by Ohio's White Motor Company specifically for national park touring, the red buses became a symbol of the nation's western parks. Yosemite, Yellowstone, Zion, Mount Rainier, Grand Canyon, and Bryce had their own fleets, and so did Glacier. Nearly 500 red buses toured visitors in Glacier, Yosemite, and Yellowstone alone.

Although red bus fleets disappeared from the other parks in the 1950s, Glacier steadfastly held on to its 33 scarlet prizes, upgrading parts as necessary. The canvas tops rolled back to create an open-air touring car, so guests rode in historic style over Going-to-the-Sun Road, covering up with blankets if temperatures chilled down. Nicknamed "jammers" or "gear jammers" for the tremendous noise their gears made while shifting, the vintage 25-foot-long 17-passenger vehicles first drove Glacier's curvy roads in 1937 as the park's second generation of touring sedans. Decades later, as automatic transmissions replaced the manual transmissions and power steering eased driving Going-to-the-Sun Road's curves, jammers continued to tour folks through Glacier until 1999, when safety concerns sidelined the red rigs.

Glacier Park, Inc., operator of the historic park lodges, owned the jammers but donated the fleet to the National Park Foundation. Ford Motor Company rehabilitated the vehicles in keeping with their historic appearance. In the process, Ford also converted them to bifuel to run on gasoline or propane. New wiring, interiors, and paint jobs completed the project. (Check a jammer up close: You'll see both White and Ford logos.) Thirty-two of the red buses are back in service; one was kept intact for historical value.

Uniformed park employees pedal red retro bikes to match the historic buses – part of a National Park Service program to employ alternative transportation in the park, save fuel costs, and reduce emissions. The bikes were purchased with help from The Glacier Fund, a nonprofit organization.

minutes, with stops at the Apgar Transit Center, Sprague Creek Campground, Lake McDonald Lodge, Avalanche Creek, The Loop, and Logan Pass. The 32-mile ride from the Apgar Transit Center to Logan Pass takes 90 minutes or more. Several different routes service the west side: Confirm your destination when boarding to be sure you catch the right bus.

On the east side, free shuttles depart every 30 minutes from St. Mary Visitor Center. The one-hour shuttle travels 18 miles to Logan Pass, stopping at Rising Sun, Sun Point, Sunrift Gorge, St. Mary Falls, Gunsight Pass Trailhead, and Siyeh Bend. At St. Mary, for a fee you can connect with the **Glacier Park, Inc.** (406/892-2525, www.glacierparkinc.com, no reservations, cash only) daily van service, running early June–late September, linking St.

Mary with East Glacier, Two Medicine, Many Glacier, and Waterton ($10–50 one-way; kids 11 and younger half price). For hikers on The Highline or Piegan Pass trails dropping to Many Glacier, GPI runs an afternoon shuttle July–Labor Day (4:45 P.M., $10) from Many Glacier to St. Mary.

For those arriving by Amtrak with reservations at Lake McDonald Lodge, GPI runs a shuttle late May–late September ($10 adults, $5 child) to or from the Belton Depot in West Glacier. Reservations are mandatory.

Flathead-Glacier Transportation (406/892-3390 or 800/829-7039) runs shuttles by reservation between Glacier International Airport and Lake McDonald Lodge ($55 one-way for one person, $3 each additional person).

Red Bus Tour

In historic style, red jammer buses tour visitors over Going-to-the-Sun Road in vintage 1930s White Motor Company sedans operated by **Glacier Park, Inc.** (406/892-2525, www.glacierparkinc.com, mid-June–mid-Sept., $45–75; kids 11 and younger half price, meals and park entrance fees not included). On good weather days, the jammers (tour bus drivers known for their storytelling) roll the canvas tops back for spectacular views of the Continental Divide. Without a roof, it's one of the most scenic ways to feel the expanse of the glacier-carved terrain. From Lake McDonald Lodge, tours depart daily to explore Going-to-the-Sun Road: The 7.5-hour Crown of the Continent tour departs at 9 A.M., and three-hour Logan Pass tours depart several times daily. You can make reservations by phone or at hotel activity desks. Evening tours are available in July and August.

For those staying at Rising Sun Motor Inn, daily tours originating at Many Glacier Hotel or Glacier Park Lodge will stop to pick up riders. Inquire at the motel's front desk.

Native American Tour

A Blackfeet-led tour provides a different perspective, with emphasis on Native American cultural and natural history. **Sun Tours** (406/226-9220 or 800/786-9220, www.glaciersuntours.com, June–Sept., meals and park entrance fees not included) drives air-conditioned 25-passenger comfortable coaches with extra-big windows for taking in the massive mountains on Going-to-the-Sun Road. You can catch four-hour Logan Pass tours (adults $40, kids $15) daily from St. Mary (9 A.M.) with a Rising Sun pickup shortly following or from Apgar Visitor Center (9 A.M.). Seven-hour daily tours (adults $70, kids $20) leave East Glacier (8 A.M.) and Browning (8:30 A.M.) to drive up the east side of Going-to-the-Sun Road, explore Logan Pass, and drive down the west side to Big Bend to see the Weeping Wall before returning. Make reservations at least one day in advance.

Boat Tours

Lake McDonald and St. Mary, the park's largest lakes, dominate the lowlands here, and **Glacier Park Boat Company** (406/257-2426, www.glacierparkboats.com) runs boat tours on both. You buy tickets (cash only) at the boat docks. In high season, purchase your spot a few hours in advance; midday, cocktail, and sunset cruises fill up. Check *Ranger-Led Activities,* available at visitors centers, for launches that have ranger naturalists aboard.

At the boat dock behind Lake McDonald Lodge, hop on the historic *DeSmet* (late May–late Sept., adults $15, kids half price) for a one-hour tour down the lake. Tours depart at 11 A.M., 1:30, 3, 5:30 (after July 1), and 7 P.M., although the early and late cruise end in early September. With a 90-passenger capacity, the 1930 vintage 57-foot wooden boat motors to the lake's core, where surrounding snow-clad peaks pop into sight. Go for a prime seat on the top deck, even in marginal weather—just bring along a jacket.

At the Rising Sun boat dock on St. Mary Lake, catch a ride on *Little Chief* (mid-June–early Sept., adults $22, kids half price) as it braves the lake's choppy waters. Views of Sexton Glacier and Wild Goose Island can't be beat, but be ready for some healthy wind. Daily departures launch for 90-minute cruises: 10 A.M., noon, 2, 4, and 6 P.M. See Baring Falls at a stop or take a guided two-hour hike to St. Mary Falls.

SERVICES

Prepare for driving Going-to-the-Sun Road, because no services exist on Logan Pass. The closest gas stations are outside the park at St. Mary and West Glacier. With no food services available at the pass, you'll enjoy your time better in less of a rush if you pack a lunch.

Restrooms are few and far between on this historic highway. Flush toilets and running water (at least cold) are available at Lake McDonald Lodge, Logan Pass Visitor Center, and Rising Sun. Vault toilets (no running water for washing your hands) are available at Avalanche Picnic Area, Logan Creek, The Loop, Jackson Glacier Overlook, and Sun Point.

Hot showers (one token $1.25 for eight minutes) are available at Rising Sun. For laundry, you'll have to hit West Glacier or St. Mary.

Find ATM machines at Lake McDonald Lodge and Rising Sun Motor Inn. The Lake McDonald Lodge area also has a small seasonal post office across from the camp store; see current hours posted on the door.

Find local newspapers in gift shops and camp stores at Lake McDonald Lodge and Rising Sun. They carry the *Great Falls Tribune* and Flathead Valley's *Daily Interlake.*

Cell Phones and Internet

While some cell phones pick up service at Logan Pass and upper elevations, most do not work throughout the road's length due to the high surrounding peaks and narrow valleys. No service is available in McDonald Valley except around Apgar; St. Mary Valley gets service only in St. Mary. Granite Park Chalet receives cell service, but be aware that many visitors go there to get away from that. Be discreet in your use on trails. Public pay phones are at Lake McDonald Lodge and Rising Sun as well as Avalanche Campground. No Internet service is available on the Sun Road.

Shopping

Find gift shops in Lake McDonald Lodge, Two Medicine Grill at Rising Sun, and camp stores in both locations. They carry a good selection of guidebooks, coffee-table photo books, maps, and natural-history books, along with gifts, T-shirts, postcards, and jewelry.

Emergencies

If you have an emergency on Going-to-the-Sun Road, contact the park service (406/888-7800). If you cannot leave the scene to make a phone call, flag down a vehicle heading up or down the pass to notify the nearest ranger (usually at Logan Pass, St. Mary Visitor Center, or by phone from Lake McDonald Lodge). The nearest hospitals are North Valley Hospital (1600 Hospital Way, Whitefish, 406/863-3500), Kalispell Regional Medical Center (310 Sunny View Ln., Kalispell, 406/752-5111), or Northern Rockies Medical Center (802 2nd St. E., Cut Bank, 406/873-2251).

DRIVING TOUR

Of all the driving tours in Glacier National Park, **Going-to-the-Sun Road,** the 52-mile historic transmountain highway bisecting Glacier's heart, stands in a class by itself. For some, scary tight curves that hug cliff walls produce white-knuckled driving. But for most, its beauty, diversity, color, flora, fauna, and raw wildness will leave an impression like no other. For that reason, many park visitors drive it more than once during their stay.

In July and August, expect crowds, especially around Logan Pass. To avoid the hordes, drive in early morning or early evening, when lighting is often better for photography and wildlife is more active. In midsummer, Logan Pass parking lot crams full by 11 A.M. Signs at the entrance will indicate so and include an estimated wait of 30–60 minutes for a parking space. If the parking lot is full, forego Logan Pass for the time being and return later in the day. While pullouts sit a half mile east and west of the pass, the shoulderless road does not afford safe walking to the pass, and tromping across the fragile alpine Oberlin meadows is

DRIVING TIPS: GOING-TO-THE-SUN ROAD

© BECKY LOMAX

Keep your wits about you when driving Going-to-the-Sun Road.

FOUR SIGNS OF A ROOKIE GOING-TO-THE-SUN ROAD DRIVER

A burning brake smell.

Hint: Use second gear for slowing speeds on descents rather than riding the brakes all the way down the mountain.

A dangling extension mirror.

Hint: Retract or remove those extension mirrors for fifth wheels or trailers before driving the narrow west side below Logan Pass.

A center-line hugger.

Hint: Stay in your own lane. You're more apt to scrape another vehicle on the skinny road than drive off the cliff. Acrophobes should let someone else drive.

A traffic slug.

Hint: Rather than holding up traffic by slowing to a stop in the road to take pictures, pull off into one of the many pullouts.

OTHER TIPS

Follow posted speed limits and turn on your headlights.

During high season (mid-July–mid-August), Logan Pass parking lot fills up by late morning, with long waits for parking spaces. Consider getting an early start for touring Going-to-the-Sun Road.

Take lunch, snacks, and drinks. Between Lake McDonald Lodge and Rising Sun, no food or drinks are sold.

Watch for bicyclists. Although bicycle restrictions are in effect during July and August on Going-to-the-Sun Road's west side, the narrow roadway, lack of shoulders, and curves squeeze cyclists. Show them courtesy by slowing down to ease around them.

Expect construction delays. Reconstruction work usually reduces traffic to a single lane controlled by construction personnel. When workers are not present, timed traffic lights control flow. Obey both, for the single lanes allow for no pullover room for passing.

Check for summer closures. Heavy rains, snowstorms, fires, and accidents may close portions of the road – even in July and August. Entrance and ranger stations as well as lodges have current updates of the road status available.

Be prepared for all types of weather. Sunny skies may prevail in the valleys while visitors at Logan Pass creep along slowly in a dense fog on icy pavement.

Passengers with a fear of heights should sit on the driver's side of the car for ascending the west side and descending the east. This will put you farthest away from the cliff edges.

Your cell phone might pick up spotty service on portions of the Sun Road, but turn it off and enjoy the views.

For updates on Going-to-the-Sun Road status, call 406/888-7800 or check www.nps.gov/glac.

taboo. Parking lots at Avalanche, The Loop, and St. Mary Falls also pack full.

Although you can drive its 52 miles in less than two hours with no stops, most visitors take all day. Construction, sightseeing, and traffic slow travel. Don't be anxious with it; just sit back and enjoy the view. Pack drinking water, snacks, and a lunch to avoid frustration over lack of food services. Most restaurants around Glacier sell box or sack lunches; order them the day before you want them. The road passes through a wonderland whose development has been kept in check; no one wants to see that changed to accommodate hunger.

Season

Going-to-the-Sun Road is undergoing a decade of federally funded construction to rehabilitate the aging and ailing roadway. Shoulder seasons are used to accelerate construction, while keeping the entire length open mid-June–mid-September for sightseers. That's provided snow allows for a mid-June opening. On heavy snow years with stormy springs, Logan Pass has opened as late as July 3. During summer, the road may close temporarily for snowstorms, washouts, or accidents. The park updates road status reports regularly: 406/888-7800 or www.nps.gov/glac.

During spring and fall, when parts of Going-to-the-Sun Road are closed to vehicles during construction, sometimes bicyclists and hikers can tour the snow-free road, especially on weekends when construction crews may not be working. Call the park first, as construction changes daily. The traditional vehicle closure runs from Avalanche to Rising Sun mid-September–mid-June. During winter, the road is closed from St. Mary to Lake McDonald Lodge, but cross-country skiers and snowshoers trek lowland corridors.

Vehicle Restrictions

Large vehicles are restricted on Going-to-the-Sun Road between Avalanche Campground and Sun Point. Because the road is narrow and overhung, vehicles must be smaller than 21 feet in length, 10 feet high, and 8 feet wide. These dimensions include side mirrors, bumpers, towed units, and bike racks. Remember to pull in side extension mirrors; you'll see broken ones in the gutter claimed by the cliff wall. Even though smaller truck-camper units may be legal, drivers will feel pinched on the skinny road.

Road Construction

Maintenance is interminable on Going-to-the-Sun Road. Avalanches, torrential downpours, and snows wreak havoc. Constantly. Summer snowstorms and heavy rains cause washouts requiring annual repairs. Here, road construction is a fact of life, but it's also a unique chance to watch how workers cling to the side of thousand-foot cliffs.

The alpine section of Going-to-the-Sun Road has been undergoing a decade-long $240–270 million rehabilitation project since 2007. The critical state of the road requires repairs for weather damage and wear and tear from the 475,000 vehicles that travel the road annually. Because heavy snows constrict repairs to four to six months, summer means construction. The work has improved road safety, pavement, parking, guardrails, drainage, cracks, and deteriorating road beds—all while maintaining the historic character, fabric, and width of the road and done without closing the road during the peak visitor season.

From mid-June to mid-September, construction reduces driving to one skinny lane in places. Traffic delays are scheduled for a maximum of 30 minutes total while crossing the road. Usually this is true. Longer delays are scheduled for early mornings, evenings, and nights. During fall and spring, some sections of the road close completely to speed up construction. Usually Logan Pass is accessible in fall from one direction, but not as a through-drive.

While road construction elicits complaints and moans, repairing this road is not like repaving a local highway. You can watch state-of-the-art road technology at work in a cliff-ridden environment: Cranes and bobcats jockey for position along one narrow lane, somewhat akin

GOING-TO-THE-SUN ROAD

to working on a tightrope. Anyone with a mild engineering interest will be blown away, and you get a feel for the immensity of the original road's building.

Plowing Going-to-the-Sun Road

Every April, snowplows take to Going-to-the-Sun Road to heave over 100,000 cubic yards of snow off the pavement. It's a big deal. Avalanche piles range 30–50 feet thick from The Loop to Logan Pass. Just east of the pass, a 50- to 80-foot-deep snowdrift, the Big Drift, clings to a 40-degree slope. No wonder the job takes several months! For the duration, 25–30 equipment operators, mechanics, and snow specialists dig in with more than 20 different machines—excavators, bulldozers, sweepers, loaders, and rotary blowers.

More than 60 avalanche swaths between The Loop and Siyeh Bend smash snowslides onto the road. Sometimes crews replow the same pavement over and over, or plow themselves out at night. Heavy rains, fog, and whiteouts hamper progress, too.

© BECKY LOMAX

Plowing on Going-to-the-Sun Road usually takes a couple months.

When spring snows prohibit the road opening beyond mid-June, everyone gets nervous: from local businesses to the governor of Montana. The opening of the road is bound to the local economy. Glacier Park's website tracks plow progress with daily reports (www.nps.gov/glac), and the park's communications center (406/888-7800) posts updates.

SIGHTS

Going-to-the-Sun Road is a sight to behold! The following sights are listed as visitors see them driving from Lake McDonald to St. Mary. Approximate mileposts are listed parenthetically, with eastbound first, beginning at the road's junction with Highway 2, followed by westbound mileposts, beginning with the junction with Highway 89. The total mileage is actually 50.8 miles, yet maps claim 52 miles. Where the missing 1.2 miles has gone, no one knows, nor is anyone too concerned about the math.

⟨ Lake McDonald

The largest lake in the park, Lake McDonald (2.8–11, 39.9–47.9) hogs a valley hollowed out by a monstrous several-thousand-foot-deep glacier. Lining both sides, Howe and Snyder Ridges are lateral moraines left from that ice age bulldozer. At 10 miles long and 1.5 miles wide, the lake is big enough to plummet to a frigid depth at 472 feet. Its deep waters collect from melting glaciers and snow fields high atop the Continental Divide. Kayakers and boaters tour the shoreline, anglers pull trout from its pool, and a few water-skiers brave the cold. The road hugs its southeastern shore, with frequent pullouts for access. If rare glassy waters reflect Stanton Peak, shoot off photos!

⟨ Lake McDonald Lodge

At Lake McDonald's east end, the historic Lake McDonald Lodge (11.2, 39.2) was designed to resemble a hunting lodge. A taxidermist's delight or an animal-rights activist's nightmare, the tall, stately cedar-log lobby is cluttered with stuffed goats and mounted heads of bighorn sheep, deer, elk, and moose. Look for the woodland caribou—still represented among the furry creatures here, even though it no longer exists in the park. Because the lodge was built prior to the road, the front door actually opens on lakeside, facing the original boat approach. In 1976, the lodge was listed on the National Register of Historic Places. Explore the lobby, take a boat tour, or sit a spell in a log rocker on the back porch.

McDonald Creek

Originating near the Continental Divide, McDonald Creek (12.8–22, 29.6–38) is the longest river in the park at 25.8 miles and definitely more than a creek, but we won't quibble about nomenclature. The Sun Road follows the river path until it begins its ascent to Logan Pass. In the seven miles where the road borders the river, several tumbling rapids and waterfalls are worth a stop. But be extremely cautious of hazardous slippery rocks. Unseen algae, mosses, and swift cold waters have been lethal for the unwary. At **Upper McDonald Creek Falls** (14.7, 36.2), waters roil through scoured rock; wooden stairs drop you onto a convenient observation platform right over the falls.

Trail of the Cedars

Trail of the Cedars (16.6, 34.1) travels through a rainforest, the easternmost in the country. On a 0.7-mile wheelchair-accessible boardwalk and pavement, the shaded trail passes water-carved Avalanche Gorge. Several-hundred-year-old western red cedars, hemlocks, and towering black cottonwoods form a dense canopy that cools the forest floor, where mosses, lichens, Pacific yew, and devil's club grow in the rich duff. Fire has bypassed this small ecosystem, leaving gigantic old grandfather trees—some toppling from heavy rains, snows, and winds. You'll need many arms to hug one large cedar growing through the boardwalk.

Avalanche Paths

As the road sneaks through a slim corridor between the Glacier Wall and Mount Cannon (19.5, 31.3), look for avalanche paths. Snow, set in motion thousands of feet above, roars down gullies, uprooting trees and snapping them like toothpicks. In early summer, scour the slope for remnants of avalanches—ice, snow, and rock rubble piled up. Grizzly and black bears forage for carcasses along these avalanche paths in hopes of stumbling across some unfortunate mountain goat. Bring binoculars or spotting scopes to aid in bear-watching from a safe distance.

West Side Tunnel

An engineering marvel, the West Side Tunnel (24, 26.8) is 192 feet long, with two stunning alcoves framing Heavens Peak. In early season, the alcoves drip with thin-sheeted waterfalls, but hop through the spray to reach the dry rock-hewn guardrails. Photographers especially will enjoy working the alcoves into framing pictures of Heavens Peak. To walk into the tunnel, park below in large pullouts on both sides; above the tunnel, the road narrows, making walking hazardous. In early season, a

© BECKY LOMAX

A waterfall drops next to the uphill side of the West Side Tunnel.

waterfall on the tunnel's uphill side splatters car windshields. If you're driving a convertible, too bad.

The Loop

Going-to-the-Sun Road has one massive hairpin turn known as The Loop (24.7, 26.1). With parking lots both below and above the switchback, it's a popular stop for views and the trailhead to Granite Park Chalet. Across the valley, the 8,987-foot **Heavens Peak** makes a stunning backdrop for a family photo. In early season, it will be snow covered; by late August, only a few snow fields remain. In 2003, the **Trapper Fire** blew through The Loop; evidence of the burn lingers in skeletal trees.

Bird Woman and Haystack Falls

About two miles past The Loop, look for the sign marking Bird Woman Falls (27, 24.7). Many tourists assume the sign denotes the cascade crossing under the road. That stairstep waterfall is **Haystack Creek,** whose ledges evolved from eroding layers of Belt Sea sedimentary rock created between 800 million and 1.6 billion years ago. To see Bird Woman Falls, look across the valley for waters tumbling nearly 500 feet from a hanging valley, carved by a glacier in the last 6,000 years and lounging like a hammock in between Mount Oberlin, Mount Cannon, and Clements Peak. Early summer runoff pumps both falls full of water that dwindles to late-August trickles.

Glaciation Exhibit

Look for an interpretive pullout (28.3, 22.5) with terrific views of McDonald Valley. Once filled with several-thousand-foot thick ice, the valley's U shape shows the gouging, scouring, and carving of the behemoth glacier as it chugged around the Glacier Wall approximately two million years ago. Through the trough, McDonald Creek courses 26 miles and ends at Lake McDonald. Test your vertigo by gazing 2,500 feet below; you'll see Going-to-the-Sun Road, with cars looking tiny like ants as they drive the narrow corridor.

THE CONTINENTAL DIVIDE

At Logan Pass, you can take your photo next to a sign that says you're atop the Continental Divide. But what is it?

The Continental Divide runs the length of North America from Alaska and the Yukon to Mexico. Along the Rocky Mountains, it is the highest point in the land, dividing stream runoff in two directions: the Pacific and the Atlantic. In Glacier Park, the Continental Divide runs along the tops of the Livingston Range from Canada south to Trapper Ridge and West Flattop, where it leaps to the Lewis Range.

To cross the Continental Divide, drive over Logan or Marias Pass. You can hike across the divide on several passes: Brown's, Swiftcurrent, Hidden Lake, Gunsight, Cut Bank, Dawson, Two Medicine, and Firebrand. Beginning in New Mexico, the 3,100-mile Continental Divide Trail finishes its length, with its last 110 miles in Glacier National Park.

Glacier's Continental Divide also stands in a class by itself, for it houses a tri-oceanic divide – the only one in the United States. (Canada's Mount Columbia is the continent's other significant three-way oceanic divide.) Not particularly high by Glacier Park standards, Triple Divide Peak stands at only 7,397 feet above sea level. But its placement on the Continental Divide with connecting ridge spurs splits waters in three streams: Hudson Bay Creek, Atlantic Creek, and Pacific Creek. Their names cite their eventual destinations in the continent's major watersheds of the Saskatchewan, Missouri, and Columbia.

On the southeast corner of St. Mary Lake, Divide Mountain with St. Mary Ridge forms the division between waters flowing to Hudson Bay and the Gulf of Mexico. To drive over this unmarked divide, head from St. Mary south on Highway 89.

The Weeping Wall wails in June, but slows to a trickle in late summer.

Weeping Wall and Big Bend

As its name implies, the Weeping Wall (29.5, 21.3) does weep, but it's a moody thing. In early summer, the wall wails profusely, enough to douse cars driving the inside lane. Roll up your windows unless you want a shower! In August, drips slow to a simper. At the Weeping Wall, the road affords no room to pull over; instead, drive ahead into the bowl named Big Bend (29.7, 21) to find ample parking on both sides of the road. Here, where avalanches careen from Mount Gould into the bowl, snow often remains until mid-July.

Triple Arches

One of the most striking engineering marvels on Going-to-the-Sun Road, Triple Arches (30.4, 20.2) requires a slow drive to see, for no pullouts offer a good view. You can see this feature only driving uphill, for it sits at the back of downhill traffic. Approximately one and a half miles past Big Bend, you'll come upon the arches abruptly. Start watching for them as you enter a very narrow, curvy part of the road.

At several sharp S turns, you'll see them. As you drive over the arches, don't think about the stonework repairs that overhang hundreds of feet of air!

Garden Wall

From Big Bend to Logan Pass (29.7–32, 18.8–21), the peaks above the road actually form an arête, a wall carved by glaciers on two sides. Below its top cliffs, wildflower meadows bloom with every color of the rainbow: white cow parsnip, pink spirea, yellow columbine, purple nodding onion, and blue gentian. In a short half mile, you may pass more than 30 varieties of plants. For this reason, this wild botanical wonderland has been dubbed the Garden Wall. For the best look at the Garden Wall, hike the Highline Trail from Logan Pass.

Oberlin Bend Overlook

As Going-to-the-Sun climbs its final mile to Logan Pass, it sweeps around a large curve below Mount Oberlin. Park on the uphill lane side for the wheelchair-accessible walk to

Oberlin Bend Overlook (31.4, 18.4). Mountain goats wander in the subalpine fir thickets; look for newborns with only nubbins for horns. The overlook provides the best spot for photographing the road's west-side climb, as well as viewing the Continental Divide and peaks marching toward Canada. Look far north for Mount Cleveland, the park's highest peak.

◖ Logan Pass

Logan Pass (32.6, 18.2) sits atop the Continental Divide at 6,646 feet. With its altitude and location between mountainous hulks, weather can be chilly even in midsummer. For evidence, look at the gnarled trees, growing low in krummholz or thick mats for protection against the elements. Explore the visitors center and scan surrounding slopes for goats, bighorn sheep, and bears. In late July, the wildflowers reach their prime—pink alpine laurel, paintbrush, and monkeyflower. Logan Pass is designated an Important Plant Area, with more than 30 rare plants and mosses. Meadows at this elevation are fragile with short-lived flora,

so stick to the paths. Two must-do trails depart from Logan Pass: Hidden Lake and the Highline Trail to Granite Park Chalet.

Big Drift

Those driving over Logan Pass when it first opens get a treat: Big Drift (32.8, 18.1) towers on both sides of the road, making a thin corridor bounded by immense snow walls. Winds deposit heavy snows in this zone just east of Logan Pass. At a record 98 feet thick, Big Drift remains the last obstacle for spring road clearing. By August, snow piles disappear. In the next few miles east of Big Drift, the guardrail is sporadic—just for some added thrill.

Lunch Creek

Spilling from a cirque between Piegan and Pollock peaks, Lunch Creek (33.4, 17.4) makes for a scenic stop at the first bend east of Logan Pass. Sans picnic tables, the pullout's rock guardrail serves as a good impromptu lunch counter. Drag out your binoculars; often bighorn sheep cruise the slopes above, but they're

Logan Pass sits atop the Continental Divide.

hard to see with their camouflage tan matching the rocks. Fed by a glacier melting into an underground stream, waterfalls spew from the side of Piegan Mountain.

East Side Tunnel

The largest tunnel, the East Side Tunnel (33.8, 17), was excavated entirely by hand—all 408 feet. For safety, flip your headlights on as you drive through this tunnel. To stop for photos, drive through to its downhill side to find pullouts, also good stops for spotting bighorn sheep. Photograph the large peak looming ahead—**Going-to-the-Sun Mountain**—from which the road acquired its name.

Siyeh Bend

Three miles below Logan Pass, the road swoops through Siyeh Bend (35.5, 15.5), with ample parking above and below the curve. The trailhead leads to Piegan and Siyeh Passes via Preston Park, a meadowland of fuchsia paintbrush and purple fleabane. For a short stroll, walk up the creek crossing under the road to

© © BECKY LOMAX

Siyeh Bend is one of two hairpins on the Sun Road.

the junction of two creeks. The city-block-long walk passes gorgeous wildflower blooms in late July. From Siyeh Bend (*Siyeh* means Mad Wolf), named for the 10,014-foot barren peak towering above, you can see Blackfoot Glacier toward the south.

Jackson Glacier Overlook

This is the best view of a glacier on Going-to-the-Sun Road, but binoculars are handy to aid vision. Although trees are beginning to occlude the view from Jackson Glacier Overlook (mile 37.3, 13.4), you can still spot Jackson Glacier six miles away. One of the six highest peaks in the park, Jackson Peak rises to its west. Jackson Glacier joined its neighboring Blackfoot Glacier in the early 1900s, but the two glaciers melted into separate ice fields by 1939. A trail departs here for Gunsight Lake and Pass. More views are available in the next pullouts east.

Sunrift Gorge

A narrow canyon, Sunrift Gorge (40, 10.5) requires a short 75-foot uphill stroll to see it. Baring Creek cascades through the dark gorge like a knife slicing cake. The dank rock walls create a perfect grotto for ferns and mosses. Parking on both sides of the road is cramped, and it is a trailhead for Siyeh Pass, although most hikers opt to start at Siyeh Bend instead.

Sun Point

The often windy Sun Point (40.6, 10) on St. Mary Lake marks the site of the park's most popular early chalet colony: Going-to-the-Sun Chalets. Accessed via boat from St. Mary, the chalet launched visitors into Glacier's interior. For the best views, walk five minutes on the nature trail from the parking lot to the top of the red-rock promontory, where you'll see Going-to-the-Sun Peak, Fusillade, and the Continental Divide. A trail leads 0.6 mile to Baring Falls and connects to the St. Mary Falls Trail.

St. Mary Lake

The second-largest lake in the park, St. Mary Lake (42.2–49.8, 1–8.6) fills a much narrower

© BECKY LOMAX

The Sun Road climbs above St. Mary Lake.

valley than its larger counterpart—Lake McDonald. At nine miles long and 292 feet deep, it forms a blue platform out of which several stunning red argillite peaks rise. Its width shrinks in The Narrows (44.1, 6.6) to less than half a mile, where buff-colored Altyn limestone resisted erosion—the most ancient exposed rock sediments in the park. While its waters attract boaters, anglers, water-skiers, and sailboarders launching from Rising Sun, frequent high winds whip up wicked white-caps in minutes.

◖ Wild Goose Island Overlook

One of the most photographed spots in Glacier Park, tiny Wild Goose Island (43.8,

7) is dwarfed in St. Mary Lake's blue waters. Locate parking on both sides of the road from the signed viewpoint and walk the few steps to the overlook. The Continental Divide serves as the backdrop for the tiny island, with Fusillade Mountain as the prominent central pyramid. For the best lighting, visit this spot in early morning or at sunset. Shoot a photo, then check the nearest gift shop for the same photo—you'll find it on postcards, on calendars, and in books.

Rising Sun

Rising Sun (44.5, 6.3) on St. Mary Lake is not really a scenic stop so much as one for necessity and services. A picnic area, campground, boat dock and ramp, camp store, restaurant, and cabins make up the area's amenities. It's also a jumping-off spot for hiking to Otokomi Lake and touring St. Mary Lake on the *Little Chief.* To access a beach, head to the picnic area (44.7, 6), but hold on to your hat, for winds often rage.

Two Dog Flats

A series of grassland meadows interspersed by aspen groves lines the road from Rising Sun to St. Mary. Known as Two Dog Flats (46.5–49, 1.8–4.3), the meadows can be good elk-, coyote-, bear-, and bird-watching areas in early morning or late evening. From here, you can see two hydrological wonders to the south—Triple Divide Peak and Divide Mountain. Triple Divide Peak sits atop the Continental Divide, where its waters head to three seas—the Pacific Ocean, Hudson Bay, and the Caribbean. Divide Peak, along with the sweeping moraine heading east, marks the division between the huge Saskatchewan and Missouri watersheds.

Recreation

HIKING

Hikes off Going-to-the-Sun Road are top-notch, no matter what time of the summer. Around Lake McDonald, trails all begin in the forest, but several climb to undaunted heights. At Logan Pass and eastward, most trails provide quicker access to alpine meadows and spectacular glacially carved scenery. Shorter trails are crowded in midsummer: You may feel like you're walking in a parade to St. Mary Falls or Hidden Lake Overlook. If you want to get away from the masses, head for longer hikes that will take you farther into the backcountry: Granite Park Chalet, Siyeh Pass, Piegan Pass, or Gunsight Lake. The hikes described here are in order of their trailheads from west to east—all serviced by shuttle stops.

Mount Brown Lookout

- Distance: 10.8 miles round-trip
- Duration: 6 hours
- Elevation gain: 4,325 feet
- Effort: strenuous
- Trailhead: Sperry Trailhead across from Lake McDonald Lodge parking lot

One word describes this hike: *steep*. While the trail starts out climbing through moderate switchbacks, once you turn off the Sperry Trail at 1.8 miles, the next five switchbacks are lung busters. After these, the remaining 20-some switchbacks level out into a more reasonable ascent.

While trees preclude views for most of this trail, snippets of Mount Edwards poke through now and then. Toward the top, alpine meadows bloom with beargrass and huckleberry patches as the trail works its way along the ridge to the renovated lookout. From this false summit (Mount Brown is higher to the east), you'll get dizzy peering down to Lake McDonald and the lodge. While you zoom binoculars in on Granite Park Chalet, Swiftcurrent Lookout, and the Continental Divide, protect your lunch from the overly curious mountain goats.

Sperry Chalet

- Distance: 12.8 miles round-trip
- Duration: 6.5 hours
- Elevation gain: 3,432 feet
- Effort: strenuous
- Trailhead: Sperry Trailhead across from Lake McDonald Lodge parking lot

The historic chalet is an attraction in itself, serving lunch and homemade desserts to hikers, but many overnight at the chalet, especially to access Sperry Glacier. The climb begins with moderate switchbacks through a hemlock forest. After crossing Snyder Creek at two miles, the trail takes a long traverse around Mount Edwards, slowly easing up in elevation before switchbacking again up alder-strewn avalanche slopes. Because of the mule and horse trips using this same route, the trail sometimes smells like a barnyard and can be miserable, as you dodge equine droppings buzzing with blackflies.

With more than a mile still to climb, you'll spot the chalet clinging to a cliff top high above. The trail crosses Sperry Creek before ascending its final switchbacks, passing the turnoff to Sperry Glacier en route. If mountain goats don't stand in your way, you'll arrive at the dining hall's door, ready for lunch and home-baked pie served inside 11:30 A.M.–5 P.M. To spend the night, you'll need reservations.

Sperry Glacier

- Distance: 8 miles round-trip
- Duration: 4 hours
- Elevation gain: 1,600 feet
- Effort: strenuous
- Trailhead: Sperry Chalet

From the chalet, drop down several switchbacks to the Sperry Glacier trail sign. From here, the trail wraps upward around a glacial cirque below waterfalls and immense cliffs. It switchbacks up past alpine tarns, flower gardens, snow fields

© BECKY LOMAX

A narrow, steep stairway cuts through the headwall to reach Sperry Glacier basin.

A boardwalk guides hikers through the lush rainforest with interpretive signs. Here, fallen cedars become nurse logs, fertile habitat for hemlocks and tiny foamflowers. Immense black cottonwoods furrow with deep-cut bark. Huge western red cedars dominate the forest. At the boardwalk's end, the trail crosses Avalanche Creek, spitting from its narrow gorge. To make a loop, continue on the paved walkway past large burled cedars to return to the trailhead.

Avalanche Lake

- Distance: 4 miles round-trip
- Duration: 2–3 hours
- Elevation gain: 500 feet
- Effort: moderately easy
- Trailhead: use Trail of the Cedars, adjacent to Avalanche Campground

One of the most popular hikes, Avalanche Lake is the easiest-to-reach subalpine lake on the west side. Sitting in a steep-cliffed cirque tumbling with waterfalls, the lake attracts anglers and hikers alike. High season sees an endless stream of people, some incredibly ill prepared, with no drinking water and inappropriate footwear like flip-flops or heels. Avoid midday crowds by hiking this trail earlier or later in the day, but not at dawn or dusk.

When Trail of the Cedars crosses Avalanche Creek, turn uphill onto the lake's trail. A short grunt leads above the carved gorge. Be extremely careful: Far too many people have had fatal accidents here. From the gorge, the trail climbs steadily through woods littered with glacial erratics—large boulders strewn when the ice receded. Some still retain scratch marks left from the ice abrading the surface. At the lakeshore, enjoy watching waterfalls, mountain goats, and bears.

lingering into August, and glacially carved rock ledges before it seemingly disappears into a cliff. But, voilà: A steep stairway leads through the cliff into the basin above.

In the Sperry Glacier basin, a different world awaits. Snow fields, moraines, and ice mark this environment, with trees and flowers very sparse. From here, follow vertical markers across the snow-covered trail to the glacier overlook. Do not walk out on the glacier, which has hidden crevasses and waterways. Seasoned hikers pull a 21-mile round-trip Sperry Glacier hike off in one day from Lake McDonald Lodge: It's a 10-hour-plus day with a 5,000–foot climb followed by a knee-pounding descent.

◖ Trail of the Cedars

- Distance: 0.7-mile loop
- Duration: 30 minutes
- Elevation gain: none
- Effort: easy
- Trailhead: adjacent to Avalanche Campground and Picnic Area

Granite Park Chalet via The Loop Trail

- Distance: 8 miles round-trip
- Duration: 4 hours
- Elevation gain: 2,400 feet

- Effort: moderately strenuous
- Trailhead: The Loop

The Loop trail is mostly used by hikers exiting the Highline Trail; however, when the road is only open to The Loop, this trail makes a worthy hike with Granite Park Chalet as a scenic destination. Since the 2003 Trapper Fire, views improved, but lack of shade offers little relief from the sun's blazing heat.

At its beginning, the trail crosses a tumbling creek before joining up with the Packer's Roost trail at 0.6 mile. Note this junction: You do not want to miss it hiking back down. From here, the trail climbs two long switchbacks before it crests into the upper basin to the chalet. In June, you'll have snow in the last mile. Open July–mid-September, the chalet has no running water but does sell candy bars. Bring cash to purchase bottled water, carry your own, or filter water from the campground stream just below the chalet.

◖ Highline Trail and Granite Park Chalet

- Distance: 7.6 miles to Granite Park Chalet, 11.6 miles to The Loop

- Duration: 5–6 hours
- Elevation gain: 830 feet
- Effort: moderate
- Trailhead: across Going-to-the-Sun Road from Logan Pass parking lot

Many first-time hikers stop every ten feet to take photos on this hike, which scares severe acrophobes with its exposed thousand-foot drop-offs. The trail drops from Logan Pass through a cliff walk above the highway before crossing a flower land that gave the Garden Wall arête its name. At three miles, nearly all of the elevation gain packs into one climb: Haystack Saddle appears to be the top, but it is only halfway. After the high point, the trail drops and swings through several large bowls before passing Bear Valley to reach Granite Park Chalet atop a knoll at 6,680 feet.

En route, side trails lead to Grinnell Glacier Overlook (1.6 steep miles round-trip) and Swiftcurrent Lookout (4.6 miles round-trip). To exit the area, some hikers opt to hike out over Swiftcurrent Pass to Many Glacier (7.6 miles) and catch the Glacier Park, Inc. shuttle; backpackers continue on to Fifty Mountain (11.9 miles farther) and Goat Haunt (22.5

© BECKY LOMAX

Hidden Lake, from the overlook above Logan Pass

GOING-TO-THE-SUN ROAD

miles farther). Most day hikers head down The Loop trail (4 miles) to catch the hiker shuttle.

The chalet (open July–mid-September) does not have running water. Plan on purchasing bottled water here, carrying your own, or filtering water from the campground stream below the chalet. Day hikers may also use the outdoor picnic tables or chalet dining room but do not have access to the kitchen. On a rainy day, a warm fire offers respite from the bluster and a chance to dry out. Pop and candy bars are sold, too.

Hidden Lake Overlook

- Distance: 3 miles round-trip
- Duration: 2 hours
- Elevation gain: 550 feet
- Effort: moderate
- Trailhead: behind Logan Pass Visitor Center

Regardless of crowds, Hidden Lake Overlook is a spectacular hike. The trail is often buried under feet of snow until mid-July or later, but tall lodgepoles mark the route. Once the trail melts out, a boardwalk climbs the first half through alpine meadows where fragile shooting stars and alpine laurel dot the landscape with pink. The trail ascends through argillite: Look for evidence of mud-cracked and ripple-marked rocks from the ancient Belt Sea.

The upper trail climbs past moraines, waterfalls, mountain goats, and bighorn sheep. At Hidden Pass, the trail reaches the overlook, with views down to Hidden Lake's blue waters. For ambitious hikers or anglers, the trail continues 1.5 miles down to the lake. Just remember: What drops 675 feet must come back up!

Piegan Pass

- Distance: 9 miles round-trip, 12.8 miles to Many Glacier
- Duration: 4–5 hours
- Elevation gain: 1,670 feet
- Effort: moderate
- Trailhead: Siyeh Bend

Piegan Pass, named for the Pikuni or Piegan tribe of Blackfeet, is a reasonably unpopulated trail. After climbing two miles through subalpine forest and turning north at the first trail junction, the trail breaks out into Preston Park, bursting with purple fleabane, blue gentians, white valerian, and fuchsia paintbrush. As the trail gains altitude, Piegan Glacier is visible above. A signed trail junction splits the Piegan Pass trail from the Siyeh Pass trail.

Shortly after the junction, the Piegan Pass trail heads into the seemingly barren alpine zone as it crosses the base of Siyeh Peak. But look carefully, for all kinds of miniature flowers bloom—food for pikas. In a long traverse, the trail sweeps around a large bowl to Piegan Pass, tucked under the Continental Divide. Rather than returning to Siyeh Bend, some hikers opt for continuing another 8.3 miles to Many Glacier Hotel, where they can link in with Glacier Park, Inc.'s east-side shuttle.

◖ Siyeh Pass

- Distance: 10.3 miles
- Duration: 5 hours
- Elevation gain: 2,240 feet
- Effort: strenuous
- Trailhead: Siyeh Bend

Siyeh Pass trail crosses through such different ecosystems that the entire trail nearly captures the park's diversity in one 10-mile segment. The trail begins with a two-mile climb through subalpine forest broken by meadows, where it passes two well-signed junctions. (Go left at the first, right at the second.) The trail waltzes through Preston Park, one of the best flower meadows, with purple fleabane and fuchsia paintbrush, before switchbacking above tree line.

The switchbacks appear to lead to a saddle—a false summit. Eight more turns climb above the saddle before swinging through a cliff to the pass. Be wary of your lunch—there are aggressive golden-mantled ground squirrels here. Due to the elevation, snow can bury switchbacks south of the pass until mid-July.

Siyeh Pass trail drops past Sexton Glacier.

The trail descends past goats, bighorn sheep, and a multicolored cliff band before traversing the flanks of Goat Mountain and dropping to Going-to-the-Sun Road.

Gunsight Lake and Pass

- Distance: 12.4 miles round-trip
- Duration: 6 hours
- Elevation gain: 550 feet
- Effort: moderate
- Trailhead: Jackson Glacier Overlook

Gunsight Lake is a tantalizer. For those who hike in for the day, more high country lures beyond. The trail begins with a one-mile drop down to Reynolds Creek before gently climbing through a forest of boggy moose ponds that kick up mosquitoes. After passing a spur trail leading to Florence Falls, the trail breaks out into flower meadows, climbing along the flanks of Fusillade Mountain. Incomparable views of the wild Blackfoot and Jackson Glaciers sprawl across the scoured basin.

Surrounded by avalanche corridors, the lake sits at the base of Jackson Peak (10,064 feet), one of the six highest peaks in the park. From here, a two-mile spur trail wanders back into Jackson Glacier basin before disappearing in meadow seeps. Another trail climbs to Gunsight Pass (3 miles farther) and on to Sperry Chalet (7.8 miles farther) before descending to Lake McDonald Lodge (20 miles total). Seasoned hikers do the entire trail over Gunsight Pass to Lake McDonald Lodge in one day.

Jackson Overlook to Sun Point via St. Mary and Virginia Falls

- Distance: 7.5 miles one-way
- Duration: 2 hours
- Elevation gain: 280 feet
- Effort: easy
- Trailhead: Jackson Glacier Overlook

With shuttles, you can do a point-to-point hike from Jackson Overlook to Sun Point, with side trips to St. Mary and Virginia Falls. From Jackson Overlook, drop to Reynolds Creek, where the trail forks eastward along the river. At the falls junction, turn right to explore mesmerizing blue-green St. Mary Falls and climb several switchbacks to misty Virginia Falls, less than one mile farther. Return to the junction to continue east over bluffs blooming with stonecrop overlooking St. Mary Lake. (Ignore two signs for Going-to-the-Sun Road parking lot spurs.) Tally up your third waterfall—Baring Falls—just before the trail climbs to Sun Point.

St. Mary and Virginia Falls

- Distance: 3.6 miles round-trip
- Duration: 2 hours
- Elevation gain: 280 feet
- Effort: easy
- Trailhead: St. Mary Falls Trailhead

In midsummer, the trail sees a constant stream of people, but the two falls are still gorgeous. The trail drops through two well-signed junctions en route to St. Mary Falls, where a wooden bridge crosses blue-green pools. From here, the trail switchbacks up to Virginia Falls, a broad falls whose waters spew mist. A 0.2-mile spur climbs to the base of Virginia Falls. Be wary of slippery rocks and strong, cold currents at both falls. Also, spot water ouzels, or American dippers, dark gray birds recognized by their dipping action, up to 40 bends per minute, that nest near waterfalls.

Baring Falls

- Distance: 1.2 miles round-trip
- Duration: 1 hour
- Elevation gain: 50 feet on return
- Effort: easy
- Trailhead: southeast corner of Sun Point parking lot

Start by popping up to Sun Point, a large promontory in St. Mary Lake, the site of the original Sun Point Chalets. From here, a sign identifies

peak names circling the often windy lake. After returning to the trail, follow it around the knoll as it gradually descends to lake level. The trail crosses the creek below Baring Falls (originally named Weasel Eyes in Blackfeet), meaning "huckleberries."

Otokomi Lake

- Distance: 10.4 miles round-trip
- Duration: 5 hours
- Elevation gain: 1,882 feet
- Effort: moderate
- Trailhead: behind Rising Sun Motor Inn

Otokomi Lake makes a good early or late season hike, with its elevation lower than other area trails. Climbing immediately uphill, the trail soon levels out into a gentle timbered ascent above Rose Creek. Pause for breaks at the scenic sections where fragile shooting stars grow next to rock slabs sliced by the creek. As the trail motors uphill, it has minimal views until the last mile of open beargrass meadows and red argillite talus slopes. At the lake, scan the cliffs above for mountain goats, and wade the outlet to get to open lunch spots on its west shore.

Guides

Mid-June–mid-September, park naturalists (406/888-7800, www.nps.gov/glac) guide free hikes at Avalanche, Sun Point, and Logan Pass. Both the Avalanche Lake and Hidden Lake Overlook hikes are extremely popular, so expect to walk in a rather long train. They also guide longer hikes, like Siyeh Pass, and hikes with boat tours on St. Mary Lake. Pick up a copy of *Ranger-Led Activities* from visitors centers for current destinations and schedules, also online.

Glacier Guides (11970 Hwy. 2 E., 406/387-5555 or 800/521-7238, www.glacierguides.com) lead several types of day-hiking trips. Solo travelers can hook up with their Tuesday Hikes ($75 per person, July–Aug.), while families and small groups can arrange their own day hikes ($375, 1–5 people, June–Sept.). Both depart from their West Glacier office. Custom Day Hikes ($450, up to five people) will depart from your lodge or campground. Many of their favorite haunts use Sun Road trailheads. All hikes require reservations and include guide service, deli lunch, and transportation to the trailhead. The guide service also leads three-day trips to Granite Park Chalet ($697, all meals, transportation from West Glacier to trailhead, guide services, linens, and lodging included), and a very popular six-day Ultimate Chalet trip ($1,805) spends two nights at Sperry Chalet, a night at Belton Chalet for a shower, and two nights at Granite Park Chalet. All meals (except one dinner), transportation, and lodging are included. The company also has three-, four-, and six-day backpacking trips that depart weekly ($140 per day, June–mid-Sept.), some via Sun Road trailheads. Tip your guides 15 percent.

BIKING

Going-to-the-Sun Road is a bicycle trip you won't forget. While the 3,500-foot climb in elevation seems intimidating, it's not steep…just a constant thigh-burning grind. During construction in the 1920s, the road grade stayed at 6 percent because cars shifted with 7 percent grades.

Locals relish spring and fall riding when the Sun Road is closed to cars; new blacktop in 2010 smoothed the riding. Biking begins in early April as soon as snowplows free pavement while the road remains closed to vehicles on the west side from Lake McDonald Lodge or Avalanche, and closed on the east side from Rising Sun. Riders climb up as far as plowing operations and construction permits. Even tricycles and training wheels hit the west-side flats! After mid-September, the road closes again to vehicles but permits bicycling. Call the park (406/888-7800) to check on access as construction limits bicycling some days.

When Logan Pass opens, riders head for the top, some returning the way they came, others continuing on to the other side. Local racers make a 142-mile one-day loop (Going-to-the-Sun Road, Highway 89, Highway 49,

Bicyclers relish riding Going-to-the-Sun Road sans cars in shoulder seasons.

© BECKY LOMAX

and Highway 2); tourers ride the loop in two days. Locals also celebrate the full moon with a bone-chilling night ride. It's dangerous (injuries and at least one fatality have occurred), but it's an otherworldly experience.

Restrictions and Safety

Bicycles are restricted on the shoulderless Going-to-the-Sun Road during summer due to heavy midday traffic. From June 15 to Labor Day, 11 A.M.–4 P.M., bicycles are not permitted between the Apgar Road junction and Sprague Creek or climbing uphill between Avalanche Campground and Logan Pass. If starting from the west side, head out from Lake McDonald by 6:30 A.M. for adequate time to pedal to Logan Pass. In late June and early July, long daylight hours allow for riding after 4 P.M., when traffic lessens.

While helmets are not mandatory by law, it's stupid not to wear one here—considering most drivers are gaping at views rather than paying attention to the road. Wear bright colors for visibility and consider tacking a flag on

GOING-TO-THE-SUN ROAD

your bike. At dusk or night, tail reflectors and a front light are required. Be sure to carry plenty of water: exertion, wind, and altitude can lead to a fast case of dehydration. Before heading out, check your brake pads, for the screaming downhill off the Continental Divide can wear them down to nubbins. Both mountain bikes and road bikes are appropriate here, but with skinny tires, be wary of obstacles: debris, grates, rockfall, and ice. Because shoulderless Going-to-the-Sun Road is so narrow, it is not the place for a family ride—except when the road is closed to cars. Pick up bike rentals in Flathead Valley.

HORSEBACK RIDING
◖ Swan Mountain Outfitters

Only one trail-riding concession operates along Going-to-the-Sun Road. Swan Mountain Outfitters (mile 11.2 or 39.2, 406/888-5121 or 877/888-5557 summers, 800/919-4416 winters, www.swanmountainoutfitters.com) depart from the horse barn across from McDonald Lodge parking lot. Early July–mid-September, their specialty all-day ride ($160)—the best trail ride in the park—departs at 8:45 A.M. and climbs to Sperry Chalet, where you can lunch in the historic dining hall. The last two miles of the ride break out of thick trees into avalanche chutes, where you'll have better views of the steep-walled valley. Lunch is not included in the rate, so be sure to bring cash, and plan on ordering fresh homemade pie for dessert. Late May–mid-September, one-hour forest ($40) and two-hour McDonald Creek ($60) rides depart several times daily on a trail through lichen-laden cedars and firs with peek-a-boo views of peaks. Wear long pants and hiking boots or tennis shoes. Kids need to be at least seven years old (10 for Sperry ride), and they cost the same as adults.

BOATING

Lake McDonald and St. Mary permit motorized boats, kayaks, sailboards, and canoes on both lakes, but Lake McDonald imposes a 10-horsepower limit on motorboats. As with all lakes in the park, Jet Skis are banned. Due to vehicle length restrictions (21 feet), towed boats may not cross Going-to-the-Sun Road between Avalanche and Sun Point.

Lake McDonald

Because Lake McDonald has only one boat ramp, you must drive to Apgar to launch anything larger than what you can carry. For hand-carried crafts, you can launch from Sprague Creek Picnic Area or several pullouts along the lake. At the Lake McDonald Lodge boat dock, **Glacier Park Boat Company** (406/888-5727 summers only, 406/257-2426, www.glacierparkboats.com) rents rowboats for $18 per hour and eight-horsepower motorboats for $23 per hour. Paddles, lifejackets, and fishing regulations are included. Find the rentals at the boat dock behind Lake McDonald Lodge. Bring cash; the company doesn't accept credit cards.

St. Mary

St. Mary Lake permits motorboats with unlimited horsepower. No boats are available to rent, but launch your own from the boat ramp at Rising Sun. Hand-carried crafts can also launch easily from Rising Sun Picnic Area. Be aware: Wild winds whip up quickly here, so keep your eye on conditions.

KAYAKING AND CANOEING

Both sea kayaking and canoeing are popular on Lake McDonald and St. Mary Lake. On calm days, shoreline tours are exceptionally scenic, and evening paddles yield stunning alpenglow. On Lake McDonald, launch from any of the Going-to-the-Sun Road pullouts for shoreline tours or from the Apgar Boat Launch. On St. Mary Lake, launch from Rising Sun boat ramp to paddle to Silver Dollar Beach below Red Eagle Mountain; however, watch the weather, as high winds churn up monstrous waves quickly in the narrow valley. Although river kayakers drool at the rapids on McDonald Creek, the creek is closed to all boating due to nesting harlequin ducks.

© BECKY LOMAX

Kayakers paddle Lake McDonald's east end.

FISHING
McDonald Valley

Heavily fished, Lake McDonald is a haven for kokanee, lake trout, whitefish, and cutthroat. Lake McDonald has no limit on lake trout or lake whitefish. Use catch-and-release fishing for westslope cutthroat trout. Boat fishing tends to produce better results than shore fishing, but you'll see plenty casting from beaches.

Other than Lake McDonald, fishing in McDonald Valley is sporadic at best. Although scads of anglers rim McDonald Creek, the river has a reputation for leaving hooks bare. As for Fish Lake, a three-mile climb from Lake McDonald Lodge accesses the tiny lily-padded shallow lake, where a few westslope cutthroats reside. Snyder Lake, a 4.4-mile climb from Lake McDonald Lodge, also has small cutthroat and is a little more open than Fish Lake's brushy shore. Ignore Avalanche Creek and head instead for Avalanche Lake, where indigenous westslope cutthroat have been kept genetically pure by the gorge's falls. This lake is fished extensively, so drop your line far away from the log-jammed outlet or wade to one of the chilly inlet streams to its south end.

Logan Pass

With a quick three-mile access from Logan Pass, Hidden Lake holds good-size Yellowstone cutthroat trout in spite of its elevation and its reputation as the highest lake in the park with fish. However, the outlet and lake near the outlet are closed through July 31.

St. Mary Valley

St. Mary Lake's reputation is similar to Lake McDonald's: beautiful scenery, but not spectacular fishing. It's best fished from boats rather than the shoreline. Upper St. Mary River doesn't fare much better: You often see anglers up and down its reaches, especially around St. Mary Falls, but few catching fish. Gunsight Lake, the best fishing lake, requires a 6.2-mile hike from Jackson Glacier Overlook; expect wind, late snowpack, and brush along the shore.

Rentals and Guides

For those in need of fishing gear, the camp stores at Lake McDonald Lodge and Rising Sun sell a few items, like line and flies. The nearest rental-gear location is **Glacier Outdoor Center** (11957 Hwy. 2 E., 406/888-5454 or 800/235-6781, www.glacierraftco.com) in West Glacier. The park has no fishing guides, but West Glacier has four companies that guide on rivers bordering the park. Glacier requires no fishing license, but be aware of regulations (as detailed in the *Background* chapter) and learn to recognize westslope cutthroat trout and protected bull trout, which must be thrown back.

WATERSKIING

While both Lake McDonald and St. Mary permit waterskiing (although Lake McDonald has a 10-horsepower limit), you won't find the lakes packed shore to shore with skiers. Frankly, these glacier-fed lakes are frigid. Those who do water-ski wear wetsuits. Precocious winds also whisk up sizable whitecaps—especially on St. Mary Lake. Serious water-skiers head to Flathead Valley's warmer, less whimsical lakes. Flathead Valley also has the nearest ski boat and water-ski rentals.

SAILBOARDING

Of all the park's lakes, St. Mary Lake is the one sailboarders occasionally use. Lake McDonald attracts a few, but inconsistent winds can leave sails slack. On St. Mary Lake, easterlies rage down the valley; however, high mountains and erratic valley confluences create swirly winds on its west end. For that reason, the lake is really not a beginner sailboarding area; experience in self-rescue is paramount. Those who sail its frigid waters usually launch from Rising Sun Picnic Area and wear a wetsuit. No sailboarding equipment is available for rent in the region.

CROSS-COUNTRY SKIING AND SNOWSHOEING

Since winter buries Going-to-the-Sun Road with snow from Lake McDonald Lodge to St. Mary, the road attracts skiers and snowshoers November–April. They tour up the gated road's lower elevations through relatively avalanche-free zones. The gentle grade makes for good gliding suitable for beginners. For snowshoers, etiquette requires blazing a separate snowshoe trail rather than squishing the parallel ski tracks flat. Some park ski trails are mapped online (www.nps.gov/glac).

In McDonald Valley, ski tours lead past McDonald Creek and Upper McDonald Creek Falls to Avalanche Campground (6 miles). Some skiers cross the bridge at Sacred Dancing Cascade to loop back on the river's north side, but snow coverage is more variable in the trees. A gentle forest ski leads to John's Lake, but as a destination, it's not much. Some skiers head up to Snyder Lakes, but the narrow trail descending through tight trees on the way back down makes for a hair-raising adventure. Bluesky days attract snowshoers to Mount Brown Lookout.

On the east side, a good six-mile flat ski heads to Rising Sun along Two Dog Flats; however, high winds often strip sections of the roadway bare.

Between Rising Sun and Avalanche Creek, Going-to-the-Sun Road sees significant avalanche activity. Do not attempt to ski any of this section without experience, know-how, and gear—avalanche transceivers, shovels, and probes. Check current conditions at www.glacieravalanche.org.

Rentals and Guides

Cross-country skis and snowshoes are available to rent for $15–22 in West Glacier at **Glacier Outdoor Center** (11957 Hwy. 2 E., 406/888-5454 or 800/235-6781, www.glacierraftco.com). The company also guides half- and full-day tours. Expect to pay $155–185 per day for one person for a full-day tour. The more people, the less the per-person rate. A full day trip for four people will run about $310. Plan on tipping the guide 15 percent. **Glacier Adventure Guides** (406/892-2173, www.glacieradventureguides.com) guides full-day and overnight ski tours—cross-country touring and backcountry telemark and randonee skiing. If you're a solo traveler, it's the best way to get accompanied into the backcountry with avalanche-certified guides to find pristine powder stashes. Lunch, snacks, and equipment are included. For deep backcountry, ski in to an igloo to spend the night.

ENTERTAINMENT
Park Naturalists
Lake McDonald Lodge, Avalanche Campground Amphitheater, and Rising Sun Amphitheater offer 45-minute evening park naturalist programs usually starting around 8 P.M. Check for schedules at campground information boards and hotel activity desks, or pick up a copy of *Ranger-Led Activities* at visitors centers. Topics range from fires to birds.

Best of all, they're free. Once a week at Rising Sun, the program features a Native American speaker, a great way to gain an understanding of the park's rich Native American culture and history.

Jack Gladstone
Grammy-nominated Jack Gladstone, a Blackfeet, presents his multimedia *Legends of Glacier* (adults $5, kids 12 and under free) usually once a week at the Lake McDonald Lodge auditorium. The show blends slides, storytelling, and original music. His highly entertaining show provides insight into Blackfeet history, culture, and animal legends that have sprung from parklands. For showtimes and days, pick up the current copy of *Ranger-Led Activities* at visitors centers or check online: www.nps/gov/glac.

Accommodations

Accommodations on Going-to-the-Sun Road are scarce. The west side has Lake McDonald Lodge, 16 miles west of Logan Pass. Twelve miles east of the pass, Rising Sun offers plain cottages and motel units. For those with the feet to carry them, the incomparable Granite Park and Sperry Chalets require hiking and, for Granite Park, the ability to carry your own food. All chalets and inns—all nonsmoking—are listed on the National Register of Historic Places and have limited amenities—no televisions, air-conditioning, or Internet. Add the 7 percent state bed tax to rates.

LAKE McDONALD
Historic **⟨** **Lake McDonald Lodge** (milepost 11.2 or 39.2 on Going-to-the-Sun Road, 406/892-2525, www.glacierparkinc.com, late May–late Sept., $125–178) sits on the lakeshore, with boating, trail riding, red bus, and boat tours. Centered around a massive stone fireplace and its hunting-lodge-themed lobby full of trophy specimens hung by John Lewis, the complex offers three types of accommodations: main lodge rooms, adjacent cottage

Lake McDonald Lodge is one of the park's historic hotels.

© BECKY LOMAX

GOING-TO-THE-SUN ROAD

TWO CHALETS: GETTING AWAY FROM IT ALL

To sample a few of Glacier Park's top trails and historic charm, head to the backcountry chalets. You'll get away from the hubbub of modern life – no phones, no televisions, no electricity, no hot running water, and no flush toilets. Load up day packs with a few extras like toothbrushes; you'll relish backpacker advantages without lugging huge heavy packs. Backcountry solitude, sunrises, and sunsets are prime amenities at the two rustic chalets, reached only by trail. Plan a five-night lodging itinerary that includes two nights each at Granite Park and Sperry Chalets. In between the two chalet stays, treat yourself to a night at Lake McDonald Lodge for a shower. Make chalet reservations early, for high season often books up by March.

Trails to the chalets usually open in early July, although heavy snow years may delay some high-elevation access routes until mid-July. Open until mid-September, the chalets often have rooms available at the last minute midweek in early fall. With the park's hiker shuttles, you can hike in one trail and out another.

The two historic chalets still stand as enclaves of comfort in the backcountry and as tributes to a bygone era of horse tours. Their stone and log edifices are set in spectacular surroundings, and each offers different amenities. Don't forget earplugs, for noise from heavy snorers travels between rooms.

SPERRY CHALET

Start from Lake McDonald Lodge for a slog up 6.5 miles on a horse-manure-laden trail that climbs 3,500 feet in elevation to the chalet. Set in a cirque, the full-service Sperry Chalet provides everything, including mountain goats clomping on walkways. With the package including meals – dinner, breakfast, and sack or dining room lunch – and rooms complete with fresh linens and bedding, you need to carry only your water, clothes, and a few snacks. If you can handle the weight in your pack, throw in a bottle of your favorite beverage for evening sipping.

On your second day at Sperry, grab your lunch and head for **Sperry Glacier.** The eight-mile round-trip trail climbs past bedrock tarns before it squeezes up a narrow stairway through a cliff into the ice-scoured basin housing the glacier, moraines, and crevasses. To exit Sperry on your final day, hike the long 14-mile route over two passes. As the trail crosses the Continental Divide at **Gunsight Pass,** it drops roughly 3,500 feet to Jackson Overlook. Catch shuttles over Logan Pass back to **Lake McDonald Lodge,** where hot showers await.

GRANITE PARK CHALET

Hop an early hiker shuttle to Logan Pass. Walking with the goats, hike the **Highline Trail,** heading north along the Garden Wall. With only an 800-foot climb, the 7.6-mile trail heads out to a knoll with a 360-degree view of surrounding peaks and glaciers.

Granite Park Chalet functions as a hiker hostel: You bring and cook your own food in a fully equipped kitchen or purchase packaged meals on-site to cook yourself. Either tote your sleeping bag or order linen service. In the evening, bring your binoculars outside to watch bears foraging in the valley below; at sunset, walk to the chalet's northwestern side as orange and pink hues spread across the sky.

On your second day, pack in two half-day hikes: one to **Swiftcurrent Lookout** for views of the park from end to end, and the other to **Grinnell Glacier Overlook** to see the melting glacier from the crest of the Continental Divide. Together, the hikes total eight miles.

To depart on your last day at Granite, either drop four miles downhill to The Loop to catch the shuttle, or cross over Swiftcurrent Pass. The 7.6-mile Swiftcurrent Trail descends through a spectacular cliff wall dripping with waterfalls before leveling out for an easy walk past moose browsing in lakes along the valley floor. From Swiftcurrent, grab a GPI shuttle to St. Mary to link in with the Sun Road shuttle back to your car.

rooms, and motel rooms a five-minute walk away. The lodge and cottage exteriors have a quaint cabin look, with lakeside rooms having views, but the 1950s-style motel sits in deep cedars with no views. While all rooms are small, cottage rooms tend to be the tiniest, many with space for only two twin beds; main lodge rooms are the largest. Be prepared for all rooms to have petite bathrooms—dinky sinks and skinny elbow-knocking shower stalls—in many cases closets converted into bathrooms. Rooms have phones, but upstairs rooms do not have elevator access. While the rooms are small, this is a place to get out and explore—not sit in a room. Dial back your expectations to the 1940s or 1950s, and you'll be delighted with its location and historic ambience. Restaurants, a lounge, gift shop, and camp store are in the lodge or within a five-minute walk. Best of all, trails to Mount Brown Lookout, Snyder Lake, Sperry Chalet, and Sperry Glacier depart right across the street. Reservations are highly recommended in June and September and an absolute must in July and August.

RISING SUN

Rising Sun Motor Inn (milepost 44.7 or 6 on Going-to-the-Sun Road, 406/892-2525, www. glacierparkinc.com, mid-June–mid-Sept., $121–136) became the answer for motorists traveling to Glacier during World War II, as it was the only facility that stayed open. Built in 1940, the inn still retains its old-time feel with no in-room phones. (A pay phone is in front of the camp store.) The compound spreads with cottages and motel units, all with very diminutive private bathrooms; expect to bump your elbows in the shower stalls. The motel also has a restaurant, camp store, and hiker shuttle stop. The trail to Otokomi Lake begins right behind the inn, and access to St. Mary Lake is right across the street, along with the boat tour dock.

While not much has changed at this funky old-time motor inn with its board-and-batten construction, it's hard to beat its location 12 miles from Logan Pass. Although the rooms don't have much in the way of amenities, you won't spend your time there anyway with so much outside to explore. In the evening, go on a gorgeous sunset cruise on St. Mary Lake or drive to look for wildlife on Two Dog Flats between Rising Sun and St. Mary.

BACKCOUNTRY CHALETS

Glacier has two historic gems remaining in its backcountry—part of a series of backcountry chalets built by Great Northern Railway. Both Sperry and Granite Park Chalets are rustic stone and log buildings owned by the National Park Service and operated by Belton Chalets, Inc. (406/387-5654 or 888/345-2649, www.sperrychalet.com, www.graniteparkchalet.com, early July–early Sept.). They are set in the scenery-packed territory of mountain goats and grizzly bears. Pack along earplugs, because snores resound through the thin walls. With no electricity or phones, evening entertainment entails quietly watching wildlife and sunsets. Take a flashlight to find the composting vault toilets in the dead of night. No alcohol is sold on the premises or allowed in the dining halls; you can pack along your favorite beverage for your room, but pack the containers out with you. To reach the chalets requires hiking 6–14 miles, depending on routes. Reservations are required, often filling by March. Hiker shuttles stop at all Sun Road trailheads for the chalets.

◖ **Sperry Chalet** offers hikers and horseback riders three meals and a warm bed, which means hauling only a day pack with some extra clothing. Set in a timbered cirque, the chalet has a dining hall, a dorm, and several park service buildings. Seventeen dorm rooms sleep 2–6 people each in bunks or beds with bed linens included ($180 for first person per night, $125 for each additional person per night in same room). Country meals with roasted turkey sate ravenous hiker appetites, but the menu has maintained culinary sensibilities from the 1950s with canned fruits and vegetables. Trail lunches packed for you are plain, with a meat sandwich (no lettuce nor tomato), candy bars, and fruit leather. However,

© BECKY LOMAX

Sperry Chalet offers full service, with meals and lodging.

bakery goods—cookies, freshly baked breads, and pies—are outstanding, using traditional decades-old recipes. To reach Sperry, hike 6.5 miles up from Lake McDonald or 14 miles over two passes from Jackson Glacier Overlook.

Set at the same elevation as Logan Pass, **◖ Granite Park Chalet** sits atop a knoll, where the 360-degree view alone makes the stay worth it. Granite comprises the main chalet (kitchen, dining room, and guest rooms), a dorm, a park service building, and the composting outhouse. Twelve guest rooms sleep 2–6 people each ($85 for the first person, $73 for each additional person in the same room). This chalet functions somewhat like a hostel: Bring your own sleeping bag, or if you don't want to carry one, purchase linen service ($16 for sheets, pillow, blankets). Meals are not supplied; hikers haul their own food to cook in the kitchen. If you don't want to carry food, you can preorder freeze-dried food to be there for you. Candy bars, pop, and bottled water are sold on-site. Pots and pans are available for cooking on the huge 12-burner propane

stove (oven, too), but you'll need to bring your own mugs, plates, bowls, eating utensils, and water filter. (You can purchase environmentally friendly disposable plates and utensils.) Running water is not available; you haul water for cooking and washing from 0.2 mile away. Most hikers reach the chalet from Logan Pass (7.6 miles), The Loop (4 miles), or Swiftcurrent (7.6 miles).

CAMPING

In the 52 miles of Going-to-the-Sun Road, five campgrounds stretch along the corridor, but none sit in the 28-mile central Logan Pass section. On the west side, Apgar, Sprague Creek, and Avalanche offer more sites than Rising Sun and St. Mary on the east side. (Details on Apgar and St. Mary are listed in their respective chapters.) In midsummer, the coveted Avalanche, Sprague Creek, and Rising Sun campgrounds can fill by noon; all sites are first come, first serve. For all campgrounds on Going-to-the-Sun Road, amenities include shuttle stops, flush toilets, cold running water, picnic tables, and fire rings with grills; bring your own firewood, as collecting is prohibited. For hookups, hit commercial campgrounds outside the park in St. Mary or West Glacier. For bicyclists, hikers, and motorcyclists, shared hiker-biker sites ($5 per person) with bear-resistant food storage are held until 9 P.M. and are available at all three.

If campgrounds are full, oversized RVs must backtrack because vehicles over 21 feet cannot travel the Sun Road between Avalanche Campground and Sun Point. On the west side, head to Fish Creek and commercial campgrounds in West Glacier. On the east side, aim for commercial campgrounds in St. Mary.

West Side

Sprague Creek Campground (milepost 10.2 or 40.5 on Going-to-the-Sun Road, 406/888-7800, mid-May–mid-Sept., $20 per site) sits right on Lake McDonald's shore one mile west of the lodge in a timbered setting with shaded sites—a few with prime waterfront. Unfortunately, several sites also abut Going-to-the-Sun Road, with a nice view of cars driving by. After dark, the road noise plummets, so it's not like tenting next to a major highway. As the smallest campground—only 25 sites accessed via a paved road—Sprague Creek does not allow towed units; however, a few sites can accommodate small RVs up to 21 feet. No trailheads depart from here, but beach sunsets rank as spectacular. Kayakers and canoers have lakefront access. At 23 miles from Logan Pass, it still has quick access to the high country and is five minutes from Lake McDonald Lodge and camp store.

Set in a cedar-hemlock and fern rainforest, **(Avalanche Campground** (milepost 16.6 or 34.1 on Going-to-the-Sun Road, 406/888-7800, mid-June–early Sept., $20 per site) opens its 87 sites for a shorter season than Sprague Creek. Six miles east of Lake McDonald Lodge, Avalanche makes the closest west-side base for exploring Logan Pass, 16 miles away, and is convenient for hiking to Avalanche Lake since the trailhead departs from the campground's rear. You'll know you're in a rainforest, with its dark overgrown forest canopy allowing little sunlight to hit your picnic table. The moist area sprouts thick patches of thimbleberries and sometimes a good collection of mosquitoes. Although the campground can fit RVs up to 26 feet in over half of its sites, no disposal station is available.

East Side

Located only 12 miles east of Logan Pass and six miles west of St. Mary, **(Rising**

Sun Campground (milepost 44.5 or 6.3 on Going-to-the-Sun Road, 406/888-7800, late May–mid-Sept., $20 per site) tucks at the base of Otokomi Mountain by St. Mary Lake. Adjacent to Rising Sun Motor Inn, the 83-site campground is a few minutes' walk to a restaurant, camp store, and hot showers. Beach access is across Going-to-the-Sun Road, with a picnic area, boat ramp, and boat tours. Otokomi Lake trailhead sits behind the adjacent inn. The campground has a dump station but only 10 sites that can accommodate RVs up to 25 feet. Here, the sun drops down early behind Goat Mountain, casting a long twilight on the campground.

Backcountry Campsites

Some of the park's most popular trails depart from the Sun Road for backcountry campsites high along the Continental Divide. The Highline Trail connects with **Granite Park** and **Fifty Mountain,** both set near wildflower meadows with stunning views. It also makes a loop to Packer's Roost via **Flattop.** The Gunsight Trail has three popular campsites at **Gunsight Lake, Lake Ellen Wilson,** and **Sperry.** From Rising Sun, **Otokomi Lake** also makes a scenic overnight. Pick up permits ($5 per person per night; kids 8–18 $2.50, kids 7 and under free) in person at ranger stations, visitors centers, or the Apgar Permit Office (406/888-7900) 24 hours in advance or by reservation ($30). Check additional requirements online: www.nps.gov/glac.

Food

No food services are available at Logan Pass. The nearest restaurants on the west side are at Lake McDonald Lodge, 21 miles below the pass. On the east side, Rising Sun has the only restaurant, 12 miles from Logan Pass and 6 miles from St. Mary. Most restaurants in and adjacent to the park sell box or sack lunches ($7–10) to accommodate hikers and sightseers spending the day driving the Sun Road.

RESTAURANTS
Lake McDonald

Three distinctly different nonsmoking restaurants are located at Lake McDonald Lodge (milepost 11.2 or 39.2 on Going-to-the-Sun Road, 406/892-2525, daily late May–late Sept.)—all operated by the same concessionaire. The headliner dining room inside the lodge is **(Russell's Fireside Dining**

Room, with woven seats and painted Native American chandeliers. The north windows have a peek-a-boo lake view, but during dinner the blinds usually need to be pulled down as the sun blazes in hot. Breakfasts (6:30–10 A.M.) are the same in all the lodges run by Glacier Park, Inc.—a massive buffet ($8–14) spread with fruit, pastries, waffles, eggs, pancakes, French toast, sausage, and bacon. It offers a huge selection and enough to fill big eaters, but entrées will not be steaming hot off the grill. Those looking for something smaller can order à la carte. The dining hall opens for lunch 11:30 A.M.–2 P.M. ($8–13), and dinner 5–9:30 P.M. ($16–27). Wild game, pasta, and trout take on a decidedly Montana taste, and the menu features local ingredients and new vegetarian entrées, such as stuffed butternut squash. No reservations are taken, so you may have to wait for a seat. You can order $9 hiker lunches a day in advance.

If you want a lighter dinner without leaving the lodge, drop in the cozy **Stockade Lounge,** open 11:30 A.M.–midnight. It serves a respectable $9–15 appetizer and sandwich menu 2–10 P.M., which includes the requisite burger and fries. The bar also stocks plenty of local microbrews along with wine and cocktails.

Opposite Lake McDonald Lodge, **Jammer Joe's Grill and Pizzeria** (11:30 A.M.–9:30 P.M., $8–16, closes in early Sept.) serves lunch and dinner in a cafeteria atmosphere with a pizza and salad bar. Pasta and sandwiches, including a black bean and Swiss cheese burger, dominate the menu.

Rising Sun

Located at Rising Sun Motor Inn, **Two Dog Flats Grill** (milepost 44.7 or 6 on Going-to-the-Sun Road, 406/892-2525, 6:30–10 A.M. and 11 A.M.–9:30 P.M. daily mid-June–mid-Sept.) serves breakfast ($5–10) and an all-day menu ($8–17) in its building, reminiscent of an old coffee shop. Ask for a south window table for views of Red Eagle Peak. The menu has taken on a more modern flair with emu or buffalo burgers. Get soups, salads, sandwiches, steaks, and fish. Montana microbrews

and wine, too. No reservations are taken for the nonsmoking restaurant, which sometimes crowds with bus tours. You may have to wait for a table in high season. If the line is really long, you can bop six miles down the road to St. Mary for more dining options; the evening return drive offers good wildlife-watching along Two Dog Flats. Order $9 hiker lunches a day in advance.

GROCERIES

Camp stores are located at Lake McDonald Lodge, 21 miles west of Logan Pass (a five-minute walk from Lake McDonald Lodge), and Rising Sun, 12 miles east of the pass. Open 7 A.M.–9 P.M. daily mid-June–mid-September, both camp stores carry limited brand selections, but you can pick up ice, firewood, stove gas, and other camping supplies, as well as convenience-store groceries, beer, wine, gifts, and newspapers. For hikers, both stores are a suitable place to buy trail lunch supplies—crackers, cheese, chips, fruit, and cookies.

PICNICKING

Only four areas accommodate the picnic basket on Going-to-the-Sun Road: Sprague Creek, Avalanche Creek, Sun Point, and Rising Sun. All but Sun Point permit fires in the fire rings with grills, but you'll need to bring your own firewood, as gathering is prohibited. All four sites have picnic tables. At no time should you leave your picnic gear unattended, due to bears. (Read the fines stapled to the tables.) To the right as you drive in the campground, **Sprague Creek Picnic Area** (milepost 10.2 or 40.5) is tucked tightly in the trees between Going-to-the-Sun Road and Lake McDonald, with more road view than scenery; however, short paths access the shoreline. It has access to flush toilets. ❰ **Avalanche Creek Picnic Area** (milepost 16.6 or 34.1) sits across the street from the campground and has larger rebuilt vault toilet restrooms. Picnic sites sit under cedar shade adjacent to McDonald Creek. Trailheads for Trail of the Cedars and Avalanche Lake are across the street. **Sun Point Picnic Area** (milepost 40.6 or 10) is more or less a parking lot with tables scattered around its perimeter; however, it has great views up St. Mary Valley to the Continental Divide. Its trails access spectacular Sun Point and Baring Falls. Watch the paper plates, for the wind can blow here. It also has vault toilets. **《 Rising Sun Picnic Area** (milepost 44.7 or 6) sits adjacent to St. Mary Lake, with open sites slightly buffered from wind by aspen trees. If winds rage, however, hold down everything. Short paths through the trees access the shoreline. It has flush toilets.

Logan Pass has no picnic area, and the park service does not allow coolers outside of vehicles except for picnic areas...although you can eat a sandwich anywhere. If you want to "picnic" up with the views, the best method is to pack a sack lunch to eat on a trail or at one of the many pullouts along the road. Most restaurants in and around the park sell takeout lunches ($7–10) that you can order a day in advance of your trip. Especially scenic and aptly named, Lunch Creek pullout (1.4 miles east of Logan Pass) has a good historic rock wall that makes a great place for a tailgate party, but keep the cooler inside the car. On the west side, many picnic on the rock retaining walls at The Loop or big boulders at Big Bend (2.3 miles west of Logan Pass).

ST. MARY AND MANY GLACIER

On Glacier's east side, mountains don't pinch the sky here, but instead drop abruptly to wide open grassland prairies. Below sheer cliffs, elk browse. Aspen leaves chatter in only a hint of breeze. From valley floors, a wild panorama of Glacier's peaks draws across the western skyline, dominated by red sediments and milky-blue sapphire lakes. Ice fields cling for dear life to cliffs as the summer sun strips them smaller each year. It's a place of extravagant color, where pink, purple, white, and yellow wildflowers intoxicate the eyes as much as the tumbling waterfalls.

Due to the Continental Divide, wind is a constant companion. It shapes trees into gnarled, bent wonders and whips up whitecaps on lakes in seconds. But every minute yields another view to burn up pixels on rugged scenery. No wonder the Blackfeet called Glacier the "Backbone of the World."

While St. Mary is the eastern portal to Glacier's famed Going-to-the-Sun Road, Many Glacier is a setting of dreams: distinctive peaks, idyllic lakes, pastoral meadows. The morning sunrise gleams gold across a rampart of peaks speckled with the most accessible glaciers in the park. Loons call across glassy lakes. Grizzly bears forage on hillsides, clawing at the ground for glacier lily bulbs. By evening, when trails vacate, the sunset paints royal hues above the Continental Divide. Dark descends, with a multitude of stars. And if you're lucky, the northern lights dance across the sky.

© BECKY LOMAX

HIGHLIGHTS

◖ Boat Tours: Jump aboard the Many Glacier boat tour that combines two scenic rides with a short stroll. Launch on Swiftcurrent Lake and walk to Lake Josephine for the second boat – both with unbeatable views (page 120)!

◖ Many Glacier Road: Enjoy a scenic evening drive into Many Glacier. Sunsets turn the peaks rosy with alpenglow, and wildlife is frequently afoot. At its terminus, the NPS often sets up a spotting scope for its Watchable Wildlife program (page 123).

◖ Divide Mountain: Look for a pyramid southwest of St. Mary. This aptly named peak separates waters flowing north to the Saskatchewan drainage and those heading south into the Missouri (page 124).

◖ Grinnell Glacier: Hear ice calve off Grinnell Glacier while waterfalls tumble from Salamander Glacier above (page 125). Hikers on this trail to the glacier (page 130) often spot grizzly bears.

◖ Many Glacier Hotel: Visit the grandest of the park's lodges. This historic hotel lives up to its reputation for beauty with its enormous four-story log lobby and two-story floor-

to-ceiling dining room windows matching the majesty of its idyllic setting (page 125).

◖ Iceberg Lake: Swim with icebergs! Tucked below goat-studded cliffs, the lake gleams with icebergs floating its blue waters... even in August (page 126). But you have to hike to get here (page 131)!

◖ Ptarmigan Tunnel: Climb to a hiker's tunnel built in the 1930s (page 126). A walk through its dark corridor spits you out with a burst of color: Red argillite smears across hillsides, with Elizabeth Lake's indigo waters below (page 132).

◖ Swiftcurrent Valley and Lookout: Haul out gumption to hike and stand atop the Continental Divide. You'll survey glaciers and peaks for as far as the eye can see (page 131).

◖ Duck Lake: Fish the world-famous lake known for its large rainbow trout. The views aren't bad either, with Chief Mountain looming above the blue waters (page 137).

◖ Native America Speaks: Gain an understanding of Blackfeet culture and heritage by catching one of these programs, which feature storytellers, singers, and dancers. Popular shows have standing room only (page 137).

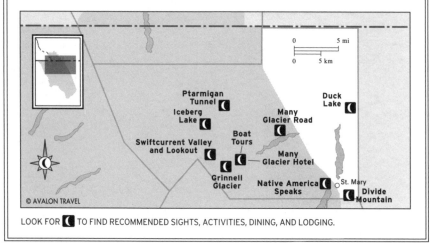

LOOK FOR ◖ TO FIND RECOMMENDED SIGHTS, ACTIVITIES, DINING, AND LODGING.

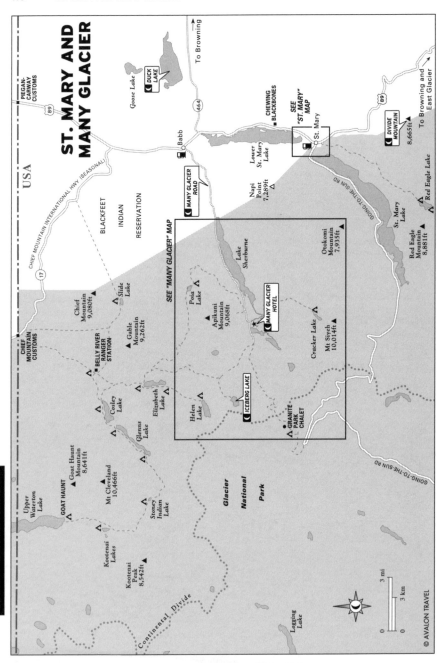

ST. MARY AND MANY GLACIER

PIEGAN-CARWAY CUSTOMS

To Browning

Goose Lake

DUCK LAKE

Babb

464

USA

BLACKFEET

INDIAN

RESERVATION

CHIEF MOUNTAIN INTERNATIONAL HWY (SEASONAL)

89

CHEWING BLACKBONES

SEE "ST. MARY" MAP

St. Mary

DIVIDE MOUNTAIN 8,665ft

To Browning and East Glacier

89

MANY GLACIER ROAD

Lower St. Mary Lake

Napi Point 7,289ft

GOING-TO-THE-SUN RD

Red Eagle Lake

17

CHIEF MOUNTAIN CUSTOMS

Chief Mountain 9,080ft

Slide Lake

Gable Mountain 9,262ft

BELLY RIVER RANGER STATION

SEE "MANY GLACIER" MAP

Poia Lake

Apikuni Mountain 9,068ft

Lake Sherburne

MANY GLACIER HOTEL

Cracker Lake

Mt Siyeh 10,014ft

Otokomi Mountain 7,935ft

St. Mary Lake

Red Eagle Mountain 8,881ft

Cosley Lake

Elizabeth Lake

Helen Lake

ICEBERG LAKE

GRANITE PARK CHALET

GOING-TO-THE-SUN RD

Goat Haunt Mountain 8,641ft

GOAT HAUNT

Mt Cleveland 10,466ft

Glenns Lake

Stoney Indian Lake

Glacier National Park

Upper Waterton Lake

Kootenai Lakes

Kootenai Peak 8,542ft

Continental Divide

Logging Lake

3 mi

3 km

0

0

© AVALON TRAVEL

HISTORY
Parkhood

George Bird Grinnell first set eyes on his namesake glacier in 1887. The editor of *Forest and Stream,* the precursor to *Field and Stream,* made several excursions to Glacier over two decades, during which he lobbied Congress for support for the area's preservation. Congress agreed to purchase lands from the Blackfeet to open to the public, and Grinnell helped negotiate the sale.

After the federal government purchased the land from the Blackfeet, Glacier became a forest reserve, thrown open to prospecting and hunting. The Many Glacier Valley attracted hordes of would-be miners, digging for copper, silver, and gold. In 1898, the mining boom gave rise to Altyn, a town site located where Sherburne Reservoir is today. At its peak, the burg housed 800 residents, but by December of 1902 it was a ghost town, its yields meager and its inhabitants lured north into Klondike's gold rush.

Grinnell pressed on in his efforts to preserve Glacier. Finally, in 1910, President Taft signed the act creating Glacier National Park, America's 12th national park. In recognition of Grinnell's efforts, a glacier, a peak, a point, and two lakes have been named after him, all in Swiftcurrent Valley.

Lodges and Chalets

On old wagon roads, Great Northern Railway built a dirt road between 1911–1912 from Midvale (East Glacier) to St. Mary and Swiftcurrent Valley—soon to be the home of the "Showplace of the Rockies," Many Glacier Hotel. When dry, the road was drivable; when rains fell, it mutated into treacherous muck. In the hustle to create guest lodging for train riders, the train company threw up Many Glacier and St. Mary Chalets in 1912–1913. Guests rode the 36 miles from Midvale to St. Mary by car in two and a half hours or stagecoach in four hours. Others arrived via the Inside Trail on an overnight saddle horse trip, stopping at Cut Bank Chalets. After avalanches demolished two of the Many Glacier chalets and the dining hall, poor site selection prompted choosing another location for the grand Many Glacier Hotel. Finally, the luxury hotel on Swiftcurrent Lake opened its doors in 1915 with running water—both hot and cold—steam heat, telephones, and electric lights in every room.

Blackfeet Highway

In the late 1920s, the State of Montana rerouted and paved the Midvale to St. Mary road—the Blackfeet Highway, found on most maps today as Highways 49 and 89. The new route bypassed St. Mary Chalets, which fell into disuse as growing automobile traffic diverted toward Going-to-the-Sun Road and sprouted the town of St. Mary. Saddled with the Depression and fewer people who could afford pricey hotels, the park service pressured the railroad company into building Swiftcurrent Cabins in 1933—immediately a popular place to stay at $2.25.

1936 Fire

When high winds forced the 1936 Heavens Peak fire over the Continental Divide, it beelined down Swiftcurrent Valley, eating up 33 of the auto cabins en route to Many Glacier Hotel. Employees doused the hotel roof with water to protect their lodge. After the fire spared the hotel, employees telegrammed the railway vice president, apprising him of the success. His reply: "Why?" The hotels and chalets had become a financial noose around the railway's neck. The St. Mary chalets were torn down in 1948; Many Glacier chalets succumbed to fire and avalanches. Only the historic showplace Many Glacier Hotel remains.

Exploring St. Mary and Many Glacier

Glacier's eastern ecosystem sprawls across national park lands and the Blackfeet Reservation—divided by an artificially straight border. Bears and elk know no boundaries, and sometimes neither do cattle, ranging astray inside Glacier.

Blackfeet Reservation
Bordering the park's eastern boundary are one and a half million acres of Blackfeet Nation tribal lands. The boundary slices across the summits of Chief Mountain, Napi Point, and Divide Peak, crossing the lower end of Sherburne Reservoir and sliding between the two St. Mary Lakes. Tribal permits are required for recreating on the reservation: camping, fishing, hiking, and boating.

St. Mary
St. Mary is the eastern portal to Going-to-the-Sun Road. Sitting at the junction of the Sun Road and the Blackfeet Highway (Highway 89,) the town clusters at the park boundary. Only the visitors center and St. Mary Campground are within the park; the town, restaurants, grocery stores, lodging, and commercial campgrounds sit on the Blackfeet Reservation.

Many Glacier
You'll have to become used to the lingo here: Although the popular Many Glacier Hotel sits in the Swiftcurrent Valley, locals refer to the whole valley area simply as Many Glacier, even though that technically is not its name. (Only two features actually use that name—the hotel and the campground.) Many Glacier derived its name from the string of small glaciers that populated its peaks: Grinnell, Salamander, Gem, North Swiftcurrent, and South Swiftcurrent.

Babb
Between St. Mary and Many Glacier sits Babb, a blink-and-you'll-miss-it village about one block long. A few houses cluster behind a petite year-round grocery store, along with two bars, two restaurants, and a tiny motel. It seemingly has no purpose in the middle of nowhere, but its year-round post office and elementary school service families ranching between St. Mary and the Canadian border.

Belly River
A confluence of two valleys lined with good fishing lakes, the Belly River, north of Many Glacier, is home to tales of one of the park's most notorious rangers—Joe Cosley. Guides and rangers tell stories of his exploits—from poaching to womanizing. The Belly, as locals call it, is undeveloped backcountry; there are no hotels or restaurants. While hikers can reach a couple of The Belly's lakes in one long day, it's an area best explored by backpacking.

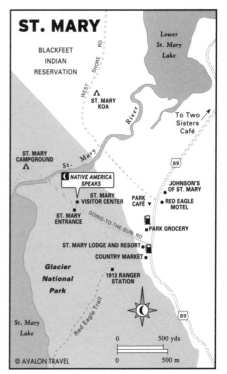

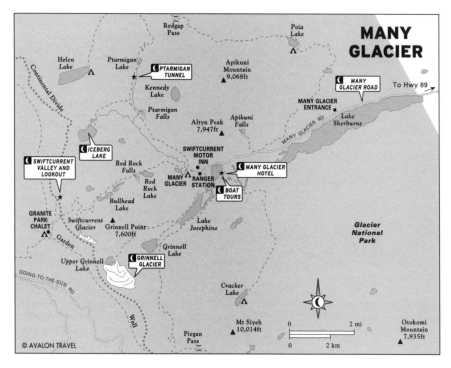

PARK ENTRANCE

The park staffs entrance stations at St. Mary at the eastern gateway of Going-to-the-Sun Road and in Many Glacier just inside the park boundary. Both have self-pay cash-only kiosks for when the stations are unstaffed. If you don't have an annual pass, seven-day passes cost $25 per vehicle or $12 for individuals on foot, bicycles, or motorcycles.

VISITORS CENTERS

In St. Mary, **St. Mary Visitor Center** (0.4 mile west on Going-to-the-Sun Rd., 406/732-7751, 8 A.M.–8 P.M. mid-May–late June and Labor Day–Sept., open until 9 P.M. late June–Labor Day) is the largest visitors center in the park. Renovated indoor facilities comprise displays with emphasis on Native American cultural history, a small Glacier Natural History Association bookstore, and an enlarged theater.

Inside the center, you'll find backcountry permits, fishing regulations, Going-to-the-Sun Road updates, Junior Ranger Activity Guides, and information on free guided park-naturalist hikes and presentations in *Ranger-Led Activities.* The indoor theater also hosts slide presentations, evening naturalist programs, and the popular Two Medicine Lake Singers and Dancers.

The visitors center is also a shuttle stop: To avoid parking hassles at Logan Pass, you can park your car here all day for free and catch the free shuttle up Going-to-the-Sun Road.

Between the picnic area and Swiftcurrent parking lot adjacent to the campground in Many Glacier, the small **Many Glacier Ranger Station** (milepost 12.4 on Many Glacier Rd., 406/732-7740, 8 A.M.–5 P.M. daily late May–mid-Sept.) has hiking info, maps, trail conditions, bear-sighting information, guidebooks, and backcountry permits available.

TOURS AND SHUTTLES
Shuttles

St. Mary Visitor Center serves as the east-side transit hub. You can catch the **free shuttle** heading up Going-to-the-Sun Road here. No tickets needed; no reservations taken. Starting at 7 A.M., the shuttle leaves every half hour for Logan Pass, with six stops en route at trailheads. It's a one-hour ride. At Logan Pass, you can catch the west-side shuttles into the Lake McDonald Valley. The last buses leave Logan Pass at 7 P.M. to return to St. Mary.

For hikers, **Glacier Park, Inc.** (406/892-2525, www.glacierparkinc.com, $10 adults one-way, kids half price) runs two shuttle routes on the east side of the park. For those heading to the Highline-Swiftcurrent Pass or Piegan Pass trails that end in Many Glacier, a shuttle runs from Swiftcurrent Motor Inn and Many Glacier Hotel to St. Mary Visitor Center (7 and 8:30 A.M., 4:45 P.M., July–Labor Day). For details of point-to-point hikes ending in Many Glacier, see the *Going-to-the-Sun Road* chapter. Between late May and late September, the east-side hiker vans run north–south connecting Waterton, Many Glacier, St. Mary, Cut Bank, Two Medicine, and East Glacier ($10–50 one-way, kids half price). Schedules are available online and at hotel activity desks, visitors centers, and ranger stations. No reservations are accepted for either shuttle; pay cash when you board.

Flathead-Glacier Transportation (406/892-3390 or 800/829-7039) runs shuttles by reservation only between Glacier International Airport and points on Glacier's east side. You can get to St. Mary, Many Glacier, or Chief Mountain Customs ($220–260 one-way for first person, $3 each additional person).

Tours

Glacier Park, Inc. (406/892-2525, www.glacierparkinc.com, mid-June–mid-Sept., adults $35–75, kids half price, prices do not include meals or park entrance fees) runs daily tours leaving Many Glacier Hotel and St. Mary on the historic red buses. Departure times vary based on location. These scenic buses are charmers; on good weather days, the jammers (tour bus drivers) roll the canvas tops back for unlimited skyward views—no air-conditioning needed! Two tours head to Logan Pass, hitting almost every scenic stop on Going-to-the-Sun Road: the seven-and-a-half-hour Crown of the Continent tour and the four-hour Eastern Alpine Tour. Both of these tours stop in St. Mary to pick up riders at St. Mary KOA and St. Mary Lodge. The International Peace Park Tour departs for an excursion to Waterton and arrives at Prince of Wales Hotel in time for afternoon tea. Passports are required. This tour, which originates in East Glacier, picks up riders in St. Mary (six-and-a-half-hour tour) and Many Glacier (five-hour tour). Other tours are available, too. Reservations can be made by phone or at Many Glacier Hotel's activity desk.

Departing St. Mary daily, **Sun Tours** (406/226-9220 or 800/786-9220, www.glaciersuntours.com, June–Sept., $40 adults, $15 kids, meals and park entrance fees not included) drives 25-passenger air-conditioned buses with extra-large windows for big scenery, an asset on the historic Going-to-the-Sun Road. Led by local Native American guides who grew up on the reservation, the tours highlight Glacier's rich connection with the Blackfeet—tribal history in the park, plants used for traditional medicines, stories behind peak names, and life in buffalo days. A four-hour tour departs at 9 A.M., with pickups at various St. Mary locations. Call for reservations 24 hours in advance.

◖ Boat Tours and Shuttles

In Many Glacier, jump on a pair of historic wooden boats for a tour of two lakes with **Glacier Park Boat Company** (406/257-2426, www.glacierparkboats.com, early June–mid-Sept., adult round-trip $22, kids half price). Catch the 1961-vintage *Chief Two Guns* at Swiftcurrent Lake's boat dock behind Many Glacier Hotel. In an hour and fifteen minutes, you'll cruise across the lake, hike 0.2 mile over a hill, hop aboard the 1945 *Morning Eagle,* and return. On this tour, you're right in the thick of moose, bear, and wolverine country. Don't

boat tour on Lake Josephine

forget your camera, but you may have difficulty cramming the view into the lens. Tours depart seven times daily: 8:30, 9, and 11 A.M., 1 (July–Aug. only), 2, 3 (July–Aug. only), and 4:30 P.M. Two of the daily launches offer a guided two-mile round-trip walk to Grinnell Lake. The guided hike tours fill up fast, so buy your tickets (cash only) at the dock a few hours early. Once the Grinnell Glacier trail melts out, the boat company adds the 8:30 A.M. launch to the schedule, allowing hikers quicker access across the valley. The park service runs a guided hike via this launch. Hikers may also catch a return boat at the upper Lake Josephine dock (pay as you board); you may have to wait for a few launches to get on, but the captain runs the boat until all hikers are shuttled.

On St. Mary Lake, boat tours on the *Little Chief* depart from Rising Sun. Check the *Going-to-the-Sun Road* chapter for details.

SERVICES

Two gas stations are in St. Mary on Highway 89, one on either side of the Going-to-the-Sun Road junction. One more gas station sits in Babb across from Thronson's General Store. Many Glacier has no gas services.

In Many Glacier, public showers ($1.25 for eight minutes)—which are often cold to lukewarm—and laundry facilities are available behind Swiftcurrent Campstore; purchase tokens for both in the store. In St. Mary, you'll find showers ($4–5) and a coin-op laundry at St. Mary KOA and Johnson's Campground. Find ATMs and pay phones at Many Glacier Hotel, Swiftcurrent Motor Inn, Country Market in St. Mary, and St. Mary Lodge and Resort. At the junction of Many Glacier Road and Highway 89, Babb has the nearest post office to Many Glacier; St. Mary has a seasonal post office in the Country Market. The local newspaper is the *Great Falls Tribune*. In St. Mary, find public restrooms at the visitors center and behind Curly Bear Café.

Cell Phones and Internet

Planning to use your cell phone in Many Glacier? Keep dreaming. There's no coverage.

© BECKY LOMAX

If you require cell service, stay in St. Mary. Likewise with the Internet.

Shopping

Several gift shops in St. Mary offer a break from the same selections found in all the park hotel gift shops, but expect to see merchandise heavily branded with popular moose and bear themes. **Trail Creek Outfitters** (junction of Hwy. 89 and Going-to-the-Sun Rd., 406/732-4431, June–Sept.) carries minimal hiking, fishing, and camping gear at specialty-store prices.

Emergencies

If you are inside the park, contact a ranger or call 406/888-7800 for emergencies. The nearest hospital is in Cut Bank—the Northern Rockies Medical Center (802 2nd St. E., 406/873-2251).

Rangers like to keep apprised of all bear sightings and encounters—especially bears close to the trail. Report your sightings to the St. Mary Visitor Center or Many Glacier Ranger Station.

Find the **Many Glacier Ranger Station** (milepost 12.4 on Many Glacier Rd., 406/732-7740, 8 A.M.–5 P.M. daily late May–mid-Sept.) between the picnic area and Swiftcurrent parking lot adjacent to the campground in Many Glacier. Backpackers who need assistance in The Belly can find the **Belly River Ranger Station** in the backcountry at the junction of the Cosley Lake, Elizabeth Lake, Gable Pass, and Chief Mountain Customs trails.

DRIVING TOURS

St. Mary is the eastern portal for Going-to-the-Sun Road. Winding along St. Mary Lake and Two Dog Flats, the road reaches Logan Pass in 18 miles before dropping 32 miles to West Glacier. The seasonally open Chief Mountain Highway connects the St. Mary Valley with Waterton and crosses the Canadian-U.S. border.

Blackfeet Highway

The Blackfeet Highway, otherwise known as Highway 89, runs entirely on the Blackfeet Reservation along the east side of Glacier Park from the Canadian border at Piegan-Carway to Browning. Its only gas services are at Babb, St. Mary, and Browning.

Be prepared for impediments on the Blackfeet Highway! Much of the road crosses open range where you may encounter cattle or horses. Slow down and give them room. Ole Bessie may just stand there staring at you and refuse to budge. If so, a toot on the horn can sometimes help, but avoid being obnoxious. If necessary, carefully pass in the other lane. Due to livestock, slow down at night, even though the speed limit sign says 70 mph. You'll frequently hear the screech of brakes as drivers come too quickly upon a cow in the middle of the road.

Driving north from St. Mary, the highway undulates on a fairly wide road past **Lower St. Mary Lake,** where you'll see Thunderbird Island. As you round the lake's outlet, watch for waterfowl and spectacular views to the north of Chief Mountain and Old Sun Glacier on Mount Merritt. This section of the highway is one of the few roads with shoulders, making the driving significantly easier. The road travels through aspen ranchland, passing Duck Lake Road (7.3 miles), Many Glacier Road and Babb (9 miles), and Chief Mountain Highway (14 miles) before reaching the Canadian border (24 miles). At the boundary, the highway turns into Alberta Highway 2 as it continues north in Canada.

Driving south from St. Mary, the Blackfeet Highway heads toward **Two Medicine, Browning,** and **East Glacier.** Even if you have only a couple of minutes, bop southward two miles up the hill from town to grab a panoramic view of the St. Mary Valley and see the results of the 2006 Red Eagle Fire. Several unmarked wide pullouts afford good places to stop for a photo. As the road climbs St. Mary Ridge at 6,015 feet, it crosses the Hudson Bay Divide—sending waters to the Missouri or Saskatchewan. Several lanes allow for passing, but within a few miles the road shrinks to a curvy, rolling, narrow shoulderless trek through willow bogs and beaver ponds divided by aspen groves. Turns are blind; take them slowly in case bicyclists or cows are on the road. At 20 miles, you can turn off onto Highway 49—a road with more curves than a snake and part of the original Blackfeet Highway—toward Two Medicine (38 miles) or East Glacier (33 miles). If you continue on Highway 89, you'll reach Browning (32 miles).

C Many Glacier Road

The 12-mile-long Many Glacier Road—also called Glacier Route Three on some maps— is a stunning drive into **Swiftcurrent Valley.** On this road, there are two reasons to drive slowly: Motorists here have a good chance of spotting wildlife, and the road is chock-full of potholes and torn-up pavement. From Babb, the road follows Swiftcurrent Creek upstream across Blackfeet Nation lands, where open range may put you nose to nose with cows on the road. Give them room, and drive at a snail's pace around them. Watch for bears, particularly around dusk. If you spot a bear, drive by

slowly to watch rather than stopping and creating a bear jam, which conditions bears to be around cars. Above all, stay in the car for safety. Several sections of road are denoted by signs as wildlife corridors; no stopping is permitted in these.

After the road rises to reach Sherburne Dam (mile 4.8), it follows the reservoir's north shore, crossing into the park over the cattle grate, but you won't reach the park entrance station for another three miles. Check the shoreline for deer, bears, and sometimes errant cows straying into the park. Aspen groves and wildflower meadows with July's pink sticky geraniums line the road. Scenic stops lend views of Sherburne Reservoir and up the valley to **Grinnell, Salamander,** and **Gem Glaciers.**

At **Many Glacier Hotel** (turn south at 11.6 miles), stop to tour the historic building. After the hotel turnoff, the road passes Swiftcurrent Lake, the picnic area (mile 12.2), the ranger station, campground, and Swiftcurrent Motor Inn, where it terminates in Swiftcurrent parking lot.

© BECKY LOMAX

bridge over outlet of Swiftcurrent Lake on Many Glacier Road

ST. MARY AND MANY GLACIER

Duck Lake Road

Montana Highway 464, known locally as the Duck Lake Road, leaves the Blackfeet Highway at the east end of Lower St. Mary Lake (7.3 miles north of St. Mary, 1.7 miles south of Babb). Locals tend to use this road via Browning for a faster access between the park's northeast sections and East Glacier. Although the mileage is longer (53 miles from St. Mary to East Glacier rather than 33 miles via Highway 89), the straighter road affords easier driving. It's also faster: Speed limits reach 70 mph on stretches, and fences keep cattle off the road. RV drivers and those pulling trailers in particular find it easier to handle than the curvy Blackfeet Highway. The road climbs over St. Mary Ridge, passing Duck Lake at three miles. From the top of the ridge above Duck Lake—the divide between the Missouri and Saskatchewan river drainages—the highway heads southward across the Blackfeet Reservation to Browning (34 miles from Highway 89) through bison and cattle ranchland, with Glacier's peaks dominating the western skyline across the prairie.

Chief Mountain International Highway

A seasonal road only, Chief Mountain International Highway links Glacier and Waterton Parks. Its season and hours operate around the Canadian and U.S. customs stations at the border (open mid-May–Sept.; May and after Labor Day 9 A.M.–6 P.M., June–Labor Day 7 A.M.–10 P.M.). With its start 14 miles north of Babb, the 30-mile road undulates over rolling aspen hills and beaver ponds on the Blackfeet Reservation as it curves around blocky Chief Mountain to the border and trailhead entrance to the Belly River. A few unmarked pullouts offer good photo ops. Drive this open range carefully, for cows wander the road.

As the road rounds Chief Mountain, it enters Glacier Park. No entrance station is here; no payment required. The road reaches the international border and Chief Mountain Customs at 18.6 miles. Passports are required for crossing.

SIGHTS
St. Mary River

Between St. Mary Visitor Center and St. Mary Campground, Going-to-the-Sun Road crosses St. Mary River, a waterway connecting the two St. Mary Lakes. You can park near the stone bridge to take a look—the same bridge Forrest Gump jogged across in his run across America. But find better parking at the visitors center and walk 0.3 mile through prairie smoke flowers to a scenic wooden bridge that connects to the campground. Watch for killdeer, among other birds. For anglers, this river offers some of the best local fishing. You can drop a line in from the wooden bridge, but not the Going-to-the-Sun Road Bridge.

St. Mary Lakes

In pockets left from 1,200-foot-deep Pleistocene ice age glaciers that gouged out St. Mary Valley, **St. Mary Lake** and **Lower St. Mary Lake** fill most of the valley floor. The lakes collect water from snowmelt and some of the largest glaciers left in the park—Blackfoot and Jackson Glaciers. Their waters then meander toward the Canadian border and into the Saskatchewan River to Hudson Bay. With the valley sucking air down from the Continental Divide, frequent winds swirl up large whitecap waves. See the lakes from Going-to-the-Sun Road and Highway 89.

◖ Divide Mountain

Divide Mountain rises 8,665 feet in elevation, the last in a string of peaks guarding St. Mary Valley's south. Charred remnants of the 2006 Red Eagle Fire flank its slopes. From its summit, it drops to St. Mary Ridge, running for miles onto the prairie. The ridge is a lateral moraine, deposited by the Pleistocene glacier that formed the valley. This ridge, along with Divide Mountain, separates the waters flowing into the Saskatchewan drainage and those heading toward the Missouri.

1913 Ranger Station

Follow the signs on a five-minute drive off Going-to-the-Sun Road (0.2 mile from the

Highway 89 junction and just south of St. Mary Visitor Center) to the 1913 Ranger Station. A small parking area leads uphill on a three-minute walk to the historic building. Adjacent to it stands the Lubec Ranger Station Barn, which was moved here in 1977 for its preservation. However, with its restored weather-split logs and chinking, the barn is more photo worthy than the original ranger station.

◖ Grinnell Glacier

Like all glaciers in northwest Montana, Grinnell Glacier is melting. Located in Many Glacier, the ice field reached its peak size around 1850, when it filled the entire upper lake pocket under Mount Gould and connected with Salamander Glacier. Lateral moraines mark its original size. By 1930, the glacier receded—forming a lake at its snout and separating from Salamander. Today, the ice has shrunk to less than one third its 1850 size. By 2020, the glacier's moving ice will be gone, leaving only icebergs. You can see the glacier with binoculars from the Many Glacier

Road. For a closer inspection, hike to the most visited glacier in the park.

Swiftcurrent Lake

Originally called McDermott Lake, Swiftcurrent Lake took its name from the Blackfeet term for swift-flowing water—a name that George Bird Grinnell promoted for the area and also used on a peak, glaciers, creek, falls, and ridge. The lake, however, does not have fast-flowing waters. Located in Many Glacier, its bays attract loons and mergansers. Moose browse in the willows along the shoreline. A beaver lodge sits at the inlet of Swiftcurrent Creek. Enjoy the lake from Many Glacier Hotel's deck, launch a canoe from its boat ramp, ride across it on the tour boat, or walk an easy two miles around it.

◖ Many Glacier Hotel

Built in 1915 and placed on the list of National Historic Landmarks, the five-story 211-room Many Glacier Hotel (milepost 11.5 on Many Glacier Rd., 406/892-2525, www.glacierparkinc.com, mid-June–mid-Sept.) sits on

© BECKY LOMAX

Grinnell Glacier is fast melting into a lake.

© BECKY LOMAX

Take a guided tour of historic Many Glacier Hotel.

Swiftcurrent Lake's shores. Listed as one of the 11 most endangered places in the country, the hotel—owned by the National Park Service and operated by Glacier Park, Inc.—began a $30 million restoration in 2001. Workers repaired structural damage, exterior walls, windows, doors, decks, the roof, and siding. Further interior improvements are scheduled for 2011, closing half the hotel rooms for the summer. Warm up on a cold day around the huge fireplace in the massive lobby or lounge on its large deck, checking out dramatic views of the Continental Divide. Join park naturalists for a one-hour tour of the historic hotel: Check *Ranger-Led Activities* for the current schedule.

Altyn-Henkel Wildlife

Bears congregate heavily in the Swiftcurrent Valley due to abundant food sources. One of the best places to see them is feeding on the slopes of Mount Altyn and Mount Henkel on the north side of the Many Glacier Road. With binoculars, you can see bears from the Many Glacier Hotel deck. Mountain goats and bighorn sheep, too. Rangers set up a spotting scope daily 5:30 to 7:15 P.M. in the Swiftcurrent Parking Lot for wildlife-watching.

(Iceberg Lake

Tucked in a cirque below Mount Wilbur and Iceberg Peak in Many Glacier, Iceberg Lake is a treat for the eyes. The lake itself sits in a glacial pocket, once carved by the moving ice that left a small moraine along the beach. With winter snows depositing heavy drifts in the bowl protected by Wilbur's shadow, summer icebergs float in the lake—even on the hottest of August days. It's worth a quick dive in, just to say you swam with the icebergs. But icy waters will suck the air out of your lungs!

(Ptarmigan Tunnel

Built in 1931 to access the Belly River Valley from Many Glacier, Ptarmigan Tunnel is a phenomenon found on few trails. Large steel doors prevent winter snows from piling up inside; good thing, too, as those snows would never melt out. The doors open usually in July and close in early October. The 183-foot-long tunnel is high enough to permit riders on horseback without scraping heads. A walk through its dark corridor doesn't require a flashlight, but more than one hiker has encountered a bear racing through its bowels.

BELLY RIVER COUNTRY

North of Many Glacier, the Belly River is wild backcountry. No roads access the valley, making the entrance via foot or horseback. From Many Glacier, two routes cross into the Belly – Ptarmigan Tunnel and Red Gap Pass via Poia Lake. Three other trails reach the Belly via other routes: the shortest from Chief Mountain Customs, one from Goat Haunt over Stoney Indian Pass, and one from Lee Ridge. To locals, the area is simply known as The Belly.

The Belly houses two headwaters of the Saskatchewan River, which flows to Hudson Bay. The **Belly River** may have been named for the Gros Ventre (French for Big Belly) tribe, and the **Mokowanis River** for a Blackfeet term that refers to a buffalo's stomach. Thirty-three backcountry campsites string up and down their two valleys. Lakes, too: Elizabeth, Helen, Cosley, Glenns, and Mokowanis. At the confluence of the two valleys, the historic Belly River Ranger Station, which is staffed in summer, sits idyllic amid aspen groves and fields of wild sticky geraniums staring up at the three spires of Stoney Indian Peaks and Mount Cleveland, the park's highest peak.

THE LEGEND OF JOE COSLEY

The Belly is rife with legends of the park's favorite renegade ranger – **Joe Cosley.** A fur trapper long before Glacier became a national park, Cosley hunted The Belly for hides, trapped in Glacier and Waterton, and carved his name on thousands of trees.

When Glacier achieved parkhood in 1910, Cosley was hired as The Belly's first ranger. But for Cosley, ranger duties became a vehicle for poaching – even near West Glacier right under the superintendent's nose. He sold hides in Canada and furnished paying clients with big game.

Cosley's mountain man reputation grew due to his self-generated legends. He told more than one woman he named Elizabeth Lake for her, said he buried a diamond ring in a Belly poplar, and claimed to have hiked 35 miles between Polebridge and Waterton in three and a half hours for a dance.

Finally in 1914, after sending rangers to

© BECKY LOMAX

Backpackers hike near Helen Lake in The Belly.

nab him poaching, the superintendent threw Joe off the payroll, despite lack of evidence. After serving with Canadian forces in World War I, Joe weaseled back into The Belly to trap and hunt. Meanwhile, 24-year-old **Joe Heimes,** who inherited The Belly's ranger badge, crossed a footprint leading to one of Cosley's caches. Heimes arrested Cosley, who was double his age. After repeated attempts at escape, Cosley succumbed only when Heimes tied his feet. Heimes made Cosley carry a pack with evidence – traps and beaver pieces – for the long snowy hike over a pass, a drive, and a train ride to jail in Belton (West Glacier).

In 1929, Glacier Park saw its most notorious trial. Cosley pled guilty but claimed Heimes framed him with the evidence. The commissioner judged him guilty with a $125 fine and 90 days in jail. Claiming a fatal disease, Cosley asked for clemency. To avoid death in his jail, the commissioner suspended the sentence due to Joe's visibly fast-failing health. Friends paid his fine; Cosley walked free.

Two hours later, supplied with snowshoes and trail grub, the cured Cosley hiked over the Continental Divide to his cache in The Belly. Within two days after his trial, he sold 55 beaver, 21 marten, and 22 mink hides for $4,129 in Canada.

For more of Cosley's adventures, read *Belly River's Famous Joe Cosley* by Brian McClung.

ST. MARY AND MANY GLACIER

Recreation

HIKING

Hiking in Many Glacier offers a wealth of trails in contrast to St. Mary. Most **St. Mary** visitors choose to travel back up Going-to-the-Sun Road or bop 21 miles to Many Glacier, where well-marked paths access high alpine meadows, lakes, glaciers, and passes. Around St. Mary, easy trails access mosquito-ridden beaver ponds, while rough trails or scrambles lead to high peaks and bluffs. St. Mary Visitor Center has a free nontopographical map of hiking trails in St. Mary Valley, and it's also online (www.nps.gov/glac). For hiking outside the park on Blackfeet tribal lands, pick up a $10 per person annual Tribal Conservation Permit at the St. Mary Visitor Center.

Using the hiker shuttle that runs between Many Glacier and St. Mary and the park shuttle on Going-to-the-Sun Road, visitors can do point-to-point hikes: the Highline over Swiftcurrent Pass or Piegan Pass to Many Glacier Hotel. (For trail descriptions, see the *Going-to-the-Sun Road* chapter for details).

Hiking **Many Glacier** is a treat. Trails trot up fast into the high country, and not much old-growth forest obliterates views. Most trailheads are accessed from Many Glacier Hotel, Swiftcurrent parking lot, or the picnic area. Although trail junctions are extremely well signed, you'll find a map helpful to navigate the maze—especially trails crisscrossing the Grinnell Valley. Free area nontopographical hiker maps are available at St. Mary Visitor Center, Many Glacier Ranger Station, park lodge front desks, and online (www.nps.gov/glac). In Many Glacier, seasonal footbridges are usually installed in late May and removed in October. Check with the ranger station or the trail status report online for exact dates.

Because of dense bear populations and high hiker traffic in Many Glacier, trails see closures from time to time to let an aggressive bear cool off. Check for current trail status with the ranger station, Many Glacier Hotel's activity desk, or online.

Backcountry camping permits are available at St. Mary Visitor Center or Many Glacier Ranger Station. From St. Mary, backpackers can hike to Red Eagle Lake and Triple Divide Pass. From Many Glacier, trails lead to backcountry campsites at Cracker Lake, Poia Lake, and The Belly, but no backcountry camping is permitted at Iceberg, Ptarmigan, Red Rocks, Bullhead, and Grinnell Lakes, or at Grinnell Glacier and Piegan Pass.

Hikes listed below begin in the south at St. Mary and move north to the Canadian border.

Divide Peak

- Distance: 5 miles round-trip
- Duration: 3.5 hours
- Elevation gain: 1,800 feet
- Effort: strenuous
- Trailhead: unmarked end of dirt road
- Directions: Take Highway 89 south of St. Mary; depart from the dirt road at milepost 25.5, on top of St. Mary Ridge.

On Blackfeet land, this hike requires a Tribal Conservation Permit ($10 per person) available at St. Mary Ranger Station. You'll have to poke around a bit to find the trail (of which there are several) that wanders through the 2006 Red Eagle Fire. Not only is the trail unmarked, but it's very steep—only those confident in their backcountry scrambling skills should attempt this. Several routes lead up to an old hexagonal fire lookout on Divide's northeast ridge. Pick one, scouting constantly ahead for where it goes. If you don't like the steepness of what's ahead, back down and try another trail.

At the lookout, incredible views span the St. Mary Valley up to the Continental Divide and sprawl to prairies. From the lookout, a 45-minute scramble leads to the top of the peak, where you can stand atop the division of the Saskatchewan and Missouri drainages.

Red Eagle Lake

- Distance: 15 miles round-trip
- Duration: 7.5 hours
- Elevation gain: 300 feet
- Effort: easy, but long
- Trailhead: at 1913 Ranger Station parking lot at St. Mary

After following an old road for one mile, the trail climbs gently through the 2006 Red Eagle Fire, where wildflowers are madly growing back. The burn continues to the lake, where it started. Watch for bear diggings—places where grizzlies rototill for glacier lily bulbs or chase after ground squirrels. Red Eagle Mountain looms ahead, and grand views northwest to Going-to-the-Sun Mountain unfold. About halfway, the trail crosses Red Eagle Creek twice on swinging bridges. In between the two bridges, the St. Mary Lake trail splits off.

In the 1920s, Red Eagle Lake held a large tent camp, famous for its fishing. Today, die-hard anglers hike in with float tubes hitched to their packs.

Apikuni Falls

- Distance: 2 miles round-trip
- Duration: 1 hour
- Elevation gain: 550 feet
- Effort: moderate
- Trailhead: Grinnell Glacier Interpretive site, 10.4 miles west on Many Glacier Road

Apikuni Falls springs forth from a hanging valley, which you can see from the trailhead. The short walk starts out across a flat meadow but soon climbs uphill. In July, wildflowers bloom thickly here: geraniums, arrowleaf balsamroot, paintbrush, lupine, and stonecrop. The trail climbs to the cliffs between Altyn Peak and Apikuni Mountain, where the falls drops out of the basin above. Those with scrambling skills can climb a rough trail into the upper scenic basin.

Poia Lake

- Distance: 13 miles round-trip

- Duration: 6 hours
- Elevation gain: 1,765 feet
- Effort: moderate
- Trailhead: Grinnell Glacier Interpretive site, 10.4 miles west on Many Glacier Road

One of Many Glacier's less crowded routes, the trail to Poia Lake climbs through aspen groves and wildflower meadows blooming with pink sticky geranium to crest the forested Swiftcurrent Ridge before dropping to the lake. Cows wandering into the Poia drainage sometimes wreak havoc on the trail before the lake. Pass through the campground and drop to the lake, where spur paths cut through the willows to the beach. The return trip requires a 400-foot climb back over the ridge. Backpackers continue on from Poia over Red Gap Pass.

Cracker Lake

- Distance: 12.2 miles round-trip
- Duration: 6 hours
- Elevation gain: 1,400 feet
- Effort: moderate
- Trailhead: south end of Many Glacier Hotel parking lot

If you can stand the muddy, horse-rutted, manure-filled first 1.3 miles where trail rides travel four times a day, the rest of the hike is extremely scenic and not nearly as crowded as other Many Glacier hikes. If you meet horses, step below, not above the trail to let them pass. At the Cracker Flats junction, leave the messy trail behind and stomp the mud and manure from your boots. Climb up switchbacks into the Cracker Valley, where the forested trail breaks out into bluebell and lupine meadows about halfway up.

Once you reach Cracker Lake, bypass the backcountry campground and drop to the inlet for the best lunch spot on the shore. Glacial flour clouds the lake water, turning it a rich milky turquoise. Some historic mining debris still litters the cirque above the lake; it's protected by law, so leave items be. Siyeh Peak, at 10,014 feet, rises abruptly up a gigantic cliff face, a skyscraping 4,000 feet above the lake.

Josephine and Grinnell Lakes

- Distance: 1.8–7.8 miles round-trip
- Duration: 1–4 hours
- Elevation gain: minimal
- Effort: easy
- Trailheads: on the south side of Many Glacier Hotel, at Swiftcurrent Picnic Area, or via the tour boat

With the maze of trails through Grinnell Valley, a map is helpful to navigate even though trails are well signed. Pick up a free nontopographical map from the hotel desk or the ranger station. For a two-mile round-trip walk, catch the tour boat across Swiftcurrent and Josephine Lakes to hike to Grinnell Lake. For a longer hike, begin from Many Glacier Hotel, following the trail winding around Swiftcurrent Lake to the boat dock opposite the hotel. A third starting point begins at the picnic area, where it follows Swiftcurrent Lake to that same boat dock.

From here, bop over the hill to Josephine Lake, where the trail hugs the north shore until it splits off to Grinnell Glacier. Stay on the lower trail to wrap around Josephine's west end until you reach the Grinnell Lake junction. Turn toward the lake and follow the trail over a swinging bridge. At the lakeshore, enjoy Grinnell's milky turquoise waters and the falls tumbling into the lake from the glacier basin above. Although you can return to the trailheads via the south lakeshore trail, it is not as scenic, buried in deep forest. Shorten the hike by catching the tour boat back.

◖ Grinnell Glacier

- Distance: 11 miles round-trip
- Duration: 6 hours
- Elevation gain: 1,600 feet
- Effort: moderately strenuous
- Trailheads: on the south side of Many Glacier Hotel, at Swiftcurrent Picnic Area, or via the tour boat

In early summer, a large steep snowdrift

Grinnell Glacier is the most accessible glacier in the park.

frequently bars the path into the upper basin; check with the ranger station for status before hiking. The most accessible glacier in the park, Grinnell Glacier still requires stamina to access, for most of its elevation gain packs within two miles. For that reason, many hikers take the boat shuttle, cutting the length to 7.8 miles round-trip or just trimming 2.5 miles off the return. To hike the entire route from the picnic area, follow Swiftcurrent Lake's west shore to the boat dock. From Many Glacier Hotel, round the southern shore to meet up with the same dock. Bop over the short hill and traverse around Lake Josephine's north shore.

Toward Josephine's west end, the Grinnell Glacier trail diverts uphill. As the trail climbs through multicolored rock strata, Grinnell Lake's milky turquoise waters come into view below. The trail ascends on a cliff stairway where a waterfall douses hikers before passing a rest stop with outhouses. A final grunt up the moraine yields a stunning viewpoint. Trot through the maze of paths crossing the bedrock to Upper Grinnell Lake's shore, but do not walk out on the glacier's ice, harboring deadly hidden crevasses.

🍁 Swiftcurrent Valley and Lookout

- Distance: 3.6–16 miles round-trip
- Duration: 2–8 hours
- Elevation gain: 100–3,500 feet
- Effort: easy to strenuous
- Trailhead: Swiftcurrent parking lot in Many Glacier

This popular trail provides various destinations along a scenic path dotted with lakes, waterfalls, moose, glaciers, and wildflowers. The trail winds through pine trees and aspen groves as it rolls gently up to Red Rocks Lake and Falls at 1.8 miles. At the top of the falls, a knoll provides a viewpoint to scan hillsides with binoculars for bears. The trail continues level through meadows rampant with Sitka valerian in July to Bullhead Lake at 3.9 miles, a good destination with bighorn sheep wandering above on scree slopes.

From the lake, the trail knows nothing but uphill switchbacks. It cuts through a cliff face before reaching the pass at 6.6 miles. From here, Granite Park Chalet is 0.9 mile downhill. To reach the lookout, take the spur trail up 1.4 miles of more switchbacks—you'll lose count of them. From the lookout, you'll survey almost the entire park: glaciers, peaks, wild panoramas, and the plains. Many Glacier Hotel looks minuscule. (Enjoy the one-of-a-kind view from the outhouse!) For a different descent, drop to The Loop to catch a shuttle.

🍁 Iceberg Lake

- Distance: 9.8 miles round-trip
- Duration: 5 hours
- Elevation gain: 1,200 feet
- Effort: moderate
- Trailhead: behind Swiftcurrent Motor Inn cabins in Many Glacier

One of the top hikes in Glacier, the trail to Iceberg Lake begins with a short-lived steep

© BECKY LOMAX

Hikers en route to Iceberg Lake can see the jagged Iceberg Wall.

ST. MARY AND MANY GLACIER

THE EXTINCTION OF GLACIERS

"Where's the best place to go to watch the glaciers go by?" Locals chuckle when someone who slept through seventh grade earth science asks this question. Glaciers don't move like a herd of elk, but they are moving ice that scientists from the United States Geological Survey (USGS) estimate will melt by 2020 – a decade earlier than originally predicted.

WHAT ARE GLACIERS?

Glaciers are moving ice. A glacier's upper end – the accumulation zone – piles with snow, adding to the ice's mass that presses downslope. Contrary to Alaska's giant glaciers that move several feet a day, most of the park's glaciers move less than an inch. A glacier needs to be 25 acres in size to have the mass necessary to move. That movement separates glaciers from static snow fields. When summer heat melts the ice, water departs its snout. A glacier shrinks when the math doesn't add up – when more ice melts annually than accumulates.

Many of the park's glaciers now look similar at first glance to snow fields, but they aren't. They have crevasses, debris bands, and moraines. When ice inches over rocky humps, the rigid surface cracks into crevasses – some hundreds of feet deep. Bands of rock debris pile atop the ice, carried along in lines that reveal the glacier's movement. When the ice melts, rock rubble is left in moraines – lateral or terminal piles. Snow fields lack these features.

HOW MANY GLACIERS REMAIN?

Once glamorous diamonds, the park's glaciers are relics from a mini ice age that peaked around 1850 with more than 150 glaciers. Since then, glaciers thinned, shrunk, broke into pieces, or disappeared entirely like a silent Wicked Witch of the West, miming "I'm melting." While early melt rates tended to be slow, by the 1920s, warmer summers and less snows triggered rapid melting for two decades. Since the 1970s, melt rates skyrocketed to more than 50 percent. By 2010, less than 17 percent of the 150 glaciers remained, the number shrinking to 25.

WHY ARE GLACIERS MELTING?

Glacier Park is a laboratory for studying climate change around the globe because the

---

jaunt straight uphill with no time to gradually warm up the muscles. However, within 0.4 mile you reach a junction. Take note of the directional sign here and watch for it when you come down. Some hikers in zombie-walk mode blaze right on past it on the return heading on this high-bear-traffic spur.

From the junction, the trail maintains an easy railroad grade to the lake. Make noise on this trail, known for frequent bear sightings. Wildflowers line the trail in July: beargrass, bog orchids, penstemon, and thimbleberry. A mile past the junction, the trail rounds a red argillite outcropping with views of the valley. As the trail swings north, it enters a pine and fir forest and crosses Ptarmigan Falls at 2.6 miles, a good break spot where aggressive ground squirrels will steal your snack. Do not feed them; feeding only trains them to be

more forceful. From here, the trail traverses avalanche paths until it climbs the final bluff, where a view of icebergs stark against blue waters unfolds.

⟨ Ptarmigan Tunnel

- Distance: 10.4 miles round-trip
- Duration: 5 hours
- Elevation gain: 2,300 feet
- Effort: moderately strenuous
- Trailhead: behind Swiftcurrent Motor Inn cabins in Many Glacier

Depending on snowpack, the tunnel doors usually open in July and close in early October; check with the ranger station to confirm status. Traversing the same trail as Iceberg Lake, the route begins with a steep uphill climb park has warmed two times the rate of the overall planet. Average temperatures in Glacier now run two degrees hotter than they did in the mid-1900s. The park now sees 30 fewer days with below-freezing temperatures and eight days more above 90 degrees. Warmer summers and less snowpack are now the norm. The USGS monitors the park's glaciers as climate barometers, using surface measurements, aerial photography, and repeat photography for comparisons between years.

HOW ARE THE GLACIERS MELTING?

As glaciers retreat, they fracture into patches, form lakes at their snouts, or split in two. In 1850, Sperry Glacier stretched across 960 acres, but today it covers less than one fourth that area. Likewise, 27 glaciers clustered over 5,300 acres in the Mount Jackson area; now 15 of those glaciers have disappeared, and those remaining broke into multiple pieces. Grinnell and Salamander Glaciers – once joined – split into two separate glaciers. In 1927, Grinnell Glacier's recession formed a lake, growing in size as the glacier receded. Within two decades of its onset, the lake ballooned to 20 acres and was named Upper Grinnell Lake, now nearing equal size with the shriveling glacier. Harrison Glacier, at 465 acres, is the largest, while Waterton and Two Medicine have no glaciers left.

WHAT WILL HAPPEN WHEN THE GLACIERS MELT?

Glacier's ecosystem will change, the most obvious being an increase in forest elevations. More trees aren't necessarily disastrous, but animals and birds, especially those living on the fringes of their habitat, may seek a food base elsewhere. Heat intolerant pikas, for instance, may not survive warmer temperatures. Water, which is seemingly so abundant, may not shed from the mountains in the same volume or at temperatures kept cool by the ice, threatening the survival of cold-loving bull trout and affecting irrigation and salmon runs. With more forests eventually come more fires.

Follow the ongoing study of Glacier's glaciers and see repeat photography at www. nrmsc.usgs.gov. Pick up the *Climate Change* flier at visitors centers and ranger stations for more information.

---

before leveling out into a gentle ascent around Mount Henkel. Just past Ptarmigan Falls at 2.8 miles, the Ptarmigan Tunnel route leaves the Iceberg Trail. From here, it climbs aggressively uphill for nearly a mile before assuming an easier uphill grade through meadows to Ptarmigan Lake.

From the lake, the route to the tunnel switchbacks another 800 feet up a scree slope. Tiny fragile alpine plants struggle to survive on this barren slope: protect them by staying on the trail rather than cutting switchbacks. The 183-foot tunnel (6 ft. wide by 9 ft. long) cuts through Ptarmigan Wall. Walk through for the burst of red rock greeting you on the other side. Admire the trail engineering along the north side's cliff wall and drop down a quarter mile to see Old Sun Glacier on Mount Merritt.

Belly River Ranger Station

- Distance: 12.6 miles round-trip
- Duration: 6 hours
- Elevation gain: 750 feet on return
- Effort: moderate
- Trailhead: Chief Mountain Customs parking lot on Chief Mountain Highway

A trail used by backpackers to access Elizabeth, Helen, Cosley, Glenns, and Mokowanis Lakes, Ptarmigan Tunnel, and Stoney Indian Pass, the Belly River Trail attracts day hikers more for the views en route of Chief Mountain and Pyramid Peak in the distance. Anglers also drop lines into the Belly River. The trail begins with a descent down to the valley floor. Look for scratches in the aspen bark where elk have rubbed to remove the velvet from their antlers.

As the trail undulates gently across the valley floor, it traverses aspen groves and open meadows blooming with lupine and paintbrush. At the pastoral Belly River Ranger Station, listed on the National Register of Historic Places, you can envy the backcountry rangers who spend their summers staring at Gable Mountain's colorful strata, the spires of the Stoney Indian Peaks, and Mount Cleveland, the highest peak in the park.

Guides

In Many Glacier and St. Mary, options abound for guided hikes. The National Park Service leads hikes to various scenic destinations mid-June–mid-September, including full-day hikes to Grinnell Glacier and Iceberg Lake in Many Glacier. Some trips combine with boat tours to cross Swiftcurrent and Josephine Lakes. Although park naturalist hikes are free, you'll need to pay for the boat. The park's guided hikes are great for solo hikers to be in the company of others in bear country and to glean tidbits of natural history, but be prepared for hiking in very large groups—some upwards of 30 people midsummer. For schedules, pick up a copy of *Ranger-Led Activities* from the visitors centers, online (www.nps.gov/glac), at ranger stations, or hotel activity desks. For full-day hikes, pack along water, snacks, lunch, and extra clothes.

Glacier Guides (406/387-5555 or 800/521-7238, www.glacierguides.com) lead several types of day-hiking trips. While solo travelers can hook up with their Tuesday Hikes ($75 per person, July–Aug.) and Group Day Hikes ($375, 1–5 people, June–Sept.), those depart from their West Glacier office, more than two hours away. Their Custom Day Hikes ($450, up to five people) will depart from your lodge or campground in St. Mary or Many Glacier. Many of their favorite day hikes are in Many Glacier. All hikes require reservations and include guide service, deli lunch, and transportation to the trailhead. You bring a day pack with extra clothes, water bottle, bug spray, and sunscreen. The company also has three-, four-, and six-day backpacking trips that depart weekly

($140 per day, June–mid-Sept.)—some via St. Mary and Many Glacier trailheads and frequently in The Belly.

BIKING

Bicycling the east side of Glacier Park is relegated to road biking as trails do not permit mountain bikes. No bike rentals are available, so bring your own.

St. Mary and Many Glacier park service campgrounds provide shared biker-hiker campsites on a first-come, first-served basis for $5 per person. The sites have bear-resistant food storage containers and are held daily until 9 P.M. for cyclists.

Going-to-the-Sun Road

Bicyclists riding on Going-to-the-Sun Road have no restrictions heading westbound until reaching Sprague Creek Campground on the west side. Due to heavy traffic during July and August, riding earlier or later in the day is easier on the narrow, shoulderless road. See the *Going-to-the-Sun Road* chapter for details.

Blackfeet Highway

Cycling the Blackfeet Highway (Highway 89) from the Canadian border to St. Mary is easier than pedaling other roads in the area. The undulating road is wider, straighter, and has at least a bit of a shoulder. However, the wide-open space means only one thing—high winds. Expect strong easterlies. If you're heading the right direction, it will be a nice tailwind. Otherwise, you'll be cursing under your breath as you push against its bluster.

Riding south from St. Mary to East Glacier on Highway 89, however, is a different story. A wide thoroughfare with big shoulders climbs atop St. Mary Ridge, luring you into breathing comfortably with the width in spite of the huffing climb. But atop the ridge, the spacious road suddenly squeezes into a narrow, curvy ribbon with blind corners and little place to go when large vehicles hog the road. From a cycling perspective, it's a fun ride with the rolling terrain, but you'll find yourself nearly steering off the road while watching for vehicles coming up behind you. Blind corners have a tendency to make riders brake for safety and then curse the loss of momentum. To avoid the heavier midsummer traffic, ride early or late in the day. Since the highway is open range, be prepared to encounter cow pies and brake; you may round a corner into cattle.

Many Glacier Road

Bicycling Many Glacier Road is extremely picturesque. However, keep at least one eye on the road for potholes, cattle grates, and a few short gravel sections. Also, be prepared for possible bear encounters, especially early or late in the day. While riding this road, some cyclists even whoop or holler to make noise to alert bears to their presence. With bears capable of running up to 40 mph, you won't be able to outbike a bear, so muster up all your bear-country savvy when riding here.

HORSEBACK RIDING

Adjacent to the Many Glacier Hotel parking lot, **Swan Mountain Outfitters** (406/732-4203 or 877/888-5557 summer, 800/919-4416 winter, www.swanmountainoutfitters.com, early June–late Sept., $40–160) guides one- and two-hour rides departing several times daily for Josephine Lake and Cracker Flats. Half-day rides leave twice daily for Grinnell Lake's milky blue waters or Swiftcurrent Ridge. All-day rides (lunch not included) head through aspen parklands and wildflower meadows to Poia Lake or Cracker Lake. Be aware that this is trail riding; the nose of one horse will be in the tail of another—sometimes in a long string of 15 horses. This is not the horse riding of the movies where you're galloping across Montana's prairies. However, the scenery is well worth a ride. Wear long pants and hiking boots or tennis shoes for these rides. Unfortunately, kids under eight are not allowed. Reservations are highly recommended.

In St. Mary, **Wounded Bear Trail Rides** (Hwy. 2 across from St. Mary Resort gas station, 406/450-5739, $50–145) guides horseback rides on the Blackfeet Reservation.

BOATING

Powerboating is restricted in Many Glacier. The public boat dock on **Swiftcurrent Lake** sits adjacent to the picnic area, but no motorized boats are allowed on the lake. Sans motors, only sailboats, kayaks, rowboats, and canoes ply the waters quietly. **St. Mary Lake** permits motorized craft with no horsepower limit as well as nonmotorized boats such as canoes, kayaks, rowboats, and rafts. The boat launch sits at Rising Sun. Boating regulations in Glacier Park require motorized vehicles to have free permits. Boaters must show that their boats have been cleaned, drained, and dried to avoid bringing Aquatic Invasive Species into park lakes. Permits for up to 14 days are available at the St. Mary Visitor Center.

On the Blackfeet Reservation, you can launch onto **Lower St. Mary Lake** via the public boat ramp at Chewing Blackbones Campground (milepost 37.3 on Highway 89). It's no longer a campground, but you can still access the boat ramp. Boating is also allowed on the reservation at **Duck Lake,** at milepost 29 on Duck Lake Road (Highway 464). Both lakes require a $20 Blackfeet recreation label, which you can purchase at St. Mary KOA (103 West Shore, 406/732-4122) or Montana's Duck Lake Lodge (milepost 32 on Duck Lake Rd., 406/338-5770) to affix to your boat. If you plan on fishing, your boat label is included in your tribal fishing permit.

No motorized boat rentals are available in St. Mary, Rising Sun, or Many Glacier. However, on Swiftcurrent Lake at the boat dock behind Many Glacier Hotel, **Glacier Park Boat Company** (406/732-4480 summers only, 406/257-2426, www.glacierparkboats.com, early June–mid-Sept.) rents rowboats for $18 per hour. Bring cash; no credit cards are accepted.

KAYAKING AND CANOEING

High east-side winds deter many kayakers and canoers from the larger lakes. Instead, most paddlers head to more protected waters, such as Many Glacier's smaller lakes that are less prone to kicking up big whitecaps. A popular kayak

© BECKY LOMAX

Rent boats at Many Glacier Hotel to paddle Swiftcurrent Lake.

trip crosses **Swiftcurrent Lake** and paddles the connecting slow-moving Cataract Creek upstream to Lake Josephine, where a shoreline loop makes a wonderfully scenic tour. Launch this tour from the public boat dock adjacent to Swiftcurrent Picnic Area.

Rent canoes and kayaks at the boat dock behind the Many Glacier Hotel. **Glacier Park Boat Company** (406/732-4480 summers only, 406/257-2426, www.glacierparkboats.com, mid-June–mid-Sept., $15–18 per hour) rents boats for use on Swiftcurrent Lake. Paddles and lifejackets are included. Bring cash; no credit cards are accepted.

FISHING

Glacier's east side is more noted more for lake fishing than streams or rivers. Glacier's Red Eagle Lake has yielded state record trout, and Duck Lake on the Blackfeet Reservation claims a reputation for world-class fishing.

Inside Glacier, no license is required for fishing, although you must be aware of fishing regulations (for details, see the

Background chapter). Outside park boundaries, visitors on the Blackfeet Reservation need a tribal fishing permit ($20–65), which may be purchased at St. Mary KOA (103 West Shore, 406/732-4122) or Duck Lake Lodge (milepost 32 on Hwy. 464, 406/338-5770, www.ducklakelodge.com).

St. Mary

St. Mary Lake doesn't support much in the way of good fishing with its raging winds. But it does have lake whitefish, brook trout, and rainbows. For better fishing, head instead to St. Mary River's deep channels below the lake for rainbow trout. The best local fishing requires a 7.5-mile hike to **Red Eagle Lake;** here a 16-pound state record native westslope cutthroat was caught. Those with a serious commitment and willpower hike in float tubes.

Many Glacier

With its number of lakes, the Many Glacier Valley offers lots of fishing holes. Grinnell, Josephine, Swiftcurrent, Red Rocks, Bullhead,

Windmaker, and Ptarmigan Lakes all support varying trout populations, but don't be deceived into carrying your rod to Iceberg, Upper Grinnell, or Poia Lakes, which have no fish. Cracker and Slide Lakes are closed to fishing. Sherburne Lake—a dam-controlled reservoir partly on tribal lands and partly in the park—supports northern pike. Cataract Creek between Josephine and Swiftcurrent Lakes contains brookies, but other creeks in the area don't offer much.

Those willing to heft a backpack should hike through Ptarmigan Tunnel or from Chief Mountain Customs into **The Belly.** Pools and riffles along the Belly and Mokowanis Rivers, plus Elizabeth, Cosley, Glenns, and Mokowanis Lakes, provide endless angling for arctic grayling and trout.

◖ Duck Lake

Outside the park boundary, the Blackfeet Reservation houses Duck Lake (milepost 29 on Highway 464), attracting serious lake anglers year-round. One can easily spend a day of catch-and-release, pulling eight-pound rainbow trout from its waters. Some anglers commonly catch 10–12 pounders, and a rainbow or brown trout may reach 15 pounds! Although you can keep the fish from this tribally stocked and managed fishery, you may find your fishing over within an hour or so if you don't throw some back. The fishing is better from a boat or a float tube: Motorized boats are allowed with a 10 mph speed limit, and lots of float tubers launch from shore. In winter, the lake permits ice fishing. The lake is surrounded by tribal and private land; be conscious of private property.

WATERSKIING

Waterskiing is not a big sport on Glacier's east side. But for diehards, waterskiing is permitted on both Upper and Lower St. Mary Lake; however, brisk winds and cold waters inhibit the activity for most. All folks choosing to water-ski here wear wetsuits or drysuits, as the water is extremely cold. On **Lower St. Mary Lake,** the public boat launch is at Chewing Blackbones Campground (milepost 37.3 on Highway 89). For Lower St.

Mary, a tribal recreation permit ($10 per year per person) and boat permit ($20 per year) are required for waterskiing. Purchase the permits at St. Mary KOA (103 West Shore, 406/732-4122). Duck Lake does not permit waterskiing.

SAILBOARDING

Because St. Mary Lake kicks up good winds, it attracts a few skilled sailboarders, launching from Rising Sun Picnic Area. (See the *Going-to-the-Sun Road* chapter for details.) Most serious sailboarders head instead for **Duck Lake** (seven miles north of St. Mary and three miles up Duck Lake Road #464), where winds blow more consistently—usually in the afternoon—and waters are warmer. Be conscious of private property surrounding much the shoreline. Tribal recreation permits ($10 per person per year and $20 per sailboard per year) are required for sailboarding; purchase them at Duck Lake Lodge (milepost 32 on Hwy. 464, 406/338-5770, www.ducklakelodge.com).

ENTERTAINMENT
Park Naturalist Programs

Evening programs about natural history and wildlife are presented by park naturalists in Many Glacier Hotel, Many Glacier Campground Amphitheater, and St. Mary Visitor Center during summer. The free 45-minute programs run nightly at 8 P.M. in Many Glacier Hotel and the campground amphitheater, and at 7:30 P.M. at St. Mary Visitor Center. Indoor programs include slide shows; outdoor programs feature park naturalists.

◖ Native America Speaks

For more than two decades, Glacier's naturalist programs have included the extremely well-liked Native America Speaks program. Once a week, the free 45-minute campground evening amphitheater shows feature members of the Blackfeet, Salish, and Kootenai tribes. Speakers use storytelling, humor, and music to share their culture and heritage. You'll walk away with a new appreciation of Glacier's Native American history.

Two acclaimed Native American programs

ON STAGE WITH NATIVE AMERICANS

During summer months, Native Americans feature their talents around Glacier Park. Look for shows in park lodges, at campground amphitheaters, and in various Flathead Valley venues.

Renowned storytellers of the Blackfeet, Salish, and Kootenai tribes share stories and legends from their history in the **Native America Speaks** program, free 45-minute presentations. You can catch the Native America Speaks series at the Apgar, Many Glacier, Rising Sun, and Two Medicine campground amphitheaters and Lake McDonald Lodge. Check *Ranger-Led Activities* newspaper for the current times and days.

An award-winning and Grammy-nominated singer, songwriter, and storyteller, **Jack Gladstone** combines music and slides to create a narrative weaving Native American tradition with current cultural history. Gladstone packages a unique vision that gives insight into Blackfeet roots and Glacier's roots as sacred tribal land. Look for his **Native Anthropology** (adults $5, kids 12 and under $2) performances at Many Glacier Hotel and Lake McDonald Lodge; check *Ranger-Led Activities* newspaper for showtimes and dates.

At St. Mary Visitor Center, the **Two Medicine Lake Singers and Dancers** give a glimpse into Blackfeet heritage. Dancers in full regalia perform traditional dances as well as jingle, fancy, and grass dances – each with different footwork, body movement, and regalia. For the finale, visitors can join in their Round Dance. This show packs out, so buy your tickets early (adults $5, kids 12 and under free). Check *Ranger-Led Activities* for current showtimes and dates.

draw standing-room-only crowds. At St. Mary Visitor Center's auditorium, the **Two Medicine Lake Singers and Dancers** demonstrate Blackfeet dances in full traditional regalia once a week during the summer. Tickets go fast for this popular show. At Many Glacier Hotel, Jack Gladstone, a Blackfeet, presents his multimedia *Legends of Glacier* show, blending slides, storytelling, and music into a walk through Glacier's history from the Blackfeet perspective. For showtimes and days, pick up the current copy of *Ranger-Led Activities* at visitors centers or check online: www.nps/gov/glac. Tickets (adults $5, kids 12 and under free) for both shows help support the Native America Speaks program.

David Walburn Programs

Montana singer-songwriter-guitarist David Walburn (adults $8, kids six and under free) performs multimedia shows Monday–Saturday in Many Glacier Hotel at 9 P.M. He entertains with live folk music, scenic photography, and stories in a series of rotating 90-minute shows. Celebrate the west's most famous explorers and their epic trip with Walburn's outstanding narrative *Lewis and Clark: West for America,* or catch his re-creation of homesteading in Alaska in *Cabin Song,* or the colorful regional history with *Montana: Life Under the Big Sky.* Check the sign in the hotel lobby for a current schedule.

Accommodations

St. Mary has access to Going-to-the-Sun Road and a modern luxury hotel; Many Glacier has location. While St. Mary is convenient for exploring Logan Pass and taking day trips to Many Glacier, Waterton, and Two Medicine, Many Glacier is the best place to be smack in the heart of hiking country. You can park the car for a few days without getting back in it. In both locations, that 7 percent Montana bed tax will still find its way to your bill.

ST. MARY

The headliner lodge at the east portal of Going-to-the-Sun Road, **(** **St. Mary Lodge and Resort** (junction of Hwy. 89 and Going-to-the-Sun Rd., 406/732-4431 or 800/368-3689, www.stmarylodgeandresort.com, May–Sept.) is the biggest complex in town, with 122 rooms. Rooms span both sides of the highway, with audible road noise in some. After

Stay in a luxury tepee at St. Mary Lodge and Resort.

the resort changed ownership in 2007 to the Delaware North Company, reviews have not been as favorable as they once were. Although the resort surrounds itself mostly with parking lots rather than natural grounds, it provides convenience with shopping, restaurants, cafés, and a bar as part of the complex adjacent to the park entrance. Portions of the resort have access to high-speed Internet.

Five different lodging options run from family accommodations to luxury ($119–399 per night). The three-story, 48-roomed **Great Bear Lodge,** built in 2001, contains modern hotel comforts of satellite televisions, air-conditioning, and wet bars, as well as the sound of the creek and private decks with stunning views from the top floor. The lodge's 13 suites also include fireplaces and Jacuzzis. Pricey 700-square-foot **tepees** standing 27 feet tall include queen beds, cedar wood floors, and private bathrooms with Jacuzzis. Tepees do not have doors that lock nor electricity. Less-pricey rooms cluster in the resort's older lodges and smaller cabins. Upgraded rooms in the **West Lodge** include satellite television and air-conditioning. Older **East Lodge** rooms do not have either. The small, cozy **Glacier Cabins** each have kitchenettes and are great for families.

Located 2.5 miles north of St. Mary, the **Glacier Trailhead Cabins** (milepost 34.4 on Hwy. 89, 406/732-4143 or 800/311-1041, www.glaciertrailheadcabins.com, mid-May–mid-Oct. $130–150) are quiet, removed from the bustle of town, and set back from the highway in aspens. The 12 spartan, smoke-free knotty pine log cabins built in 1999 maintain a silence without televisions, Internet, and phones (a guest phone is available in the office). Each cabin has one or two queen beds with a private bathroom, electric heat, and a porch with a mountain view; one cabin is wheelchair accessible. Cook your own dinner at the community outdoor grill, where a covered kitchen area has sinks, a stove, picnic tables, and running water. St. Mary restaurants are five minutes away by car.

© BECKY LOMAX

ST. MARY AND MANY GLACIER

Two lodging options sit on a bluff above St. Mary with views into the park, where a five-minute walk connects to restaurants and shopping. The **Red Eagle Motel** (above Hwy. 89 just 0.5 mile north of Going-to-the-Sun Rd. and Hwy. 89 junction, 406/732-4453, May–Oct., $100–125) has the cheapest rooms in town. Its 23 rooms are plain, tiny, and old, but with Napi Point views. The third-generation family-owned **Johnson's of St. Mary** (0.5 mile north of Going-to-the-Sun Rd. and Hwy. 89 junction, 406/732-5565, www.johnsonsofstmary.com, May–late Sept.) rents a few cabins, a modular home, and rooms. None have phones, Internet, or TVs. Rates start around $150 per night. Johnson's Café is right next door.

Eight miles northeast of St. Mary, **Montana's Duck Lake Lodge** (milepost 32 on Hwy. 464, 406/338-5770, www.ducklakelodge.com, open year-round, $99–199) is a family-owned lodge mostly attracting anglers, hunters, and snowmobilers, with Duck Lake one mile away and access to local Native American hunting and fishing guides. The rooms are simple: two twin beds with a shared bathroom and shower down the hall to a queen bed with in-room bathroom. West-facing rooms have views of Glacier. A great room has a guest phone, satellite television, fireplace, restaurant, and bar.

MANY GLACIER

❮ **Many Glacier Hotel** (milepost 11.5 on Many Glacier Rd., 406/892-2525, www.glacierparkinc.com, mid-June–mid-Sept., $142–285 double) is the most popular of the park's historic lodges due to its stunning setting. Sitting on Swiftcurrent Lake with access to activities from boating and trail riding to red bus and boat tours, the nonsmoking lodge centers around its massive four-storied lobby, with a large fireplace. The hotel rooms and suites facing lakeside stare at the Continental Divide's peaks. East-side rooms get the sunrise, with a unique morning wake-up as the horses jangle to the corral.

From being the "Showplace of the Rockies," the hotel slipped into disrepair, prompting Congress to fork over funds to renovate the

Many Glacier Hotel sits on Swiftcurrent Lake.

National Historic Landmark. An extensive five-year rehabilitation straightened the structure, repaired decks, and replaced windows. But bathrooms are small—many created from the original closets—with tiny sinks and skinny shower stalls. Some rooms have old-fashioned claw-foot tubs. The rooms have phones, but no television, Internet, air-conditioning, or elevator access—even up to the fourth floor. A restaurant, lounge, convenience store, and gift shop are on-site. When the hotel opened in 1915, it was considered the epitome of luxury; today, that is hardly the case, but what the hotel lacks in amenities it makes up for in historical ambience, unbelievable scenery, and convenience to trailheads. Trails to Cracker Lake, Grinnell Lake, Piegan Pass, and Grinnell Glacier depart from the hotel. Other trails depart from Swiftcurrent, one mile away. Early reservations are mandatory at this prized location, especially for summer 2011, when the north half of the hotel—including half of the 214 rooms—will be closed for further renovation by the park service.

At Many Glacier Road's terminus, **Swiftcurrent Motor Inn** (end of Many Glacier Rd., 406/892-2525, www.glacierparkinc.com, early June–late Sept., $89–136 with private bath, $68–79 without bath) has austere cabins and a single-story motel. Units come with or without baths. For those without, a central comfort station and shower house awaits. It's similar to camping, especially with the lukewarm to cold shower, but with a bed, heat, walls, and a roof for inclement weather. The nonsmoking rooms have no televisions, air-conditioning, Internet, or in-room phones. Pay phones are outside the camp store; the complex also has a laundry and restaurant. Historic charm isn't the lure, but rather its price and utter convenience. Trailheads for Red Rocks and Bullhead Lakes, Granite Park Chalet, Swiftcurrent Pass and Lookout, Iceberg Lake, and Ptarmigan Tunnel depart from the inn.

CAMPING

While Many Glacier has only one park service campground with no hookups, St. Mary has both commercial campgrounds and a park service campground. The commercial campgrounds have flush toilets, hot showers, picnic tables, and hookups for electric, water, and sewer (and will add a 7 percent state tax to your bill), while the in-park campgrounds are limited to flush toilets, dump stations, picnic tables, fire rings with grills, and running water. Bring your own firewood for the park service campgrounds; collecting it is illegal within the park. If the park service campgrounds fill up, head to a commercial one in St. Mary rather than up Going-to-the-Sun Road to Rising Sun, which usually fills up first. In September after the campground water is turned off, you can camp primitively ($10, pit toilets only) through late October.

St. Mary is convenient for exploring Going-to-the-Sun Road, and it works as a home base for day trips to Waterton, Many Glacier, and Two Medicine. However, if you envision parking the car, setting up a tent for a couple days, and hiking straight from the campground, then Many Glacier is where you need to be.

St. Mary

Inside Glacier Park, ◖ **St. Mary Campground** (milepost 0.9 on Going-to-the-Sun Rd., 406/888-7800, late May–late Sept., $23) has 183 sites—some in open meadows, others tucked between aspens. For the best views, the C loop sites stare at Divide and Red Eagle mountains, but in August heat, they can be hot. The campground can fit RVs up to 35 feet in 25 sites. Reservations here are highly recommended through the National Park Service Reservation System (877/444-6777, www.recreation.gov). This campground also opens late April–May for primitive camping ($10). A trail crosses St. Mary River on a wooden bridge to connect with the visitors center, St. Mary's restaurants, shuttles, and shops but has no access to St. Mary Lake.

Away from the hubbub of St. Mary and one mile down a paved road, **St. Mary KOA** (106 West Shore, 406/732-4122 or 800/562-1504, www.goglacier.com, May–Sept., tents $28–32, RV hookups $39–60, cabins $66–400) sits on the St. Mary River and Lower St. Mary Lake in a huge meadow where elk often browse. Open, with views of surrounding peaks, the campground has little shade and can be quite windy, but it has the only swimming pool in the area. It rents canoes, kayaks, and paddleboats; mountain bikes; and cars for driving Going-to-the-Sun Road—a great option for RVers whose rigs are too big. In addition to the usual commercial campground amenities, it has a grocery store, espresso, outdoor hot tubs, splash park, putting green, laundry, gift shop, free Wi-Fi, playground, and the A-OK Grille (June–August), which serves sourdough pancake breakfasts and pizza.

Sitting atop a bluff with premium RV sites that have a gorgeous view of Glacier, the older **Johnson's Campground** (0.5 mile north of Going-to-the-Sun Rd. and Hwy. 89 junction, 406/732-4207, www.johnsonsofstmary. com, late Apr.–late Sept.) sprawls in a grassy setting broken up by chattering aspens just above St. Mary. With 75 tent sites ($25) plus 82 RV sites with hookups ($29–45)—some with fire rings—the campground can usually accommodate latecomers when park service campgrounds are full. The bathrooms are old. Amenities include a camp store, laundry, dump station, and 18-hole mini golf. Restaurants and shops in St. Mary are a five-minute walk away.

Many Glacier

At the end of Many Glacier Road in the park, **C Many Glacier Campground** (406/888-7800, late May–late Sept., $20 per site) packs 110 shaded sites into a treed setting at the base of Grinnell Point. Because of the popularity of its location, it fills up by early morning in midsummer. Plan to arrive by 11 A.M. to claim a site, as they are all first come, first serve. Thirteen sites can accommodate RVs up to 35 feet. Nearby trails depart for Red Rocks, Bullhead, and Iceberg Lakes as well as Ptarmigan Tunnel and Swiftcurrent Pass. From the picnic area, a five-minute walk down the road, trails depart to Josephine and Grinnell Lakes, Grinnell Glacier, and Piegan Pass. Across the parking lot at Swiftcurrent Motor Inn, you have access to a restaurant, laundry, hot showers, and a camp store. If bears frequent the campground, tent camping may be restricted, with only hard-sided vehicles allowed. Check www.nps.gov/glac or 406/888-7800 for status.

Backcountry Camping

From St. Mary, you can catch a series of backcountry campsites on the Continental Divide Trail to Cut Bank and Two Medicine. The most popular campsites sit on both ends of **Red Eagle Lake,** a fishing mecca. Hikers then continue southward over Triple Divide Pass to **Atlantic Creek** or farther on to **Morningstar Lake.** The first campground is buggy in thick doghair timber, but the lake tucks under sunrise-catching cliffs housing mountain goats and a golden eagle nest.

Most of Many Glacier's spur valleys are reserved for day hiking only; however, **Cracker Lake** campground sits on a bluff above a turquoise lake at the base of Mount Siyeh's monstrous face. North of Many Glacier via Ptarmigan Tunnel, The Belly houses seven gorgeous lakeshore backcountry campgrounds. **Elizabeth, Helen,** and **Cosley** are the most popular, but all offer outstanding scenery and good fishing. Accessing the same lakes, the trail from Chief Mountain Customs leads first to **Gable Campground,** hidden in aspens and surrounded by wildflower meadows near the Belly River Ranger Station.

Pick up permits ($5 per person per night, kids 8–15 $2.50, kids 7 and under free) at Many Glacier Ranger Station, St. Mary Visitor Center, or the Apgar Permit Office (406/888-7900). Permits must be picked up in person 24 hours in advance. A limited number can be reserved beginning in mid-April ($30). Check additional requirements online: www.nps.gov/glac.

Food

Because Many Glacier has only two restaurants, locals staying here for several days will drive to Babb (12 miles away) or St. Mary (21 miles away) to hit their favorite eateries. Nothing beats driving back in to Many Glacier at sunset, with ample opportunities for wildlife-watching. Be aware that restaurants and grocery stores in Babb and St. Mary do not serve alcohol during Indian Days, a reservation-wide four-day celebration beginning the second Thursday in July. Other select days also prohibit alcohol sales, such as graduation in June. Because of their location in the park rather than on the reservation, the restaurants in Many Glacier can still serve alcohol on those days.

RESTAURANTS
St. Mary

Located in St. Mary Lodge and Resort (junction of Going-to-the-Sun Rd. and Hwy. 89, 406/732-4431 or 800/368-3689, www.st-marylodgeandresort.com, May–Sept.), the

Snowgoose Grille is the resort's headliner restaurant. Overlooking Divide Creek, the dining room (7 A.M.–10 P.M. daily) serves breakfast ($5–14), lunch ($9–15), and dinner ($16–40 for entrées). Reservations are advised for dinner midsummer. Dinner specialties feature bison, elk, beef, and chicken. The whitefish comes from Lower St. Mary Lake. Those looking for a less-expensive option can order lunch and dinner in the **Lobby Bar,** or on warm days sit on the deck overlooking Divide Creek to watch the sunset. Try, if you dare, one of the martini concoctions—the Montini with chocolate or the Huckletini with huckleberry-infused vodka.

Also in the resort, **Curly Bear Café** (junction of Going-to-the-Sun Rd. and Hwy. 89, 406/732-4431, May–Sept., 11 A.M.–7 P.M. daily, $4–20) is the best place to take the kids, as it has the closest thing to a fast-food menu: buffalo burgers, pizza by the slice, and hand-scooped ice-cream cones. Try the gourmet

© BECKY LOMAX

The Park Café specializes in fresh-baked fruit pies.

house specialties—buffalo chicken or puttanesca pizza. During midsummer, hours for the pizza shop extend to 10 P.M. You can also order pizza to go.

The **■ Park Café** (0.2 mile north of Hwy. 89 and Going-to-the-Sun Rd. junction, 406/732-4482, late May–Sept., 7 A.M.–10 P.M. daily, shoulder season hours shorten) cranks out the best homemade fruit pies daily ($4.50 per slice). Try the triple berry or peach. If your heart is set on a particular pie, order it when you order dinner, in case they run out. The restaurant serves breakfast, lunch, and dinner with an eclectic menu all of its own: creative veggie meals, burgers, and Southwest style. Most items range $7–17. Be ready for long waiting lines midsummer, for they don't take reservations, and it's a favorite haunt of locals. No alcohol is served in the restaurant, but you can get a Moose Moss shake made with chocolate chunk mint ice cream.

Four miles north of St. Mary, in a bright purple building with the walls inside covered with license plates and bumper stickers, **Two Sisters Café** (milepost 36 on Hwy. 89, 406/732-5535, late May–early Sept., 11 A.M.–10 P.M. daily) serves up homemade fare, with big portions for lunch and dinner. Most menu items range $7–21, with Cajun grilled chicken dinners accompanied by corn on the cob and fresh baked bread. The Red burger is topped with bacon, cheese, grilled mushrooms and onions, and Creole sauce. Montana microbrews and margaritas are available, and monstrous ice-cream sandwiches for dessert.

For a throwback experience, **Johnson's World Famous Historic Restaurant** (a half mile north of Hwy. 89 and Going-to-the-Sun Rd. junction, 406/732-5565, www.johnsonsofstmary.com, late May–late Sept., 7 A.M.–9 P.M. daily, $7–20) serves up its daily specials family style. Located at Johnson's Resort of St. Mary, the small old-fashioned restaurant with red-checked tablecloths serves its eggs, bacon, and hash browns all on one big platter for the entire table. Lunch soup shows up in a large tureen; you ladle it yourself. Dinner features country foods, with fried chicken on Sunday. On

Sunday, lunch is replaced by the dinner menu starting at 11:30 A.M. No alcohol is served.

Babb

Not for vegetarians, the **Cattle Baron Supper Club** (junction of Hwy. 89 and Many Glacier Rd., 406/732-4033, or before 3 P.M. 406/732-4532, weekends only mid-May–mid-June, daily mid-June–Sept., 5–9 P.M.) is a steak palace. Up the log spiral staircase in the Babb Bar, once known as the roughest bar in Montana, the restaurant serves dinners ($16–32) where the baked potato isn't the biggest thing on the plate. Be ready to gorge, for steak cuts are humongous—16–20 ounces. Salads, grilled veggies, baked bread yanked from the oven, and potato accompanies most entrées. The log lodge gives tribute to Blackfeet history with painted wall stories and a sculpture of a buffalo jump. Make reservations for midsummer.

Many Glacier

Many Glacier has three nonsmoking options, all operated by the same concessionaire and open daily mid-June–mid-September. No reservations are accepted for any of them, so you may have to wait for a table in midsummer. Hiker lunches are available for $9; order them one day in advance.

In Many Glacier Hotel, the **■ Ptarmigan Dining Room** (milepost 11.6 on Many Glacier Rd., 406/892-2525) gains a reputation more for its views than its cuisine. The restaurant's massive two-story floor-to-ceiling windows look out on Swiftcurrent Lake, Grinnell Point, and Mount Wilbur. For the best views to watch bears, ask to sit near the north windows facing Altyn Mountain. Breakfast (6:30–10 A.M., $8–14) is a multitable spread of fruits, pastries, eggs, French toast, bacon, sausage, biscuits and gravy, and pancakes. While the buffet has selection and quantity to feed hikers carbo-loading for a long day, entrées are sometimes lukewarm, but you can get a waffle hot off the iron. The menu also has à la carte breakfasts. The dining hall is also open for lunch (11:30 A.M.–2 P.M., $8–13) and dinner (5–9:30 P.M., $16–27), which features chicken, fish, beef, pasta, and vegetarian entrées. In summer 2011, the dining room will be closed by the park service for renovation that will include removing the drop ceiling to restore the original railroad beams; however, the restaurant will accommodate diners in the neighboring dining room.

Grab lighter meals—appetizers, sandwiches, and burgers ($8–15)—in the **Swiss Room** lounge 11:30 A.M.–10 P.M. The traditional Swiss Après Fondue, featuring four cheese or chocolate ($18, serves two), may appear as an appetizer on the 2010 menu but will resume its 2–4 P.M. service in 2011 in the Interlaken Lounge.

At Swiftcurrent Motor Inn, **Italian Garden Ristorante** (milepost 12.5 on Many Glacier Rd., 406/892-2525) is open for breakfast (6:30–10 A.M. daily, $5–10), lunch (11:30 A.M.–2 P.M. daily, $8–13), and dinner (5–9:30 P.M. daily, $13–16). Breakfast is standard café fare; lunch and dinner menus include burgers, sandwiches, and pasta. Montana microbrews and wines are available, but no cocktails. It's popular for families and because of its convenient location near the campground.

CAFFEINE

Located in St. Mary Lodge, the **Glacier Perk** (junction of Going-to-the-Sun Rd. and Hwy. 89, May–Sept., 406/732-4431, 8 A.M.–8 P.M.) is the place to grab an espresso before driving over Going-to-the-Sun Road. If temperatures outside are too hot, order it iced. Many folks enjoy the huckleberry fudge, too, although it's incredibly sweet. In Many Glacier, get espresso drinks at **Heidi's Snack Shop** in the Many Glacier Hotel basement.

GROCERIES

In Many Glacier, you'll find only two options for groceries—both convenience-type stores open daily mid-June–mid-September. In the basement of Many Glacier Hotel, **Heidi's Snack Shop** (406/892-2525, 8 A.M.–9 P.M.) sells hot dogs, coffee, espresso, pop, snacks, newspapers, beer, wine, and other convenience-store items. Located across the parking lot from

Many Glacier Campground and adjacent to Swiftcurrent Motor Inn, the **Swiftcurrent Campstore** (milepost 12.5 on Many Glacier Rd., 406/892-2525, 7 A.M.–10 P.M.) carries groceries, camping and hiking supplies, T-shirts, gift items, newspapers, beer, wine, firewood, and ice. Hikers can put together lunches from either store.

In St. Mary, you can stock up on supplies at two grocery stores on Highway 89. The largest grocery store, but by no means a supermarket as its sign says, **Country Market** (open year-round, summers 7 A.M.–10 P.M. daily, off-season 9 A.M.–5 P.M. daily), is just south of the Going-to-the-Sun Road junction. It has fresh produce, a bakery, butcher shop, beer, wine, and some fishing supplies. The **Park Grocery and Gift Shop** (0.2 mile north of Hwy. 89 and Going-to-the-Sun Rd. junction, 406/732-4482, late May–Sept.) carries a great selection of Montana microbrews, along with convenience-store items and some groceries. During high season, hours are usually 7:30 A.M.–10 P.M., but the store will open a half hour later and close one hour earlier in early June and after Labor Day. Neither shop sells alcohol during Indian Days celebrations (second Thursday–Sunday in July).

Located in Babb, **Thronson's General Store** (0.2 mile north of Hwy. 89 and Many Glacier Rd. junction, 9 A.M.–6 P.M. daily in summer, weekdays only in winter) stocks convenience-store items but no beer or wine.

PICNICKING

Many Glacier's small picnic area (milepost 12.2 on Many Glacier Rd.) is a great place to sit with binoculars and scan for bears on Altyn Peak—even if you aren't picnicking. It's a popular picnic site and can be crowded in midsummer at lunchtime. If you want to roast marshmallows in one of the fire pits, bring your own firewood, because gathering wood is prohibited. The picnic area is also one of the trailheads for hiking to Lake Josephine, Grinnell Lake, Piegan Pass, and Grinnell Glacier.

TWO MEDICINE AND EAST GLACIER

Quiet and removed, Glacier's southeast corner harbors a less-traveled wonderland. It's away from the harried corridor of Going-to-the-Sun Road with its endless line of cars. With no hotel in Two Medicine, you'll find trails far less clogged on day hikes than at Many Glacier. Just because it sees fewer people, however, does not make it less dramatic. For many locals, it's their favorite park locale.

A string of three lakes curves through the Two Medicine Valley below Rising Wolf—a red hulking monolith. Its sheer mass is larger than any other peak in the park. Even though glaciers vacated this area within the past 150 years, their footprints are left in swooping valleys, blue-laked cirques, and toothy spires. Two Medicine Lake—the park's highest road-accessible lake, sitting a mile high in elevation—shimmers in a valley strewn with hiking trails.

Around the corner, the tiny burg of East Glacier buzzes in summer. Great Northern Railway's historic headliner hotel, Glacier Park Lodge, dominates the town with its immense Douglas fir lobby. Those coming by train taste the history as they step from the depot across a garden walkway to the hotel, framed by the mountains of Dancing Lady and Henry. Hiking, golf, Native American and red bus tours, horseback riding, and swimming delight guests. Yet at night, quiet stretches across the sky, broken only by the rumble of trains rolling by.

HISTORY

Two Medicine acquired its name from Blackfeet legends. According to one story, two

© BECKY LOMAX

HIGHLIGHTS

◖ Boat Tour: Hop on the historic *Sinopah* for the best way to see Two Medicine Lake. The boat has plied the waters here since 1927 and knows its way around (page 150).

◖ Looking Glass Hill-Browning Loop: Drive up the dramatic and sometimes scary Highway 49. The narrow, bumpy, curvy road lends stupendous views of Two Medicine Valley (page 153).

◖ Running Eagle Falls: Catch sight of water cascading from underground chutes. Named for Pitamakin, a Blackfeet woman warrior, the falls also has another name – Trick Falls (page 155).

◖ Glacier Park Lodge: Walk the gardens leading up to the front door of the headliner hotel for the historic chain of Great Northern park hostelries. Lounge in its massive lobby held up by three-story Douglas firs (page 155).

◖ Museum of the Plains Indian: Sample Blackfeet history and culture in Browning at this museum, crammed with intricate beadwork. Local artisan crafts also fill the gift shop (page 156).

◖ Scenic Point: Hike high above Two Medicine Lake to a top-of-the-world view. Stare across the plains to the Sweet Grass Hills, spy the tiny towns of East Glacier and Browning, and maybe if it's clear enough, you'll see Minneapolis (page 158).

◖ Dawson-Pitamakin Loop: Skitter on a narrow trail along the Continental Divide thousands of feet above blue lakes and green forested valleys. Bighorn sheep summer on the high passes here (page 159).

◖ North American Indian Days: Join the Blackfeet celebration for four days. Visitors are welcome at the colorful early July festival in Browning (page 164).

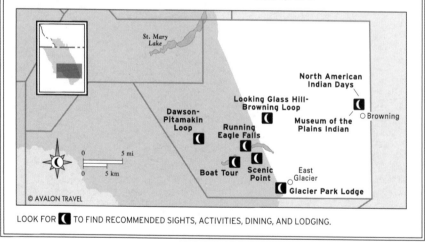

LOOK FOR ◖ TO FIND RECOMMENDED SIGHTS, ACTIVITIES, DINING, AND LODGING.

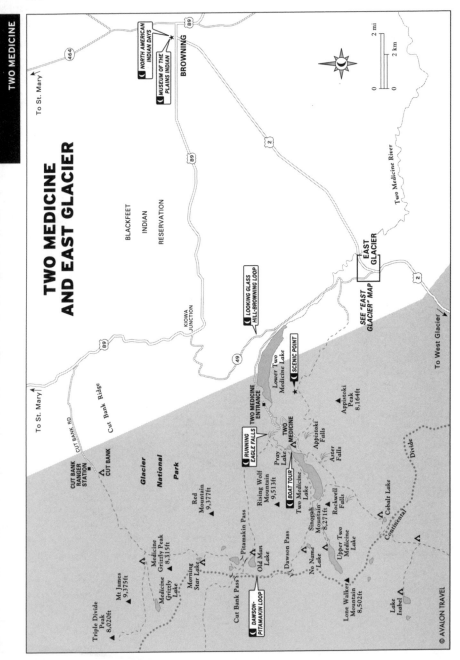

TWO MEDICINE AND EAST GLACIER

To St. Mary

464

89

NORTH AMERICAN INDIAN DAYS

MUSEUM OF THE PLAINS INDIAN

BROWNING

2

89

Two Medicine River

BLACKFEET

INDIAN

RESERVATION

KIOWA JUNCTION

49

LOOKING GLASS HILL-BROWNING LOOP

EAST GLACIER

SEE "EAST GLACIER" MAP

2

To West Glacier

To St. Mary

Cut Bank Ridge

CUT BANK RD.

CUT BANK RANGER STATION

▲ CUT BANK

Glacier

National

Park

Red Mountain
9,377ft ▲

Triple Divide Peak
8,020ft ▲

Mt James
9,375ft ▲

Medicine Grizzly Peak 8,315ft ▲

Medicine Grizzly Lake

Morning Star Lake

Pitamakin Pass

Rising Wolf Mountain
9,513ft ▲

Old Man Lake

Cut Bank Pass

DAWSON-PITAMAKIN LOOP

Dawson Pass

No Name Lake

Sinopah Mountain
8,271ft ▲

RUNNING EAGLE FALLS

Pray Lake

TWO MEDICINE ENTRANCE ▲

TWO MEDICINE ▲

Appistoki Falls

Aster Falls

Appistoki Peak
8,164ft ▲

Lower Two Medicine Lake

SCENIC POINT ★

BOAT TOUR

Two Medicine Lake

Rockwell Falls

Upper Two Medicine Lake

Lone Walker Mountain
8,502ft ▲

Cobalt Lake

Lake Isabel

Continental Divide

▲

▲

© AVALON TRAVEL

2 mi

2 km

0

0

Piegan tribes planned to meet for a medicine ceremony in the valley. Failing to find each other, they both celebrated independently. In another version, two lodges for the Sun Dance sat on either side of Two Medicine Creek. Either way, the name stuck.

The 1896 land sale between the Blackfeet and the federal government included the Two Medicine area. Starving and nearly decimated as a tribe, the Blackfeet swapped part of their reservation land from the Continental Divide to the current reservation boundary for $1.5 million—a mere pittance considering what the parklands are worth.

In April 1891, Great Northern Railway began laying tracks from Cut Bank to Midvale (East Glacier) and over Marias Pass toward West Glacier. As railroad developer James J. Hill sought means to increase ridership on his new line, he spawned a grand plan: a lodge to greet eastern guests first arriving to Glacier and several chalets sprinkled in the park's most scenic spots for places to tour. For early visitors debarking the train in Midvale in 1911, Two Medicine Lake was the first stop in Glacier's backcountry after a bumpy wagon ride. Originally a tepee enclave with canvas walls and wooden floors, the hugely successful camp prompted the railroad to add two log chalets—a dormitory and a dining hall. By 1915, guests arrived on horseback via trail, the first leg on the Inside Trail connecting to Cut Bank and St. Mary Chalets on Park Saddle Horse Company tours—a three-day trip costing $13.25.

In 1913, Great Northern's headliner hotel—the Glacier Park Lodge—finally welcomed arriving train guests, awed at the first glimpse of Glacier. Built on reservation land purchased from the Blackfeet, the posh lodge with a plunge pool in the basement erected its elegantly large lobby with 500- to 800-year-old Douglas firs sent from western Washington and Oregon. Rooms touted such high-class amenities as electric lights and steam heat. The nine-hole golf course followed 14 years later—on which employees were not allowed to play for fear of upsetting high-class tourists.

In 1929, Great Northern introduced the Empire Builder, named after J. J. Hill, as its modern train for the 2,200-mile Chicago–Seattle trip that packaged Glacier Park travel for its passengers. This is still the name for the Amtrak line here. It's the only U.S. train outside Alaska that stops regularly at a major national park.

In the wake of the Depression, World War II closures, and increasing auto traffic, the Two Medicine chalets met their demise and were torn down building by building until only the dining hall remained. It's now the Two Medicine store.

Exploring Two Medicine and East Glacier

ENTRANCE STATION

East Glacier sits outside park boundaries, but Two Medicine is within the park, with an entrance station location approximately four miles up Two Medicine Road. It is staffed during daylight hours seven days a week in the summer. During shoulder seasons, staffing reduces to weekends only or not at all, but you can use the self-pay cash-only kiosk. If you don't have an annual pass, seven-day passes cost $25 per vehicle or $12 for individuals on foot, bicycles, or motorcycles. Maps and the biannual *Waterton-Glacier Guide* are available.

Even though the Cut Bank Road enters the park, it lacks both an entrance station and self-pay kiosk.

RANGER STATIONS

The **Two Medicine Ranger Station** (406/888-7800, summers only, 8 A.M.–4:30 P.M. daily), at the terminus of Two Medicine Road at the campground junction, has current trail information and issues backcountry campsite permits. You can also pick up copies of *Ranger-Led Activities* for park naturalist programs, fishing information, and free nontopographical maps of trails in the area. The ranger station plots bear sightings on a large wall map worth a look just for bear trivia. The ranger station sells tribal conservation permits ($10 per person per year) for those hiking over Scenic Point to East Glacier. The **East Glacier Ranger Station** (824 Hwy. 49, 406/888-7800) houses a small year-round staff, but the station doesn't maintain public hours.

SHUTTLES AND TOURS
Shuttles
The hiker shuttle operated by **Glacier Park, Inc.** (406/892-2525, www.glacierparkinc.com, $10–50 one-way, kids half price) aids getting to trailheads. The east-side shuttle runs daily early June–late September, connecting East Glacier, Two Medicine, Cut Bank Road Junction, St. Mary, Many Glacier, and Waterton. Pay cash when you board. Shuttles heading to Two Medicine hook up with tour boat departure times. Ask for schedules at the hotel front desk. At St. Mary Visitor Center, riders can link into the free Going-to-the-Sun Road shuttles running July–Labor Day. No shuttle runs directly from East Glacier to West Glacier via Highway 2. For trailheads at Marias Pass, for instance, you must drive yourself or hitchhike, which is legal in Montana.

While in theory the shuttle is a great way to access trailheads, consider where you are and how long it will take you to get to Logan Pass—three hours. For the most efficient use of your time while staying in East Glacier, you're better off hiking in Two Medicine; then, move north to St. Mary or Many Glacier to hike trails in the park's core.

Flathead-Glacier Transportation (406/892-3390 or 800/829-7039) runs shuttles by reservation only between Glacier International Airport and East Glacier ($130 one-way for first person, $3 each additional person).

Bus Tours
Historic **Red Buses** (406/892-2525, www.glacierparkinc.com, adults $45–80, kids half price) depart from Glacier Park Lodge in East Glacier. Driven by storytelling jammer drivers who roll the canvas tops back when the weather permits, the vintage tour buses are not just a treat for their historic ambience, but for the whole-sky views. The eight-and-a-half-hour **Big Sky Circle Tour** (mid-June–mid-Sept.) packs in the best of the park for those who have limited time to explore all its corners. Departing daily, the tour travels over Marias Pass to Lake McDonald Lodge, then crosses Logan Pass on Going-to-the-Sun Road to St. Mary and back to the lodge. The three-hour **Two Medicine Tour** (late May–late Sept.) departs twice daily and includes a boat tour on Two Medicine Lake. For an excursion to Many Glacier and Waterton, the eight-and-a-half-hour **International Peace Park Tour** (early June–mid-Sept.) departs daily for Waterton Lakes National Park. Prices do not include meals or park entrance fees. Reservations are required and can be made by phone or at the hotel front desk.

Departing East Glacier daily at 8 A.M., **Sun Tours** (406/226-9220 or 800/786-9220, www.glaciersuntours.com, June–Sept., adults $70, kids $20, meals and park entrance fees not included) drives 25-passenger air-conditioned buses with extra-large windows to catch the big views on Going-to-the-Sun Road. Tours travel through St. Mary to Logan Pass and back. Led by local guides who live on the reservation, the eight-and-a-half-hour tour highlights Glacier's connection with the Blackfeet. You'll get to know the background of peak names as well as the cultural history of the park. The guides, most of whom are excellent storytellers, also know about plants, wildlife, and geology. Those staying in Browning can hop on the bus at 8:30 A.M. While last-minute spots are sometimes available on the day of the tour, reservations at least 24 hours in advance are best. Call or stop at the East Glacier office on Highway 2 across from the train depot.

◖ Boat Tour and Shuttle
The *Sinopah* (Glacier Park Boat Company, 406/257-2426, www.glacierparkboats.com,

© BECKY LOMAX

The *Sinopah* provides boat tours and shuttles hikers across Two Medicine Lake.

who runs the Lodgepole Tipi Village and Art Gallery in Browning, leads private **Blackfeet Cultural Historical Tours** (2.5 miles west on Hwy. 89, 406/338-2787, www.blackfeet-culturecamp.com, May–Sept.) to buffalo jumps and old tepee ring sites on the Blackfeet Reservation. He accompanies you in your car for a half-day tour that runs $100 for up to four people; full-day tours run $160. Additional participants cost $25 or $50 each. He also conducts art workshops.

SERVICES

Two Medicine has no gas station, but East Glacier has two: an Exxon at the Bear Track Travel Center at the east end of town on Highway 2 and Grizzly Gas on Highway 49 at the Sears Motel. Browning has several gas stations. ATMs are at Glacier Park Trading Company and Glacier Park Lodge. The post office is in East Glacier (15 Blackfoot Ave., 8:30 A.M.–noon and 1:30–5 P.M. weekdays only). The area's daily newspaper is the *Great Falls Tribune*.

A launderette is at Y Lazy R RV Park on Lindhe and Meade, and it offers coin-op showers available to drop-ins.

From May–September, you can rent cars in East Glacier through Dollar Rent-A-Car at **Sears Motel** (1023 Hwy. 49, 406/226-4432 or 800/800-4000, www.dollar.com) or Avis at **Two Medicine Grill** (316 Hwy. 2, 406/226-9227, or 800/230-4898, www.avis.com).

Cell Phones and Internet

Some cell phones have reception in East Glacier and Browning. No reception is available at Two Medicine. Internet access is available at Brownie's, Bear Track Travel Center, and a few motels.

Shopping

East Glacier has few gift shops, but not even a block full of shops to browse. But it is home to the unique **Spiral Spoon** (1012 Hwy. 49, www.thespiralspoon.com) that boasts the world's largest purple spoon and artfully hand-carved spoons made with different woods.

mid-June–early Sept., adults $11.25 round-trip, kids half price) started service on Two Medicine Lake in 1927 and has never left its waters. The 45-foot, 49-passenger wooden boat cruises uplake four times daily for 45-minute tours (10:30 A.M. and 1, 3, and 5 P.M.) while the captain narrates a little history, trivia, and natural phenomena. Two launches daily also incorporate a short, guided hike to Twin Falls (0.9 mile one-way). For July–August, the boat company adds on a 9 A.M. hiker express. Purchase tickets (cash only) at the boat dock. To shorten the 10-mile round-trip Upper Two Medicine Lake hike to four miles, catch the boat both directions. For a three-mile jaunt, hike one-way along the northern lakeshore through avalanche gullies under Rising Wolf's flanks and hop the boat back. You can pay (cash only) for one-way return rides upon boarding. At the end of the day, the boat retrieves all hikers waiting at the upper dock, even with extra trips.

Blackfeet Reservation Tours

Darrell Norman, a Blackfeet tribal member

BLACKFEET NATION

Bordering Glacier National Park on the east side, Blackfeet tribal lands extend from the Canadian border to south of East Glacier, covering 1.5 million acres. About half of the tribe's 15,000 members live on the reservation.

Originally from north of the Great Lakes, the Blackfeet are related by language to the Algonquin tribes. As Europeans landed in North America in the 1600s, the Blackfeet were one of the first tribes to move westward, adopting a nomadic lifestyle hunting buffalo in Saskatchewan, Alberta, and Montana. Small bands, each led by a chief, met for summer medicine lodge or sun dance rituals and separated for winter.

The loose Blackfeet Confederacy contained three tribes: The **North Blackfeet** and **Bloods** gravitated into Alberta, and the **Piegan** to Montana. All three hunted using buffalo jumps, lighting fires to stampede bison over a cliff. ("Siksika," or Blackfeet, may have referred to moccasins ash-darkened from these prairie fires.) When the Blackfeet acquired horses in the 1700s from the Kootenai, Flathead, and Nez Perce and guns from French fur traders, their hunting methods altered.

The 1800s brought devastating misery to the Blackfeet. A smallpox epidemic in 1837 killed 6,000 people, wiping out two thirds of the population. Buffalo herds declined, leading to Starvation Winter in 1884, claiming the lives of 600 Blackfeet. By midcentury, the first treaty with the U.S. government defined Blackfeet territory as two thirds of eastern Montana, starting at the Continental Divide. White settlers arrived, rankling the Blackfeet who raided settlements. To squelch hostilities, the U.S. Army sent Colonel E. M. Baker in 1870 to eradicate the raid leader Mountain Chief. But Baker mistakenly attacked Heavy Runner's peaceful tribe, slaughtering 200 and capturing 140 women and children.

Tribal leaders, desperate to help their destitute people, bargained with the U.S. government for their survival. They sold off portions of the reservation in trade for tools, equipment, and cattle. Glacier Park, from the Continental Divide to the eastern boundary, was one of these trades – purchased by the U.S. government for a mere $1.5 million in 1896.

Today, the Blackfeet economy is based on some cattle ranching, but 90 percent of the tribe's income depends on oil and gas extraction. Browning, the center of Blackfeet culture, houses the small but outstanding **Museum of the Plains Indian,** which chronicles their history and displays amazing beadwork. In July, the tribe celebrates **North American Indian Days,** hosting regional tribes for the four-day powwow that includes rodeos, games, dancing, traditional costumes, singing, and drumming (406/338-7521, www.blackfeetnation.com).

East Glacier is on the Blackfeet Reservation.

Those seeking Native American art should stop in Browning at the **Blackfeet Heritage Center and Art Gallery** (333 Central Ave., 406/338-5661, www.blackfeetnationstore.com, 9 A.M.–6 P.M. daily), which houses the works of more than 500 artists and craftspeople. You can find beadwork, jewelry, paintings, sculptures, rawhide, and buffalo hides and skulls.

Water

Since East Glacier draws its water from surface sources, both East Glacier and Browning struggle with water quality. When bacteria get into the water, all water must be boiled (five minutes) before drinking. To be safe, it's best just to drink bottled water in East Glacier, rather than tap water. All restaurants serve bottled water, so you don't have to worry—but ask just to be sure. Glacier Park Lodge heavily chlorinates its water (you'll taste it) to eliminate the bacteria.

Emergencies

In Glacier Park, contact a park ranger for emergencies (406/888-7800). You can also walk into the **Two Medicine Ranger Station** (summers only, 8 A.M.–4:30 P.M. daily), on Two Medicine Road at the campground junction. The nearest hospital is in Cut Bank—the **Northern Rockies Medical Center** (802 2nd St. E., 406/873-2251).

DRIVING TOURS
Two Medicine Road

Four miles north of East Glacier off Highway 49, Two Medicine Road heads up the Two Medicine Valley for 7.5 miles. It begins on the Blackfeet Reservation and winds through quaking aspen above Lower Two Medicine Lake into the park. In September, the aspens turn bright yellow, almost emitting a light of their own. **Scenic Point** rises across the lake, and the red flanks of Rising Wolf hog the upper valley. You'll enter the park at 2.9 miles, crossing over a cattle guard, but you won't reach the entrance station until 4.1 miles. A few minutes past the entrance station (5.2 miles), stop for the short nature walk heading to **Running**

Eagle Falls. As the road climbs into the Two Medicine Basin, look for blue camas, fleabane, paintbrush, and lupine. Once you cross the apex, the peaks of Two Medicine pop out: Sinopah, Lone Walker, and Rising Wolf. After passing the campground and picnic area entrance (7.1 miles), the road terminates in the parking lot at **Two Medicine Lake,** where you can catch a boat tour on the lake or stop in the historic chalet, now a camp store selling ice-cream cones.

◖ Looking Glass Hill-Browning Loop

From East Glacier, drive Highway 49 north up Looking Glass Hill, an original part of the Blackfeet Highway. Because this section from Two Medicine Road to Kiowa Junction is closed in winter (November–April), this tour is a summer drive only. State law restricts the size of trailer combinations and RVs to 21 feet on the shoulderless Highway 49, which has more curves than a snake, but you'll see many anyway. But be aware that wet downpours cause landslides; the road frequently closes for repairs, and you'll hit rough sections with chewed pavement. As the road climbs to a high vantage point above **Lower Two Medicine Lake,** it twists through aspen groves. Three miles past the Two Medicine junction you'll find unmarked pullouts overlooking the valley for great photo ops before descending to Kiowa Junction.

Drive slowly, for *open range* means no fences. Cattle wander willy-nilly where they please here. Often, you'll round a corner into cows standing smack in the middle of the road and may have to wait for them to move. They are not particularly speedy creatures, but they can dent your car with a good kick, so give them room. Because the road is narrow and curvy, take it slow. You'll have less chance of putting a cow imprint across your grille.

At Kiowa, you can choose the **Looking Glass-Browning** tour making a 49-mile scenic loop through the Blackfeet Reservation for grand views of peak panoramas from the plains. Take Highway 89 east toward Browning, stop at the Museum of the Plains Indian, and turn back to East Glacier on Highway 2 past the Blackfeet National Bison Preserve. From Kiowa, you can also continue north on the **Blackfeet Highway to St. Mary** (Highway 89) along the Rocky Mountain Front—a scenic, but narrow, curvy drive.

Looping south and east of Browning, a 70-mile **Blackfeet Trail Tour** winds on mostly paved roads through the Blackfeet Reservation following 15 historical markers. The sites paint a picture of the West as seen through the eyes of the Blackfeet. Download a map online (www.blackfeetcountry.com/blackfeettrailtour.html).

SIGHTS
Two Medicine Lake

The largest of three lakes, Two Medicine Lake is the highest road-accessible lake in Glacier,

sitting almost one mile high in elevation. Its waters collect from snowmelt on peaks over 8,000 feet high but devoid of glaciers. The lakes are all that remain of the monster thousand-foot-thick ice field that covered nearly 500,000 acres, flowing out onto the prairie past Browning. To explore Two Medicine Lake, jump on the historic *Sinopah* tour boat for storytelling by Glacier Park Boat Company's captains. If waters are calm, rent a canoe to paddle its shoreline, swim in its chilly clear waters, or fish for brook trout.

Family Peaks

Rich with Blackfeet history, the peaks in Two Medicine Valley tell a story. **Rising Wolf,** climbing straight out of the north shoreline to 9,513 feet, was named for Hugh Monroe, a Hudson Bay Company fur trapper who came to the Glacier area in the early 1800s.

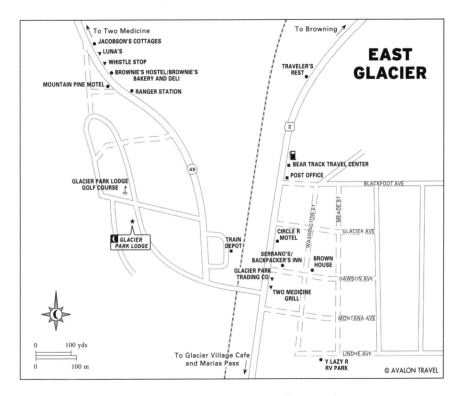

After living with the Piegans, he bargained with **Lone Walker,** the tribal chief, to marry his daughter. At Upper Two Medicine Lake, find Lone Walker rising from the lake's head. Rising Wolf married Lone Walker's daughter—**Sinopah,** the dramatic eroded pyramid directly across Two Medicine Lake.

Two Medicine Chalets

All that remains of historic Two Medicine Chalets is the dining hall, now operating as the Two Medicine Campstore and designated as a National Historic Landmark. Built 1912-1913, the chalets replaced the original tepee camp for visitors. The log two-story chalet was once the hub of the small colony, the first stop on the Inside Trail horse trip with Park Saddle Company in the 1920s. The dining hall's most famous guest—Franklin Delano Roosevelt—addressed the nation from here in an unofficial fireside chat in 1934.

◖ Running Eagle Falls

A short nature trail (0.6 mile round-trip) leads to Running Eagle Falls, also known as Trick Falls. In high runoff, water gushes over the top of the falls, spraying those standing nearby. But in lower flows, you can see the trick. Part of the falls runs underground and spits out through a cavern halfway down the cliff face. Running Eagle, the Blackfeet name for the falls, honors a female warrior named Pitamakin who had her vision quest here. She gained renown for stealing horses from the Kootenai but was eventually killed during a raid.

◖ Glacier Park Lodge

In East Glacier, Glacier Park Lodge stands as the headliner hotel for the historic chain of Great Northern hostelries built throughout Glacier. Set within the Blackfeet Reservation, the 155-room hotel built in 1915 started its life providing train visitors with the first taste of Glacier. Since the advent of Going-to-the-Sun Road, additional avenues into the park stole some of the lodge's thunder. Today, the hotel is listed on the National Register of Historic Places. Even if you are not staying

© BECKY LOMAX

Running Eagle Falls in autumn reveals its trick.

RISING WOLF

Without a doubt, the most prominent feature in Two Medicine Valley is the hulk of 9,513-foot **Rising Wolf Mountain.** It's named for the first European descendent to meet the Blackfeet. Born Hugh Monroe in Quebec, Canada, in 1798, the 16-year-old traveled west as an apprentice for the Hudson Bay Company.

With an intense interest in the Indians, he was sent to live with the Small Robes band of Piegans (a Blackfeet tribe) to learn their language and find beaver-trapping territory. The tribe's chief, **Lone Walker,** took a liking to the congenial Monroe. After several seasons with the Piegans, Monroe married **Sinopah,** Lone Walker's daughter, and lived permanently with them.

When officially admitted to the tribe, Monroe was ascribed the name Rising Wolf. Despite lack of written records, it is presumed that Monroe was the first European descendent to set eyes on St. Mary Lake and much of Glacier's eastern lands. He served as a guide and interpreter for territorial survey teams and early reconnaissance of Glacier Park. He later left Hudson Bay Company for the American Fur Company, which established trading posts on the Marias River in Blackfeet country. Rising Wolf died in 1892, the same year Great Northern Railway laid tracks over Marias Pass.

While there is some discrepancy on Monroe's birth date, it is apparent he lived to a ripe old age, even after losing sight in one eye in a fight with a Sioux. Many of Monroe's descendents still live on the Blackfeet Reservation. Lone Walker peak sits at the head of Upper Two Medicine Lake; Sinopah rises straight out of Two Medicine Lake opposite Rising Wolf.

here, walk the gardens leading up to the front door, lounge in its massive lobby held up by three-story Douglas firs, and catch the historic photo display chronicling the hotel's glory days.

Blackfeet Sentries

Blackfeet artist Jay Laber gives new life to garbage in what he calls "Reborn Rez Wrecks." Using farm tools, jewelry, hubcaps, and barbwire, he sculpted a not-to-be-missed sculpture series—*Blackfeet Reservation Sentries*—posted on the reservation's four boundaries. Each pair of life-size sentries rides atop horses. Posted in East Glacier, one pair guards the reservation's western entrance (0.2 mile west of town on Highway 2).

Blackfeet Nation Bison Reserve

While driving between East Glacier and Browning, stop at the Buffalo Viewing Area on the north side of Highway 2 to catch sight of the herd managed by the tribe. Bison provided food, shelter, and clothing for the nomadic Blackfeet until the buffalo were exterminated in the 1800s.

【 Museum of the Plains Indian

Located in Browning, 12 miles from East Glacier, the Museum of the Plains Indian (junction of Hwy. 2 and 83, 406/338-2230, 9 A.M.–4:45 P.M. daily June–Sept., 10 A.M.–4:30 P.M. Mon.–Fri. Oct.–May, adults $4, kids 6–12 $1, under 6 free, all ages free in winter) is a small but very informative center for Blackfeet culture and history. A multimedia five-screen show narrated by Vincent Price tells the story of the Blackfeet people, well worth the 20 minutes it takes to watch it. Displays cluster phenomenal beadwork, leather, tools, and clothing to tell the story of the Northern Plains Indians. Seeing the life-size beaded ceremonial regalia is worth the price of admission.

Recreation

HIKING

Hiking at Two Medicine is in a class by itself. Except for a few short hikes from the lake's upper boat dock, hikers here find solitude even on the most crowded hot summer days. For hikes on reservation land (those leaving directly from East Glacier or the latter half of the Scenic Point trail), a tribal recreation permit ($10) is required, available at the Two Medicine Ranger Station or Bear Track Travel Center (Exxon gas station) in East Glacier.

With a maze of trail junctions breaking off the north- and south-shore Two Medicine Lake trails, you'll find one of the park's nontopographical trail maps helpful. These are available at the ranger station and the Glacier Park Lodge activity desk. For longer hikes, such as the Dawson-Pitamakin Loop, tote a good topographical map: You can buy one in the Two Medicine Campstore.

In Two Medicine, hikers use the tour boat as a shuttle up the lake to prune miles off hikes and get farther into the backcountry faster. Glacier Park, Inc. also runs a shuttle from Glacier Park Lodge to Two Medicine for hiking; the shuttles arrive in time to catch the boat across Two Medicine Lake.

Aster Park

- Distance: 3.8 miles round-trip
- Duration: 2 hours
- Elevation gain: 670 feet
- Effort: easy
- Trailhead: adjacent to Two Medicine boat dock

Beginning on the south shore trail, Aster Park is reached via a spur trail just past Aster Creek. About 1.2 miles southwest of the boat dock, turn left at the signed junction and follow the trail past Aster Falls as it switchbacks up to a flower-covered knoll. This overlook

© BECKY LOMAX

Aster Park affords a short hike to an overlook of Two Medicine Lake.

provides grand views of Two Medicine Lake and Rising Wolf.

Twin Falls and Upper Two Medicine Lake

- Distance: 1.8–10 miles round-trip
- Duration: 1–5 hours
- Elevation gain: 0–350 feet
- Effort: easy
- Trailhead: Two Medicine Lake west boat dock or Pray Lake Bridge in Two Medicine Campground

Set in a subalpine bowl, Upper Two Medicine Lake is reached by a trail passing Twin Falls—a double flume of cascades. Taking the boat both ways on Two Medicine Lake shortens the hike: Twin Falls, 1.8 miles round-trip; the upper lake, 4.4 miles. Taking the boat one-way and hiking the remaining distance shortens the hike to 7.2 miles. For the longest route, you can hike both up and back on the north shore trail or loop around Two Medicine Lake.

Two separate falls comprise Twin Falls, one of Two Medicine's most popular hikes.

The trail climbs gently, passing the short spur trail to Twin Falls. After crossing avalanche gullies thick with huckleberries, you'll crest a prominent rock ledge to the lake. If you are eating lunch at the lake, help maintain the safety of those sleeping in the backcountry campground here by not eating in the sleeping sites. Sit in the cooking area to eat or in late season hike up the north shoreline. Early season high water floods the beach.

◀ Scenic Point

- Distance: 6.2 miles round-trip
- Duration: 3–4 hours
- Elevation gain: 2,350 feet
- Effort: moderately strenuous
- Trailhead: milepost 6.9 on Two Medicine Road

Scenic Point is one short climb with big scenery. The trail launches up through a thick subalpine fir forest. A short side jaunt en route sneaks a peek at Appistoki Falls. As switchbacks line up like dominoes, stunted firs give way to dead silver, twisted limber pines. Broaching the ridge, the trail enters seemingly barren alpine tundra. Only alpine bluebells and pink mats of several-hundred-year-old moss campion cower in crags.

The trail traverses across a talus slope, covered in early season with steep snows to be avoided. (You can climb a worn path that circumvents the snow field.) The trail descends to Scenic Point. To reach the actual point above the trail, cut off at the sign, stepping on rocks to avoid crushing fragile alpine plants. Atop, you can swan dive several thousand feet straight down into Lower Two Medicine Lake. Return the way you came, or drop seven miles to East Glacier, passing outside the park boundary, where cow pies buzz with flies. Tribal recreation permits are required for this option, available at the ranger station.

Rockwell Falls and Cobalt Lake

- Distance: 6.8–11.4 miles round-trip
- Duration: 4–5.5 hours

LEAVE NO TRACE

To keep Glacier pristine, visitors to this unique park need to take an active role in maintaining its well-being.

- **Plan ahead and prepare.** Hiking in Glacier's backcountry is inherently risky. Three miles here may be much harder than three miles through your neighborhood park back home. Choose appropriate routes for mileage and elevation gain with this in mind, and carry hiking essentials.

- **Travel and camp on durable surfaces.** In both frontcountry and backcountry campgrounds, camp in designated sites. Protect fragile plants by staying on the trail, refusing to cut switchbacks, and walking single file on trails – even in the mud. If you must walk off the trail, step on rocks, snow, or dry grasses rather than wet soil and delicate plants.

- **Leave what you find.** Flowers, rocks, and goat fur tufts on shrubs are protected park resources, as are historical cultural items. For lunch stops and camping, sit on rocks or logs where you find them rather than moving them to accommodate your camp.

- **Properly dispose of waste.** Whatever you bring in, you must pack out. Pack out all garbage. If toilets are not available, pack out toilet paper. Urinate on rocks, logs, gravel, or snow to protect soils and plants from salt-starved wildlife, and bury feces 6-8 inches deep at least 200 feet from water.

- **Minimize campfire impacts.** Make fires in designated fire pits only, not on beaches. Use small wrist-size dead and downed wood, not live branches. Be aware that fires and firewood collecting are not permitted in many places in the park.

- **Respect wildlife.** Bring along binoculars, spotting scopes, and telephoto lenses to aid in watching wildlife. Keep your distance. Do not feed any wildlife, even ground squirrels. Once fed, they become more aggressive.

- **Be considerate of other visitors.**

For more Leave No Trace information, please visit www.LNT.org or call 303/442-8222.

- Elevation gain: minimal to 1,400 feet
- Effort: easy to moderate
- Trailhead: adjacent to the Two Medicine boat dock

Follow the gentle south shore trail along Two Medicine Lake past beaver ponds and bear-scratched trees to Paradise Creek, where a swinging bridge makes you think of Indiana Jones movies, but it's not as scary. At 2.3 miles, turn left at the signed junction. The trail wanders through avalanche paths with uprooted trees shredded like toothpicks. At 3.4 miles, you reach Rockwell Falls. Spur trails explore the falls.

Continuing on to Cobalt Lake, the trail climbs up several switchbacks into an upper basin, crossing back and forth over the creek. The trail packs all of its elevation gain into the last two miles. Tucked in the uppermost corner of the basin, Cobalt Lake sits below talus slopes covered with mountain goats.

【 Dawson-Pitamakin Loop

- Distance: 16.9 or 18.8 miles
- Duration: 7–9 hours
- Elevation gain: 2,935 feet
- Effort: strenuous
- Trailhead: Two Medicine Lake west boat dock or Pray Lake Bridge in Two Medicine Campground

Although this loop can be done from either direction, both with the same elevation gain up to 8,000 feet, the approach to Dawson Pass is much steeper than to Pitamakin Pass. It crams all of its elevation gain within three miles, while Pitamakin Pass sprawls it less steeply out over eight. So pick your route based on your preference for uphill grunts and knee-pounding descents. If you catch the Two Medicine boat one direction or the other, you'll chop off 1.9 miles.

In its loop around Rising Wolf, the route actually crosses three passes: Pitamakin, Cut Bank, and Dawson, the latter two passes seeing frequent winds raging enough to force crawling. Starting toward Pitamakin, the trail crosses Dry Fork and follows it up to Old Man Lake (6.8 miles), a good fishing lake, before climbing to the pass (8.8 miles), where you'll often see bighorn sheep. With the narrow trail exposed high on a several-mile goat traverse between Cut Bank and Dawson (12.1 miles) passes, those with a fear of heights will be uncomfortable. For most, it's the best part of the trail, walking a tightrope between vertigo and soaring.

Medicine Grizzly Lake and Triple Divide Pass

- Distance: 12 or 14.4 miles round-trip
- Duration: 6–7.5 hours
- Elevation gain: 540 or 2,380 feet
- Effort: easy to strenuous
- Trailhead: terminus of Cut Bank Road
- Directions: Locate the signed Cut Bank Road six miles north of Kiowa Junction on Highway 89. Follow the narrow dirt road over cattle grates into the park and past the ranger station. The trailhead is about four miles up just before the campground.

Due to its location up the rough Cut Bank Road, many hikers are deterred. But it's a popular trail for anglers as Medicine Grizzly Lake harbors 12-inch rainbows. Check with the ranger station before leaving, as bear activity frequently closes the lake and its spur trail. The trail follows Atlantic Creek up a forested drainage to a signed junction at four miles. Turn right, climbing (0.6 mile) past the Atlantic Creek campground to the junction for the pass or lake. For Medicine Grizzly Lake, continue straight for 1.4 miles.

© BECKY LOMAX

Hikers reach Triple Divide Pass below the peak that sends waters to three oceans.

For Triple Divide Pass, climb north at the junction. The trail bursts out of the trees, traversing up a rocky face below Mount James as it looks down on the lake. After winding into a large bowl, look for bighorn sheep frequently browsing. Tucked at the base of Triple Divide Peak, the pass actually stands on the split between the Saskatchewan and Missouri River drainages, beginning here as Hudson Bay Creek and Atlantic Creek.

Guides

The National Park Service guides free hikes mid-June–mid-September to a variety of destinations in Two Medicine: Upper Two Medicine Lake, Scenic Point, Dawson Pass, Rockwell Falls, and Cobalt Lake, as well as a daily boat ride and hike to Twin Falls. (The hike is free, but you still need to pay for the boat ride.) Grab a copy of *Ranger-Led Activities* from the ranger station for the current schedule.

Glacier Guides (406/387-5555 or 800/521-7238, www.glacierguides.com) will pick you up at the lodge, transport you to the trailhead, and bring along a deli lunch and snacks. You just need to bring your pack, sunscreen, bug juice, water, and extra clothes. Reservations are mandatory. Their Custom Day Hikes ($450, up to five people) will depart from East Glacier or Two Medicine. Solo travelers can also hook up with their Tuesday Hikes ($75 per person, July–August) and Group Day Hikes ($375, 1–5 people, June–September), which depart from their West Glacier office, an hour from East Glacier. The guide service also has three-, four-, and six-day backpacking trips that depart weekly ($145 per day, June–mid-September)—some on routes out of Two Medicine.

BIKING

Bicycling around the park's southeast corner is usually restricted to narrow, curvy, shoulderless roadways. Although most drivers are fairly courteous toward bicyclists, be prepared to have large RVs nearly shove you off the road, simply due to their size in comparison to the skimpy pavement. It's an area where you may encounter bears on the roadway, especially on Two Medicine Road; on Highway 49 with open range, you can round a corner into a small herd of cows. For some reason, no matter which direction you're riding, a strong headwind always blasts. Since mountain biking is not permitted on trails within Glacier, riding is restricted to roadways and the campground loops for kids. Bicyclists do day tours from East Glacier to Two Medicine Lake and back. No bike rentals are available.

For bicyclists, Two Medicine Campground has shared hiker-biker campsites for $5 per person. These are reserved until 9 P.M. for bikers and have bear-resistant food storage containers on-site.

TRAIL RIDING

Across the street from Glacier Park Lodge on Highway 49, **Glacier Gateway Outfitters** (0.4 mile north of Hwy. 2 and 49 junction, 406/226-4408, June–Sept.) leads trail rides and cowboy-style horseback rides—ones that tour cross-country rather than riding single file. Led by Native American guides, the

© BECKY LOMAX

Early-season bikers can reach Two Medicine before the road opens completely to cars.

tours roam outside Glacier Park on adjacent Blackfeet Reservation land. Rides wander along Two Medicine River Gorge through aspens and blooms of early-season shooting stars and late-summer lupine—all at the foot of the park's front range. One-, two-, and three-hour rides depart several times daily ($30 per hour). Those dreaming of riding the open range rather than head to tail can take a full-day ride ($185 per person with minimum of six people, bring your own lunch). Wear long pants and sturdy shoes, such as hiking boots or tennis shoes. Kids must be at least seven years old and have some experience riding. Reservations are recommended, especially midsummer.

BOATING, CANOEING, AND KAYAKING

Two Medicine is the highest lake you can drive to in the park; it's also one of the windiest. Boaters need to keep an eye on waves; if white-caps pop up, paddlers should consider getting off the lake. Two Medicine Road terminates at the public boat ramp, so it's easy to find. Hand-powered craft and motorized boats are allowed with 10 horsepower or less, but no Jet Skis, so the lake maintains a nice quiet. On calm days, kayakers and canoers tour the lake's shore. On Lower Two Medicine Lake, you won't see many boats. Lack of a boat ramp and no access trails preclude most people.

Boating regulations in Glacier Park require free permits for motorized boats. Boaters must show that their boats have been cleaned, drained, and dried to avoid bringing Aquatic Invasive Species into park lakes. Permits for up to 14 days are available at the Two Medicine Ranger Station.

Located at the Two Medicine boat dock, **Glacier Park Boat Company** (406/226-4467 summers only, 406/257-2426, www.glacier-parkboats.com) rents canoes, kayaks, and small motorboats for $15–20 (cash only) per hour.

FISHING

Two Medicine River links together the three lakes by the same name, with brook trout populating much of the waters. For fishing **Upper**

© BECKY LOMAX

Glacier Park Boat Company rents canoes, kayaks, and boats at Two Medicine.

Two Medicine Lake, hike two miles after taking the boat shuttle across Two Medicine Lake. It's an attractive lake to fish, but its shoreline is brushy and the outlet clogged with downed timbers. Anglers in **Two Medicine Lake** may have more success tossing in a line from a boat rather than fishing from shore, with its heavy timber and brush. On the valley's south side, Paradise Creek harbors some trout, but Aster and Apistoki Creeks are void. On the dam-controlled **Lower Two Medicine Lake,** which is half in the park, half on the Blackfeet Reservation, only a few anglers go after the 10- to 12-inch rainbows and brookies here; difficult access with no trails or boat ramp keeps most anglers away. Other area lakes— **No Name** and **Old Man**—support trout, but Cobalt is barren. In the Cut Bank Valley, **Medicine Grizzly Lake** lures anglers, but reality doesn't live up to legend, and the lake frequently sees bear closures.

Licenses and Regulations

No fishing license is required in the park, but pick up park fishing regulations at the ranger station in Two Medicine. On Lower Two Medicine Lake or Two Medicine River, you will need a tribal fishing permit. (See the *Background* chapter for details.) Purchase fishing licenses at **Bear Track Travel Center** (Exxon station in East Glacier, 20958 Hwy. 2, 406/226-5504, 7 a.m.–8 p.m. daily in winter, 7 a.m.–10 p.m. daily in summer).

GOLF

Built in 1927, the **Glacier Park Lodge Golf Course** (406/892-2525, www.glacierparkinc. com, late May–early Oct.) is the oldest grass greens in Montana. The nine-hole course winds through aspen groves with views of Dancing Lady, Henry, Calf Robe, and Summit peaks. Don't be surprised if bears (or more commonly stray dogs) roam across the course. Because the course is on Blackfeet tribal lands, each of the nine holes is named after former Blackfeet Nation chiefs—Rising Wolf, Bad Marriage, Long Time Sleeps, and Stabs-By-Mistake. Nine holes cost $18, and an 18-hole round

© BECKY LOMAX

The Glacier Park Lodge Golf Course names each hole for a Blackfeet chief.

costs $27. Clubs rent for $14–21 and power carts for $18–37. For tee times, call 406/226-5342 or the hotel front desk. The lodge often offers special spring and fall rates for golf-lodging packages.

A public, nine-hole pitch-and-putt miniature golf course covers half of the front lawn of Glacier Park Lodge. Pick up clubs and a souvenir ball ($8 per person) at the front desk. Ground squirrel holes add a challenge to the course.

CROSS-COUNTRY SKIING

Late December–April, **Two Medicine Road** (15 miles round-trip) makes a delightfully moderate but long ski, with frozen Two Medicine Lake as the destination. Snow piles up enough to bury the restrooms. While the going is not tough and the gentle terrain undulates except for one long hill, winds can scour the road free of snow in places, requiring skiers to take skis off and on. Headwinds also frequently blow both directions. Nevertheless, it's a stunning trip, with relatively little avalanche danger.

When snow permits, skiing **Looking Glass Hill** on Highway 49 is also popular. An eight-mile round-trip tour leads from the junction with Two Medicine Road to spectacular overlooks of Two Medicine Valley and Lake Creek drainage to Divide Mountain by St. Mary. Sometimes winds blow the pavement bare, so be prepared to take skis off and put them on again.

No equipment rental is available in East Glacier; the nearest rentals are at the Izaak Walton Inn on Highway 2 and at Glacier Outdoor Center in West Glacier. Winter shuts down East Glacier and much of the park; be prepared for winter trips. Do not venture out without a complete pack full of emergency gear, ready for self-rescue.

ENTERTAINMENT

On summer evenings National Park Service naturalists present free 45-minute talks on natural history and wildlife in the Two Medicine Amphitheater, usually at 8 P.M. Once a week, the presentations feature **Native America Speaks**—storytellers who bring to life the history of local tribes and their involvement in Glacier. For a current schedule, pick up a copy of *Ranger-Led Activities* at visitors centers and ranger stations.

Glacier Park Lodge sponsors entertainment from time to time—Native American speakers and entertainers as well as musicians, such as the Trapp Family Singers. Check the sign in the lobby near the front desk for the current schedule.

◖ North American Indian Days

Over four days beginning the second Thursday in July, North American Indian Days (406/338-7406, www.blackfeetnation.com) celebrates native culture in vibrant, stunning color. In Browning, behind the Museum of the Plains Indian, the powwow grounds (4th Avenue NW and Boundary Street) become home to tepees, dancing, drumming, singing, games, rodeos, horse racing,

North American Indian Days features four days of dancing.

sporting events, food, and crafts. Hosted by the Blackfeet, the family event, which bans alcohol on the reservation for the duration, draws regional tribes from the United States and Canada. Traditional regalia show off exceptional craftsmanship with feathered headdresses and beadwork. Nonnative people are welcome to attend. Watching is free.

Casino

Gaming and slot machines on the Blackfeet Reservation are at **Glacier Peaks Casino** (406/338-2274 or 877/238-9946, www.glaciercash.com, 10 A.M.–2 A.M. daily). The 33,000-square-foot casino, sitting in Browning at the junction of Highways 2 and 89, contains 400 slot machines, live poker, and a restaurant.

Accommodations

East Glacier is divided in half by the railroad tracks. You may want to bring earplugs; most motel rooms catch the rumble and clatter of passing trains. On one side, historic Glacier Park Lodge sits on Highway 49 followed by a compact motel strip—think very rustic here, not a highway megastrip—which ends abruptly within one mile. On the south side of the tracks along Highway 2, East Glacier tucks several motels within a few-block radius of restaurants. All fill to the brim midsummer, so reservations are highly recommended. Two Medicine has no lodging available—only a campground.

EAST GLACIER
Lodges and Cabins

Historic (**Glacier Park Lodge** (0.1 mile north on Hwy. 49, 406/892-2525, www.glacierparkinc.com, mid-June–late Sept., $140–449) sits outside the park boundary on Blackfeet tribal land right across from the train depot. It's the

© BECKY LOMAX

A large garden walkway leads up to Glacier Park Lodge.

only historic lodge with an outdoor swimming pool (heated, but still chilly), golf course, and pitch-and-putt. Main lodge rooms are connected to rooms in the west wing via a scenic enclosed walkway off the gigantic lobby, where huge western red cedars hold aloft a several-story ceiling. The west rooms tend to be larger than rooms in the other historic park hotels. Get a room facing the mountains to enjoy the sunrises and sunsets casting orange glows. Lodge rooms, suites, and family rooms are available, along with a chalet. All rooms are nonsmoking. Expect rustic—tiny bathrooms converted from original closets, thin walls, slanted floors, cantankerous hot water, and no television, Internet, air-conditioning, or elevators; revel in the historical ambience instead. Reservations are highly recommended in June and September, an absolute must in July and August.

A restaurant, lounge, snack shop, and gift shop sit off the lobby, and Remedies Day Spa offers massages for trail-weary muscles. Red bus tours depart from the hotel, and trail riding is across the street. Trails to Scenic Point and Firebrand Pass depart nearby, crossing reservation land before entering park boundaries. In the evening, Native American speakers often give fireside talks.

Built in 2004, **◖ Traveler's Rest Lodge** (0.3 mile east of Exxon station on Hwy. 2, 406/226-9143 summer, 406/378-2414 winter, www.travelersrestlodge.net, May–Sept., $115–160 double occupancy) has clean, roomy nonsmoking log mortise and tenon cabins with gas fireplaces and fully equipped kitchenettes on eight acres amid aspen trees. Each is positioned for its covered deck to gain privacy and views of the Bob Marshall Wilderness. The nicely decorated cabins sleeping 2–4 people in log-hewn beds have televisions and CD players but no phones. (One is available in the office.) Because of East Glacier's frequent "boil orders" for water, each cabin is equipped with five gallons of drinking water. In one of the cabins, the owners, Diane and Bob Scalese, have their engraving workshop. They are well-known artisans who design, craft, and engrave spurs, bits, belt buckles, and saddle silver.

Motels

East Glacier has seven small plain motels, some with cabins, and all within walking distance to restaurants and stores. Four small seasonal (May–September) ones line Highway 49's motel strip north of Glacier Park Lodge. The area hops midsummer, but highway traffic virtually disappears at night. You can hear train noise even though the motels are shielded from the tracks by trees. Three other year-round motels sit in "downtown" East Glacier, with both highway and train noise. Advance reservations midsummer are wise.

Sitting right on Highway 2 across from the train depot, **Glacier Park Circle R Motel** (402 Hwy. 2 E., 406/226-9331, www.circlermotel.net, open year-round, summer $48–159, late Sept.–mid-June $62–75) just added more new rooms in 2007. Year-round, the motel rents nonsmoking rooms with cable television and wireless Internet. The second-floor rooms have good views of Dancing Lady. One suite has a full kitchen and air-conditioning. In summer, the motel also rents its older smoking-permitted rooms. Pets cost $10. Rates increase by $50 per night July 7–13 for North American Indian Days.

On Highway 49, 0.6 mile north of the junction with Highway 2, **Mountain Pine Motel** (between Midvale St. and First St., 406/226-4403, www.mtnpine.com, May–Sept., $48–165) offers 25 tidy rooms—some connecting—lined up surrounding a shady lawn. The nonsmoking rooms have queen beds, wireless Internet, and television. Early- and late-season discounts are available.

Guesthouses

Art aficionados may enjoy renting a room from a professional potter and sculptor at **The Brown House** (402 Washington St., 406/226-9385, June–Sept., $70 double occupancy), which has three remodeled nonsmoking rooms, each furnished with antiques and having a private entrance and bath. The upstairs room has a view of the park's peaks. Originally a 1920s store, the building still has some of the fixtures from that era. The gift shop also sells the works of local artisans.

Hostels

For the budget minded, East Glacier has two hostels open May–September.
Backpacker's Inn (29 Dawson Ave., 406/226-9392, www.serranosmexican.com) has three dorms, plus two cabins located in the backyard of Serrano's Mexican Restaurant—a little outdoor oasis in the middle of town that serves for a common area. The buildings are the renovated original prefab cedar Sears and Roebuck 1920 homes. Beds in the dorm rooms are $12 per person per night; bring your own sleeping bag ($1 to rent a bag). The cabins with one queen bed start at $30. **Brownie's Hostel** (1020 Hwy. 49, 406/226-4426, www.browniesshostel.com) is in an old renovated two-story 1920s building on the Highway 49 motel strip. An easy six-block walk from the train station and adjacent to restaurants, the hostel has a fully equipped communal kitchen and three dorms with beds ($21 per night; Hostelling International members get a discount). Private bedrooms are also available ($28–38 double). Cinnamon rolls scent the air in the morning

from the downstairs bakery. It has a deli and convenience store with Internet access, too.

CAMPING

RVers requiring hookups will need to stay in East Glacier or Browning, as Glacier Park campgrounds have no hookups. If campgrounds are full, check the *Marias Pass and Essex* chapter for alternatives, such as Summit (11 miles west) or Glacier Meadow RV Park (17 miles west).

Glacier Park Campgrounds

Two national park campgrounds sit in Glacier's southeast corner—one with easy paved access and the other via a dirt road. Both offer campsites outfitted with picnic tables and fire rings with grills. Bring your own firewood; gathering is prohibited. All campsites are first come, first serve.

Two Medicine Campground (406/888-7800, late May–late Sept., $20) yields views of bears foraging on Rising Wolf Mountain, especially from the A and C loops. In early summer,

© BECKY LOMAX

A few campsites at Two Medicine get river frontage.

ruby-crowned kinglets call out "teacher, teacher" from the trees. The campground is set back from Two Medicine Lake, surrounding the calmer waters of small Pray Lake, a good place for paddling and chilly swimming or fishing. With 99 sites, the campground fills up midsummer, but often not as early in the day as those on Going-to-the-Sun Road; try to claim a campsite by early afternoon. Flush toilets, water, and a dump station are provided. The north shore trail departs right from the campground, leading two directions around Rising Wolf Mountain. A seven-minute walk or few-minute drive puts you at the boat tour and rental dock, and the Two Medicine Campstore can cover what you've forgotten. Only 13 sites can handle RVs up to 32 feet. In late September and October, the campground allows primitive camping ($10) with pit toilets and no running water.

Located 19 miles north of East Glacier off Highway 89, **Cut Bank Campground** (406/888-7800, late May–early Sept., $10 per night) sits at the end of a five-mile potholed dirt road. Large RVs shouldn't attempt the rough access road. To locate the road, look for the campground sign six miles north of Kiowa Junction. The campground is rustic, with only pit toilets and no running water. Atlantic Creek runs nearby, but you'll need to boil (for five minutes) or filter the water. With only 14 sites, set in deep shade under large firs, it's a great place to escape crowds. The campground has fishing in Atlantic Creek and the trailhead to Medicine Grizzly Lake and Triple Divide Pass nearby.

Glacier Park Backcountry Camping

Two Medicine has plenty of backcountry campsites that work as good destinations for kids as well as connections on the Continental Divide Trail. For kids, chop off mileage with the boat and head to **Upper Two Medicine** or **Cobalt Lake.** Those backpacking the Dawson-Pitamakin Loop will need permits for **No Name** and **Old Man Lake.** Those backpacking the Continental Divide Trail to St. Mary

will want to continue on to **Morningstar,** with its lake tucked against a cliff wall with a golden eagle nest and mountain goats, before hitting **Atlantic Creek** and **Red Eagle Lake.** Pick up permits ($5 per person per night, kids 8–15 $2.50, kids 7 and under free) 24 hours in advance in person at Two Medicine Ranger Station or the Apgar Permit Office (406/888-7900) or by reservation ($30). Check additional requirements online: www.nps.gov/glac.

East Glacier

A small campground set on three grassy acres on the Blackfeet Reservation, **Y Lazy R RV Park** (junction of Lindhe Ave. and Meade St., 406/226-5505, mid-May–Sept., tents $18, hookups $20–23) is two blocks off Highway 2. With only a few aspen trees, its open setting overlooks Midvale Creek and affords big views of surrounding mountains. Amenities include flush toilets, picnic tables, coin-op showers, dump station, a large laundry, and hookups for electricity, water, and sewer. The campground sits an easy few-block walk from restaurants.

Browning

On a prairie wildflower knoll west of Browning staring at Glacier's peaks, the ◖ **Lodgepole Gallery and Tipi Village** (2.5 miles west on Hwy. 89, 406/338-2787, www.blackfeetculturecamp.com, May–Sept.) is different—and not just because a small herd of nearly extinct Spanish mustangs, the original Indian horse, runs free on the property (they're not for riding, just for watching). Ten traditional double-walled canvas tepees with a fire pit inside each serve as tents. Supplied wood heats the tepees on cooler nights. You bring your sleeping bag, air mattress, and flashlight; or rent them for $8 (the sleeping bags come with linen). A central bathhouse with flush toilets and showers services all the tepees. Overnight rates run $50 for first person in tepee, $15 each additional person, and $10 for kids under 12. Meals—breakfast or a traditional southern Blackfeet dinner—are available by reservation. A Blackfeet art gallery and art classes are available on-site. The owners can arrange Blackfeet-guided tours, fishing trips, and horseback riding.

West of Browning, with views of Glacier's eastern front range, **Aspenwood Resort** (9.5 miles west of Browning or 2.3 miles east of Kiowa Junction on Hwy. 89, 406/338-3009, www.aspenwoodresort.com, mid-May–mid-Oct., $18–35) sits on the Blackfeet Reservation

with two beaver ponds that offer fishing, paddleboating, wildlife-watching, and walking. The campground includes flush toilets, hookups for electricity and water, tent and RV campsites, showers, a disposal station, and a restaurant. The resort also arranges for Native American–guided fishing trips, tours, and horseback riding. Reservations are required for powwow weekends. Pets and horses are welcome.

Food

Because Two Medicine has no restaurants, campers must hit East Glacier to dine out. However, the road between the two is short, and the evening can be a good time to spot wildlife on the return drive. During special days, such as graduation and North American Indian Days on the Blackfeet Reservation, none of the restaurants or bars serves alcohol. The four-day celebration is usually scheduled beginning the second Thursday in July. During that time, all alcohol sales in restaurants, lounges, and grocery stores are banned on tribal lands—including all restaurants in East Glacier.

Only one restaurant is open year-round. **Two Medicine Grill** (314 Hwy. 2, 406/226-9227, www.whistlingswanmotel.com, 6:30 A.M.–9 P.M. daily but closes earlier in winter, $4–12) is the local hangout for favorite greasy-spoon foods, espresso, home-baked cinnamon rolls, and hard ice cream. This small hole-in-the-wall diner, owned by Mark Howser and Colleen O'Brien, who also own the Whistling Swan Motel and Glacier Park Trading Company, was built in 1935 in Choteau and moved to East Glacier.

RESTAURANTS
East Glacier
In the historic Glacier Park Lodge, the **Great Northern Steak and Rib House** (on Hwy. 49 across from train depot, 406/892-2525, late May–late Sept.) has the best views compared with any restaurant in town. Ask to be seated

near the west windows facing Dancing Lady Mountain: The sunrise smears it with pink, and the sunset casts orange alpenglow across its face. The nonsmoking restaurant serves up three meals per day with a menu similar to all the park lodges. It has kids' menus, too. Breakfast (6:30–10 A.M., $6–14) has two options—a huge buffet or à la carte. The buffet stacks with fruit, pastries, eggs, sausage, bacon, French toast, and pancakes. You won't walk away hungry, but the mass-produced entrées are sometimes only lukewarm. Lunch is served 11:30 A.M.–2 P.M. ($8–15). Dinners (5–9:30 P.M., $15–26) specialize in prime rib, wild game, chicken, ribs, and trout. The restaurant doesn't take reservations, so high season can see waiting lines. Order hiker lunches ($9) one day in advance.

Adjacent to the restaurant, the **The Sunset Lounge** serves up Montana microbrews, along with wines and cocktails, with a terrific view of Dancing Lady and Mount Henry. If you need a television fix, this is the place to go. For a quick, light meal in a nonsmoking atmosphere, appetizers and sandwiches ($8–15) are served 2–10 P.M., but the bar stays open until midnight.

Waiting lines on the front porch of **Serrano's Mexican Restaurant** (29 Dawson Ave., 406/226-9293, www.serranos-mexican.com, May–Sept., 5–10 P.M. daily) attest to its tasty food. Most dinners run $8–18, with the made-from-scratch Veggie Delight and Enchilada Especial topping the choices of house specialties. Nachos as appetizers and huge plateloads of food pacify hungry hikers. The smoke-free building is the oldest house in East Glacier; you can eat inside in its cozy dining room with wooden booths or sit on the deck out back while watching the sunset. Either way, the margaritas here are easy to down.

Run by the same owners of Brownie's Hostel and Grocery, the **(Whistle Stop Restaurant** (0.5 mile north on Hwy. 49, 406/226-9292, June–Sept., 7 A.M.–9 P.M. daily, $6–24) sits in a funky rickety-looking old building with outside seating in good weather. The breakfast specialty of stuffed French toast is crammed with huckleberries or hazelnut-vanilla filling. For kids, the Grizzly Paw French toast is served with chocolate sauce. The house dinner features barbecue ribs and chicken in different styles and portions ($11–24). Beer and wine are available, and the huckleberry pie is a must.

(Luna's Restaurant (1112 Hwy. 49, 406/226-4433, mid-May–Sept., 6:30 A.M.–9 P.M. daily, $6–17) opened in 2009 after new owners remodeled the old Thimbleberry. Luna serves up café fare, with popular biscuits and gravy or egg burritos for breakfast. Design-your-own burgers, fry bread tacos, and salads make up the menu favorites, as well as home-fried red potato chips. Dinners add comfort foods like Momma's Meatloaf. Luna's huckleberry pie is made with a graham cracker crust and cream cheese layer. The restaurant does not have an alcohol license, but you can bring in your own beer and wine for dinner.

With historic park photos on the wall, the **Glacier Village Cafe** (304-308 Hwy. 2 E., 406/226-4464, June–Sept., 7 A.M.–9 P.M. daily, $7–20) is one place you can get vegetarian and low-fat meals. The café—now run by the owners of Izaak Walton Inn—is a hiker haunt for home-baked pastries and espresso to go en route to the trail. The restaurant serves breakfast, lunch, and dinner, with specialties such as buffalo brats, wraps, entrée-size salads, and buffalo meat loaf. Beer and wine are available. You can also get picnic lunches to go.

CAFFEINE

Find that espresso jolt at three places in East Glacier: **The Empire Café** in Glacier Park Lodge, **Two Medicine Grill,** and **Brownie's.**

GROCERIES

The only full-size grocery stores (not superstores) are located in Browning, 12 miles east of East Glacier. In East Glacier, three small stores sell groceries, but don't expect them to carry every brand available. Two Medicine has a camp store.

Open year-round, **Glacier Park Trading Company** (316 Hwy. 2, 406/226-9227, 8 A.M.–9 P.M. daily in summer, 9 A.M.–8 P.M. daily in winter) sells fresh veggies, dairy products, wine, meat, and staples. It also carries a broad selection of Montana microbrews. The deli makes sandwiches ($6), good for hiker lunches, and pizzas to go. On the east end of East Glacier and also open year-round, **Bear Track Travel Center** (Exxon station, 20958 Hwy. 2, 406/226-5504, 7 A.M.–8 P.M. daily

© BECKY LOMAX

Two Medicine Grill and Glacier Park Trading Company are open year-round.

in winter, 7 A.M.–10 P.M. daily in summer) sells convenience-store foods, ice, firewood, camping and fishing supplies, beer and wine, propane, and fishing licenses. On Highway 49 in the same building that houses a hostel and a grocery, **Brownie's Bakery and Deli** (406/226-4426, June–Sept., 7 A.M.–9 P.M. daily) is an everything place—a bakery, a deli, a convenience store, an ice cream shop, an espresso stand, and an Internet café. It's a great place to pick up a deli sandwich ($6) for hiking or grab a light breakfast of muffins or bagels. Daily, the bakery churns out cookies and brownies.

On the shore of Two Medicine Lake, **Two Medicine General Store** (terminus of Two Medicine Rd., 406/892-2525, mid-June–mid-Sept., 7 A.M.–9 P.M. daily) now operates in what used to be the historic dining hall for Two Medicine Chalets. It sells a few groceries, camping and hiking supplies, newspapers, maps, gifts, books, beer, wine, ice, and ice cream. Hikers can build a trail lunch from convenience items.

PICNIC AREA

Two Medicine has the only picnic area, adjacent to the campground. It sits in a scenic spot right on the shore of Two Medicine Lake amid cottonwoods, and it has running water and

© BECKY LOMAX

Two Medicine picnic area offers lakeside tables and fire rings with grills.

flush toilets. Most the sites have some trees, which provide a good windbreak on howling days and scant shade on hot days. Sites include a picnic table and fire ring with grill, but bring your own firewood. (It's illegal to gather firewood here.)

MARIAS PASS AND ESSEX

The Theodore Roosevelt Highway (Highway 2) runs 2,119 miles from Minnesota to Washington; 57 of its miles border Glacier National Park. Small mountain enclaves are part of the charm. Both Marias Pass and Essex gained their notoriety through the railroad: Marias Pass as the route the railroad chose to cross the Continental Divide, Essex as a train community to work the tracks. The history of this Rocky Mountain corridor, as much as its scenery, adds to its appeal.

Running through John F. Stevens Canyon, the year-round highway accesses some of the wildest country around. With one and a half million acres of the Bob Marshall Wilderness Complex to the south and Glacier's one million acres to the north, the road bisects the largest grizzly bear habitat in the Lower 48. The Wild and Scenic Middle Fork of the Flathead River races through the canyon, creating a playground for rafters, kayakers, and anglers. The canyon also draws mountain goats in search of minerals and bighorn sheep and elk for wintering. From this passageway, hikers also launch onto one of Glacier's more remote trails, while horseback riders, anglers, and hunters dive into the Bob Marshall Wilderness.

Backwoodsy and removed from the usual accoutrements of civilization, the southern route around Glacier is pleasantly devoid of fast-food restaurants and chain stores. You're in wild country, where services are few and far between.

HISTORY
Marias Pass
When Lewis and Clark passed through

© BECKY LOMAX

HIGHLIGHTS

◖ Marias Pass: Drive over the Continental Divide on one of the lowest passes through the Rockies. From the pass, peaks sweep up above 8,000 feet, revealing remarkable geology (page 178).

◖ Lewis Overthrust Fault: Catapult back in time 65 million years ago to when the Lewis Overthrust pushed older rock on top of younger sediments. See this stone story in the cliff face along Summit and Little Dog Mountains (page 178).

◖ Goat Lick: Mountain goats congregate May-early July at the Goat Lick for minerals. Bring your binoculars to see the shaggy white beasts strutting across death-defying cliffs (page 179).

◖ Izaak Walton Inn: Stop for lunch at the historic inn that used to house Great Northern Railway workers. The hotel now attracts train aficionados, cross-country skiers, and those looking for a taste of history (page 179).

◖ Firebrand Pass: Climb uphill through wildflowers. Fields below the pass make you want to break out in songs from *The Sound of Music* (page 181).

◖ Stanton Lake and Grant Ridge Loop: Hike in the Great Bear Wilderness to one of the best panoramic views of the park's southern monoliths. You'll spot Stimson, Jackson, and St. Nicholas (page 183).

◖ River Rafting and Kayaking: Float the Middle Fork of the Flathead River below the Goat Lick. You'll stare up at the nimble creatures cavorting along the cliffs (page 184).

◖ Autumn Creek Trail: Cross-country ski or snowshoe beneath the ramparts of Marias Pass. Elk Mountain and Little Dog make a dramatic backdrop for the trail, which winds through lodgepole forest (page 187).

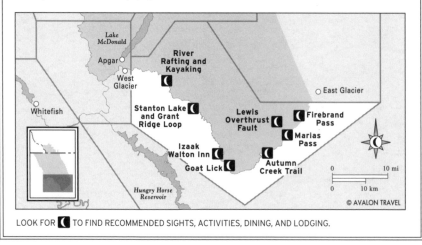

LOOK FOR ◖ TO FIND RECOMMENDED SIGHTS, ACTIVITIES, DINING, AND LODGING.

MARIAS PASS AND ESSEX

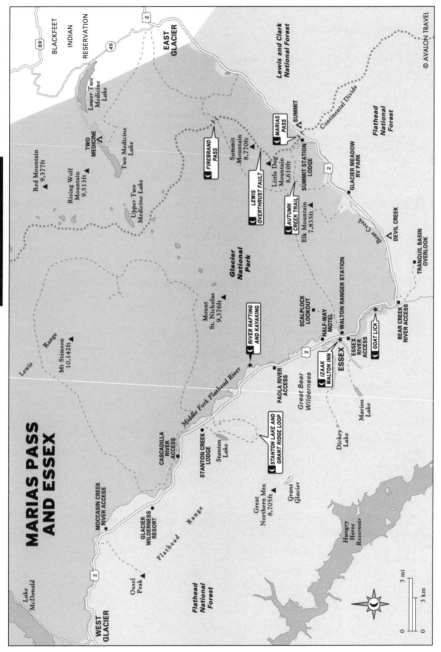

MARIAS PASS AND ESSEX

© AVALON TRAVEL

BLACKFEET INDIAN RESERVATION

EAST GLACIER

Lewis and Clark National Forest

Continental Divide

Flathead National Forest

SUMMIT

MARIAS PASS

SUMMIT STATION LODGE

GLACIER MEADOW RV PARK

Lower Two Medicine Lake

TWO MEDICINE

Two Medicine Lake

FIREBRAND PASS

Summit Mountain 8,770ft

Little Dog Mountain 8,610ft

Red Mountain 9,377ft

Rising Wolf Mountain 9,513ft

Upper Two Medicine Lake

LEWIS OVERTHRUST FAULT

AUTUMN CREEK TRAIL

Elk Mountain 7,835ft

Bear Creek

DEVIL CREEK

TRANQUIL BASIN OVERLOOK

Glacier National Park

Mount St. Nicholas 9,376ft

RIVER RAFTING AND KAYAKING

WALTON RANGER STATION

SCALPLOCK LOOKOUT

HALF-WAY MOTEL

ESSEX

ESSEX RIVER ACCESS

GOAT LICK

BEAR CREEK RIVER ACCESS

Lewis Range

Mt Stimson 10,142ft

Middle Fork Flathead River

PAOLA RIVER ACCESS

IZAAK WALTON INN

Great Bear Wilderness

Dickey Lake

Marion Lake

CASCADILLA RIVER ACCESS

STANTON CREEK LODGE

Stanton Lake

STANTON LAKE AND GRANT RIDGE LOOP

MOCCASIN CREEK RIVER ACCESS

GLACIER WILDERNESS RESORT

Great Northern Mtn 8,705ft

Grant Glacier

Flathead Range

Hungry Horse Reservoir

Ousel Peak

Flathead National Forest

Lake McDonald

WEST GLACIER

0 3 mi

0 3 km

© BECKY LOMAX

Amtrak and freight trains make use of the tracks over Marias Pass.

Montana in 1805, they failed to find Marias Pass. They came within 25 miles but swung south on the Missouri River to cross the Continental Divide on a much higher and more difficult pass. Lewis named the Marias River, christening it "Maria's River" after his cousin. The apostrophe got lost through history, much like the pass with the same name.

Reports of a "lost" pass filtered through the ranks of fur traders and mountain men. Government-funded expeditions went looking, but to no avail, while mountain men and Native Americans wandered through the real Marias Pass—yet "undiscovered." Rumors of the pass reached Great Northern Railroad developer J. J. Hill, prompting him to dispatch railroad engineer John F. Stevens and his Flathead guide Coonsa to see if the fable was true. While temperatures plummeted to 40 degrees below zero in December 1889, the pair traveled on rawhide snowshoes through deep snow. Unable to slog on, Coonsa stayed behind with a fire as Stevens ventured on solo. He found the lost pass, deeming it appropriate

for the railroad crossing. Within two years, Hill shoved the railroad across the Continental Divide at Marias Pass in his push to complete his transcontinental railway.

Building a Highway

As auto travel enchanted Americans, the demand for a road through John F. Stevens Canyon rose to a clamor. To transport an auto over the Continental Divide, you had to cough up $12.50 to put your car on a Great Northern Railway flatbed. While building Going-to-the-Sun Road dragged on for 20 years, the road over Marias Pass went through in a jiffy. Finished in 1930, the road over Marias Pass was simply much easier than chipping a route through cliffs over Logan Pass.

Lodges

In 1906, Great Northern Railway built Summit Station at Marias Pass as one of its early depots. When Glacier Park Lodge and its depot in East Glacier attracted more tourists, Summit's use died.

In 1939, Great Northern Railway constructed Izaak Walton Inn to house railroad workers who cleared the tracks of snow in winter. The railroad planned to convert it to guest lodging when the park service built a southern road entrance into Glacier. When the Depression and World War II sent park visitation plummeting, the park scrapped the south entrance. Today, Glacier's southern valleys remain remote bastions of wilderness, accessible only by trail, some only after fording the Middle Fork. The building eventually became an inn, but not under Great Northern Railway's umbrella.

Exploring Marias Pass and Essex

With two and a half million acres of public lands surrounding Highway 2—Glacier National Park, Lewis and Clark National Forest, Flathead National Forest, and the Bob Marshall Wilderness Complex—only small strips of private parcels line the valley floor. The result is a necklace of tiny mountain communities, none barely large enough to warrant the title of "village." Truly, if you blink, you will miss them.

SEASONAL CONCERNS

Highway 2 is considerably easier to maintain than Going-to-the-Sun Road. It is wider, more gradual, and for the most part, follows a fairly long, gentle 2,000-foot ascent from West Glacier to Marias Pass. However, even though Marias Pass is 1,500 feet lower than Logan Pass, the road still has its share of winter difficulties. While plows clear and sand the road frequently to keep it passable for winter travel, cornices thousands of feet above break loose, careening avalanches down across its path. Some winters the highway is closed for several days while road crews clear a path through ice, rock, and tree debris.

SHUTTLES AND TOURS

No hiker shuttles regularly run across Highway 2. You either have to drive yourself to trailheads or use your thumb, which is legal in Montana. By reservation, you can arrange for a shuttle with **Flathead-Glacier Transportation** (406/892-3390 or 800/829-7039). They accommodate backpackers hiking point-to-point trails, dropping you off at one trailhead and

picking you up at another several days later ($40–130 one-way for one person, $3 for each additional person). The company will also run a shuttle between Glacier International Airport and Izaak Walton Inn ($90).

The historic **red buses** run by Glacier Park, Inc. (406/892-2525 www.glacierparkinc.com, mid-June–mid-Sept., adults $80, kids half price) drive over both Marias and Logan Passes on their eight-and-a-half-hour loop. For $5–10 more, the buses will pick up riders at Glacier Meadows RV Park or Izaak Walton Inn for tours originating in East Glacier. For details, check the *Two Medicine and East Glacier* chapter.

SERVICES

This 60-mile corridor through wild untamed wilderness is a road where the usual expectancies of civilization are not readily available. You won't find gas stations between East Glacier and West Glacier; fill up in either of those towns before you leave.

While you can find some newspapers sold in the inns and restaurants along the highway, you'll need to head to East or West Glacier for ATMs, laundry, and anything resembling espresso. For hot showers ($5), you can pop in to Glacier Meadow RV Park. **The Half-Way Motel** (milepost 178, Essex, 406/888-5650) runs a tiny post office.

Even though Highway 2 lacks many services, public restrooms are plentiful. Most are vault toilets with no running water and are open spring–fall. Find these at all river access points, Walton Picnic Area, the Goat Lick, and Marias Pass.

PUBLIC LANDS: WHAT'S THE DIFFERENCE?

Many people are confused by the various types of public lands. In the greater Glacier ecosystem, national park lands border national forest and wilderness area. So what are these? National parks, national forests, and wilderness areas are each managed differently, with different purposes:

- **National parks** fall under the U.S. Department of the Interior. Parks are set aside for their historical, geological, cultural, or biological significance and geared toward public recreation. Hunting is not permitted, nor is picking mushrooms or berries for commercial use. Mining and logging are also taboo. Leases for developing recreation like ski resorts are not available. Generally, dogs are not allowed on trails; neither are mountain bikes. Permits are needed for backcountry camping.

- **National forests** come under the U.S. Department of Agriculture. With permits, hunting, timber harvesting, and commercial berry picking are generally allowed. National forest land is leased for recreational development, such as ski areas. Your pooch can go with you on hikes; you can mountain bike as long as no special designation says otherwise. Permits are not needed for backcountry camping.

- **Wilderness areas** are administered usually by the national forest that contains the wilderness boundaries. Two concepts set wilderness apart: no mechanical transports and no permanent human inhabitants. Wilderness areas do not have roads inside them. While hunting is permitted and Fido can go along on the trail, mountain biking is not allowed. Permits are not needed for backcountry camping.

For maps, guidebooks, and information on outdoor activities in the Great Bear Wilderness and the Bob Marshall, contact the **Hungry Horse Ranger Station** (10 Hungry Horse Dr., 406/387-3800, www.fs.fed.us/r1/flathead), nine miles west of West Glacier. It is the place for information on river rafting, fishing, hiking, hunting, and horse packing in the national forest. For Lewis and Clark National Forest information, call the Rocky Mountain Ranger Station in Choteau (1102 Main Ave. NW, 406/466-5341, www.fs.fed.us/r1/lewisclark).

Cell Phones and Internet

Because of John F. Stevens Canyon and surrounding steep mountains, you'll find cell reception intermittent to nonexistent on Highway 2, but you can stop to use old-fashioned public pay telephones at Stanton Creek Lodge, Izaak Walton Inn, and Snow Slip Inn. The nearest Internet services are in East and West Glacier, except for Glacier Meadow RV Park and Izaak Walton Inn.

Emergencies

If the emergency permits a choice, most people head to the large hospitals in Flathead Valley, 35 minutes from West Glacier—Kalispell Regional Medical Center (310 Sunny View Ln., Kalispell, 406/752-5111) and North Valley Hospital (1600 Hospital Wy., Whitefish, 406/863-3500). The nearest east-side and smaller hospital is the Northern Rockies Medical Center (802 2nd St. E., Cut Bank, 406/873-2251), 46 miles from East Glacier. For river emergencies along the Middle Fork of the Flathead, just get to a phone and dial 911.

The **Walton Ranger Station** (milepost 180.5, 406/888-7800), at Walton Picnic Area on the southernmost tip of Glacier National Park, is staffed only in summer, and not full time, as the rangers patrol miles of backcountry trails. If you need assistance, use the pay phone at Izaak Walton Inn (0.8 mile west of the Walton Ranger Station) to call Glacier Park Headquarters (406/888-7800).

DRIVING TOUR
Highway 2

After driving the dramatic Going-to-the-Sun Road, most visitors are less than impressed with this southern highway. You can drive the highway from East Glacier to West Glacier in a little over an hour. Locals use the road as a faster route across the Continental Divide when too many cars clog Going-to-the-Sun Road midsummer. All large RVs and trailers use it, as they are precluded from driving Going-to-the-Sun Road. In spite of its use as a year-round thoroughfare, it still is a scenic highway. Drive it from either direction: from East or West Glacier.

Montana has an oddity on its highways—white crosses marking fatalities. One cross equals one traffic fatality. Begun in 1953, the American Legion–sponsored program operates in conjunction with the Montana Department of Transportation to use the crosses as safety reminders. An estimated 2,000 sobering crosses line the state's highways—several on this highway.

SIGHTS

Highway 2 sights are listed here from East Glacier to West Glacier.

Lewis and Clark National Forest

From south of East Glacier to Marias Pass, Highway 2 passes through the Lewis and Clark National Forest. Its 1.7 million acres serve as the headwaters for the mighty Missouri River. High prairies at 4,500 feet in elevation climb up to Rocky Mountain Peak, at 9,362 feet, along the Rocky Mountain Front in an extremely diverse ecosystem that harbors species like lynx and grizzly bears. Around milepost 198, you'll get good views south of 46,000 burned acres from the 2007 Skyland Fire.

◖ Marias Pass

At 5,220 feet, Marias Pass (milepost 197.9) is the lowest Continental Divide saddle north of New Mexico. Two monuments mark the pass: A statue of John F. Stevens commemorates his discovery of the passage, and a tall obelisk stands in memory of Theodore Roosevelt, for whom the highway is named. Legend has it that he visited Many Glacier in 1910, but no official records indicate so. The 3,100-mile Continental

The Marias Pass obelisk commemorates Theodore Roosevelt.

Divide Trail crosses into Glacier National Park here, where hikers and skiers launch onto Autumn Creek Trail. If signs and the monuments weren't here, you'd be hard pressed to realize you were crossing the Continental Divide, with the area's broad flat forest.

◖ Lewis Overthrust Fault

Opposite Marias Pass, the Lewis Overthrust Fault shoved older 1.6-billion-year-old rocks on top of 80-million-year-old stones. This fault exposed some of the oldest sediments in the world—ancient Precambrian rocks that formed as Belt Sea sediments solidified. On the face of Summit and Little Dog Peaks, look for an obvious upward line where the younger Cretaceous rock from the dinosaur age shows up as black or brown. This is the site where in the 1890s geologists discovered the Lewis Overthrust Fault, which extends into Canada and sets Glacier apart as a World Heritage Site.

Silver Stairs Falls

Tumbling thousands of feet, an unmarked

© BECKY LOMAX

Silver Stairs Falls

Bob Marshall Wilderness Complex

While Glacier rises to the north of the highway, to the south the Bob Marshall Wilderness Complex spans nearly one and a half million acres. It actually comprises three wilderness areas: The Bob (as locals call it), the Great Bear, and the Scapegoat. The Great Bear is the section bordering Highway 2. The Bob Marshall was one of the country's first wilderness areas, dedicated in 1964 concurrent with the Wilderness Act. Scapegoat was added in 1972, and Great Bear six years later. While roads do not enter the wilderness areas and mechanized vehicles are prohibited (no mountain bikes or snowmobiles), a plethora of trails lead off Highway 2. Short day hikes access the Great Bear, while longer overnight treks reach The Bob, a world-class area for horse packing, fishing, and big-game hunting.

◖ Izaak Walton Inn

Listed on the National Register of Historic Places, Izaak Walton Inn (milepost 179.7) sits opposite the southernmost point of Glacier National Park at Essex. The hotel stands adjacent to the train tracks, luring train aficionados, cross-country skiers, and those looking for something a bit different, like sleeping in a renovated caboose. Loaded with historical photos and memorabilia, the inn makes you feel almost like you've been transported back to a different era. In the downstairs bar, check out photos of avalanches burying the railroad tracks. Eat lunch on Great Northern Railway plates in the small dining room, and cozy up to the warm lobby fire.

Mount St. Nicholas

The toothy 9,376-foot spire of St. Nicholas is easy to pick out on the skyline—especially rimmed with winter snow. Look for a notched spire with precipitous cliffs on its southern face. Grab good views of this forbidding-looking peak driving eastward on Highway 2. For more in-your-face views of it, hike Grant Ridge Loop counterclockwise or climb to Scalplock Lookout.

John F. Stevens Canyon

Named for the Great Northern Railway

and unsigned pullout on the highway's south side stares up at Silver Stairs Falls (milepost 188.2). The waterfall cascades down a series of stairsteps created from eroding sedimentary layers. In June and July, water rages down in torrents, but by late August it slows to a trickle. You can catch quick views with a drive-by, but with alder and brush surrounding the falls, you'll get a better view by stopping.

◖ Goat Lick

Much of Glacier National Park's wildlife tends to be mineral deficient. Because their bodies crave minerals from their winter-deprived condition, during spring and early summer mountain goats congregate at the Goat Lick (milepost 182.6). The lick is actually a huge mass of gray rock cliffs, an exposed fault containing salts like calcium, magnesium, and potassium. Goats hop sure-footed along the steep cliff faces as if they were on flat land to slurp the minerals. The well-marked overlook has a couple of viewing areas with interpretive signs. Bring your binoculars for better viewing.

BOB MARSHALL WILDERNESS COMPLEX

The largest wilderness area in Montana, the Bob Marshall Wilderness Complex straddles 1.5 million acres along 110 miles of the Continental Divide. It harbors a huge ungulate population of deer, elk, moose, mountain goats, and bighorn sheep. They feed predators like lynx, grizzlies, black bears, mountain lions, and wolves. Over 1,000 miles of trails crisscross its ranges, with peaks reaching 9,000 feet high. The 1,000-foot-high Chinese Wall escarpment runs for 22 miles along the Continental Divide.

The complex is named for Bob Marshall, a young forester who became a local legend in 1925 with marathon 30-mile mountain treks around the Missoula area. Later, he penned *The Problem of Wilderness*, a treatise defining principles that would shape the movement to preserve America's wilds. In a one-man crusade as the Forest Service's Lands Division chief, he placed 5.4 million acres of vulnerable lands under wilderness protection. Along with Aldo Leopold and others, he launched the Wilderness Society in 1935, but he died four years later at age 38.

In 1941, the South Fork, Pentagon, and Sun River areas south of Glacier were set aside as primitive zones. But finally after 66 drafts, the 1964 Wilderness Act protected them from development. As part of the act, the three primitive zone areas combined to create the one-million-acre **Bob Marshall Wilderness.**

Unprecedented lobbying by a Lincoln citizen group led by a hardware store owner resulted in the adjacent **Scapegoat Wilderness,** adding 239,936 acres to the south in 1972. Scapegoat houses 50 miles of the 3,100-mile-long Continental Divide Trail.

Six years later, a third wilderness was added to the complex – the **Great Bear Wilderness,** adjoining its 286,700 acres of land to the northwest. Tucked between Hungry Horse Reservoir and Glacier National Park, the Great Bear houses 300 miles of trail and tops out at 8,700 feet on Great Northern, the sweeping peak seen from Flathead Valley.

Together these three wilderness areas along with Glacier Park comprise 2.5 million acres of habitat for species such as grizzly bears, lynx, and wolves. The wilderness complex is managed jointly by Flathead, Lewis and Clark, Lolo, and Helena National Forests.

engineer who verified the feasibility of Marias Pass as a railroad route, John F. Stevens Canyon begins just west of the pass and follows Bear Creek and the Middle Fork of the Flathead until its terminus near West Glacier. Highway 2 and the railroad traverse the canyon's entire 40-mile distance. In places the canyon broadens into wide valleys; in others it tightens up into narrow channels, frothing with wild waters. Although its more dramatic sections are seen best from a raft or kayak on the river, several highway pullouts still offer good photo ops.

Flathead National Forest

From the Continental Divide west past Flathead Valley and extending 120 miles south of the Canadian border, Flathead National Forest is broken up by state and private land but still tallies up a healthy 2.3 million acres. Within its glaciated mountains, it has 2,600 miles of trails. Over 46 percent of the forest is designated wilderness area. Spruce, Douglas fir, lodgepole, larch, and pine cover its slopes—home to wolverines, grizzly bears, and wolves.

Middle Fork of the Flathead River

Draining Glacier National Park and the Bob Marshall Wilderness Complex, the Middle Fork of the Flathead River is no small tributary. Designated a Wild and Scenic River, its 95-mile length is known for some of the best white-water rafting and kayaking in Montana. Dropping at 35 feet per mile, the Great Bear section teems with Class III and IV rapids; the lower waters break up long scenic floats with Class II and III rapids with such names as Jaws and Bonecrusher. Hook up with one of the four West Glacier rafting companies to splash in its waves: **Glacier Raft Company** (6 Going-to-the-Sun Rd., 406/888-5454 or 800/235-6781, www.glacierraftco.com), **Great Northern Whitewater** (12127 Hwy. 2 E., 406/387-5340 or 800/735-7897, www.gnwhitewater. com), **Montana Raft Company** (11970 Hwy. 2 E., 406/387-5555 or 800/521-7238, www. glacierguides.com), or **Wild River Adventures** (11900 Hwy. 2 E., 406/387-9453 or 800/700-7056, www.riverwild.com).

Wintering Range

Belton Mountain, to the road's north (milepost 155–157), is quite a different ecosystem from the heavily forested south slopes. Fires, winds, and a dry exposure have minimized forest growth. Winds create a lower snowpack, and south-facing slopes melt off early—both keys to making the area a prime wintering range for ungulates such as deer, elk, and bighorn sheep. Grizzly and black bears also forage on its slopes. Even in summer, it's worth a stop at one of the several pullouts to scan slopes with binoculars.

Recreation

HIKING

Highway 2 is one road where hiker shuttles are not available; you must get to trailheads on your own. Most of Glacier's trails on the south end are long valley hikes accessing little-used areas. Additional short hikes, mostly in the Great Bear Wilderness, fill out the options—especially for hikers with Fido. While trails within Glacier do not allow dogs, your canine friend can tag along on a leash in the wilderness area. Be aware, however, that hiking with pets in bear country poses certain dilemmas; a dog will not protect you from a bear encounter.

While trails within Glacier National Park are well signed and frequently maintained, trails in the wilderness areas are not; signs, if any, may be just a wooden trail number or name nailed to a tree—no mileages. Take a good topographical map, which you can purchase from the Hungry Horse Ranger Station (10 Hungry Horse Dr., Hungry Horse, 406/387-3800), and know how to read it! Be prepared to encounter deadfall, downed trees, and heavy brush. Trail crews in the national forests do not have the staff numbers of the national park trail crews; it takes them longer to get to damaged or buried trails. Contrary to Glacier, bear-warning signage does not exist, except in extreme cases. Make noise and take precautions in bear country.

Hikes are listed here from east to west on Highway 2.

◖ Firebrand Pass

- Distance: 9.6 miles round-trip
- Duration: 4.5 hours
- Elevation gain: 2,210 feet
- Effort: moderate
- Trailhead: at milepost 203 on Highway 2

From the trailhead, the path wanders by beaver ponds, crosses into Glacier Park, passes the old Lubec ranger station site, and follows Coonsa Creek northward. At 1.4 miles, turn right at the Autumn Creek Trail junction and ascend through aspens and meadows thick in July with valerian, lupine, paintbrush, and penstemon to another junction about one mile later. Take a left, gaining elevation as the trail circumvents Calf Robe's lower slopes. Make noise, for this is prime bear country.

As the trail breaks out of the trees, you'll have views of Dancing Lady and East Glacier. The trail rounds Calf Robe into a hanging basin and then ascends to the pass, where you can look down Ole Creek and into Glacier's remote southern peaks. Scrambles up Calf Robe or Red Crow lend even better views, but don't go off trail unless you're ready to deal with steep scree hillsides.

Elk Mountain

- Distance: 7 miles round-trip
- Duration: 6 hours
- Elevation gain: 3,355 feet
- Effort: strenuous
- Trailhead: turn north off Highway 2 at Fielding (milepost 192) and follow the dirt road #1066 about a half mile to the trailhead

Hike up through private logged land to the railroad tracks and cross into Glacier Park. The trail starts off deceptively easy enough, but shortly after turning right at the junction near a ranger cabin, the trail climbs and climbs. *Steep* does not come close to describing the pitch as it ascends to an open saddle. No wonder you have so much solitude here. From here, you can see the remainder of the trail, climbing sharply again across a talus slope to the summit.

From the top, among debris from what was once the lookout, the views make the grunt worthwhile. Panoramas both north and south line up peak tops for miles into Glacier's remote southern sector and the Bob Marshall Wilderness Complex. A knife ridge leads east toward the Continental Divide, and the view down Autumn Creek is dizzying.

Scalplock Lookout

- Distance: 9.4 miles round-trip
- Duration: 5 hours
- Elevation gain: 3,079 feet
- Effort: strenuous
- Trailhead: Walton Picnic Area (milepost 180.5)

This can be a gorgeous early July hike, with bluebells in the high meadows, but be prepared for snow on top in June. Beginning in the Walton Picnic Area, the trail wanders along the Middle Fork of the Flathead in the first mile, crossing Ole Creek on a swinging bridge over a small gorge and ascending to the Ole Creek trail. Turn west on this trail for 0.4 mile to a second junction where the climb begins. In the remaining

Hikers descend the Scalplock Lookout trail.

© BECKY LOMAX

three miles, the trail grunts up switchbacks at nearly 1,000 feet per mile as sounds of the highway and train reverberate from below.

Peek-a-boo views of the Middle Fork of the Flathead River are the only respite from the relentless ascent. Near the top, the trail breaks out of the trees to climb up a ridge flanked with wildflower meadows. At the top, Scalplock Lookout has a commanding view of the entire Middle Fork drainage, with Mount St. Nicholas spire in your face.

Marion Lake

- Distance: 3.4 miles round-trip
- Duration: 2 hours
- Elevation gain: 1,810 feet
- Effort: short, but strenuous
- Trailhead: turn south on the Dickey Lake Road (milepost 178.7, Road #1640) at Essex and follow the left fork 2.3 miles to the Flathead National Forest–signed trailhead

Due to the trail's popularity, it sees quite of bit of summer traffic, making it well worn and quite obvious to follow until you encounter heavy foliage. From the start, it taxes your lungs on its steep climb up Marion Creek Valley. You will encounter thick, heavy brush in the trail's midsection. Cow parsnip, nettle, elderberry, and false huckleberry nearly suffocate the trail. Make noise here to avoid surprising a bear.

You know you're nearing the lake when the trail assumes a more moderate pitch. Marion Lake sits in a photo-worthy glacial cirque surrounded by cliffs and the outlet congested with logs. Anglers should bring rods, for the lake harbors westslope cutthroat trout up to 12 inches.

Dickey Lake

- Distance: 4.8 miles round-trip

- Duration: 2.5 hours

- Elevation gain: 1,460 feet

- Effort: moderate

- Trailhead: turn south on Dickey Lake Road (milepost 178.7, Road #1640) at Essex and follow the right fork three miles to an unmarked spur where the Flathead National Forest trail begins

This short trail in the Great Bear Wilderness gives rather decent rewards for its efforts, and anglers will want to tote a fishing rod. After wading Dickey Creek, the forested trail climbs up a large bowl riddled with avalanche paths, which means deadfall, limbs, and uprooted and downed trees. In places, thick brush chokes the path, but you can still follow it to the headwall near the basin's end. From here, a rock cairn, which may be buried in snow that hangs late in the season, marks the trail, ascending steeply through false huckleberry bushes dangling with pale apricot blossoms into a hanging valley.

Upon reaching the upper basin, the trail pops out on the edge of Dickey Lake. The shallow tarn flanked by meadows and steep talus slopes is a scenic lunch spot. You'll most likely find solitude here. Anglers will enjoy fishing for cutthroats in the small lake.

◖ Stanton Lake and Grant Ridge Loop

- Distance: 2 miles round-trip or 10.2-mile loop

- Duration: 1 or 5 hours

- Elevation gain: 600 or 3,605 feet

- Effort: easy or strenuous

- Trailhead: Stanton Lake Trailhead on Highway 2 at mile marker 169.9 in the Flathead National Forest

An easy short hike plops hikers and anglers on the shores of Stanton Lake, or a longer strenuous loop explores the ultrascenic Grant Ridge, both in the Great Bear Wilderness. From the trailhead, a steep grunt heads straight uphill. But never fear, for it levels out soon into a nice forested walk that leads into the basin cradling Stanton Lake. For a short hike to a well-traveled destination, stop here. Anglers should bring

© BECKY LOMAX

Stanton Lake makes a great kids' destination.

rods to fish for westslope cutthroat, rainbows, and mountain whitefish. Some maps show the trail continuing above Stanton Lake; however, that trail peters out promptly in willow bogs.

For the Grant Ridge Loop, take the left fork before the lake and ford the outlet creek. The trail climbs a forested hillside with peek-a-boo views of Great Northern, the highest peak in the Great Bear Wilderness. At the ridge top, follow a faint, intermittent trail a quarter mile south to a rocky outcrop overlooking Grant Peak and the waterfall springing from the glacier's snout. With views of Glacier's southern monoliths, the trail wanders north below the ridgeline before descending switchbacks to the highway a half mile from the starting point. Many hikers prefer to do this loop clockwise, staring at Grant and Great Northern during the ridgeline walk.

Ousel Peak

- Distance: 5.2 miles round-trip
- Duration: 3.5 hours
- Elevation gain: 3,260 feet
- Effort: very strenuous
- Trailhead: mile marker 159.6 on Highway 2 in the Flathead National Forest

Do the math: This trail gains well over 1,000 feet per mile and from the first minute makes no bones about heading straight uphill. If the uphill doesn't tax your lungs, the downhill will pound your knees. Nevertheless, the view from the top is outstanding and well worth the effort or pain. Sitting on the northern edge of the Great Bear Wilderness, the trail climbs through a forest canopy littered with various microclimates, from wet seeps to dry, arid slopes. The path finally breaks out of the forest with glimpses of Glacier's peaks. At the top, remnants of the old lookout scatter across the hillside amid tiny yellow stonecrop. Look into Glacier to see Mounts Jackson and Stimson along with Harrison Glacier.

BIKING

Cross-country bicyclists use Highway 2 to cross the Continental Divide when Going-to-the-Sun Road is not open. However, many use it also to make a big loop through and around Glacier (Going-to-the-Sun Road and Highways 89, 49, and 2). Compared to the rest of Glacier's roads, Highway 2 is definitely an easier ride, for it has shoulders in some sections and is a bit wider and less curvy. However, due to heavy traffic in summer, it can be downright dangerous, with large rigs that nearly blow cyclists off the road. Tackle it only if you can handle riding with semis and RVs whipping by your elbows at 60 mph.

Be prepared for winds, especially at Marias Pass. They are usually blowing eastward, so those riding toward West Glacier encounter substantial headwinds. Also, be extra cautious in the five curvy miles east of West Glacier, as severe turns reduce the visibility of drivers on the road. Even though no law requires a helmet, think twice about leaving your brain bucket off. Most drivers here are gawking at scenery or trying to spot wildlife rather than keeping their attention totally on the road.

Mountain bikes are not permitted on trails in the wilderness areas nor in Glacier Park.

◖ RIVER RAFTING AND KAYAKING

Designated as Wild and Scenic, the **Middle Fork of the Flathead River** is the local hot spot for rafting and kayaking. The river comes in two sections—the wilderness above Bear Creek and the lower section below Bear Creek.

With headwaters starting in the Great Bear Wilderness, you'll need to fly in to Schaeffer Meadows or pack in on a horse to float the upper 26 miles. Contact the Flathead National Forest Hungry Horse Ranger Station (406/387-3800) for details on rafting and floating this upper wild section. The normal float season (Class III and IV) runs mid-May–mid-July. During peak runoff in May, the trip can often be more challenging, with several rapids becoming Class V and spring snows chilling the air.

From Bear Creek to the confluence with the North Fork of the Flathead, the river runs 46 miles, with easy river access from locations on Highway 2: Bear Creek (milepost 185), Essex

© BECKY LOMAX

Rafters splash in white water on the Middle Fork of the Flathead River.

Natural History Association (406/888-5756, www.glacierassociation.org, $12.95) for location of rapids and public land for camping. No permits are needed for overnights. In the Great Bear Wilderness, sites are not restricted, but in the section below Bear Creek, private lands abut national forest land, much of it unmarked. No camping is permitted on the Glacier Park side of the river.

Guides

Four local river companies operate out of West Glacier, guiding half-day, full-day, and overnight trips on the Middle Fork of the Flathead. **Glacier Raft Company** (406/888-5454 or 800/235-6781, www.glacierraftco.com) is the only one that guides trips in the wilderness section above Bear Creek. Check for details in the *West Glacier and Apgar* chapter.

Rentals and Shuttles

Two West Glacier raft companies rent rafts, kayaks, camping gear, toilet systems, and fire pans: **Montana Raft Company** (406/387-5555 or 800/521-7238, www.glacierguides.com) and **Glacier Raft Company** (406/888-5454 or 800/235-6781, www.glacierraftco.com). Glacier also provides shuttle services on the Middle Fork in your rigs ($30–200) or theirs ($50–315). Overnight vehicle storage is included for free.

FISHING
Rivers and Streams

In Glacier Park, Ole, Park, Muir, Coal, and Nyack Creeks are closed to fishing. However, anglers can drop lines in Summit, Railroad, and Badger Creeks, which flow from Marias Pass east through Lewis and Clark National Forest and onto the Blackfeet Reservation. **Badger Creek,** in particular, has a good reputation for rainbow trout. **Bear Creek,** good for westslope cutthroat, mountain whitefish, and some rainbow trout, drops west from Marias to its confluence with the Middle Fork of the Flathead River. The **Middle Fork** has plenty of river accesses for fishing: Bear Creek, Essex, Paola, Cascadilla, and Moccasin.

(milepost 180), Paola (milepost 175.2), Cascadilla (milepost 166), Moccasin Creek (milepost 160.5), and West Glacier (follow signs to the golf course). With the float season running mid-May–early September, the river accesses make for easy half- or full-day float trips. Between Bear Creek and Cascadilla, rapids rate Class III and IV. Waters flatten to a float trip from Cascadilla to Moccasin Creek, but be aware of deadly log jams. From Moccasin to West Glacier, rapids range Class II and III, with some IVs during late May high water. The average float time in July from Bear Creek to Cascadilla usually takes six and a half hours, and from Moccasin Creek to West Glacier two and a half hours.

Flathead National Forest manages the river, even though it borders Glacier National Park. Consult Hungry Horse Ranger Station (10 Hungry Horse Dr., 406/387-5243), located nine miles west of West Glacier, for assistance in planning a self-guided overnight trip. Toilet systems are required for overnights and fire pans recommended. Rafters and kayakers should purchase the *Three Forks of the Flathead Floater's Guide,* available through Glacier

MARIAS PASS AND ESSEX

Lakes

Inside the park, good cutthroat trout fishing lakes such as Ole, Harrison, and Isabel usually require backpacking or fording the Middle Fork of the Flathead. It's actually easier to get to lakes in the Great Bear Wilderness on the south side of the highway. **Stanton Lake** is a quick destination with westslope cutthroat trout, mountain whitefish, and rainbow trout, but it's somewhat overfished because of its ease of access. Dickey and Marion Lakes also harbor cutthroat.

Guides

For guided fishing on Blackfeet Nation lands, contact **Blackfeet Fish and Wildlife** (406/338-7207, www.blackfeetfishandwildlife.com) for a list of licensed outfitters. From West Glacier, four fishing companies guide fly-fishing trips on the Middle Fork of the Flathead River. Check for details in the *West Glacier and Apgar* chapter.

Licenses and Regulations

Fishing regulations along Highway 2 vary depending on land ownership. Check carefully where you are before dropping a line into waters. The road passes through Blackfeet tribal lands, Glacier National Park, and national forests. For details on each of these permits, see the *Background* chapter. You can purchase Tribal fishing permits at Bear Track Travel Center (Exxon station in East Glacier, 20958 Hwy. 2, 406/226-5504, 7 A.M.–8 P.M. daily in winter, 7 A.M.–10 P.M. daily in summer). For Montana State licenses, go to Glacier Outdoor Center in West Glacier (11957 Hwy. 2 E., 406/888-5454 or 800/235-6781, www.glacierraftco.com).

HUNTING

Hunting is illegal in Glacier National Park. But just south of Highway 2, the famed Bob Marshall Wilderness boasts world-renowned big-game hunting for bighorn sheep, elk, and black bear. East-side grasslands are also famous for bird hunting. For hunting in the Bob Marshall Wilderness or in national forests,

get regulations and license info from Montana Fish, Wildlife, and Parks (406/444-2535, www.fwp.mt.gov). The Blackfeet Reservation (406/338-7207, www.blackfeetfishandwildlife.com) has separate regulations and licenses for tribal lands. Check also with each for names of licensed outfitters.

CROSS-COUNTRY SKIING AND SNOWSHOEING

In winter, ski and snowshoe routes off Highway 2 are popular for their ease of access. You'll find everything from groomed skate and classic skiing trails to snowmobile-packed tracks and off-piste break-your-own-trail treks.

Izaak Walton Inn

With 20 miles of track groomed daily for skate and classic skiing late November–mid-April, Izaak Walton Inn (290 Izaak Walton Inn Rd., 406/888-5700, www.izaakwaltoninn.com) makes a great cross-country skiing destination at milepost 179.7 on Highway 2. At the

Izaak Walton Inn grooms an intricate system of ski trails.

© BECKY LOMAX

inn, trails range from easy meanders to steep grunts. One short section of trail is lit for night skiing. Trail passes for skiing are $12 per day and are available to day visitors as well as inn guests. Although the area never feels crowded, its most popular time is Christmas–Presidents' Day. Lessons are available from the lodge as well as rentals (skis or snowshoes), and the rentals can be taken elsewhere to use. The inn also guides half-day snowshoe tours and full-day ski tours in Glacier.

◖ Autumn Creek Trail

One of the most popular ski trails in Glacier is Autumn Creek Trail at Marias Pass, which can be skied point to point if you set up a car shuttle or hitchhike, which is legal in Montana. The west trailhead sits at milepost 193.8 on Highway 2. Park across the highway, then ski up the railroad access road and across the tracks. The other trailhead is at Marias Pass, across Highway 2 from the parking lot (milepost 197.9). Orange markers on trees denote the six-mile trail. Beginners will find more success in the Marias Pass section rather than the steep Autumn Creek section. Those seeking to avoid the narrow, steep 660-foot elevation drop downhill should begin on the west end and finish at the pass.

SNOWMOBILING

Snowmobilers gravitate to groomed and ungroomed roads in Lewis and Clark National Forest (406/791-7700) and Flathead National Forest (406/758-5204). The most popular snowmobiling is in the Marias Pass and Skyland/Challenge complex, both straddling the Continental Divide south of Highway 2. The Cut Bank Snowgoers and Flathead Snowmobile Association groom about 40 miles of trail, which are open for snowmobiling December 1–May 15. Contact them via the Montana Snowmobile Association (406/788-2399, www.snowtana.com). Snow depths in both of these snowmobiling areas vary 150–250 inches. Some restrictions apply to the designated connecting trails, so get a good snowmobile map through Montana Snowmobile Association. The nearest rentals are in Flathead Valley.

ENTERTAINMENT

Every Labor Day Weekend, spiffed-up and spit-shined classic cars descend on Stanton Creek Lodge for the annual **Show and Shine.** The event features evening parking lot dances, barbecues, live bands, and the car show. Call the Stanton Creek Lodge (406/888-5040 or 866/883-5040) for the current schedule and entry info.

Accommodations

Along Highway 2, lodging spans historic inns, rustic cabins, and tiny motels. Regardless of type, that 7 percent Montana state bed tax will find your bill here.

Lodges

Since 2006, the new owners at ◖ **Izaak Walton Inn** (290 Izaak Walton Inn Rd., 406/888-5700, www.izaakwaltoninn.com, open year-round, $117–400) have added new lodging options to the Essex complex. In addition to the historic lodge rooms and cabooses, the resort now features new cabins, a luxury

locomotive, and the 1920s Withrow House. From the lobby fireplace to the Dining Car Restaurant or the swinging seat on the porch, the nonsmoking inn is a place to unwind and relax. The inn maintains its historic ambience with no televisions, in-room phones, air-conditioning, or elevators; a pay phone is off the lobby. Lodge rooms vary in size, although most bathrooms are fairly small. Check out the avalanche photos in the basement Flagstop Bar, where you can also get wireless Internet access. A short walk over a footbridge above the railroad tracks leads to four heated cabooses with

© BECKY LOMAX

You can stay in a locomotive at Izaak Walton Inn.

kitchenettes and full bathrooms, set in the trees and sleeping four in each. In the same glen, six new log cabins with kitchens were built in 2008. They sleep up to six in bedrooms and lofts, and include kitchens. The luxury locomotive that sleeps four with its picture window looks out on the train tracks. Two nights minimum are required for cabins, cabooses, and the locomotive. Withrow House sleeps 10 and requires three nights.

Amenities include a sauna, coin-op launderette, wireless Internet in the Flagstop Bar, restaurant, cross-country ski trails in winter, walking trails, and railroad ambience. You can arrive and depart by train, as it's an Amtrak stop. Bring earplugs, for trains rumble by each night. You can rent skis or snowshoes in winter. In summer, red bus tours pick up riders here for an all-day loop around Going-to-the-Sun Road. To get good deals, check the inn's packages, which include skiing, rafting, park sightseeing, and special weekends for railway fans.

Motels

Several small no-frills motels dot Highway 2—all within close earshot of the highway and train noise. Bring earplugs. All three have restaurants on the premises. Under new ownership since 2009, the **Snow Slip Inn** (milepost 180, 15644 Hwy. 2 E., Essex, 406/226-4400, www.snowslipinn.com, open year-round, $75 summer, $50 off-season) has six motel rooms and wireless Internet. Aptly named for its location halfway between East and West Glacier, **⟨ The Half-Way Motel** (milepost 178, Essex, 406/888-5650) is a family-run motel with four large clean rooms ($80 for two people) with two queen beds, fridge, microwave, coffeemaker, and satellite TV. At milepost 173.8, **Glacier Haven Inn** (14305 Hwy. 2, 406/888-5720, www.glacierhaveninn.com, open year-round) has small rooms ($99–140) with two double beds and satellite TV.

Cabins

Flathead National Forest (406/387-3809, www.fs.fed.us/r1/flathead/) rents two rustic cabins with three-night maximums. Both are accessible from Highway 2 and must be reserved (877/444-6777, www.recreation.gov). Decked out with propane, mattresses, and kitchen utensils, the cabins are reasonably well equipped and warm with either propane heat or woodstoves (wood is supplied). A seven-mile ski or snowmobile ride up Skyland Road (milepost 195.8 on Highway 2), tiny one-room **Challenge Cabin** (Dec.–Mar., $30 per night) sleeps six people stacked like sardines. A much larger two-bedroom cabin sleeping eight, **Zip's Place** (June–Mar., $50 per night) is found by turning off Highway 2 (milepost 191.9) and driving two miles, following signs. In winter, it requires a ski or snowshoe trip to reach the front door. Bring your own food and sleeping bags. Both are nonsmoking; neither permit pets.

Small, simple, rustic cabins; a restaurant; a bar; and a campground make up **Stanton Creek Lodge** (milepost 170 on Hwy. 2, 406/888-5040 or 866/883-5040, www.stantoncreeklodge.com, open year-round). Six heated cabins with linens and towels vary in size ($69–99). The higher-priced cabins, those open year-round, have satellite TV and private bathrooms; other cabins share a bathhouse, which is closed in winter. Trailheads to Stanton Lake and Grant Loop sit adjacent to the lodge, and fishing on the Middle Fork River is easily accessible. Bring earplugs for highway and train noise.

The closest lodging to West Glacier, **⟨ Glacier Wilderness Resort** (milepost 163 on Hwy. 2, 406/888/5664, www.glacierwildernessresort.com, open year-round, $215–295) sits in a woodsy setting abutting the Great Bear Wilderness. With an indoor heated pool, its 11 one- and two-bedroom log cabins that sleep 4–6 people come with fireplaces, satellite televisions, DVD/VCR, fully equipped kitchens, and private hot tubs. Summertime usually requires a five-night minimum; other seasons require a two-night minimum stay. In summer, you can use an outdoor picnic pavilion and walking trails. In winter, cross-country skiing and snowshoeing trails tour the property.

Bed-and-Breakfast

Located 1.5 miles from East Glacier, **Bison Creek Ranch B & B** (milepost 207.4, 20722 Hwy. 2, 406/226-4482 or 888/226-4482, mid-May–Sept., $60–100 for two people, $12 for each additional person) combines cabin stays with a continental breakfast. Rustic remodeled one-bedroom Gandy Dancer cabins (built as bunkhouses for railroad repairmen) and two-bedroom A-frame chalets spread among firs and meadows. It appeals to those who want real quiet without phones, Internet, or televisions (but with electricity and private baths), and the hot water may take a bit to get to your cabin. The rates include the Montana bed tax, making them an even better deal. A small fishing stream runs nearby, and a restaurant on-site serves Western dinners.

CAMPING

Highway 2 has no drive-in national park campgrounds; to camp in Glacier requires backpacking. Forest Service and private campgrounds line the highway, where noise from trains and trucks permeates the night.

U.S. Forest Service Campgrounds

Two fairly small summer-only Forest Service campgrounds sit adjacent to Highway 2, tucked in doghair timbers for shade and monitored by campground hosts. Expect to find picnic tables (some wheelchair accessible), fire rings with grills, vault toilets, drinking water, but no hookups. You must also pack your own garbage away with you. Sites ($10) are first come, first serve, so get there by early afternoon in high season, especially if you want to nab one of the campsites farthest from the highway. Firewood is not available; you can collect it in the woods here. At Marias Pass, the **Summit Campground** (Lewis and Clark National Forest, 406/791-7700) has 17 sites. You can hop onto the Autumn Creek Trail across the highway and railroad tracks. At milepost 190, **Devil Creek Campground** (Flathead National Forest, 406/387-3800) has 14 sites, a few of which can handle up to 40-foot RVs. From the campground, a trail leads 5.9 miles up to Elk Lake or 8.2 miles to Moose Lake.

Private Campgrounds

Several private campgrounds are available along Highway 2. Rates add on the 7 percent Montana bed tax. Rates usually cover two people, with each additional person costing $5. Bring earplugs, for all sit near the highway and train tracks.

Located 16 miles west of East Glacier between milepost 191 and 192, **◖ Glacier Meadow RV Park** (406/226-4479, www.glaciermeadowrvpark.com, mid-May–mid-Sept.) has 41 sites on a 58-acre meadow and forest setting with dump station, laundry, playground, full hookups, flush toilets, showers, and wireless Internet. The campground sits in full view of the highway, and all the sites are open, providing good satellite dish reception for those so inclined, but you'll not get much privacy from your neighbors. Hookups cost $34, and tent sites are $20. In the evening and early morning, elk sometimes browse in the meadow. Red bus tours heading over Logan Pass pick up here.

Between milepost 173 and 174 west of Essex, **Glacier Haven Inn** (14297 Hwy. 2 E., 406/888-5720, www.glacierhavenrv-campground.com) built a new treed campground in 2009 between the highway and railroad tracks. It has 19 RV campsites ($35), including three that can accommodate large RVs, and room for five tents in a large camping zone ($25). Facilities include flush toilets, showers, full hookups, a launderette, and restaurant. Children age nine and under are free.

Two motel-bar-restaurant businesses offer a few campsites on their compounds. Under new ownership since 2009, the **Snow Slip Inn** (milepost 180, 15644 Hwy. 2 E., Essex, 406/226-4400, www.snowslipinn.com, open year-round) maintains tent campsites ($10) and six full-hookup sites ($15). Wireless Internet is available. Located 16 miles east of West Glacier, **Stanton Creek Lodge** (milepost 170 on Hwy. 2, 406/888-5040 or 866/883-5040, www.stantoncreeklodge.com, open year-round) has tent ($15) and eight full-hookup RV ($25) sites in open sight of the highway and train. Amenities include flush toilets, hot showers,

picnic tables, and fire pits. Walk a few minutes to the Stanton Lake and Grant Ridge Loop trailheads or 300 yards to fishing. While you can camp here in winter surrounded by snow, the water is turned off.

Backcountry Camping

On Highway 2's north side, trails lead up Glacier's remote, rugged valleys. With multiple creek fords and primitive or undesignated campsites, the **Coal-Nyack Loop** keeps the wimps out. Its best campground—**Beaver Woman Lake**—sits in Martha's Basin in goat-watching terrain. Pick up permits ($5 per person per night, kids 8–18 $2.50, kids 7 and

---

COAL-NYACK LOOP

Remote doesn't come close to describing the Coal-Nyack Loop, an ancient Kootenai trail. A rough 38-mile trail encircles Mount Stimson, one of the six highest peaks in Glacier Park at 10,142 feet. Where other trails require camping in designated sites, the Coal-Nyack Loop is wild, with wilderness camping at large the modus operandi…which means, wherever you can find a flat place to sleep and abide by Leave No Trace principles. Bear-resistant canisters are the way to carry food.

The loop is not a place for the faint of heart. Without bridges, creeks require fording, and there are plenty of them, for the mountains spew water in spring. Frequent avalanches splinter trees across trails. Thick brush cloaks routes. And the only access is via more trails or fording the Middle Fork of the Flathead River. Only those with experienced backcountry savvy should tackle its primitive isolation. For the few intrepid souls tackling the loop on foot or horseback, wilderness solitude awaits.

Permits are required for backcountry camping in the Coal-Nyack Loop. Call 406/888-7800 or check for details online: www.nps.gov/glac.

under free) in person at ranger stations, visitors centers, or the Apgar Permit Office (406/888-7900) 24 hours in advance or by reservation beginning in mid-April ($30). Check additional requirements online: www.nps.gov/glac.

Backcountry camping on Forest Service land south of Highway 2 requires no special permit. Any destination works as long as you follow Leave No Trace ethics. Campsites are not maintained, nor designated. Overused campsites attest to the popularity of **Marion** and **Stanton Lakes**—short destinations good for anglers and families with young kids. **Tranquil Basin** ranks as one of the most scenic places for 1–2 nights. Call Hungry Horse Ranger Station (406/387-3800) for information.

Food

Restaurants along Highway 2 vary from old dives to family restaurants—no fine dining. Off-season, don't be surprised if one is closed when its hours say otherwise—if fish are biting, owners will lock up.

RESTAURANTS

At Izaak Walton Inn, the **◖ Dining Car Restaurant** (290 Izaak Walton Inn Rd., Essex, 406/888-5700, www.izaakwaltoninn. com, year-round, 7:30 A.M.–8 P.M. daily) serves up scrumptious meals on replicas of Great Northern Railway's historic dinnerware. (The gift shop sells the dishes, too!) The cozy restaurant is a great place to grab a huckleberry pancake breakfast ($7–9) before hiking or lunch favorites ($8–11) like a buffalo burger or shredded pork wrap with red onion marmalade and a Montana microbrew. Enjoy a leisurely dinner ($12–26) of grilled rainbow trout with lemon-pepper pesto or huckleberry glazed pork shanks accompanied by a glass of wine as trains rumble past your window. You'll find vegetarian dishes and a kids' menu, too ($3.50–5). Be sure to head downstairs to the Flagstop Bar for a nightcap or at least to look at the historic photos of local railroad disasters.

Located 1.5 miles from East Glacier at milepost 207.4, **◖ Bison Creek Ranch** (20722 Hwy. 2, 406/226-4482 or 888/226-4482, May–Sept., 5–9 P.M. daily, $10–18) has served up the Schauf family's Western home cooking since the 1950s. The house favorite is fried chicken. Come hungry, for dinners are large, complete with salad bar, soups, rolls, veggie, potato, and ice cream. If anglers bring their own catch along, the Schaufs will cook it up for them.

CAFÉS

Inexpensive cafés, faves for locals and good for posthiking burgers, are the mainstay of Highway 2. Lighter meals run $5–10; full dinners run up to $18. Under new ownership since 2009, the circa 1945 **Snow Slip Inn** (milepost 180, 15644 Hwy. 2 E., Essex, 406/226-4400, www.snowslipinn.com, open year-round, 7 A.M.–10 P.M. daily), six miles west of Marias Pass, revamped its menu to home-style cooking. Some nights have music. Open year-round, **The Half-Way Motel** (milepost 178, Essex, 406/888-5650, 8 A.M.–9 P.M. Mon.–Sat. in summer, call for off-season hours) features good portions of simple, tasty café fare. Open Memorial Day–Labor Day weekend, the **Healthy Haven Cafe** (milepost 173.8, 406/888-5720, www.glacierhaveninn.com, 8–10 A.M. Tues.–Sun. and 6–8 P.M. Tues.–Sat.) serves breakfasts of homemade granolas, breads, and seasonal fresh fruit, and home-style dinners of Alaska salmon, rib eye steak, and buffalo burgers. Open mid-May–October, the small **Stanton Creek Lodge** (milepost 170, 406/888-5040 or 866/883-5040, www.stantoncreeklodge.com, 11 A.M.–7 P.M. daily, bar stays open later on Fri. and Sat. nights) serves lunch and dinner, and runs a full-service bar—perfect for a burger and beer after hiking the Grant Ridge Loop. If you see the buck sing in the funky bar, you've stayed too long.

GROCERIES

Highway 2 lacks grocery stores, but the Half-Way Motel near Essex (milepost 178, 406/888-5650) carries convenience-store items: chips, pop, and a few staple groceries. To stock up for camping, you'll find seasonal grocery stores in East and West Glacier. Larger food markets are in Browning on the east side and Hungry Horse and Columbia Falls on the west.

PICNIC AREAS

Only one designated picnic area is set aside on Highway 2, and that is **Walton** (milepost 180.5). Behind the Walton Ranger Station, the small picnic area clusters under thick trees adjacent to the Middle Fork River. Picnic tables, pit toilets, and fire rings with grills are available, but you'll need to bring your own firewood; gathering wood is prohibited. The picnic area is the trailhead for the Ole Creek Trail and Scalplock Lookout.

With several river accesses along the Middle Fork of the Flathead, there are plenty of additional places sans tables for picnicking at a scenic spot and soaking your feet in cold water. Cascadilla and Paola offer the best beaches.

WATERTON

For such a small park, Waterton Lakes National Park packs a punch. It houses rare plants found nowhere else and a plethora of wildlife that rivals its large northern sisters of Banff and Jasper. It sits on a nexus of major bird migration routes and weather systems. On the Continental Divide's east side, mountains literally collide with prairies. With no transitional foothills, eastern peaks plummet to grasslands—a phenomenon due to geological overthrusts that exposed the oldest sedimentary rock in the Canadian Rockies. Although active glaciers vacated Waterton's borders years ago, the results of ice gnawing on its landscape left lake pockets strewn through the park. A long glacier-gouged trough forms Upper Waterton Lake, the deepest lake in the Canadian Rockies and one that straddles the U.S.-Canadian border. The lake frequently kicks up with winds, giving credence to the park's ranking as the second-windiest place in Alberta.

Dominated by the Prince of Wales Hotel and Waterton Lake, the park serves as a destination in itself as well as an entrance to Glacier's remote north country. On any summer day, the Waterton Townsite bustles with shoppers, bicyclists, backpackers, boaters, and campers. It's a quintessential Canadian mountain town that embodies what Banff used to be before booming commercialism. The MV *International* shuttles hikers and sightseers across Waterton Lake and the international boundary to Goat Haunt, U.S.A. Only two roads pierce the park's remarkable interior, both gateways to lakes, waterfalls, canyons, peaks, and wildlife.

© BECKY LOMAX

WATERTON

HIGHLIGHTS

Boat Tour: Hop aboard the historic MV *International* for a ride on the deepest lake in the Canadian Rockies. You'll float across the international boundary to Goat Haunt, U.S.A. (page 199).

Chief Mountain: Spot this 9,080-foot sacred mountain of the Blackfeet from Chief Mountain Highway. Sitting in Glacier Park rather than Waterton, the mountain stands adjacent to Ninaki (the mother), and Papoose peeks up behind it (page 203).

Prince of Wales Hotel: Drop in to the historic 1927 hotel sitting regally atop a knoll. Part of the chain of Swiss-style hostelries built by Great Northern Railway, the hotel maintains a British ambience with kilt-wearing bellhops and afternoon high tea (page 203).

Goat Haunt, U.S.A.: Walk to the International Peace Park Pavilion. Accessible only by boat or on foot, Goat Haunt rests at Waterton Lake's southern end in Glacier Park – a launch pad to Glacier's remote northern trails (page 204).

Cameron Lake: Rent a boat to paddle the lake, or walk the pathway to Grizzly Gardens. The lake at Akamina Parkway's terminus receives snowmelt from the remnants of

Herbst Glacier across the international boundary (page 204).

Red Rock Canyon: Tread around a colorful mosaic of sediments. Argillites in striking reds and greens layer atop one another – evidence of its ancient inland sea origins (page 206).

Maskinonge Lake: Focus your binoculars on unusual bird sightings. Located on the axis of two migration flyways, Waterton is home to trumpeter swans, yellow-headed blackbirds, and Vaux's swifts (page 206).

Bison Paddock: Drive through a paddock harboring majestic bison. In a tribute to the great wild herds that once roamed the prairies in vast numbers, Parks Canada maintains a small herd of these large mammals (page 206).

Bear's Hump: Climb up the short grunt for a grand panoramic view. The trail gives you an eagle-eye shot of Waterton Townsite and Waterton Lake (page 209).

Carthew-Alderson: Cross over a high, windswept alpine pass on a scenic trail between Akamina Lake and the Waterton Townsite. You'll be wowed by the peaks and walk past blue icy jewels (page 210).

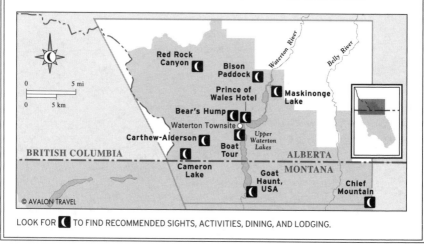

LOOK FOR **(** TO FIND RECOMMENDED SIGHTS, ACTIVITIES, DINING, AND LODGING.

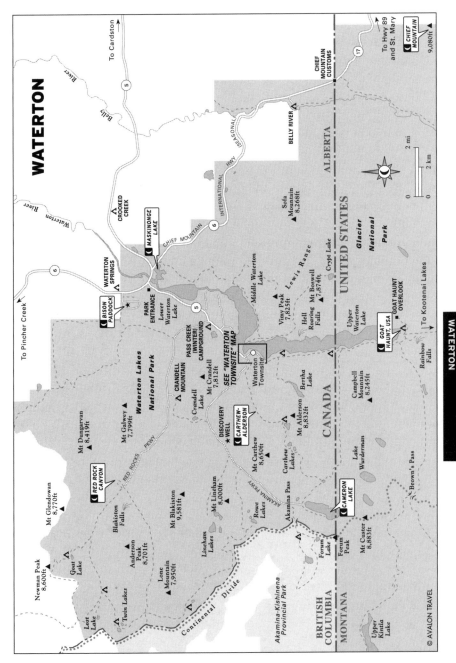

WATERTON

To Cardston

Belly River

Waterton River

To Pincher Creek

CROOKED CREEK

MASKINONGE LAKE

WATERTON SPRINGS

BISON PADDOCK

PARK ENTRANCE

Lower Waterton Lake

CHIEF MOUNTAIN

CHIEF MOUNTAIN CUSTOMS

To Hwy 89 and St. Mary

CHIEF MOUNTAIN
9,080ft ▲

BELLY RIVER ▲

ALBERTA

Waterton Lakes National Park

Mt Dungarvan
▲ 8,419ft

Mt Galwey
▲ 7,799ft

RED ROCK CANYON

RED ROCKS PKWY

Mt Glendowan
8,770ft ▲

Newman Peak
8,600ft ▲

Goat Lake

Lost Lake

Twin Lakes

Anderson Peak
8,701ft ▲

Blakiston Falls

Lone Mountain
▲ 7,950ft

Mt Blakiston
9,581ft ▲

Mt Lineham
8,000ft ▲

Lineham Lakes

Rowe Lakes

CRANDELL MOUNTAIN

Crandell Lake

PASS CREEK (WINTER) CAMPGROUND

Mt Crandell
7,812ft ▲

SEE "WATERTON TOWNSITE" MAP

Waterton Townsite

DISCOVERY WELL

CARTHEW-ALDERSON

AKAMINA PKWY

Mt Carthew
8,650ft ▲

Carthew Lakes

Akamina Pass

CAMERON LAKE

Forum Lake

Forum Peak

Mt Custer
8,883ft ▲

Mt Alderson
8,832ft ▲

Bertha Lake

Campbell Mountain
▲ 8,245ft

Lake Wurderman

Continental Divide

Akamina-Kishinena Provincial Park

BRITISH COLUMBIA

MONTANA

Upper Kintla Lake

Brown's Pass

Middle Waterton Lake

INTERNATIONAL HWY (SEASONAL)

Vimy Peak
7,825ft ▲

Hell Roaring Falls

Mt Boswell
7,874ft ▲

Crypt Lake

Lewis Range

Sofa Mountain
▲ 8,268ft

Upper Waterton Lake

GOAT HAUNT OVERLOOK

GOAT HAUNT, USA

Rainbow Falls

To Kootenai Lakes

CANADA

UNITED STATES

Glacier National Park

2 mi

2 km

© AVALON TRAVEL

SEE "WATERTON TOWNSITE" MAP

WATERTON

KOOTENAI BROWN

John George "Kootenai" Brown was influential in the formation of Waterton Lakes National Park but also became the stuff of legend. Born in Ireland in 1839, he served with the British Army in India before coming to North America in 1861. With no money, he followed the Cariboo Gold Rush to Barkerville, British Columbia, where he mined gold. He spent it all, departing several years later broke.

At 26 years old, he crossed the Continental Divide at South Kootenay Pass in what would become Waterton Lakes National Park. He fell in love with the country, called Kootenay Lakes at the time, and inherited his name through his close ties to the Kootenai Indians.

Local legend is full of Brown's escapades. When Blackfeet shot him in the back with an arrow, he reputedly pulled the arrow out himself and cleaned the wound with turpentine. In Montana, he spent 12 years as a trader, a pony express rider, a scout for Custer, and a buffalo hunter. When buffalo became scarce, he hunted wolves. While he rode for the U.S. Army pony express, Chief Sitting Bull and the Sioux captured him, stripping and tying him to a stake while they debated his fate. He escaped in the middle of the night.

In 1869, he married and started a family with a Métis woman, Olivia Lyonnais. After being hauled into a Fort Benton court on murder charges and acquitted, he and his family packed off to Alberta. He built a cabin by Upper Waterton Lake, working as a guide, commercial fisherman, hunter, rancher, trader, and scout for the Rocky Mountain Rangers during the 1885 North-West Rebellion, the same year Olivia died. He later married Isabella, a Cree.

When Canada established the Kootenay Lake Forest Reserve in 1885, Brown became its first game warden and fisheries officer. In 1910, he was promoted to Forest Ranger in Charge. A year later, when Kootenay Lakes officially became Waterton Lakes, he stepped in as its first superintendent.

Kootenai Brown died in 1916 and is buried with his two wives along the entrance road to Waterton.

HISTORY

In 1858, Lieutenant Thomas Blakiston, a European explorer, came to southern Alberta searching for a railroad route through the Canadian Rockies. He traveled to the chain of Waterton Lakes, naming them for the British naturalist Charles Waterton, who never visited the area.

When the area became Kootenay Lakes Forest Park in 1895—Canada's fourth national park and the brainchild of Pincher Creek rancher F. W. Godsal—the legendary Kootenai Brown took the reins as its first game guardian and fisheries inspector. In 1911, he became Waterton's first superintendent, and the park's name officially changed to Waterton Lakes National Park.

Waterton produced Western Canada's first oil well in 1902. But within four years, the site closed down, the yield trickling to nothing. Meanwhile, an oil well near Cameron Falls produced one barrel a day and prompted building the Waterton Townsite. When oil riches dissipated in 1910, tourists arrived, fueled in part by Great Northern Railway's Glacier development. The Townsite sprouted cottages, a hotel, tennis courts, a golf course, packhorse outfitters, and boating.

In 1913, Great Northern Railway scouted Waterton for an appropriate hotel site, but World War I and a proposed dam in Waterton tabled its construction. Ironically, the Prohibition in America prompted it to be built. Alcohol, after all, was still legal in Alberta, attracting scads of Montanans for thirst quenching. In 1927, the Prince of Wales Hotel finally opened on the wind-battered knoll above town, and the 72-foot MV *International* launched its first sightseers up Waterton Lake. Within five years, the park gained status in conjunction with Glacier as the world's first International Peace Park.

ECOLOGICAL SIGNIFICANCE

For such a tiny park, Waterton is a nexus. The park sits on a narrow north–south wildlife corridor and the axis of two major bird migratory highways. Over 250 species of birds nest or use the park's rich habitats for migration stopovers. It's one of the last places in North America where grizzly bears roam into the fringes of their original grassland habitat. Over 45 different habitats provide harbor for 10 species of amphibians and reptiles, 24 species of fish, and 60 species of mammals. Rare trumpeter swans nest here, as do Vaux's swifts.

Because Arctic and Pacific weather systems collide here, a breadth of vegetation abounds. With more than 1,370 plants, mosses, and lichens, Waterton houses more than half of Alberta's plant species, 179 which are considered rare, 22 found nowhere else in the province. Moonworts, a small fern, come in eight varieties here: One is found only in Waterton. The park's diminutive acreage has more plant diversity than the much larger Banff, Jasper, Kootenay, and Yoho parks combined! For such extremes and such rarities likewise contained in its sister park Glacier, the United Nations Educational, Scientific and Cultural Organization (UNESCO) named Waterton-Glacier a **Biosphere Reserve** and a **World Heritage Site.**

Exploring Waterton

Waterton's 52 square miles is tiny compared to Glacier. The Townsite sits at 4,200 feet in elevation, but surrounding peaks climb to 9,000 feet. While the Townsite houses about 100 people in winter, in summer it burgeons to nearly 2,000 residents. The park sees less than 400,000 annual visitors—about 20 percent of Glacier's crowds.

Waterton and Glacier span the 49th parallel (the international border), yet the parks are connected. The pair forms one ecosystem, recognized as a **World Heritage Site** and a **Biosphere Reserve.** Humans use one to access the other via Waterton Lake, and grizzly bears cross back and forth. The two parks, which include part of the longest undefended border in the world at 5,525 miles, form **Waterton-Glacier International Peace Park.**

PARK ENTRANCE

U.S. park passes are not valid in this Canadian park, although many Americans expect them to be. Even though Waterton-Glacier is an International Peace Park, no combined park pass is sold to date. To enter Waterton, you must purchase a separate Parks Canada day pass (adults CDN$8, seniors CDN$7, youth 6–16 CDN$4, kids under 6 free, family or single-vehicle group CDN$20), valid until 4 P.M. the following day.

You can also purchase year-long passes good for all Canadian National Parks (adults CDN$68, seniors CDN$58, youth 6–16 CDN$34, family or maximum per vehicle CDN$137). While the entrance gate is open 24/7 year-round, it is only staffed early May–early October. Admission to the park is free on Canada Day, July 1.

VISITORS CENTER

The **Waterton Lakes Visitor Information Centre** (4.6 miles, 7.6 km south of the park entrance station on the park entrance road, 403/859-5133, 9 A.M.–4:30 P.M. daily early May–early Oct., 8 A.M.–7 P.M. in summer) sits across from the entrance road to Prince of Wales Hotel. It is the best stop for information, wilderness use permits, road conditions, fishing licenses, and maps. The trail to Bear's Hump departs from here. During months when the center is closed, you can get the same information, licenses, and permits from the Parks Canada office (215 Mount View Rd., 403/859-2224, open year-round, 8 A.M.–4 P.M. weekdays).

GOAT HAUNT RANGER STATION

Located at the southern tip of Waterton Lake, **Goat Haunt Ranger Station** sits in Glacier

© BECKY LOMAX

Waterton Lakes Visitor Centre is the place to get maps and information.

National Park and the United States. It is only accessible by boat or foot. Visitors may debark the tour boat to walk to the International Peace Park Pavilion at Goat Haunt and back without going through customs; however, hikers must go through customs at the ranger station between 10:30 A.M. and 5 P.M. to access Glacier's trails and backcountry campsites. All hikers must have appropriate passports or passport cards. Those entering Waterton from Glacier via Goat Haunt–area trails are required to call Canadian Customs (403/653-3535 or 403/653-3009) from the Waterton Townsite.

SHUTTLES AND TOURS
Shuttles

Getting between Glacier and Waterton by shuttle is complicated by the international border. From Glacier's east side, you can get to Waterton on the **Glacier Park, Inc.** shuttle (406/892-2525, www.glacierparkinc.com, early June–mid-Sept., $10–50 depending on distance, kids half price). Originating at Glacier Park Lodge in East Glacier, the shuttle

hits Two Medicine, Cut Bank Creek, St. Mary Visitor Center, Many Glacier Hotel, and Chief Mountain Customs before reaching the Prince of Wales Hotel. It runs once a day each direction, with departure times varying depending on your starting point. For the return connection between Waterton and Glacier, riders may not originate in Canada with GPI. Instead, you must use **Tamarack Shuttles** (Tamarack Village Square, 214 Mount View Rd., 403/859-2378, www.hikewaterton.com, mid-May–Sept.). They provide transportation (CDN$20 per person) by reservation to Chief Mountain Customs departing at 2:30 P.M. from Waterton. Walk through customs to the Chief Mountain parking lot, where you catch the GPI shuttle running down Glacier's east side.

Hikers can access Waterton trailheads via shuttles—by land or water. The **Crypt Lake Water Shuttle Service** (Waterton Shoreline Cruises, 403/859-2362, www.watertoncruise.com, daily late May–early Oct., adults CDN$18 round-trip, kids CDN$9) departs from the marina daily at 10 A.M. for a

15-minute ride across Upper Waterton Lake to Crypt Landing, where the 10-mile (17.2-km) round-trip trail begins. Watch your hiking time, for the return boats depart Crypt Landing at 4:15 (early May and late Sept.) or 5:30 P.M. (late May–late Sept.). During midsummer, additional boats run at 9 A.M. and 4 P.M. No reservations are taken for this shuttle; arrive at least 20 minutes before departure. The tour boat to **Goat Haunt** functions also as a hiker shuttle (daily late May–mid-Sept., adults CDN$23 one-way, kids CDN$9–12). It accesses trailheads in northern Glacier and provides transportation back to Waterton after hiking the shoreline trail to Goat Haunt. Buy your return ticket that morning before hiking down the lake. You can also pay in cash (exact change in U.S. or Canadian dollars) when you board in Goat Haunt. Hikers may catch an early boat and return on a later boat; just notify the ticket agent of your return intentions. Boats depart the Townsite at 10 A.M., 1 and 4 P.M.; boats depart Goat Haunt at 11:25 A.M., 2:25 and 5:25 P.M. and in midsummer 8:05 P.M.

Be aware of border regulations for hiking and using this shuttle. Starting in September, there is no 5:25 P.M. Goat Haunt pickup for hikers and backpackers as Canada Customs is closed.

Departing daily at 8:30 A.M. from Tamarack Village, the **Cameron Express** (Tamarack Village Square, 214 Mount View Rd., 403/859-2378, www.hikewaterton.com, mid-May–Sept., CDN$12.50) shuttles hikers to the popular Carthew-Alderson trailhead for a point-to-point 11-mile (18-km) hike back to the Townsite. Reservations are a good idea, especially midsummer; you can make them with a credit card by phone. They'll also provide custom shuttles to other trailheads; ask for rates and details.

🄲 Boat Tour
Waterton Shoreline Cruises (at the marina at the junction of Mount View Rd. and Waterton Ave., 403/859-2362, www.watertoncruise.com, daily May–early Oct., adults round-trip CDN$36, kids CDN$12–18, kids

© BECKY LOMAX

MV *International* tours Waterton Lake.

three and under free) operates the historic MV *International* on Upper Waterton Lake. During the two-hour tour on the wooden 200-passenger boat cruising here since 1927, knowledgeable guides punctuate their patter with humor. For the best views, go for a sunny seat on the boat's top deck. If the weather is brisk, just bundle up. From June to mid-September, the boat docks for 30 minutes at Goat Haunt—time enough to walk to the International Peace Park Pavilion. Trips depart at 10 A.M., 1 and 4 P.M. June–mid-September. In May and after mid-September, they depart at 10 A.M. and 2:30 P.M. In midsummer, they add a 7 P.M. tour that stops only for 10 minutes in Goat Haunt. Because advanced reservations are only taken for large groups, get to the dock early in midsummer.

SERVICES

Gas up before you head north across the border—gas in Canada is more expensive than in the United States, usually around $0.50–0.80 per gallon more. Also, be aware that gas is sold by the liter in Canada rather than the gallon, so the price on the pump will look pretty darn good. To convert the price, remember 3.7 liters equals one gallon.

Pat's Gas Station (224 Mount View Rd., 403/859-2266) is much more than a place to gas up or buy propane for the RV. While Pat can magically perform minor car repairs, the shop's claim to fame is its rental line: surrey bikes (CDN$25 per hour), mountain bikes (CDN$40–50 per day, hourly available), baby backpacks (CDN$15), and tennis rackets (CDN$3 per hour). You can even rent Mopeds (CDN$150 per day). Pat's also sells food and convenience items as well as Cuban cigars, fishing tackle, park permits, and newspapers.

A launderette on Harebell Avenue is open during summer months 7 A.M.–10 P.M. daily. Showers (CDN$6 adults) are available at the Waterton Health Club in the Waterton Lakes Lodge. The Townsite post office (102 Windflower Ave.) is open year-round 8 A.M.–4:30 P.M. Monday–Friday. Remember: You must use Canadian postage stamps rather than U.S. stamps to post mail from Canada. ATMs

© BECKY LOMAX

Tamarack Outdoor Outfitters runs shuttles, guides hikes, and sells outdoor gear.

are located at Pat's Gas Station, Tamarack Village Square, Rocky Mountain Food Mart, and the Prince of Wales Hotel. While keying in the dollar amount, remember that the ATM gives Canadian currency. *The Calgary Sun* carries regional, national, and international news, and a free newspaper, *The Boundary,* published weekly mid-May–early September, carries the local Waterton news.

Cell Phones and Internet
Some cell phones can get service in the Townsite, but not in the rest of the park. Pearl's Café (305 Windflower Ave., 403/859-2498) and Zum's (116 Waterton Ave., 403/859-2388) have wireless Internet.

Shopping
Shopping in Waterton is a different experience. Souvenirs are decidedly Canadian, with moose and red maple leaf T-shirts. Most shops are open May–September seven days a week but close in winter. During shoulder seasons, hours are short, often 10 A.M.–5 P.M., but in midsummer, shops stay open into the evening (7–8 P.M.). Many stores and restaurants sell specialty Cuban cigars, unavailable in the United States. But remember, these cannot go back over the U.S. border.

If you need outdoor gear, **Tamarack Outdoor Outfitters** (Tamarack Village Square, 214 Mount View Rd., 403/859-2378) can outfit you from head to toe with hiking, backpacking, camping, and fishing gear. The owners expanded their shop to 5,000 square feet. They carry good reputable brands at reasonable prices, and topographic maps for hiking. Chocoholics gravitate toward a sister shop to one in Banff—**Welch's Chocolate Shop** (corner of Cameron Falls Dr. and Windflower Ave., 403/859-2363)—which stocks international chocolates and makes its own fudge and candy. Get wine, beer, and liquor at **Mountain Spirits** (504 Cameron Falls Dr., 403/859-2015, noon–10 P.M. daily, closes at 8 P.M. Sun.).

Currency Exchange
In Waterton, most businesses, including restaurants, shops, and lodges, will accept U.S. currency; however, return change will be given back in Canadian currency. For conversions, most businesses use the bank exchange rate, but some have their own policies. For the best exchange rates, use a credit card as much as possible. Waterton has no banks; the nearest banking services are in Cardston and Pincher Creek, but **Tamarack Village Square** (214 Mount View Rd., May–mid-Oct., 8 A.M.–8 P.M. in summer, closes at 6 P.M. early and late season) offers currency exchange for U.S. and Canadian dollars only.

Emergencies
For emergencies, contact the Royal Canadian Mounted Police (RCMP, 202 Waterton Ave., 403/859-2244 or 403/653-4931) during summer months or Parks Canada Wardens (215 Mount View Rd., 403/859-2224) year-round. The nearest hospitals are 30 miles (50 km) away in Pincher Creek (403/627-3333) and Cardston (403/653-4411). To contact the park's one emergency ambulance, call 403/859-2636.

DRIVING TOURS
Chief Mountain Highway
The Chief Mountain International Highway provides a summer-only connection between Glacier and Waterton Parks. Its season and hours operate around the Canadian and U.S. customs stations at the border (open mid-May–Sept.; 9 A.M.–6 P.M. daily May and after Labor Day, 7 A.M.–10 P.M. daily June–Labor Day). You may want to top off on gas in the United States since gas is generally more expensive in Canada. (The nearest gas is in Babb, Montana, or Waterton Townsite.) The 30-mile road undulates over rolling aspen hills and beaver ponds as it curves around Chief Mountain, imposing alone on Glacier's northwest corner. A few unmarked pullouts offer good photo ops. Drive this open range carefully, for cows wander the road. Your car also may need a good cleaning if wet cow pies litter the road!

From the United States as the road rounds Chief Mountain, it enters Glacier Park. No entrance station is here; no payment is required.

The road reaches the international border and Chief Mountain Customs at 18.6 miles. After customs, the road enters Alberta and Waterton Lakes National Park, but you won't reach a park entrance station until nearly at the Townsite. After the road crosses the Belly River, it briefly exits the park, crossing the Blood Indian Reserve (part of the Blackfoot family) before reentering the park. Burn from the 1998 Sofa Mountain Fire lines both sides of the road. As you crest a big rise, stop at the overlook (28 miles, 45 km) to gaze at the Waterton Valley. For the descent, shift into second gear to avoid burning your brakes.

Park Entrance Road

From Highway 6, the five-mile (eight-km) road connecting the park entrance station with Waterton Townsite is worth a drive with a pair of binoculars. Linnet, Maskinonge, and Lower Waterton Lakes attract scads of birds, as well as moose, bear, elk, and smaller wildlife. Stop at a picnic area along its route for wildlife-watching: Knight's Lake (0.6 mile, 0.9 km), Hay Barn (2.5 miles, 4 km), or Marquis (4.1 miles, 6.5 km). The Waterton Lakes Visitor Information Center is 4.8 miles (7.7 km) from the entrance station.

Akamina Parkway

A 10-mile (16-km) paved drive climbs above Waterton Townsite along the base of Crandell Mountain on Akamina Parkway. The road is open all year, although in winter only to Little Prairie. Just west of the Waterton Visitor Information Center, the signed Akamina Parkway turns off and begins climbing steeply from Waterton Townsite as it curves up above the Cameron Creek Gorge. It passes the **Oil City Historic Site** as well as trailheads to Crandell Lake, Lineham Falls, Rowe Lakes, Akamina Pass, and Forum Lake. For those looking to picnic along Cameron Creek, picnic tables, pit toilets, and shelters are at McNeally's (4 miles, 6.4 km) and Little Prairie (8.1 miles, 13 km). The road ends at **Cameron Lake.** On the return trip, shift into second gear for the steep descent back to the Townsite; you can always smell the brakes of those who forget.

Red Rocks Parkway

Red Rocks Parkway (May–Oct.) is self-descriptive, for the paved road ends at a red-rock canyon. Locate the signed turnoff on the park entrance road (2.2 miles, 3.5 km from the Townsite; 2.8 miles, 3.9 km from park

AKAMINA-KISHINENA PROVINCIAL PARK

Where Waterton Lakes National Park meets the Continental Divide, Akamina-Kishinena Provincial Park sits to the west. It follows the international boundary of Montana's Glacier National Park to the North Fork of the Flathead River. This remote 27,000-acre park is accessible only on foot from Akamina Parkway in Waterton Lakes or trails from the end of a 68-mile (109-km) dirt road that takes off 10 miles (16 km) south of Fernie, British Columbia.

The small park is part of the same narrow Rocky Mountain ecosystem that provides corridors for grizzly bears and wolves. Geologic wonders display themselves in Forum Peak's 1.3-billion-year-old sedimentary rocks, and rare plants like the pygmy poppy grow here.

From Waterton, hikers and mountain bikers can access the park via an old circa 1920 trail that connects the Cameron Valley to the North Fork of the Flathead Valley. To access Akamina-Kishinena, hike to Akamina Pass, the boundary between Waterton Park and the provincial park. From here, you can mountain-bike to Wall Lake or hike to Forum Lake.

Some Canadians want to expand Waterton Lakes National Park to include Akamina-Kishinena. The addition would increase the size of Waterton and complete the "Crown of the Continent" ecosystem, matching more of Glacier's northern boundary.

For more information, contact British Columbia Parks (205/489-8540, www.gov.bc.ca/bcparks).

© BECKY LOMAX

Imposing Chief Mountain stands in Glacier's northeast corner.

entrance station). The 9.3-mile (15-km) narrow road climbs through grasslands, squeezes through a canyon, and opens up into meadows along Blakiston Creek. Through the canyon, the road is quite narrow but passable for trailers and RVs. Bring your binoculars for watching bears and bighorn sheep. Crandell Mountain Campground (4.6 miles, 7.5 km) is accessed via this road. The parkway ends where a self-guided trail leads around **Red Rock Canyon.** To picnic along Red Rocks, you'll find tables, pit toilets, and shelters at three spots: Coppermine Creek (5 miles, 8 km), Dungarvan (8 miles, 13 km), and Red Rocks (9.3 miles, 15 km). Red Rocks picnicking, washroom, and parking facilities were upgraded in 2010.

SIGHTS
◖ Chief Mountain
Located along Chief Mountain Highway, Chief Mountain rises up 9,080 feet abruptly from aspen parklands and prairies. It marks the northeasternmost peak in Glacier National Park. Legend tells of a young Flathead brave who carried a bison skull to its summit and remained there for four nights wrestling the Spirit of the Mountain. When he finally prevailed, the Spirit gave him a protection totem to keep him safe in battle and hunting.

◖ Prince of Wales Hotel
Designated a Canadian National Historic Site, the 122-foot-tall, four-story, 90-room Prince of Wales Hotel took more than a year to build. Constructed by Great Northern Railway as a link for the Glacier chain, the hotel opened its doors in 1927. Even if you are not staying here, drop in to see its massive lobby with floor-to-ceiling windows looking down Waterton Lake. Kilt-wearing bellhops haul luggage, and the lobby serves high tea in the afternoon. Walk out on the bluff for the best photographic views of Waterton Lake. But hold on to your hat due to howling winds!

Waterton Lake
Set in a north–south trough gouged by Pleistocene ice age glaciers, Waterton Lake is

© BECKY LOMAX

Prince of Wales Hotel sits on a bluff overlooking Waterton Townsite.

WATERTON

the deepest lake in the Canadian Rockies. (It's actually Upper Waterton Lake, which feeds Middle and Lower Waterton Lakes, but no one calls it that.) Its 487-foot depths hold 50-pound lake trout and tiny ice age relics—the opossum shrimp. Spanning the international boundary, the half-mile-wide and nearly seven-mile-long lake conveys visitors over its waters in the 1927 wooden MV *International.*

The U.S.-Canadian Border

For Waterton visitors, the border inside the park is an attraction. The long, straight swath is cleared every 20 years by the International Boundary Commission. The boat tour down Waterton Lake crosses this unnatural forest line en route to Goat Haunt, where visitors can de-bark and walk to the Peace Park Pavilion without going through customs. Hikers can also walk over the border swath on the Waterton Lake Trail.

◖ Goat Haunt, U.S.A.

A tiny seasonal enclave housing rangers, Goat

Haunt, U.S.A., rests at Waterton Lake's southern end in Glacier National Park. Accessed only by boat or on foot, Goat Haunt sees hundreds of visitors per day in midsummer. Most arrive via the MV *International.* Walk the paved pathway to the International Peace Park Pavilion, where displays tell the story of the peace park. Trailheads depart to Goat Haunt Overlook, Kootenai Lakes, Rainbow Falls, and beyond.

◖ Cameron Lake

Tucked in a glacial cirque at the terminus of Akamina Parkway, Cameron Lake reflects the steep slopes of Mount Custer. Look across the glacially fed lake to Herbst Glacier: You're looking across the international boundary into Montana. Avalanches preen the slopes into good bear habitat. Rent a rowboat or canoe to paddle around the lake's shoreline, or saunter the pathway along the west shore, watching for moose, shorebirds, and bears. From here, hikers climb the Carthew-Alderson trail to trek to the Townsite.

Waterton Heritage Centre

Operated by the Waterton Natural History Association, Waterton Heritage Centre (117 Waterton Ave., 403/859-2267, mid-May–Sept., 10 A.M.–6 P.M. daily) is a small museum housed in the old fire hall with displays on Waterton's natural and cultural history, including local favorite renegade Joe Cosley. Books—from hiking guides to coffee table picture books—are also sold here.

Cameron Falls

Picturesque Cameron Falls sits on the edge of the Waterton Townsite on Evergreen Avenue. In June, water roars through its slots, but flows drop substantially by August. Cameron Creek has eroded a massive fold of the Waterton Formation, a 600-million-year-old rock layer. Sit on a bench at the base, or climb the short, steep trails on both sides of the creek to access viewpoints. Opt for the north-side switchback trail for better views.

Waterton Townsite

A quaint little tourism town, Waterton

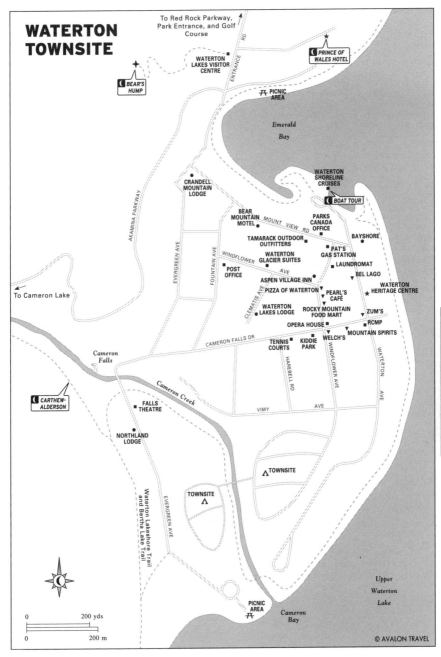

WATERTON TOWNSITE

To Red Rock Parkway, Park Entrance, and Golf Course

WATERTON LAKES VISITOR CENTRE

ENTRANCE RD

PRINCE OF WALES HOTEL

BEAR'S HUMP

PICNIC AREA

Emerald Bay

AKAMINA PARKWAY

CRANDELL MOUNTAIN LODGE

WATERTON SHORELINE CRUISES

BOAT TOUR

BEAR MOUNTAIN MOTEL

MOUNT VIEW RD

PARKS CANADA OFFICE

BAYSHORE

TAMARACK OUTDOOR OUTFITTERS

PAT'S GAS STATION

EVERGREEN AVE

FOUNTAIN AVE

WINDFLOWER

WATERTON GLACIER SUITES

LAUNDROMAT

BEL LAGO

POST OFFICE

AVE

WATERTON HERITAGE CENTRE

To Cameron Lake

ASPEN VILLAGE INN

CLEMATIS AVE

PIZZA OF WATERTON

PEARL'S CAFÉ

WATERTON LAKES LODGE

ROCKY MOUNTAIN FOOD MART

ZUM'S

OPERA HOUSE

RCMP

MOUNTAIN SPIRITS

CAMERON FALLS DR

TENNIS COURTS

KIDDIE PARK

WELCH'S

Cameron Falls

HAREBELL RD

WINDFLOWER AVE

WATERTON AVE

CARTHEW-ALDERSON

Cameron Creek

FALLS THEATRE

VIMY

AVE

NORTHLAND LODGE

Waterton Lakeshore Trail and Bertha Lake Trail

EVERGREEN AVE

TOWNSITE

TOWNSITE

Upper Waterton Lake

PICNIC AREA

Cameron Bay

0   200 yds

0   200 m

© AVALON TRAVEL

WATERTON

© BECKY LOMAX

Rent a boat to row quiet Cameron Lake.

Townsite sits in a dramatic location at the foot of Waterton Lake. Paved walking trails circumvent the town, connecting the few-block-long shopping district with the campground and picnic areas. It hums in summer with visitors riding surrey bikes but quiets in winter under snows. Bighorn sheep and deer frequent town.

Red Rock Canyon

Red Rocks Parkway begins at Blakiston Creek and terminates at Red Rock Canyon, a colorful narrow gorge. Walk the 0.4-mile (0.7-km) pathway up one side and down the other to take in all its hues. Iron-rich argillite sediments layer on top of each other, some turning red from oxidization, others remaining green. Evidence of the ancient Belt Sea, these sediments are some of the oldest exposed rock in the world, created between 800 million and 1.6 billion years ago. Look for sea evidence of mud cracks and ripple marks.

Maskinonge Lake

Birders and wildlife-watchers migrate to Maskinonge Lake for its rich diversity. Located east of the park entrance, the aspen-rimmed lake attracts waterfowl, osprey, trumpeter swans, yellow-headed blackbirds, and kingfishers. Because Waterton sits on the axis of two migration flyways, it sees over 250 species of birds. The lake also attracts everything from huge Shiras moose weighing 1,500 pounds to muskrats, mink, and tiny vagrant shrews. When rare trumpeter swans nest in July and early August, some of the area is closed to protect their offspring. Don't forget to take your binoculars and spotting scopes!

Bison Paddock

Once roaming the plains in vast numbers 150 years ago, wild bison have all but vanished from North America. On Highway 6, 1.2 miles (2 km) west of the park entrance road, the Bison Paddock contains a small herd. Bison weigh close to 2,000 pounds and look like shaggy cows. But don't be lured into thinking they are docile: They may look big, lunky, and dumb, but they are extremely unpredictable and aggressive. Drive on the narrow, roughly paved 2.5-mile loop through the grassland paddock; for safety, stay inside the car.

Discovery Well and Oil City

Located on the Akamina Parkway, two stops mark the site of the Discovery Well, Western Canada's first oil well, and its accompanying town site. The first is at 4.8 miles (8 km) up the road; it's the actual site of the first well from 1902. Continue on a bit to the original town site for Oil City. A short five-minute walk through the trees leads to the hotel foundation—all that remains of the 20-block city that was plotted out. Closed within four years, Oil City soon became a ghost town.

Recreation

HIKING

Waterton has well over 124 miles (200 km) of trails. Nearly two miles of walking trails—both paved and dirt—connect sights, restaurants, lodging facilities, the campground, and picnic areas in Waterton Townsite. From the marina to Cameron Bay, the trail follows the shoreline. Trails also connect to the Falls Theater, Cameron Falls, Bertha Lake and Waterton Lake trailheads, Emerald Bay, and Prince of Wales Hotel. Contrary to Glacier's backcountry rules, Waterton's trails permit dogs on a leash, but keep your pet under control and away from wildlife. You'll find updated trail reports on the Parks Canada website (www.pc.gc.ca, look under Waterton hiking for access). The visitors center also has trail closure and update info.

For hiking, you'll find the best Waterton topographical map at the visitors center and Tamarack Outdoor Outfitters. The Gem Trek Publishing map (CDN$10, 877/921-6277, www.gemtrek.com), also available online, includes roads, trails, bike routes, and trail descriptions for easy, moderate, and strenuous hikes. It also includes the eastern end of Akamina-Kishinena Provincial Park and the Goat Haunt area of Glacier.

For those planning to camp in the backcountry, wilderness permits are necessary (CDN$10 per person per night, ages 16 and under free) for all of the nine designated backcountry campsites. Reservations are available for CDN$12 per trip 90 days in advance beginning April 1 each year. You can get permits and reservations at the Waterton Visitor Information Center (403/859-5133) or Waterton's Parks Canada office (403/859-5140).

Shuttles by water and land make for easy trailhead access. Waterton Shoreline Cruises (403/859-2362, www.watertoncruise.com) operates the Crypt Lake and Goat Haunt boats. Waterton Visitor Services (214 Mount View Rd., 403/859-2378, www.hikewaterton.com) operates the land shuttles.

Hikers heading on trails in Glacier beyond the Goat Haunt Ranger Station must have valid passports or approved passport cards. International visitors from countries other than Canada or the United States must also have an I-94 or I-94W form available at Class A Ports of Entry, but not Goat Haunt. Customs at Goat Haunt is open 10 A.M.–5 P.M. daily.

Bertha Lake

- Distance: 7 miles (11.4 km) round-trip
- Duration: 3–4 hours
- Elevation gain: 1,480 feet
- Effort: 2 miles moderate, remainder strenuous
- Trailhead: southwest corner of Waterton Townsite off Evergreen Avenue

The trail starts as a signed interpretive path to Lower Bertha Falls. The path climbs gradually along the western shore of Waterton Lake to an overlook with views of Mount Cleveland, the highest peak in Glacier. At the junction, take the right fork and head across the dry open

WATERTON

© BECKY LOMAX

Hike to Lower Bertha Falls en route to Bertha Lake.

hillside to Lower Bertha Falls, where pounding waters crash through bedrock. For a destination, the falls is 4 miles (6.4 km) round-trip.

To continue to Bertha Lake, cross the bridge below the falls and climb incessant switchbacks up through a forested hillside beside Upper Bertha Falls, a larger sister of the lower falls. Soon, the trail crests a timbered knoll high above narrow Bertha Lake for the best view of the lake. To reach the shore, descend 0.1 mile (0.16 km) to the campground near its outlet.

Waterton Lake Trail

- Distance: 8.7 miles (13 km) one-way
- Duration: 4–5 hours
- Elevation gain: minimal
- Effort: easy by elevation gain, moderate by length
- Trailhead: southwest corner of Waterton Townsite off Evergreen Avenue

Bordering the west lakeshore of Waterton Lake, the trail begins at the Bertha Lake Trailhead.

After 1 mile (1.5 km), the trails diverge, with the Waterton Lake Trail dropping in a quick steep descent to Bertha Bay Campground on the lakeshore. The trail wanders through cottonwoods, subalpine firs, lodgepoles, and aspen, with overlooks that offer views of the lake.

The trail crosses the international boundary at 3.8 miles (6.1 km) before connecting to a well-signed maze of trails at the end of Waterton Lake. Follow signs to Goat Haunt and catch the MV *International* back to the Townsite. Before you leave in the morning, book your return trip with Waterton Shoreline Cruises. Bring your passport; you'll need it for customs in Goat Haunt. Only U.S. and Canadian citizens are permitted U.S. entry at Goat Haunt.

Crypt Lake

- Distance: 11.2 miles (17 km) round-trip
- Duration: 5–6 hours
- Elevation gain: 2,300 feet
- Effort: moderately strenuous
- Trailhead: Crypt Landing, accessible by boat from Waterton

Catch the water taxi operated daily by Waterton Shoreline Cruises to reach Crypt Landing. From Crypt Landing, the climb bolts up through a wooded hillside along Hellroaring Creek Valley. An alternate route leads to the edge of Hellroaring Creek and its waterfalls; you can take one route up and one down this short section. Soon, the trail passes Twin Falls, and lodgepole pines give way to open meadows and boulder fields.

The trail appears to dead-end in a headwall. But, an iron ladder climbs up to a four-foot-high tunnel with an awkward walk or crawl. The tunnel emerges on a cliff with a steel cable for assistance in crossing. The trail breaks into a tight cirque housing Crypt Lake, which drains from an underwater channel. The international boundary crosses the lake's southern end. In a mad dash, hikers suddenly check their watches, and all jump up to speed down the trail en masse to catch the return boat.

🌙 Bear's Hump

- Distance: 1.7 miles (2.8 km) round-trip
- Duration: 1.25 hours
- Elevation gain: 550 feet
- Effort: strenuous, but short
- Trailhead: Waterton Lakes Visitor Information Centre parking lot

The trail heads promptly uphill—piling on switchback after switchback in a vertical Thighmaster. At least it offers benches en route for rest. Partially forested and thick with thimbleberry and virgin's bower, the hike is cool in early morning or late afternoon after the hump shades the east slope from the sun. Pick up a free interpretive guide for the trail at the visitors center.

Topping out on the Bear's Hump, a rocky outcropping on Mount Crandell's ridge, the trail offers one of the best views of the Waterton Townsite, Prince of Wales Hotel, Waterton Lake, Glacier National Park, and the prairie. On top, three benches offer good spots to gaze at the scenery before you tackle the knee-pounding descent.

Rowe Lakes and Lineham Ridge

- Distance: Lower Rowe Lake, 5 miles (8.4 km) round-trip
- Upper Rowe Lakes, 7.7 miles (12.8 km) round-trip
- Lineham Ridge, 10.6 miles (17.2 km) round-trip
- Duration: 2.5–6 hours
- Elevation gain: 3,116 feet
- Effort: moderate to strenuous
- Trailhead: Rowe Tamarack Trailhead, 6.7 miles (10.9 km) up Akamina Parkway

In July, this trail bursts with wildflowers: yellow arnica, paintbrush, and purple lupine. The climb starts through thin forest broken by avalanche paths, following Rowe Creek. At 2.4 miles (3.9 km), a 10-minute spur trail splits off to Lower Rowe Lake, a destination for those wanting the

© BECKY LOMAX

Hikers walk the falls between two Upper Rowe Lakes.

WATERTON

shortest trek. Continuing on from the junction, the trail ascends into a broad meadow at the base of a giant cirque. After you cross the creek at 3.1 miles (5.2 km), the left fork climbs steep switchbacks to Upper Rowe Lakes, a pair of scenic shallow lakes fringed with alpine larch.

For Lineham Ridge, the right fork after the creek crossing swings around the cirque to climb from subalpine wildflower meadows into alpine tundra. Red argillite colors the mountainside. From the ridge, Lineham Lakes appear below. At the saddle below Mount Lineham, you can opt to climb off-trail east to the peak or continue on the rugged trail west up Lineham Ridge to look down Blakiston Creek.

Cameron Lakeshore

- Distance: 1.9 miles (3.2 km) round-trip
- Duration: 1 hour
- Elevation gain: none
- Effort: easy
- Trailhead: at the day-use facility at Cameron Lake

This short trail follows the lake's west shoreline to a wooden platform and small interpretive display called Grizzly Gardens, where trees are starting to cut the view. Although the trail is flat, watch your footing on tree roots. Several points reach the shoreline for photos of Mount Custer and Herbst Glacier. At the trail's terminus, scan the avalanche slopes for grizzly bears feeding on glacier lilies. Do not continue farther; bears depend on quiet here for denning, feeding, and cub rearing.

🄲 Carthew-Alderson

- Distance: 11.8 miles (18 km) one-way
- Duration: 6 hours
- Elevation gain: 1,440 feet
- Effort: moderately strenuous
- Trailhead: behind day-use facility at Cameron Lake

Catch the Cameron Express hiker shuttle to Cameron Lake. One of the most popular hikes in Waterton, the trail climbs 4.5 miles to

Hikers descend the north side of Carthew Summit.

© BECKY LOMAX

Carthew Summit, where alpine tundra stretches along a windswept ridge. Be prepared for strong winds here, even on a sunny summer day. Some winds may even force you to crawl over the pass. Views span deep into Glacier's interior.

The descent is a knee pounder, dropping over 3,000 feet in elevation. From the summit, the trail passes by several high tarns, sometimes flanked with snow fields into July. The path drops along a cliff wall before reaching Alderson Lake. Once you depart the lake, only peek-a-boo views of avalanche chutes break out from the thick timber en route to Cameron Falls at Waterton Townsite.

Akamina Ridge via Wall and Forum Lakes

• Distance: Akamina Ridge Loop, 11.4 miles (18.3 km)
• Forum Lake, 5.4 miles (8.8 km) round-trip
• Wall Lake, 6.4 miles (10.4 km) round-trip
• Duration: 6–7 hours
• Elevation gain: 3,199 feet
• Effort: strenuous
• Trailhead: Akamina Pass Trailhead, 9.2 miles (14.8 km) up Akamina Parkway

This hike begins in Waterton Park, but within one mile reaches low, forested Akamina Pass, where it crosses over the Continental Divide and into Akamina-Kishinena Provincial Park. Hikers looking for shorter adventures can choose either lake as a destination, but the longer loop hike gets the views. Continue 0.4 mile (0.7 km) to the Forum Lake junction, turning left (Wall Lake is to the right and the way you will return). The trail climbs to the snowmelt-fed Forum Lake, surrounded by steep talus and larch slopes. From the lake, follow the rough, unmaintained trail that ascends the western ridge up through a 16-foot rock band where you'll need to use your hands for climbing. Once above the band, the ridge walk begins.

The three-mile Akamina Ridge walk is truly spectacular. Rolling over peaks and knolls, the alpine tundra is devoid of trees but rampant with miniature plants like pink moss campion struggling to survive. To the south, Glacier's remote Kintla Peak stands with Agassiz Glacier while a sea of peaks stretches in all directions. At the end of the ridge, the trail drops steeply back into forest to Wall Lake, a dramatic cirque tucked against abrupt limestone walls. From Wall Lake, hike 1.8 miles (3 km) back to the Forum Lake junction and return to the trailhead over Akamina Pass.

Blakiston Falls

• Distance: 1.2 miles (2 km) round-trip
• Duration: 45 minutes
• Elevation gain: minimal
• Effort: easy
• Trailhead: end of Red Rocks Parkway

Turn left just after you cross Red Rocks Creek. After crossing Bauerman Creek, look for the hiker trailhead and walk through a coniferous forest. Blakiston Creek tumbles below the trail, and Mount Blakiston peeks into view from time to time. At Blakiston Falls, a wooden deck conveniently makes for easy observation of the tumbling falls.

Avion Ridge and Goat Lake

• Distance: Avion Ridge Loop, 14 miles (22.5 km)
• Goat Lake, 7.8 miles (12.6 km) round-trip
• Duration: 4 hours
• Elevation gain: 1,750 feet
• Effort: moderately strenuous
• Trailhead: at end of Red Rocks Parkway

The Avion Ridge Loop begins and ends on the Snowshoe Trail, an old overgrown roadway that permits bicycles. It's easiest done clockwise, but some hikers prefer the vertical ascent via Goat Lake in favor of a less-steep descent. At 2.4 miles (4 km) up the Snowshoe Trail, you'll reach the Goat Lake junction. Those heading to Goat Lake abruptly climb a relentless uphill into the hanging valley above to Goat Lake, known for its rainbow trout.

WATERTON

For Avion Ridge Loop, continue up the Snowshoe Trail from the Goat Lake junction. At 5.1 miles (8.2 km), you'll reach the Snowshoe Warden Cabin and campsites. Take the trail heading north toward Lost Lake and climb to Avion Ridge. A five-mile unmaintained trail ascends the ridgeline through larch before popping out of the trees on a barren, windswept ridge. The trail circles above a cirque right on the boundary line of Waterton National Park (you'll see signs). Endless peaks parade in all directions. As the trail swings north, it descends to a saddle, traverses a steep sidehill, and reaches a pass above Goat Lake. A knee-pounding descent through wildflower meadows plummets to the lake and then to the Snowshoe Trail junction. Turn left to return to the trailhead.

Rainbow Falls

- Distance: 1.4 miles (2.3 km) round-trip
- Duration: 1 hour
- Elevation gain: minimal
- Effort: easy
- Trailhead: behind ranger station at Goat Haunt in Glacier National Park

Rainbow Falls is one option for a short hike from the boat tour on Waterton Lake. (Check with Waterton Shoreline Cruises for a schedule and book a return boat that allows enough time to complete your hike. Take passports to pass through customs in Goat Haunt.)

Follow the paved trail to the first junction, taking the right fork onto dirt. The trail wanders through thick forests, mosquito filled in early summer. Just before reaching Waterton River, take a left turn at the signed junction, heading up the east bank toward Rainbow Falls. The falls is actually a series of cascades cutting troughs in bedrock, but it's a great place to sit.

Goat Haunt Overlook

- Distance: 2 miles (3.2 km) round-trip
- Duration: 2 hours

- Elevation gain: 844 feet
- Effort: very strenuous
- Trailhead: behind ranger station at Goat Haunt in Glacier National Park

Goat Haunt Overlook is another option for a short hike from the boat tour on Waterton Lake. (Check with Waterton Shoreline Cruises for a schedule and book a return boat that allows enough time to complete your hike. Take passports to pass through customs in Goat Haunt.)

Follow the paved trail past the first right-hand turn to a dirt trail and hike 0.1 mile (0.16 km) on the Continental Divide Trail, heading south toward Fifty Mountain. At the signed junction, turn left. The trail climbs gently for a few hundred feet before it turns steep straight uphill. It's a grunt, but the view is well worth the climb. At the overlook, you can flop on a conveniently placed log to eat lunch and gander downlake to the Waterton Townsite and Prince of Wales Hotel.

Kootenai Lakes

- Distance: 5.6 miles (9 km) round-trip
- Duration: 3–3.5 hours
- Elevation gain: minimal
- Effort: easy
- Trailhead: behind ranger station at Goat Haunt in Glacier National Park

Kootenai Lakes attracts hikers for its often-seen moose and sometimes-seen nesting trumpeter swans. Access is via the tour boat. (Check with Waterton Shoreline Cruises for a schedule and book a return boat that allows enough time to complete your hike. Take passports to pass through customs in Goat Haunt.)

At Goat Haunt, follow the paved trail past the first right-hand turn and hike on the Continental Divide Trail, heading south toward Fifty Mountain. The trail wanders through old growth forest. At 2.5 miles (4 km), take the right junction toward the campground. If you eat lunch here, do so on the beach or in the cook area and protect the cleanliness of the tenting sites for those sleeping in bear country.

International Peace Park Guided Hike

Twice a week during July and August, Park Service interpretive rangers from Waterton and Glacier jointly lead the International Peace Park Hike. The 8.7-mile (14-km) hike leaves at 10 A.M. from the Bertha Lake Trailhead on Wednesday and Saturday. Bring a sack lunch, water, and extra clothes, and wear sturdy walking shoes. You'll stop at the boundary for a hands-across-the-border ceremony and photos before hiking to Goat Haunt and returning by boat to the Townsite by 6 P.M. Group size is limited to 35, so you'll need to preregister at the Waterton Lakes Visitor Information Center (403/859-5133) or Glacier's St. Mary Visitor Center (406/732-7750). It's free, but you'll need to pay for the boat ride and make reservations through Waterton Shoreline Tours.

Guides

Brian and Lauren Baker, longtime Waterton folks who own the outdoor gear shop, arrange guides for custom hikes with interpretive services by reservation at **Tamarack Outdoor Outfitters** (Tamarack Village Square, 214 Mount View Rd., 403/859-2379, www.hikewaterton.com, late May–early Oct.). In general, a full-day hike for two people starts at CDN$75 per person and includes ground transportation to the trailhead. Half-day hikes are available, too. Boat shuttles cost extra. Bring your own trail snacks, lunches, and water.

BIKING

All roadways in Waterton offer good bicycling. Particular favorites are Akamina and Red Rocks Parkways. Both have minimal shoulders and narrow up tightly in spots, so be prepared to ride with cars at your elbows and encounter bears on both roads. In 2010, Parks Canada began construction of a trail paralleling the entrance road. The route, which is expected to be paved, connects the entrance station with the Townsite.

Parks Canada levies heavy fines up to CDN$2,000 for riding on sidewalks, grass, or trails designated for hiking only. For campers traveling by bicycle, both the Townsite and Crandell Mountain Campgrounds have bear-resistant food storage facilities.

Alberta law requires kids under 18 to wear a helmet while bicycling. Given the narrow roads and the fact that most drivers are gaping at the scenery or looking for bears, and that winds can be strong enough to knock you off your bike, it's a wise idea for all ages to wear helmets.

Bike Trails

Four trails in Waterton permit bikes. For these, mountain bikes are best in handling the trail rubble, roots, and terrain. For current trail conditions, check with the visitors center.

Departing from 8.4 miles (14 km) up the Akamina Parkway, **Akamina Pass Trail** is a wide but stiff and steep 0.8-mile (1.3-km) climb on a forested trail. Even though the pass offers no great scenery, it's the Continental Divide and marks the boundary of Waterton National Park and Akamina-Kishinena Provincial Park as well as Alberta and British Columbia. After crossing the pass, you can continue riding to Wall Lake—adding another 4.8 miles (8 km) round-trip.

Beginning at the end of Red Rocks Parkway, the **Snowshoe Trail** rides 9.8 miles (16.4 km) round-trip along Bauerman Creek to the Snowshoe Warden Cabin. An abandoned fire road with a fairly wide berth, the trail has some steep sections and creek fords for spice. Bikes are prohibited on the side trails. Hikers with a little savvy do biking-hiking trips here—bicycling to the Snowshoe Cabin, then hiking to Lost or Twin Lake. Those camping at Snowshoe need a permit.

Leaving Chief Mountain Highway less than a half mile from the Highway 5 junction, the 12.6-mile (21-km) round-trip **Wishbone Trail** starts off wide and easy on an old wagon road through aspen parklands, but about halfway it narrows and becomes overgrown. At 4.9 miles (8.2 km), you'll pass the Vimy Trail (hiking only) junction just before traversing above the Lower Waterton Lake shoreline.

The most challenging ride is the 12.6-mile (21-km) **Crandell Mountain Loop,** combining trails to circle the massive mountain. Be prepared to encounter rough terrain and washouts. You can start at three different trailheads: Crandell Lake Trailhead 3.6 miles (6 km) up Akamina Parkway, 3.6 miles (6 km) up Red Rocks Parkway on the Crandell Campground turnoff, or Waterton Townsite.

Rentals

Pat's Gas Station (224 Mount View Rd., 403/859-2266) rents mountain bikes by the hour (CDN$9–12) or full day (CDN$40–50). The shop carries full-suspension mountain bikes, helmets (free with rentals, otherwise CDN$10), and cycle trailers (CDN$25) for baby hauling. You'll see Pat's famous two-person four-wheel surrey bikes tootling around the Townsite (CDN$25 per hour); they're fun for a spin, but stick to the Townsite roads!

Pat's Gas Station rents surreys, mopeds, and mountain bikes.

HORSEBACK RIDING

Alpine Stables (2.4 miles, 4 km from park entrance on park entrance road, 403/859-2462, www.alpinestables.com, May–Sept.) offers guided hourly rides (CDN$35) that leave daily on the hour 9 A.M.–5 P.M., touring on open grasslands with big views of surrounding peaks. During shoulder seasons, the first ride starts at 10 A.M. With small saddles, the stables can take kids as young as four years old. You can either reserve a spot or simply show up about 20 minutes early. Wear long pants and tennis shoes or boots. Other rides range 90 minutes–8 hours (CDN$50–145). Two-hour rides that depart at 10 A.M., 1 and 5 P.M. cruise through wildlife habitat where you can often see elk. The three- to four-hour rides depart at 1:30 P.M. for the Bison Paddock. Those traveling with their own equines can board horses (CDN$10 per night, including feed). Backcountry camping with horses is allowed only at Lone Lake and Snowshoe Cabin (permits required).

BOATING

Motorized boats are permitted on two lakes: **Upper** and **Middle Waterton Lakes.** Jet Skis are banned. You can launch boats on ramps at Linnet Lake Picnic Area (0.7 mile, 1.1 km north of the Townsite) on Middle Waterton Lake or the marina on Upper Waterton Lake. The marina sells gas and also has overnight mooring services operated by Waterton Shoreline Cruises (403/859-2362).

Boaters are not permitted to camp in their watercraft, but two wilderness campsites are accessible by boat—Bertha Bay and Boundary Creek. Permits are required for these (CDN$10 per person per night, kids 16 and under free). Reservations are available for CDN$12 per trip 90 days in advance beginning April 1 each year. Both permits and reservations are available at the Waterton Visitor Information Center or Waterton's Parks Canada office. Goat Haunt's campsites require Glacier Park permits, which are available in St. Mary.

KAYAKING AND CANOEING

Canoeing, kayaking, and rowing are perfect activities for many of Waterton's road-accessible

the marina in Waterton Townsite

lakes. However, be aware that whitecaps are common, with an average wind speed of 20 mph on Waterton Lake.

Waterton Lakes

A few paddlers tackle Upper Waterton Lake; those who hug shorelines because of the wind. More kayakers and canoers gravitate toward Middle Waterton Lake, the Dardanelles (the waterway connecting the two lakes), and Lower Waterton Lake for exceptional wildlife-watching and birding—and less-hefty gales. Hay Barn and Marquis Picnic Areas are the most popular put-ins for paddling these sections.

Cameron Lake

Cameron Lake is an ideal spot for sea kayaking, canoeing, and rowing. Winds are often less cantankerous here than at Waterton Lakes and the views equally as tantalizing. Do not beach or hike on the slopes surrounding the southern half of the lake; this is prime grizzly bear habitat. Canoes, paddleboats, and rowboat rentals (403/859-2396, mid-June–Aug., 8 A.M.–6:30 P.M. daily, CDN$25–35 per hour, cash only) are available at the lakeshore. Life jackets and paddles are included in the rates.

FISHING

As in Glacier, fish are no longer stocked in Waterton Lakes National Park; however, introduced species still populate waterways: arctic grayling, British Columbia and Yellowstone cutthroat, and rainbow, eastern brook, and brown trout. Conscientious anglers practice catch-and-release, especially to protect 17 species of native fish—bull trout, ling, lake chub, deepwater sculpin, northern pike, pygmy whitefish, and spottail shiner.

In **Waterton Lake,** which harbors rainbow trout, whitefish, and pike, fish feed here on the tiny opossum shrimp, a crustacean that is a relic descended from pre–ice age days. The record lake trout caught in Waterton Lake was 51 pounds. Some hiking destinations, like **Goat Lake,** offer decent rainbow trout fishing.

Season

The general fishing season runs July–October, but mid-May–early September, anglers may fish Upper and Middle Waterton Lakes, Crandell Lake, Cameron Lake and Creek, and Akamina Lake with barbless hooks. Waters closed year-round include Maskinonge Lake and inlet, plus several creeks—Blakiston, Bauerman, Sofa, Dungarvan, and North Fork of the Belly.

Regulations

Waterton Park requires a fishing permit (daily CDN$10, annual CDN$35) to fish within park boundaries. Purchase one at the visitors center, Parks Canada office, campground kiosks, Cameron Lake boat rentals, or Pat's Gas Station. The license is valid in all Canadian mountain parks. Kids under 16 can either purchase their own permit to catch a full limit or share limits with an adult. Check for species limits when you purchase fishing licenses. Anglers planning to fish Wall and Forum Lakes in Akamina-Kishinena Provincial Park need British Columbia provincial fishing licenses.

Regulations on catch-and-release of native fish and limits of nonnative fish may see changes, due to concerns with the aquatic ecosystems. Check for current limits at the visitors center. Lead weights less than 50 grams (1.75 oz.) are not permitted due to contamination of waterfowl. As in Glacier, bull trout are a protected species in Waterton. Follow the adage "No black, put it back."

WATERSKIING

Waterskiing is permitted only on Upper and Middle Waterton Lakes; however, most waterskiers gravitate to the middle lake. It's more sheltered and less windy than its upper sister. You'll find boat ramps at Linnet Lake Picnic Area (0.7 mile, 1.1 km north of the Townsite) on Middle Waterton Lake or the marina on Upper Waterton Lake. Because the water is extremely cold, water-skiers wear drysuits or full wetsuits here. Floating debris—logs, sticks, and branches—is common; keep your eyes open for these hazards. Waterton has no water-ski boat or ski rental service.

SAILBOARDING

It's a rare day when Waterton doesn't see wind. Winds don't just blow here; they rage. For traveling sailboarders with their own gear (no rental gear is available in Waterton), Upper Waterton Lake is the best place to catch some waves with consistent wind. The glacier-fed lake, however, is freezing cold. Wear a drysuit or wetsuit to prevent hypothermia. To sailboard here, you should know how to water start and self-rescue; it's not a place for beginners. For the best launching on the upper lake, head to **Windsurfer Beach** on Waterton Avenue, one block west of Vimy Avenue. For safety, check the current weather report at the Waterton Visitor Information Center before launching into a big wind.

SCUBA DIVING

Scuba divers go after a spot in Emerald Bay where a sunken circa 1900 paddle steamer, *The Gertrude,* provides exploration at a 65-foot (20-m) depth. For the clearest waters, early spring and fall are best for diving. Just remember that historic artifacts, which include anything on the wreck, are protected by the park; leave all things where you find them. Bring your own gear, as the nearest scuba shop for rentals and repairs is 78 miles (130 km) east in Lethbridge.

SWIMMING

On warm days, the beaches at Waterton Lake attract swimmers, but the water is chilly, and winds can howl. For swimming indoors in a heated pool, head to the **Waterton Health Club** (101 Clematis Ave., 888/985-6343, open year-round but hours vary, adults CDN$6, kids CDN$4) in the Waterton Lakes Lodge. The facility is open to the public and includes a hot tub and fitness center. Children can also find outdoor water-play features at the kiddie playground area on the corner of Cameron Falls Drive and Windflower Avenue.

GOLF

Focusing on your putting can be difficult with huge scenery. Not only are sand traps a hazard,

© BECKY LOMAX

Beaches on Upper Waterton Lake attract swimmers and windsurfers.

but sometimes grizzly bears are, too. Located 1.7 miles (3 km) north of the Townsite, the 18-hole **Waterton Golf Course** (403/859-2114, www. golfwaterton.com, May–Oct.) is an original Stanley Thompson design like the Banff Springs and Jasper courses—rolling fairways bordered with aspens. The dawn-to-dusk course charges CDN$48 for 18 holes. A full pro shop rents golf carts (CDN$34) and clubs (CDN$7–20), and a licensed clubhouse keeps guests fed and watered on its patio with outstanding views. Many of Waterton's hotels offer golf packages in May and after mid-September.

TENNIS

Four hard-surface outdoor public tennis courts sit on the corner of Cameron Falls Drive and Harebell Drive. **Pat's Gas Station** (224 Mount View Rd., 403/859-2266) rents tennis rackets for CDN$3 per hour. The free unlit courts, which are snow covered in winter, are available on a first-come, first-served basis. Limit playing time to 30 minutes when other players are waiting.

CROSS-COUNTRY SKIING AND SNOWSHOEING

In winter, when heavy snows render many of the roads impassable by vehicle, the parkways become ideal cross-country ski trails. Alternatively, ski along Waterton Lake or on the lake after it freezes. With fewer than 100 residents wintering in Waterton, services are minimal, so plan on bringing skis or snowshoes. The park does not permit snowmobiles, so a quiet backcountry winter experience is guaranteed. Also, dogs are not permitted on the park's groomed ski trails, which helps maintain the tracks in good condition for gliding.

Waterton is a land of winter extremes. It records the highest precipitation levels in Alberta, much of it in snowfall. It also records winter winds over 60 miles per hour, which can plummet wind chills. With winter chinooks, the park is also one of Alberta's warmest areas, with an average of 28 days above freezing. With this diversity, you can expect all types of snow—from dry, light powder to heavy, wet glop—and conditions that change within an hour. Most cross-country skiers here sacrifice a bit of speed for reliable glide by using waxless skis.

Two designated ski trails are marked and track set for weekends: **Cameron** and **Dipper Ski Trails,** both off Akamina Parkway, which is plowed to the trailheads at Little Prairie. Other trails such as Crandell Lake, Rowe Trail, and Akamina Pass are popular trails, but skiers should be prepared with rescue beacons, probes, and shovels for avalanche travel. Popular snowshoe trails lead to Bertha Falls and Crandell Lake. Contact the Waterton Parks Canada office (403/859-2224) for details and avalanche conditions.

ENTERTAINMENT

During summer months, Parks Canada offers evening slide shows and indoor programs at 8 P.M. at the Falls Theater (across Evergreen Ave. from Cameron Falls) and Crandell Mountain Campground. Varying programs cover wildlife, ecology, and geology. Contact 403/859-2445 for current schedule. Schedules

WATERTON

are also posted in the visitors center and campgrounds.

The **Waterton Opera House** (309 Windflower Ave., 403/859-2466), which shows movies rather than staging operas, opens during summer months only. Shows change regularly, but don't expect to see world premieres at this tiny outpost.

Waterton celebrates festivals. For 10 days in late June, the **Waterton Wildflower Festival** (403/859-2663 or 800/215-2395, www.watertonwildflowers.com) pulls together hikes, art shows, photography courses, watercolor painting workshops, drawing classes, slide shows, and free evening lectures in a tribute to the park's rare and diverse wildflowers. Some events are single-day programs lasting two hours; others are multiday. All are taught by regional experts. Course fees range CDN$10–289, but several are free. You can register online. In late September when the elk bugle and animals congregate on Blakiston, the town celebrates the **Waterton Wildlife Festival** (403/859-2663, www.trailofthegreatbear.com), which includes the International Wildlife Film Festival and special wildlife-watching and photography excursions.

Accommodations

In Waterton, everything is within walking distance, with the compact town less than a mile across. You're not far from restaurants, shopping, boat tours, hiking, tennis, or movies no matter where you stay. While the town bustles in summer, minimal services remain open in winter. All accommodations add a 5 percent Goods and Services Tax and 4 percent tourism tax on to your rates; together, those add up, so don't be surprised that your final room bill tallies higher than you might have expected. Many of the hotels offer golf, seasonal activity packages, and specials; ask or check their websites for current deals. You'll get better deals in Waterton in the off-season (May–early June, late September–October, winter), when most lodging properties drop their room rates substantially, making travel cheaper at a crowd-free time. Waterton lodging is at a premium in summer during the big visitor season. If you don't want to pay the high rates, you can drive 35 minutes north to Pincher Creek for less-expensive chain motels.

Unfortunately, Waterton lost two of its lodging mainstays. In 2009, the historical Kilmorey Lodge (117 Mount View Rd., 403/859-2150 or 888/985-6343, www.thekilmoreylodge.com) burned to the ground. The owner plans to rebuild but as of 2010 is still hammering out details with Parks Canada. Call or check online for status. In 2010, the Waterton Hostel (corner Cameron Falls and Windflower Ave., 403/859-2150 or 888/985-6343) closed to the public in order to provide housing for workers. Contact Waterton Lakes Resort for updates.

Lodges and Inns

Located on a bluff above Waterton Lake and the Townsite, historic **(** **Prince of Wales Hotel** (across from the visitors center 4.6 miles, 7.6 km south of park entrance station, 406/892-2525, www.glacierparkinc.com, mid-June–mid-Sept., CDN$234–299, suites $799) is a four-storied wonder, and yes, it is named for Prince Edward. Its lobby, with floor-to-ceiling windows, swings with large rustic chandeliers. Lake-view rooms and suites allow you to shower with a view into Glacier Park while mountain-view rooms lend to spying bighorn sheep on Crandell Mountain. But in spite of its grand facade, the building is old, creaky, and thin walled, and the upper stories seem to sway in high winds. Be prepared for tiny sinks and small bathrooms—many installed in what were once closets. The nonsmoking rooms have phones, but no television, Internet, or air-conditioning. An elevator that doesn't always work accesses upper floors but requires a bellhop to run, rendering it unavailable at all hours. If you're on one of the top floors, you'll

WHAT IS GST?

In Canada, a 5 percent GST **(Goods and Services Tax)** is applied to some purchases. In British Columbia and Alberta, the GST is a tax that applies to most goods and services. In most cases, it will be added on to your bill, not included.

In general, groceries, prescription drugs, health care, and medical devices are not taxed. But you will pay GST on motels, campground fees, restaurant bills, souvenirs, clothing, gas, recreation rentals, and tours.

Visitors used to be able to get a rebate on the tax, but Canada canceled the rebate program. Only nonresidents on tours and foreign conventions can get a rebate now. Not all tours qualify – only those with short-term accommodations of less than one month (camping, motels, hotels, lodges) plus guide services, interpreter services, or transportation. In general, lodging, meals, admission fees, car rentals and gas, RV rentals, golf greens fees, recreational equipment, and park entrance fees do not qualify.

Nonresidents on tours that qualify need to save original receipts and detailed itineraries to be eligible for a 50 percent refund on the GST. Refund forms are available online: www.canadiantaxrefund.com.

get a workout climbing to your room, but the view is stunning. A restaurant, gift shop selling English bone china and Waterford crystal, and lounge surround the lobby. A 5-minute drive or 20-minute walk down a trail accesses the town for boat tours, shopping, bicycle rentals, and restaurants. Reservations are required.

The 17-room year-round country-style **Crandell Mountain Lodge** (102 Mount View Rd., 403/859-2288 or 866/859-2288, www. crandellmountainlodge.com, June–mid-Sept. CDN$140–220, mid-Sept.–May CDN$95–170) tucks beneath its namesake peak. The two-story circa 1940 inn has a variety of non-smoking, country-themed rooms—standards

to three-room suites with full kitchens and fireplaces. In a private garden area, a huge deck with a barbecue and lounge chairs begs for afternoon relaxation.

With free use of the Waterton Spa and Recreation Center's saltwater pool and facilities, **Waterton Lakes Lodge Resort** (101 Clematis Ave., 403/859-2150 or 888/985-6343, www.watertonlakeslodge.com, mid-May–mid-Sept. CDN$120–215, winters $120–185) has 80 air-conditioned all-nonsmoking hotel rooms, as well as kitchenettes and suites. Accommodations are spread throughout 11 themed chalet buildings sitting adjacent to each other on four acres. While some rooms have fireplaces and jetted tubs, all rooms have televisions, coffeemakers, and phones. A restaurant, lounge, and café complete the scene.

Motels

The motel on the lake, **The Bayshore** (junction of Mount View Rd. and Waterton Ave., summers 403/859-2211 or 888/527-9555, winters 604/708-9965, www.bayshoreinn.com, open May–mid-Oct., CDN$119–269) lakefront rooms have prime views from private balconies that make up for its room decor, reminiscent of chain hotels. The nonsmoking complex has restaurants, a lounge, saloon, hot tub, gift shop, wireless Internet, ice cream shop, and spa services. It sits adjacent to the marina, shopping, and additional restaurants. The Townsite Loop trail system passes between the inn and the lake.

Open year-round, the **◖ Waterton Glacier Suites** (107 Windflower Ave., 403/859-2004 or 866/621-3330, www.watertonsuites.com, mid-June–mid-Sept. CDN$225–289, winter CDN$139–229) has 26 units with balconies, refrigerators, microwaves, satellite televisions, air-conditioning, wireless Internet, and whirlpool tubs. Some rooms have fireplaces, and all have mountain views. A quick two-block walk reaches restaurants, shopping, and the tour boat.

The **Aspen Village Inn** (111 Windflower Ave., 403/859-2255 or 888/859-8669, www.aspenvillageinn.com, May–Sept., CDN$99–250) has standard hotel rooms and suites with kitchens in its aging two-story buildings. Rooms have televisions and wireless Internet. Cottages accommodating 2–8 people work for families and are surrounded by mowed lawns, playground, and outdoor barbecue picnic area. The large red-metal-roofed complex (you won't get lost trying to find it!) is centrally located in the Townsite.

If you're looking for the most affordable rooms in town, your answer is the **Bear Mountain Motel** (208 Mount View Rd., 403/859-2366, www.bearmountainmotel. com, late May–mid-Sept., CDN$95–195). The 1960s wood-and-masonry motel revamped its 36 nonsmoking rooms in 2004. Small bathrooms are still the same, but new carpets, beds, linens, and paint upgraded the accommodations of the one-, two-, and three-bedroom suites, several with small kitchenettes. Rooms have no phones. Pay phones are near the office.

Bed-and-Breakfast

For park-history buffs, the **Northland Lodge** (408 Evergreen Ave., 403/859-2353, www. northlandlodgecanada.com, mid-May–mid-Oct., CDN$120–215) carries a certain attraction. Louis Hill, builder of the Prince of Wales Hotel and many of Glacier Park's historic hotels, constructed the Swiss-style lodge as his private residence circa 1948, although he never had time to live there. The lodge only has nine rooms (two with a shared bath and the rest with private baths, all with wireless Internet), split between three levels. A large balcony is great for soaking up views with coffee and homemade muffins with Saskatoon berry jam in the morning. Cameron Falls is a short half-block walk away, as is the trailhead to Bertha Falls and Lake. A 10-minute walk puts you in the heart of shopping and restaurants, or you can hop on the 20-minute more-scenic Townsite Loop trail just across the street.

CAMPING
Inside the Park

Waterton Park campgrounds have flush toilets,

drinking water, kitchen shelters, and bear-resistant food storage lockers. Some sites have fire rings, and firewood is supplied, but you pay $9 per site for a burning permit in addition to your campground fee.

Smack in the middle of town, the **Waterton Townsite Campground** (403/859-2224, www. pc.gc.ca, mid-Apr.–mid-Oct., unserviced sites CDN$23–28, full hookups CDN$38) is citified with its mowed lawn, but it sits on prime real estate with gorgeous views. The 238-site campground borders the Townsite Loop trail and the beach. A few trees shade some sites, but most are open, offering little privacy. Go for the most scenic unserviced spots in the G loop—sites 26–46—but be prepared for strong winds. For more sheltered scenery, go for the Cameron Creek E loop sites (even numbers 2–16). Kitchen shelters are the only place where fires are permitted, but the campground includes hot showers and a dump station, and the trailheads to Bertha Lake and Waterton Lakeshore are within a few minutes' walk. In midsummer, the campground fills early; plan on arriving by noon to claim a site, or make reservations (CDN$11 nonrefundable processing fee) starting in early April through the National Parks Canada Campground Reservation Service (877/737-3783, www.pc-camping.ca). In early or late season, you'll have your pick of sites without a reservation; off-season the campground is virtually empty.

On the opposite side of Crandell Mountain from the Townsite and 3.8 miles (6 km) up the Red Rocks Parkway, **⟨ Crandell Mountain Campground** (403/859-2224, www.pc.gc.ca, mid-May–early Sept., CDN$22) nestles in the woods along Blakiston Creek. With many sites deep in trees, the campground has a remote feel, with greenery providing privacy between sites. Sometimes you can see bear and moose around Blakiston Creek. Its 129 sites offer no hookups; however, a dump station is available. An easy walk to Crandell Lake (3.1 miles, 5 km, round-trip) departs from here. The campground takes no reservations, so plan on claiming your site by midday in July and August. A, B, C, and D loops sit in thicker trees; E, F,

Waterton Townsite Campground sits on Upper Waterton Lake.

G, and H loops are more open, with views of surrounding peaks. A quick 10-minute drive puts you at the end of Red Rocks Parkway, where trailheads lead to Blakiston Falls and Goat Lake. Parks Canada added five tepees in 2010, available for rental at $55 per night.

On Chief Mountain Highway and 17 miles (26 km) from Waterton Townsite, the **Belly River Campground** (403/859-2224, www. pc.gc.ca, mid-May–early Sept., CDN$16) has 24 pleasant sites for small RVs and tents in aspen groves with hand-pumped well water and some pit toilets in addition to the flush toilets. Some sites are shaded; some are meadows. It is a good location for wildlife-watching and birding, and the closest campground to Chief Mountain Customs for those who want to shoot across the boundary first thing in the morning. A short trail leads up the Belly River but dead-ends just before the international boundary.

In winter, when all other campsites have closed, free sites are available at **Pass Creek Winter Campground** (403/859-2224, www.

pc.gc.ca, mid-Oct.–mid-Apr.). Located on the entrance road 3.1 miles (5 km) from the Townsite, the eight sites offer primitive camping with only a pit toilet and a woodstove in the kitchen shelter. Water from the creek may be boiled or purified for use.

Backcountry Camping

Waterton has nine backcountry campgrounds (called "wilderness campsites"). Some backpackers break up the Avion Ridge traverse with stays at **Snowshoe** and **Goat Lake.** But **Twin Lakes** and **Lost Lake** put you farther away from day hikers. Required permits (CDN$10 per person per night, kids 16 and under free) are available at the visitors center (403/859-5133) or Waterton's Parks Canada office (403/859-5140) in person 24 hours in advance or by reservation (CDN$12) up to 90 days in advance.

Outside the Park

Just outside the park boundary, three private campgrounds can handle the overload when park campgrounds are full. On the Highway 6 to Pincher Creek, **Waterton Springs Campground** (1.5 miles or 2.5 km north of the park entrance road, 403/859-2247, www.watertonspringscamping.com, May–Sept.) has 70 full-hookup sites (CDN$30) in an open, dusty parking-lot-type setting that fit big rigs, as well as 75 partial-hookup sites (CDN$24–30) and tent sites (CDN$18) set around small ponds and a creek in a rough aspen parkland. Amenities include token-operated showers and launderette, flush toilets, picnic tables,

camp store, wireless Internet, playground, and fire rings.

Operated by Waterton Natural History Association, **Crooked Creek Campground** (3.8 miles or 6 km east of park entrance road, 403/653-1100, mid-May–early Sept., hookups CDN$25–30, tents CDN$18) has 33 sites set adjacent to the highway. Amenities include flush toilets, running water, kitchen shelter, dump station, firewood, power and water hookups, and a shower-restroom and launderette facility. Reservations are accepted.

Food

Most restaurants in the Townsite cluster along Waterton Avenue and spill over to Windflower Avenue. While most of the hotel dining rooms cater to fine dining, the town has several worthy places to grab a meal without dropping an exorbitant pile of cash. You'll also find your final bill jacked up a bit in price by the GST (Goods and Services Tax).

RESTAURANTS

With the exception of the Prince of Wales Hotel, all of the restaurants congregate within a few blocks in the Waterton Townsite. In off-seasons (Sept.–mid-June), many may shorten their hours or days, and most close in winter. Since Kilmorey Lodge burned down in 2009, Waterton lost one of its most distinctive dining opportunities; however, the staff moved to ⟨ **Vimy's Lounge and Grill** (101 Clematis Ave., 403/859-2150 or 888/985-6343, www.watertonlakeslodge.com, 7:30 A.M.–10 P.M. daily) at Waterton Lakes Lodge—which is now the only restaurant open year-round. Breakfast (CDN$7–13) includes multiple variations on eggs Benedict, while lunch (CDN$11–15) stacks up burgers, sandwiches, and fish-and-chips. The lounge serves the Canadian classic poutine—homemade french fries drowning in melted cheese and gravy. You can also get Alberta elk meatballs, burgers, and appetizers. Dinner entrées

(CDN$25–30) span bison steaks, trout, and filet mignon.

Located in the Prince of Wales Hotel, the **Royal Stewart Dining Room** (406/892-2525, early June–mid-Sept.) looks out its massive floor-to-ceiling windows down Waterton Lake. The nonsmoking restaurant's claim to fame is its view more than its culinary uniqueness. Breakfast, running CDN$9–14, is served 6:30–9:30 A.M., and lunch, costing CDN$8–16, is served 11:30 A.M.–2 P.M. Dinner (5–9:30 P.M., CDN$25–30) features entrées of lamb, fish, steak, and pasta. No reservations are accepted for groups of fewer than 12 people, so you may have a waiting line in high season. The restaurant also makes hiker lunches (CDN$15); order these a day in advance. Go for lighter meals at the **Windsor Lounge,** with its cozy place to sit with a big view. A bar menu (appetizers and sandwiches) is available (2–10 P.M., US$8–16). Beer, wine, and cocktails are served until midnight.

The British atmosphere of the Prince of Wales Hotel goes into full swing with **Afternoon Tea** (406/892-2525, early June–mid-Sept.) in the hotel lobby, where huge windows overlook Waterton Lake. It's a full sugarfest meal of desserts, served 2–4 P.M. Homemade pastries, scones, fruits, and berries stack on multitiered serving dishes, and Devonshire cream comes on the side. You can go American with coffee rather than tea, if you prefer. It's a unique experience but more mood than anything else (CDN$30 adults, $16 kids). Reservations are a good idea. If you partake in high tea, you may be too full to need evening dinner.

Located in The Bayshore, the **Bayshore Lakeside Chophouse** (junction of Mount View Rd. and Waterton Ave., 403/859-2211 or 888/527-9555, www.bayshoreinn.com, May–mid-Oct., 7 A.M.–10 P.M. daily) has mostly the view going for it, as the restaurant sits right on Waterton Lake with outdoor dining on a patio. Full breakfasts run CDN$8–15, and lunch (CDN$9–15) features salads, wraps, burgers, pizza, and pasta. The chef combines steaks, chicken, fish, and pasta dinners (CDN$20–38) with a chef's choice wine recommendation to accompany each dish. The restaurant also makes hiker lunches to go (CDN$13). The Bayshore's **Glacier Bistro and Burger Barn** (7 A.M.–10 P.M. daily) serves lighter meals for breakfast, lunch, and dinner (CDN$6–11): croissants, lattes, pizza, and burgers, plus a selection of dessert goodies. If you prefer people-watching while you eat, the café has a shaded sidewalk deck.

For Italian flavors, head to **Bel Lago Ristorante** (110 Waterton Ave., 403/859-2213, www.bellagoristorante.com, May–Sept., 11 A.M.–10 P.M. daily), which has both indoor and covered outdoor seating. New owners in 2009 redecorated the restaurant, overhauled the menu, and added an extensive wine list. It now serves homemade pastas with Alberta ingredients—natural beef and organic veggies. Paninis are served for lunch, which runs CDN$9–14. Dinner entrées (CDN$15–32) include pastas as well as lamb osso buco and roasted game hen. Reservations are highly recommended for dinner midsummer.

With indoor and outdoor seating, the tiny **Pizza of Waterton** (303 Windflower Ave., 403/859-2660, May–Oct., 4–11 P.M. Mon.–Thurs., noon–11 P.M. Fri.–Sun., CDN$14–28) is known for creative hand-crafted pizzas and huge calzones. It also has big salads. For an easy takeout dinner while camping at the Townsite, order a pizza to go.

For a buffalo burger with friendly service, head to **Zum's Eatery and Mercantile**

© BECKY LOMAX

shopping and restaurants on Waterton Avenue

(116 Waterton Ave., 403/859-2388, May–Sept., 8 P.M.–9 P.M. daily). Its broad menu can serve a family with diverse cravings. Breakfast and lunch entrées range CDN$5–16. Dinners, which specialize in burgers, schnitzel, bratwurst, fish, steaks, chicken, and ribs barbecued in Guinness, run CDN$13–23. Shaded outside seating above the sidewalk allows for people-watching. To satisfy your sweet cravings, order the wildberry pie (CDN$5), a yummy combination of raspberries, blueberries, blackberries, rhubarb, and apple.

◖ Pearl's Café (305 Windflower Ave, 403/859-2498, www.pearlscafe.ca, May–Sept., 7 A.M.–7 P.M. daily, CDN$7–14) serves breakfast and lunch. Find homemade energy bars, baked goods, espresso, wraps, chili, salads, wine, beer, and wireless Internet. Make a hiker lunch with their daily bagel sandwich special.

CAFFEINE
Over the past few years, espresso shops have boomed in Waterton. Even several of the traditional longtime restaurants have added espresso machines. Although it may be the tiniest place to order a latte, the **◖ Waterton Bagel & Coffee Shop** (309 Windflower Ave., 403/859-2466, May–Oct., 7 A.M.–9:30 P.M. daily) answers the need for a caffeine fix well. Along with a full espresso menu, it serves smoothies, juices, biscotti, bagels, and muffins. The diminutive shop only seats a couple of people on stools and outside tables, but you can grab a bagel with cream cheese and head one block away to the beach to eat.

GROCERIES
While several locations in town carry convenience foods, only one grocery store—**Rocky Mountain Food Mart** (307 Windflower Ave., May–Sept., 8 A.M.–9 P.M. daily)—stocks produce, meats, dairy, deli, and baked goods. However, it is small, so expect limited brands. It also carries ice, firewood, and camping supplies. Off-season, the closest grocery stores are in Pincher Creek.

FLATHEAD VALLEY

The Flathead Valley is an outdoor paradise. Surrounded by mountain ranges and abundant lakes, back doors open on fishing, skiing, hiking, hunting, biking, and boating. Surrounded by two and a half million acres of wilderness and national parklands, there's no shortage of space to get away from it all and play outdoors. One of the country's largest national forests fringes the valley floor, which is dotted with oodles of lakes, including the largest freshwater lake west of the Mississippi. Summer brings on flat-water kayaking and floating lazy rivers. Anglers drop lines from drift boats. Golfers hit the links. Hikers climb to wildflower-strewn heights with huge views of the vast valley.

Sadly, strip-mall culture has made some inroads into the valley, paving once pastoral farmlands. Housing developments sprout between towns, blending the borders of one with another. Aspen wannabes throw multimillion-dollar mansions up on hillsides. But an underlying culture remains—one where ripped Carhartts and a duct-taped jacket rank as fashion. Rather than hit the nine-to-five office hours, lots of folks here work seasonally—in Glacier or Flathead National Forest in summer, and ski areas in winter.

When snows fall, logging roads and golf courses convert to ski and snowshoe trails, while two alpine ski areas rack up the vertical for skiers and snowboarders. Many in the valley adhere to the six-inch rule: If six inches or more of snow falls, call in late for work.

HISTORY

Originally the home of the Flathead, Salish, and Kootenai Indians, the Flathead Valley saw

© BECKY LOMAX

HIGHLIGHTS

◖ **Flathead Lake:** Sail its blue waters or drive around its perimeter. The largest freshwater lake west of the Mississippi draws waters from as far north as Canada (page 229).

◖ **Whitefish Lake:** Cool off on hot summer days in a lake hopping with water-skiers and anglers. Three parks and a marina provide different access options (page 229).

◖ **Mount Aeneas:** Hike the short trail up the highest peak in Jewel Basin. From the summit, you'll stare into the Great Bear Wilderness, down on Flathead Lake, and north at Glacier (page 231).

◖ **Danny On Trail:** Ride a chairlift up to hike down the most popular trail in the Flathead. It's a romp through mounds of wildflowers and has stunning views of Glacier Park (page 232).

◖ **Whitefish Mountain Resort:** Step into skis for this winter wonderland or ride its summer lift to huckleberry picking. From the top, you'll see one of the best panoramas of Glacier (page 237).

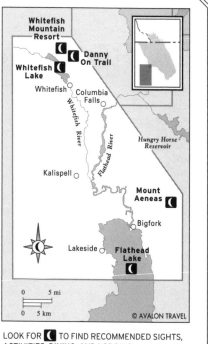

LOOK FOR ◖ TO FIND RECOMMENDED SIGHTS, ACTIVITIES, DINING, AND LODGING.

its first European descendent—famed explorer David Thompson—in 1809. Within 40 years, trappers, homesteaders, and ranchers edged their way into the valley. By the end of the century, Great Northern Railway laid tracks through the Flathead, prompting Kalispell to be plotted for township in 1890, in theory to become the next St. Paul.

Growing with ranchers, farmers, and timber harvesters, the Flathead soon sprouted other towns clustered around its lakes and rivers. In 1901, Great Northern rerouted its railroad tracks through Whitefish to access Canadian coal, catapulting the tiny Whitefish lakefront community into a train town. The mid-1900s saw tremendous change in the Flathead with the construction of the Hungry Horse dam spawning an aluminum plant, Plum Creek Timber Company, and Whitefish Mountain Ski Resort growing. Today, while original valley ranching, farming, and timber still support many families, part of the Flathead economy for its 90,000 residents comes from technology industries and tourism.

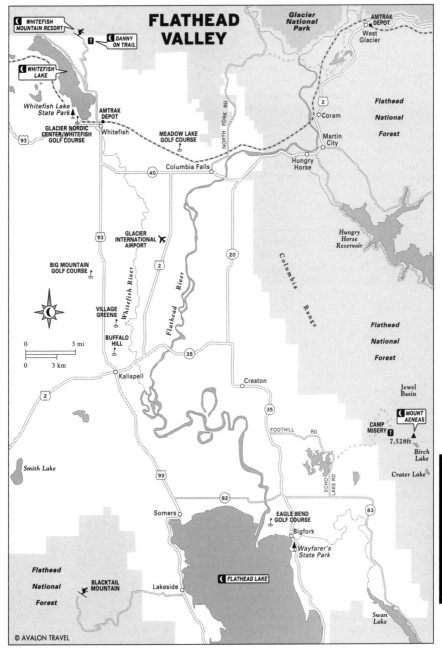

FLATHEAD VALLEY

WHITEFISH MOUNTAIN RESORT

DANNY ON TRAIL

WHITEFISH LAKE

Whitefish Lake State Park

GLACIER NORDIC CENTER/WHITEFISH GOLF COURSE

AMTRAK DEPOT

Whitefish

93

MEADOW LAKE GOLF COURSE

40

Columbia Falls

NORTH FORK RD

GLACIER NATIONAL Park

AMTRAK DEPOT

West Glacier

2

Coram

Martin City

Hungry Horse

Flathead National Forest

93

GLACIER INTERNATIONAL AIRPORT

2

BIG MOUNTAIN GOLF COURSE

Whitefish River

Flathead River

20

Columbia Range

Hungry Horse Reservoir

VILLAGE GREENS

BUFFALO HILL

0   3 mi

0   3 km

Kalispell

35

Creston

35

FOOTHILL   RD

Flathead National Forest

Jewel Basin

MOUNT AENEAS

CAMP MISERY

7,528ft

Birch Lake

Crater Lake

ECHO LAKE RD

2

Smith Lake

93

82

Somers

EAGLE BEND GOLF COURSE

Bigfork

83

Wayfarer's State Park

Flathead National Forest

BLACKTAIL MOUNTAIN

Lakeside

FLATHEAD LAKE

Swan Lake

© AVALON TRAVEL

FLATHEAD VALLEY

Exploring Flathead Valley

Flathead Valley centers around four main towns: Kalispell, Whitefish, Columbia Falls, and Bigfork. Each has its own draw, brought on by seasonal recreation in each area.

Outside the four main towns, small burgs dot Flathead Lake's shoreline. Lakeside buzzes with summer water fun and serves as the launching point to reach Blacktail Mountain Ski Area in winter. Somers is a blink-and-miss-it town but is popular for its marina.

Kalispell

The nucleus of Flathead Valley, with three golf courses, restaurants, and shopping, the area's largest town has moved beyond its cow town past. In historic downtown Kalispell, you can tour the pre-1900s Conrad Mansion and unique art spots. In August, catch the Northwest Montana Fair and Rodeo, and in October, join in the Glacier Jazz Stampede. Kalispell sits 9 miles from the airport and 34 miles from Glacier.

Whitefish

The recreation capital of Flathead Valley, Whitefish packs in summer with boating in Whitefish Lake and golf at the valley's only 36-hole course. In winter, skiing becomes the passion at Whitefish Mountain Resort. Surrounded by rampant new housing developments, downtown Whitefish fits compactly into several square blocks with boutiques, restaurants, art galleries, and theaters. It sits 11 miles from the airport and 27 miles from Glacier.

Columbia Falls

The gateway to Glacier, Columbia Falls never had a falls of its own until the town built one just off Highway 2. Those in search of old-time bargains head to one of its several antiques stores. Recently, the town has boomed with restaurants in its downtown area, upgrading its dining quality. Beside its rebuilt public outdoor swimming pool, Columbia Falls is home to Big

antique stores cluster in Columbia Falls

© BECKY LOMAX

Sky Waterslides. It sits 8 miles from the airport and 18 miles from Glacier.

Bigfork

A summer resort town, Bigfork combines easy access to the Swan Mountains with boating on Flathead Lake. Bigfork Summer Playhouse dominates the town, packing restaurants before nightly shows. Quaint shops and art galleries fill its several-block-long village, and its one-lane steel bridge crosses the Swan River. In early June, the town hops with the Bigfork Whitewater Festival, when kayakers shoot the Swan's Wild Mile. It sits 26 miles from the airport and 40 miles from Glacier.

VISITORS CENTERS

One of the easiest ways to grab additional information on the Flathead is to contact visitors centers. Flathead Valley has six: **Flathead Valley Convention and Visitors Bureau**

(406/756-9091 or 800/543-3105, www.fcvb. org), **Kalispell Chamber of Commerce** (15 Depot Park, 406/758-2800, www.kalispellchamber.com), **Whitefish Chamber of Commerce** (520 E. 2nd St., 406/862-3501, www.whitefishchamber.com), **Columbia Falls Chamber of Commerce** (233 13th St. E., 406/892-2072, www.columbiafallschamber. com), **Bigfork Chamber of Commerce** (Olde Town Center, 406/837-5888, www.bigfork. org), and **Lakeside Chamber of Commerce** (406/844-3715, www.lakesidechamber.com).

SIGHTS
◖ Flathead Lake

Stretching 28 miles long and 15 miles wide, Flathead Lake is the largest freshwater lake west of the Mississippi. Its 188 square miles, six state parks, islands, deep fishing waters, and wildlife refuges make it a summer playland. Highways encircle the lake, popping in at 13 different points to public lake accesses. The southern half of the lake falls inside the Flathead Indian Reservation, home to the Salish and Kootenai tribes.

Two boat tours offer different modes of travel. From Bigfork, **Questa Sailing Charters** (150 Flathead Lake Lodge, 406/837-5569, mid-June–Sept.) launch from Flathead Lake Lodge's dock. Two 51-foot 1928–1929 Q class sloops each carry 12 passengers. On the beautifully restored boats, trips ($39–44, ask for special senior and kids 12 and under rates) depart daily at 1:30 P.M. At 7 P.M., the popular adults-only sunset cruise includes complimentary wine and beverages. The engine-powered tour in a 23-foot cabin cruiser launches from Lakeside with **Far West Boat Tours** (7135 Hwy. 93 S., 406/844-BOAT, www.flatheadlakeboattour. com, June–Aug.). Sit upstairs in the sun for bigger views. Daily tours depart 1 P.M. Evening tours run Sun.–Tues. at 6:30 P.M. All tours cost $15 for adults; kids 4–12 are half price.

◖ Whitefish Lake

The 3,315-acre lake in Whitefish buzzes in summer. Anglers hit the lake in early morning and evening, while midday turns into a

© BECKY LOMAX

A lifeguard watches City Beach on Whitefish Lake.

frenzy of water-skiers, Jet Skiers, party barges, kayakers, and canoers. Swimmers cool off at Whitefish State Park, City Beach, and Les Mason Park. In winter when ice covers the lake, hockey players make their own rinks and anglers ice fish.

Flathead River

Outside Hungry Horse, the South, Middle, and North Forks of the Flathead River converge. Then, the Flathead River snakes 55 miles across the valley to Flathead Lake. Seven river accesses allow places for anglers, canoers, and floaters to hop onto its meandering pace. Toward Flathead Lake, the river takes several sharp S turns in sloughs and estuaries, bird habitat for ospreys and waterfowl.

Whitefish Mountain Resort

Skiers and snowboarders flock to Whitefish Mountain Resort's 3,000 acres in winter. Twelve lifts access on average 300 inches of snow per year. Snow ghosts—ice-encrusted bent firs—compete with the view of Glacier

FLATHEAD VALLEY

© BECKY LOMAX

Riders get thrills on the alpine slide at Whitefish Mountain Resort.

70 feet up in the air (you're clipped in with a safety harness).

Museums

In Kalispell, the historic Victorian **Conrad Mansion** (between 3rd St. and 4th St. on Woodland Ave., 406/755-2166, www.conrad-mansion.com, May 15–Oct. 15, 10 A.M.–5 P.M. Tues.–Sun., adults $8, seniors $7, kids $3) preserves 26 rooms with their original 1895 furniture. Vintage clothing and toys recall the days of rummaging through Grandma's attic.

Also in Kalispell, the **Hockaday Museum of Art** (302 2nd Ave. E., 406/755-5268, www.hockadayartmuseum.org, open year-round 10 A.M.–5 P.M. Tues.–Sat., adults $5, seniors $4, kids 12 and under free) features Montana pottery, jewelry, and paintings—particularly Native American and Glacier Park artists. A children's Discovery Gallery has creative hands-on exhibits for kids.

Atop Big Mountain at Whitefish Mountain Resort, the **USFS Summit Nature Center** (406/862-2900, www.skiwhitefish.com, late June–Labor Day, 10 A.M.–5 P.M. daily, free) requires a hike or a lift ride ($5–10) to reach its exhibits, but it may be the only place you can touch a grizzly bear! Free guided flower walks are offered in July and August, and there's a Junior Ranger program for kids.

National Park from the mountain's 6,817-foot summit. Late June–Labor Day, the resort runs its lift for sightseeing and mountain biking. Other summer activities include an alpine slide, zipline tours, and Walk in the Treetops, a boardwalk tour through the tree canopy

Recreation

The Flathead Valley is a four-season recreation mecca. Lakes draw summertime paddlers and swimmers, fall lures hunters, ski resorts cater to powder hounds, and spring explodes with hikers.

HIKING

Since Flathead National Forest surrounds Flathead Valley, hikers have no shortage of trails within spitting distance of the back porch. Most trails are multiuse, permitting mountain bikes and motor bikes, but a few—such as the Jewel Basin trails or the Danny

On Memorial Trail on Big Mountain—limit use to hikers.

In the Swan Mountains, **Jewel Basin** holds 50 miles of hiking paths. Open for hiking June–October, depending on snow, the 15,349-acre hiker-only area is called The Jewel, for 27 alpine fishing lakes sparkle in its basins. Paths tromp across huckleberry meadows and high ridges with top-of-the-world views. Fido can go on a leash. It's extremely popular: July Fourth weekend sees 200 people per day. Trail signage is scanty, so find maps in local sports shops or contact Flathead National Forest

HUCKLEBERRY MANIA

The huckleberry – a small dark purple berry about the size of the tip of your little finger – resembles a blueberry but is much sweeter and more flavorful. It grows only in the wild on low deciduous bushes with leaves turning red in fall. Growing mostly at elevations above 4,000 feet, they ripen late July–September.

The berry has yet to be successfully cultivated. Outside Glacier, around Hungry Horse, and in Flathead Valley, you'll find berry stands selling hucks that have been picked by commercial permit in national forests or private lands. Expect to pay about $40 per gallon of the precious purple gems. (Now you know why huckleberry pie is so expensive!) Be careful when purchasing berries early in the summer from fruit stands, as you may be buying frozen berries from last year rather than fresh-picked ones. The frozen berries are still yummy but a little softer when they thaw. Fresh ones usually hit the stands in late July.

You can pick your own huckleberries to eat – no permit needed. You'll find them on many hikes in Flathead National Forest and the park. While locals don't usually divulge their prized secret stashes in Flathead National Forest, you can usually find good huckleberry picking on Big Mountain at Whitefish Mountain Resort. Glacier Park rules permit plucking a few berries to eat, but harvesting for commercial purposes is not allowed.

Two mammals crave the berries: bears and humans. High in vitamin C, the berries are not only healthy and low in fat, but they enliven any pastry, pie, sauce, or fruit concoction. They're wonderful in smoothies and delightful on pancakes. And you'll find them here in everything, from ice cream to beer.

What huckleberry products are out there? Just about anything! Syrup, jam, and jellies top everyone's favorites. Hucks also flavor and scent chocolates, honey, cocoa, barbecue sauce, tea, salad dressing, ice cream toppings, a daiquiri mix, lotion, lip balm, bubble bath, shampoo, soap, and more.

One word of advice: Avoid using huckleberry shampoo before hiking in bear country!

(406/758-5200, www.fs.fed.us/r1/flathead) or Swan Lake Ranger Station (200 Ranger Station Rd., Bigfork, 406/837-7500).

A seven-mile narrow curvy dirt road that the Forest Service resurfaced in fall 2010 climbs up to 5,717 feet off the valley floor to The Jewel. Leave low-clearance vehicles and trailers behind, as it's riddled with washboards, rollers, and limited turnouts. To reach the Camp Misery Trailhead, with its less-than-inspiring name, catch the Swan Highway (Highway 83) two miles north of Bigfork. Follow it to Echo Lake Road and head north approximately three miles to the Jewel Basin Road (#5392).

◀ Mount Aeneas

- Distance: 5.9-mile loop
- Duration: 3 hours
- Elevation gain: 1,811 feet
- Effort: moderately strenuous
- Trailhead: Camp Misery Trailhead in Jewel Basin

Mount Aeneas, at 7,528 feet, is the highest peak in The Jewel and offers big views for little work, but don't expect solitude at the summit. From the top, you'll see Flathead Lake, Glacier National Park, the Bob Marshall Wilderness Complex, and the Swan Mountains. A lot of scenery for a short hike! Combined with Picnic Lakes, the trail loops on a ridge and through a lake basin.

Begin hiking up trail #717, a wide roadbed. In 1.5 miles, the trail reaches a four-way junction—stay on #717, heading uphill. After a few switchbacks, you'll pass an ugly microwave tower before waltzing with the mountain goats along an arête to the summit. From the summit, drop down through the Picnic Lakes Basin. At the lakes, hook onto #392, then right

© BECKY LOMAX

Picnic Lakes sits on Jewel Basin's Mount Aeneas loop trail.

onto #68, and left onto #8. (At 1.7 miles from Camp Misery, Picnic Lakes makes a good tiny-kid destination—just reverse the route.)

Birch Lake

- Distance: 6 miles round-trip
- Duration: 3 hours
- Elevation gain: 800 feet
- Effort: moderate
- Trailhead: Camp Misery Trailhead in Jewel Basin

A short hop over a ridge along with a skip down a trail plops hikers on the banks of Birch Lake—a great destination for kids. Swim in the lake's west end, but don't expect balmy waters. This clear snowmelt pond retains its chill even in August. For those with more gumption, another 2.5 miles sets hikers on the boulder shoreline of Crater Lake.

Begin hiking up the broad roadway of trail #717 to the four-way junction. Take the right fork on #7. The trail curves around the lower flanks of Mount Aeneas as it descends to Birch Lake. (You'll have to hike up this on the way out!) A trail circles the lake, but the best place to plunk yourself is on its obvious peninsula.

Danny On Trail

- Distance: 4 miles one-way
- Duration: 2 hours
- Elevation gain: 2,400 feet
- Effort: moderate
- Trailhead: next to the Chalet at Whitefish Mountain Resort
- Directions: drive seven miles north of Whitefish, following signs

The Danny On Trail chocks up over 14,000 hikers annually. At Big Mountain's summit, the USFS Nature Center provides interpretive resources for the trail. Catch the chairlift up to hike down or hike up to ride down ($5 per person one-way). While you can hike with your pooch on a leash, Fido may not ride up or down the chairlift.

After beginning in Whitefish Mountain Resort Village, the trail switchbacks up through a forested slope and crosses ski runs as it sweeps around the mountain. Valerian and penstemon bloom in July; huckleberries scent the air in August. Junctions to Flower Point are well marked: stay left at both to go directly to the top. (Loop through Flower Point for a 5.6-mile hike.) At the East Rim junction, turn left for a gentle, scenic loop before the final steep ascent. Panoramas at the top span Glacier Park to Flathead Lake.

BIKING

Oodles of two-lane highways and paved country lanes make long loops around Flathead Lake or short farmland tours for roadies, while single-track and dirt-road choices swamp mountain bikers. For the best list of itineraries to suit your palate and abilities, check Glacier Cyclery's website (www.glaciercyclery.com) for popular area routes.

In Kalispell, the **Great Northern Historical Trail** (www.railstotrailsofnwmt.com) saw its pavement finished in 2009. The 12-mile route for walkers and bikers begins at Meridian Street and ends at Smith Lake in Kila. You can also stop partway for lunch at Kila's Cottage Inn (4220 Hwy. 2 W., 406/755-8711). Find trailhead parking at Meridian Road, Derns Road, and across from Kila School. In Whitefish, the 12-mile **Whitefish Trail** provides a curvy dirt single-track open to mountain bikers, equestrians, and hikers. Current maps to trailheads can be found at www.trailrunsthroughit.org.

For single-track, lift-served mountain biking, **Whitefish Mountain Resort** (end of Big Mountain Rd., Whitefish, 406/862-2900, www.skiwhitefish.com, late June–Labor Day) hauls bikes and riders up its chairlift for $14–25, depending on age and the numbers of rides down you want. Two routes descend from the summit—one with hairpin turns and the other on a steep-pitched hair-raising downhill descent. Natural obstacles chuck both trails into the have-some-experience-first category. Bikes are available to rent (adults $39, kids $19, helmets and single ride up lift included).

© BECKY LOMAX

Ride 12 paved miles on the Great Northern Historical Trail in Kalispell.

Rentals and Repairs

Glacier Cyclery (326 E. 2nd St., Whitefish, 406/862-6466, www.glaciercyclery.com) rents touring bikes, roadies, and mountain bikes ($30–39 per day with helmets). Weekly rates are available, too. They can also equip you with car racks ($20 per day), Burleys ($19 per day), and strollers ($79 per week). **Mountain Mike's** (417 Bridge St., Bigfork, 406/837-2453, late Apr.–early Oct., 8 A.M.–4 P.M. daily) rents kid and adult mountain bikes ($35, including helmet), convenient for touring Swan Valley. You can also hire a guide (starting at $35–45 per person, reservations required) for half-day dirt-road or single-track tours. Both shops do repairs, as do several other Flathead Valley bike shops.

BOATING

Popular boating lakes dot Flathead Valley; the two largest are Flathead and Whitefish Lakes. Both have several launch sites and rentals available. Expect to pay hourly rates around $75 for Jet Skis, $85–95 for water-ski boats, and

FLATHEAD VALLEY

$85–120 for pontoon fishing boats and party barges. In addition to your rental fee, you'll need to pay for the gas used. Hand-propelled craft like canoes, kayaks, and rowboats usually run $10–20 per hour.

Flathead Lake

On Flathead Lake's north end, three communities—Bigfork, Somers, and Lakeside—service boaters with marinas usually open May–October. The lake also has 13 public accesses, six of which are state parks ($5 per day user fee) maintained by Montana Fish, Wildlife, and Parks (406/752-5501, www.fwp.state.mt.us). Boat rentals are available at **Wild Wave Watercraft** in Lakeside and Bigfork (7220 Hwy. 93 S., Lakeside; 180 Vista Lane, Bigfork, 406/253-5800 or 406/257-2627, www.wildwaverentals.com).

Whitefish Lake

For launching boats, you'll find public ramps at Whitefish Lake State Park ($5 per day user fee) and City Beach ($4 launch fee). For rentals, mooring, and fuel service, **Whitefish Lake Lodge Marina** (1390 Wisconsin Ave., 406/863-4020, mid-May–Sept.) is the only option.

WATERSKIING

Most vacationers don't come to the Flathead solely for waterskiing. Compared to other waters, glacial-fed lakes are downright cold. But locals do water-ski on Whitefish Lake and Flathead Lake—many wearing wetsuits—as well as smaller valley lakes, particularly in July and August. The marinas listed under *Boating* rent water-ski boats and gear ($85–95 per hour, plus gas).

KAYAKING AND CANOEING

Sea kayakers and canoeists paddle anywhere they can in the Flathead. Lakes such as **Flathead** and **Whitefish** provide flat water, although Flathead can kick up with big winds. The most popular Flathead Lake paddling destination is **Wild Horse Island,** launching from the public beach in Dayton. Ambling sections

The marina at the Lodge at Whitefish Lake services boaters.

© BECKY LOMAX

Kayakers and canoers paddle the Whitefish River.

of the **Flathead** and **Whitefish Rivers** flow slow enough for flat-water-like paddling, too. If you can set up your own shuttle, one two-hour float runs from Whitefish Lake on the **Whitefish River,** but take out at Highway 40, as log jams make the route nasty downstream.

White-water kayakers wearing wetsuits in freezing cold water gravitate to the Swan River outside Bigfork. For Class IV–V rapids, the **Swan River Wild Mile,** a short 1.25-mile stretch that drops 100 feet below Bigfork Dam, sees its best water May–July and Wednesday nights during the summer when the dam releases flows.

Rentals

You can rent kayaks to take to Glacier or lakes in the Flathead from several companies. Life jackets and paddles are included in rates.

With two stores, **Sportsman** (145 Hutton Ranch Rd., Kalispell, 406/755-6484; Mountain Mall, Whitefish, 406/862-3111) rents canoes and tandem kayaks ($40 for 24 hours).

A bit hard to locate, so call for directions,

Silver Moon Kayak (1215 N. Somers Rd., Kalispell, 406/752-3794, www.silvermoon-kayak.com) is convenient for Flathead River or Lake trips. Half-day canoe or sea-kayak rentals run $35–65; full-day rentals are $45–75. Per-day rates drop for those renting more than three days—a deal for paddling Glacier. Rental rates include foam blocks and straps for transporting. White-water kayaks are $40 per day.

FISHING

Lakes, estuaries, and rivers abound for fishing here. You'll need a Montana state license to fish in all of them. See the *Background* chapter for details.

Flathead Valley is sliced by the **Flathead River,** a giant highway for migrating fish. Because of dam control and cold glacial water, do not expect blue-ribbon trout fishing. But neither does the river see lots of fishing pressure. It carries many nonnative species—especially northern pike lurking in larger southern sloughs. Seven river accesses offer places to fish and to launch boats downstream: Blankenship Bridge, the Highway 2 bridge at Hungry Horse, a spur road at Bad Rock Canyon's west end, Kokanee Bend, Pressentine Bar, the old Steel Bridge, and the Stillwater mouth. Most anglers hit the stretch between Columbia Falls and the Old Steel Bridge in Kalispell.

Flathead Lake teems with cutthroat, giant trophy lake trout, mountain and lake whitefish, largemouth bass, bull trout, and yellow perch. It's good for all types of fishing: bait to lure, fly-fishing to trolling. Anglers need a Montana fishing license, good on the north half of the lake and available at sporting goods stores.

Whitefish Lake draws anglers for its lake trout and whitefish. During winter, some anglers ice fish. Northern pike, lake trout, and kokanee are common, and it is regularly stocked with westslope cutthroat trout.

Fly Shops and Guides

Hit up fly-fishing shops in the Flathead for locally made hand-tied flies and tackle, as well as advice on where fish are biting. Most of the following shops also offer guide services that range $320–450 for two people per day. Rates usually do not include Montana fishing licenses.

Lakestream Flyshop (334 Central Ave., Whitefish, 406/862-1298, www.lakestream.com) guides fly-fishing trips on a private lake as well as other local lakes. **Stumptown Anglers** (5790 Hwy. 93 S., Whitefish, 406/862-4554, www.stumptownanglers.com) guides trips on five different northwest Montana rivers, including the Flathead. **Arends Fly Shop** (7356 Hwy. 2 E., Columbia Falls, 406/892-2033, www.montanaflies.com) hits the South Fork and main Flathead River. For guided fishing on the Swan or Flathead River, head to **Two River Gear** (603 Electric Ave., Bigfork, 406/837-3474, www.tworivergear.net) or **Bigfork Anglers** (405 Bridge St., Bigfork, 406/837-3675, www.bigforkanglers.com).

Montana has no shortage of independent fly-fishing guide services operating unattached to shops. You can find them in the phone book or through the Internet. Be sure the guide service is licensed with the state before hiring them.

Charter Fishing

Charter fishing services on Flathead Lake operate May–September. Expect rates to run $350 for half days and $700 for full days, depending on the number of people. Located in Lakeside, **A Able Fishing and Tours** (688 Lakeside Blvd., 406/844-0888, www.aablefishing.com) runs two boats per day. Other charter services also operate on Flathead Lake; locate them in the phone book.

HUNTING

With Flathead Valley surrounded by Flathead National Forest, it is popular for hunting—big game and birds. Get hunting regulations, seasons, and license info from Montana Fish, Wildlife, and Parks (406/444-2535, www.fwp.mt.gov).

GOLF

Golf Digest rated Flathead Valley as one of the world's 50 greatest golf destinations—not just because the scenery is good and the prices are reasonable, but because of nine championship courses. As there are over 16 hours of daylight in early summer, courses open from dawn to dusk, adjusting tee times as daylight drops. Depending on snows, most courses are open April–October.

For playing 18 holes, expect to pay $48–95 during the day, depending on the course. Rates in April, May, and October and daily after 3 P.M. drop. Club rentals range $15–30 and carts $15–28.

One of the best resources for Flathead golf is www.golfmontana.net, where you can get stats for all the local courses. A central number (800/392-9795) provides guaranteed advanced reservations and golf packages.

Courses

Six courses—all with rentals, pro shops, restaurants, and lounges—sprawl across the northern Flathead. With the highest greens fees, **Eagle Bend Golf Course** (279 Eagle Bend Dr., Bigfork, 406/837-7310 or 800/255-5641,

Golfers line up at the Whitefish Lake Golf Course.

www.golfmt.com) is ranked in the top 50 public courses in the country. The challenging 27-hole course is a Jack Nicklaus design with big variety in its hole layouts. From different tees, you can see Flathead Lake, Swan Mountains, and Glacier Park; osprey fly overhead. With cheaper greens fees, the city-owned **Whitefish Lake Golf Course** (1200 Hwy. 93 N., Whitefish, 406/862-4000, www.golfwhitefish.com) is Montana's only 36-hole course. The north course tours through large cedars and firs; the south course runs past Lost Loon Lake. Both have mountain views.

Meadow Lake Golf Course (490 St. Andrews Dr., Columbia Falls, 406/892-2111 or 800/321-4653, www.meadowlakegolf.com) weaves its 18 holes through the woods, with some tight fairways and lots of adjacent houses. A couple of ponds and a creek separate the fairways, and some trees shade the course. **Big Mountain Golf Course** (3230 Hwy. 93 N., Kalispell, 406/751-1950, www.golfmt.com) is a Scottish links–style course. Since its 18 holes sit midvalley with few trees, views open up to Big Mountain and Glacier Park. The Stillwater River runs adjacent to the back nine.

Village Greens (500 Palmer Dr., Kalispell, 406/752-4666, www.montanagolf.com) surrounds its bent-grass greens with a few trees, ponds, and some houses. The 18 holes afford a pleasant place to play on one of the easier courses here. **Buffalo Hill** (1176 N. Main St., Kalispell, 406/756-4530, www.golfbuffalo.com) combines an older course with a newer course for 27 holes. The older Cameron Nine abuts the highway; the newer 18-hole course is moderately difficult with a lot of terrain variety.

SKIING
Whitefish Mountain Resort
Located seven miles north of Whitefish, Whitefish Mountain Resort (end of Big Mountain Rd., 406/862-2900, www.skiwhitefish.com, early Dec.–early Apr.) lives up to its former name of Big Mountain with 3,000 acres of skiing terrain, 2,400 feet of vertical, 12 lifts, and 91 named runs. Big bowls,

© BECKY LOMAX

FLATHEAD VALLEY

Whitefish Mountain Resort is known for its ice-crusted snowghosts on the summit.

glades, and long cruisers head 360 degrees off the summit. You can even find good tree skiing in the mountain's famous fog and an adult lift ticket that runs $61. The resort's village contains restaurants, shops, rental gear, ski school, day care, and lodging from economy to upscale condos.

Blacktail Mountain

Sitting above Flathead Lake, Blacktail Mountain (end of Blacktail Mountain Rd., 406/844-0999, mid-Dec.–early Apr., Wed.–Sun., plus holidays) attracts families for its smaller 1,000 acres, four lifts, and family-friendly pricing, with an adult lift ticket at $36.

Great Northern Powder Guides

Two Whitefish local skiers bought an ailing cat-ski company in 2010 to pump new life into it. Great Northern Powder Guides (855-766-9228, www.greatnorthernpowderguides.com) offers backcountry cat-ski tours on Stryker Ridge, just north of Whitefish. Trips run $350 per person per day. Multi-day packages are available as well as pick ups at Whitefish Mountain Resort and select Whitefish hotels.

CROSS-COUNTRY SKIING

Several small cross-country ski areas dot Flathead Valley, with trails groomed for classic and skate skiing mid-December–March. You need to bring your own skis for Blacktail Mountain, central Flathead Valley, Foothills, and Round Meadows. Only two ski areas in Whitefish offer rentals. At the golf course, **Glacier Nordic Center** grooms 7.5 miles, with the Glacier Nordic Shop (406/862-9498) renting skate and classic gear ($10–18) and teaching lessons in both disciplines ($30). Grooming 25 kilometers (16 miles), **Stillwater Nordic** (750 Beaver Lake Rd., 406/862-7004, $10–12) rents only classic skis, with kids under 12 renting and skiing free.

SNOWMOBILING

The Flathead Valley is surrounded by 200 miles of groomed snowmobile trails (December–mid-April, but some trails close April 1). Flathead Valley Snowmobile Association (406/756-3703

or www.snowtana.com for Montana Snowmobile Association) maintains the grooming on nine popular trails near Whitefish, Columbia Falls, and Bigfork. For those striking out on their own, be sure to check conditions with Glacier Country Avalanche Center (406/257-8402 or 800/526-5239, www.glacieravalanche.org).

Rentals are available at **Extreme Motorsports** (803 Spokane Ave., Whitefish, 406/862-8594) and **J & L Rentals** (7358 US Hwy 2 East, Columbia Falls, 406/892-7666, www.jandlrvrentals.com). Expect to pay around $180–200 per day for renting a snowmobile (helmets included); snowmobile suits, boots, and gloves are extra. J & L has the only licensed guide service.

ENTERTAINMENT AND EVENTS
Theaters

In Bigfork, the **Bigfork Summer Playhouse** (526 Electric Ave., 406/837-4886, www.bigforksummerplayhouse.com, mid-May–late Aug.) presents five shows in repertory during each summer, from Broadway musical favorites to comedies. In Whitefish, **Whitefish Theater Company** (1 Central Ave., 406/862-5371, www.whitefishtheaterco.org) sponsors plays, concerts, speakers, and art films in the O'Shaughnessey Center. Broadway veterans formed the acclaimed **Alpine Theatre Project** (Whitefish, 406/862-7469, www.alpinetheatreproject.org), which produces plays during the summer at Whitefish Performing Arts Center. Beloved musicals, classic comedies, and first-run plays highlight its summer schedule, along with big names like John Lithgow, Olympia Dukakis, and Henry Winkler for single evening shows.

While Montana may be on the dark side of the moon regarding lots of things, you can actually catch a just-released blockbuster movie in the Flathead—but don't expect a hotbed of foreign, independent, or avant garde films. Whitefish has one movie theater, **Mountain Cinema** (Mountain Mall on Hwy. 93, 406/862-3130). In Kalispell, you'll find 14 movies showing at **Stadium 14** (185 Hutton Ranch Rd., 406/752-7800, www.signaturetheatres.com).

Rodeos and Fairs

Located midvalley between Whitefish and Kalispell, **Majestic Valley Arena** (3630 Hwy. 93 N., 406/755-5366, www.majesticvalleyarena.com) is the hub for big events: concerts, rodeos, equestrian competitions, and trade shows. Special attractions include calf roping, pro rodeos, and horse jumping. For cowpoke wannabes, the annual **Northwest Montana Fair and Rodeo** opens in mid-August at the Flathead County Fairgrounds (265 N. Meridian, Kalispell, 406/758-5810). The five-day, six-night event features PRCA (Professional Rodeo Cowboys Association) rodeos, fireworks, animal and produce exhibits, pari-mutuel horse racing, team penning, musical concerts, and livestock sales.

Events

The annual **Glacier Jazz Stampede** (406/862-3814 or 888/888-2308, www.glacierjazzstampede.com) is for those who love traditional jazz, swing, ragtime, Dixieland, and big-band sounds. The October event crams four days with 12–14 bands from across the United States and Canada, pounding out nearly nonstop music in four different Kalispell venues. Bands, schedules, and ticket prices vary yearly for each event, but you can order an "all event" ticket ($65–70) online.

Attracting hundreds of spectators even in soggy weather, the **Bigfork Whitewater Festival** (406/837-5888, www.bigfork.org) runs kayakers down the Class IV Wild Mile of the Swan River at the peak of spring runoff. Traditionally held for two days over Memorial Day Weekend, competitions run the gamut from slalom to boater cross. Local pubs and restaurants party with nightly entertainment.

In the doldrums of winter, Whitefish celebrates its wacky **Winter Carnival** (406/862-3501 or 877/862-3548, www.whitefishchamber.org), a three-day spree of ski races, ice hockey, penguin plunge, a figure-skating show, torchlight parade, skijoring, and snow skate jam held the first weekend in February. Hundreds of people line the few blocks of downtown Whitefish for an old-fashioned, drive-the-old-

A Glacier Park mascot joins the Whitefish Winter Carnival parade.

© BECKY LOMAX

tractor-down-main-street parade disrupted by raucous Yetis and Viking women.

Art events abound in the Flathead. Whitefish hosts their **Gallery Nights** on the first Thursday of each month, May–October, and their three-day **Huckleberry Days** art festival in mid-August in Credit Union Park. Kalispell celebrates their three-day **Arts in the Park** in late July in Depot Park and a late-November **Art Walk** through downtown galleries. The **Bigfork Festival of the Arts** takes place in early August on the town's main street. Check with respective chambers of commerce for current schedules.

Casinos

While gambling is legal in Montana, casinos haven't rocketed to Las Vegas style—or even to the level of those found on some Native American reservations. Most Flathead bars have a few slot machines squirreled away in a corner; some even run a card table or two. In a twist to the usual gas station–convenience mart, some gas chains add small, dark, and smoky casinos featuring gaming machines and poker tables.

FLATHEAD VALLEY

Accommodations

Flathead Valley has varied lodging—motels to guest ranches—but most of the chain hotels congregate in Kalispell. Find complete lists through the area visitors bureaus and chambers of commerce. Contrary to the rustic nature of Glacier Park's lodges, you'll find most accommodations have Internet, televisions, air-conditioning, and modern amenities. You can also rent homes—nightly, weekly, and long-term. Two reputable property management companies offer short-term rentals: Hideaway Resorts (406/862-5500 or 888/836-5500, www.hideawayresorts.com) and Lakeshore Rentals (406/863-9337 or 877/312-8017, www.lakeshorerentals.net).

All accommodations listed here are open year-round unless noted otherwise. When making reservations, be sure to ask about golf or ski packages, as many places offer good deals in season—even independent motels. Rates vary according to season; the ranges listed reflect the low rates of the off-season and high rates of peak seasons. However, what is considered high and low season varies with location: Summer is high season valley wide, but in winter, it's high season in Whitefish. Fall and spring are off-seasons. A 7 percent Montana state bed tax will be added to your bill. In Whitefish, an additional 2 percent resort tax will also be added.

BIGFORK

The Bigfork high season is summer, when lake activities, hiking, and the playhouse are in full swing. Get lower rates fall, winter, and spring.

Motels and Cottages

The town's most reasonably priced lodging is **Timbers Motel** (8540 Hwy. 35 S., 406/837-6200 or 800/821-4546, www.timbersmotel.com, $69–152), which puts you within a five-minute drive to Eagle Bend Golf Course and just a couple minutes from the Bigfork Summer Playhouse. It sits on a small knoll above the

highway and has a heated pool, hot tub, and sauna.

In downtown Bigfork, **Bridge Street Cottages** (309 Bridge St., 406/837-2785 or 888/264-4974, www.bridgestreetcottages.com) offers higher-end lodging with a three-night minimum stay. Four of the units sit right on the Swan River. Surrounded by small perennial gardens, these well-furnished, well-kept one-bedroom cottages built in 2004 come with Internet access, cable television, air-conditioning, and fully equipped kitchens ($115–325 per night). Suites ($95–185) are smaller, with just a fridge and microwave.

Bed-and-Breakfast

A short 3.5 miles south of Bigfork puts you at **Candlewycke Inn Bed & Breakfast** (311 Aero Ln., 406/837-6406 or 888/617-8805, www.candlewyckeinn.com, $85–165). On 10 acres, the nonsmoking cedar-and-log inn serving a full breakfast in the morning has five folk-art-themed rooms with pillow-top beds and private baths, some with Jacuzzi tubs. Walk on trails around the property, cross-country ski in winter, or lounge on the massive decks or in the outdoor hot tub.

Flathead Lake Resorts

◀ **Averill's Flathead Lake Lodge** (Flathead Lake Lodge Rd., Bigfork, 406/837-4391, www.flatheadlakelodge.com, June–Labor Day) is a family-owned working dude ranch on 2,000 acres. Lodging, meals, and activities all wrap up in one big price for 7 or 14 days: per week rates run around $3,200 for adults, with kids rates less depending on ages. With horseback riding, fishing, swimming, waterskiing, tennis, and sailing, the ranch centers around the classy log lodge and cabins. You can park the car and dive into vacation mode for several days, as the ranch coordinates the activities.

On Flathead Lake, **Marina Cay Resort** (180 Vista Ln., Bigfork, 406/837-5861 or 800/433-6516, www.marinacay.com) has courtyard and waterfront suites ($140–220) and two- and three-bedroom condos ($250–400) along with restaurants, seasonal outdoor pool and hot tub, and marina with boat rentals. You can easily walk seven minutes to downtown Bigfork's shops and restaurants. Eagle Bend Golf Course is a five-minute drive away, and the closest hiking trails are in Jewel Basin.

COLUMBIA FALLS

Columbia Falls is the closest town to Glacier, but with minimal lodging. It does have a Super 8.

Motels

Good for those on a budget, two small motels sit near the waterslide and Flathead River. **Glacier Inn Motel** (300 Hwy. 2 E., 406/892-4341, www.glacierinnmotel.com, $50–90) has cable TV and air-conditioning. **Glacier Park Motel** (7285 Hwy. 2 E., 406/892-7686, www.glacierparkmotelandcampground.com, $110–165) is a renovated nonsmoking motel with kitchenettes, luxury tepees ($65), wireless Internet, and free cereal bar.

Bed-and-Breakfast

On 10 quiet acres 10 minutes from town, **Bad Rock Bed and Breakfast** (480 Bad Rock Dr., 406/892-2829 or 888/892-2829, www.badrock.com, $125–225) opens its four log cabins surrounding a river-rock and log-frame house to guests. Cabin rooms have hand-crafted log furniture, while the three house rooms are decorated in different styles. All have private baths. Breakfast is a large Montana-style affair, sometimes featuring Belgian waffles heaped with strawberries.

Golf Resort

Outside Columbia Falls, among big trees and quiet, **Meadow Lake Resort** (100 St. Andrews Dr., 406/892-8700 or 800/321-4653, www.meadowlake.com) sits on an 18-hole golf course, with a restaurant, indoor and outdoor swimming pools, a spa, and tennis courts. For lodging, the resort has 24 hotel rooms ($140–190), condos with one to three bedrooms and private decks ($140–475), and vacation homes

($160–620). In winter, the resort provides a ski shuttle to Whitefish Mountain Resort.

KALISPELL

Kalispell, which lacks the seasonal attractions of Bigfork, Columbia Falls, and Whitefish, holds most of the easily-recognized chain hotels.

Hotels

Right in downtown Kalispell's shopping district, the historic **⟨ Kalispell Grand Hotel** (100 Main St., 406/755-8100 or 800/858-7422, www.kalispellgrand.com, $80–150) makes you take a leap back in time. Walking in the lobby, you're greeted by a tin ceiling, ornate pump organ, and the original wide, oak banister stairway. Renovated rooms have smaller bathrooms with showers rather than tubs. Although the ambience harkens back to 1912, when the hotel opened with a room costing $2, its modern amenities now include an elevator, high-speed Internet, air-conditioning, and televisions. In the afternoon, pick up home-baked cookies in the lobby.

WHITEFISH

Bustling in summer with Whitefish Lake and busy in winter with Whitefish Mountain Ski Resort, the town supports a myriad of lodging options—including chains.

Bed-and-Breakfasts

A short walk to restaurants and nightlife in downtown Whitefish, the circa 1920 **⟨ Garden Wall Inn** (504 Spokane Ave., 406/862-3440 or 888/530-1700, www.gardenwallinn.com, $155–195, suite $255) is furnished with antiques inside, while a perennial garden blooms outside. It's an extension of Glacier Park, with historic photos and picture books in the living room, and if the weather deteriorates, you can curl up in front of a real fire in the glazed brick fireplace. Five guest rooms each have private baths—some with oversized claw-foot tubs. In the morning, awake to a coffee or tea tray delivered to your room before heading to the dining room for a breakfast of treats like huckleberry-pear crepes.

A five-minute drive from downtown and 10 minutes from the ski resort, **❰ Hidden Moose Lodge** (1735 E. Lakeshore Dr., 406/862-6516 or 888/733-6667, www.hiddenmooselodge. com, $100–200) provides three styles of upscale Montana-outdoors themed rooms with private decks and baths: lodge rooms, Jacuzzi rooms, and a suite. A great room centers around a large river-rock fireplace, and decks face the woods. Amenities include an outdoor hot tub, wireless Internet, air-conditioning, cable TV, mini fridge, and complimentary evening beverages. Breakfast is big, with Hidden Moose chorizo quiche being one of the favorite entrées.

Ski and Golf Resorts

❰ Whitefish Mountain Resort (406/862-2900 or 800/858-5439, www.skiwhitefish. com) has all lodging options—motels and condos ($60–699 per night) and vacation homes ($100–2,100 per night). Winter sees the highest rates as all restaurants and shops are open for the ski and snowboard season and all lifts operate. Summer has moderate prices when some restaurants open and one lift to the summit runs for hiking and mountain biking. Fall and spring are very inexpensive, but no lifts, shops, nor restaurants are open. Kandahar Lodge has the best reputation for upscale accommodations with an outstanding gourmet restaurant; for budget lodging, ask about the Hibernation House.

In Whitefish, one mile from downtown restaurants and nightlife, **Grouse Mountain Lodge** (Hwy. 93 and Fairway Dr., 406/862-3000, 406/892-2525, or 800/321-8822, www. grousemountainlodge.com, $110–260) sits its modern hotel rooms right on a 36-hole golf course that converts in winter to groomed Nordic skiing trails. It has an indoor pool and outdoor hot tubs, a restaurant, DSL and wireless Internet, and comfortable lobby with its huge river-rock fireplace. Rooms come in seven configurations, all with private baths— from a basic hotel room to a high-end room with oversized shower sporting multiple water heads. For accessing town, the airport, or ski resort, a complimentary shuttle bops you to

The Lodge at Whitefish Lake is the only lakeside hotel.

your destination. GPI, the company that runs Glacier's historic hotels, purchased Grouse in January, 2011.

Waterfront Lodge

With a two-story lobby draped with a giant wrought-iron chandelier and river-rock fireplace, **[C The Lodge at Whitefish Lake** (1380 Wisconsin Ave., 406/863-4000 or 877/887-4026, www.lodgeatwhitefishlake. com, $155–1,044) opened in late 2005 with more upscale furnishings than other valley hotels. Spacious balconied suites and condos (with two or three bedrooms) vary in size, with fireplaces, slate floors, granite countertops, refrigerators, tubs and walk-in showers, and high-speed Internet. Their premier rooms overlook the lake, facing sunsets; upstairs north rooms have mountain views. The lodge has a private beachfront on Whitefish Lake, outdoor pool and hot tub, full-service marina, boat rentals, day spa, restaurant, and lounge. Golf and skiing are both within a 7- to 10-minute drive.

Guest Ranch

The **Bar W Guest Ranch** (2875 Hwy. 93 W., Whitefish, 409/863-9099 or 866/828-2900, www.thebarw.com) houses guests in its 6,200-square-foot Western lodge and cabin suites adjacent to a small lake and Spencer Mountain. Ranch activities pile on trail rides, rodeos, cookouts, boating, archery, hiking, fishing, and campfires. Three-, four-, and six-night packages include all meals, lodging, and ranch activities (adults $592–3,150, kids $450–1,200). If you're looking for a deal, hit fall, spring, or winter for lower rates.

CAMPING

In Flathead Valley, state-park camping tends to cluster around lake shores, with drinking water, picnic tables, and flush toilets, but no hookups. Conversely, most private commercial campgrounds have full hookups, laundry, showers, dump stations, and camp stores, and will accommodate large RVs with pullouts as well as tents. Commercial campgrounds add

a 7 percent Montana bed tax to your bill, and Whitefish private campgrounds add another 2 percent resort tax. Most will give 10 percent discounts to AAA, Woodall's, and Good Sam members.

Bigfork

Located on Flathead Lake, **Wayfarer's State Park** (0.5 mile south of Bigfork on Hwy. 35, 406/837-4196, www.fwp.state.mt.us, May–Sept., $15) is great for boating and fishing. The park is one of the lake's largest campgrounds, with 30 sites on 68 acres, a boat ramp, a swimming area, and 1.5 miles of hiking trails. Pets are allowed on a leash. Campground amenities include firewood, fire grill, flush and vault toilets, showers, picnic tables, and drinking water. Four other state parks also rim the lake.

Columbia Falls

Two private campgrounds dot Highway 2 and 40, with Glacier Park 16–20 minutes away. Both sit right on the highway, so be prepared for road noise. The closest golf course is Meadow Lake; the closest grocery stores are in Columbia Falls. Amenities include flush toilets, hot showers, dump stations, wireless Internet, and laundries for about the same rates: tents $20–28, RV hookups $25–40.

With 55 full-hookup sites in a renovated grassy setting surrounded by trees right in town, **Columbia Falls RV Park** (103 Hwy. 2 E., 406/892-1122 or 888/401-7268, www.columbiafallsrvpark.com, open year-round) is the closest to Glacier and one mile from the waterslides, an outdoor community swimming pool, and grocery stores. A few-block walk puts you at restaurants in town. **Glacier Peaks RV Park** (3185 Hwy. 40, 406/892-2133 or 800/268-4849, www.glacierpeaksrvpark.com, open year-round) is easy to spot with its flower-painted VW bug and trailer as a sign. Under partial shade, 60 full-hookup grassy sites sprawl adjacent to a summer outdoor drive-in theater. With its location at the junction of Montana Highway 40 and U.S. Highway 2, driving access is quick to Columbia Falls, Whitefish, and Kalispell.

Kalispell

Quite a few year-round commercial campgrounds scatter in Kalispell, all within 30–40 minutes from Glacier and 15–20 minutes to Flathead Lake. Golf courses (Eagle Bend, Village Greens, Buffalo Hills) are within five miles, along with shopping, box stores, and restaurants. They have comparable rates: tents $15–25, RV hookups $25–32. Standard amenities include flush toilets, hot showers, dump stations, laundries, playgrounds, cable TV hookups, wireless Internet, picnic tables, and fire rings.

The nearest to Glacier, **Rocky Mountain "Hi" RV Park and Campground** (825 Helena Flats, 406/755-9573 or 800/968-5637, www. glaciercamping.com) sits adjacent to a spring-fed creek, with 98 grassy sites tucked between large fir trees—a few with Swan Mountain views. Tucked back from the highway, you'll hear no road noise. With swimming, fishing, and canoeing in a wide creek, it's a good campground for kids.

Convenient to downtown Kalispell (a seven-minute drive), two RV parks sit adjacent to the noisy Highway 35 truck route; however, each has something more to recommend it. **Glacier Pines RV Park** (1850 Hwy. 35, 406/752-2760 or 800/533-4029, www.glacierpines.com) has grassy sites under large trees and a seasonal outdoor heated swimming pool. **Spruce Park on the River** (1985 Hwy. 35, 406/752-6321 or 888/752-6321, www.spruceparkrv.com) accommodates 100 RVs and 60 tents in shaded sites. With its location on the Flathead River,

you can fish from the campground. A pet walk accommodates dogs, and you can wash road dust from the RV.

Whitefish

Within 30–35 minutes from West Glacier, Whitefish offers several campgrounds. Golf sits within a 5- to 10-minute drive, as are shopping and restaurants in town; Whitefish Mountain Resort is a 10-minute drive up the hill.

Set in deep woods right on Whitefish Lake, **Whitefish Lake State Park** (one mile west of Whitefish on Hwy. 93, then one mile north following signs, 406/862-3991, www.fwp. state.mt.us, open year-round, $13–15 per site) is perfect for swimming and launching boats, but not particularly for sleeping, as the train tracks cross the park, with more than 30 trains per day rumbling by. With a good set of earplugs, you can survive the night. Amenities include flush toilets, picnic tables, fire rings with grills, firewood, running water, and a biker-hiker site.

Two miles south of town, **Whitefish KOA** (5121 Hwy. 93 S., 406/862-4242, www.glacierparkkoa.com, mid-Apr.–mid-Oct., RV hookups $30–60, tents $20–36) sits on 33 acres shielded from the highway by thick forest. The outdoor pool attracts kids, while oldsters gravitate to the adults-only hot tub. Amenities include flush toilets, showers, picnic tables, fire rings, cabins, a dump station, camp store, wireless Internet, free mini-golf, free breakfast, and a restaurant serving nightly barbecues, sandwiches, and pizza.

Food

Dining in the Flathead Valley is a casual affair, even in the priciest restaurants. Don't bother with a suit and tie or fancy dinner dress; even in fine establishments, relaxed attire is common. Check the phone book for options: You'll find Mexican to Japanese, country cafés to steak houses, and ubiquitous espresso cafés.

BIGFORK

For a tiny town, Bigfork packs in the tasty restaurants, most of which sit downtown within two blocks' walking distance of the theater. On performance nights at the theater, you won't get in a restaurant for dinner unless you make reservations. For hiking lunches in Bigfork, stop by **Wild Mile Deli** (435 Bridge St., 406/838-3355) for sandwiches, and pick up oversized chocolate-chip cookies at **Brookies Cookies** (191 Mill St., 406/837-2447). You can even mail some home.

Burgers

For posthiking or kayaking burgers and beers, drop in the **Garden Bar and Grill** (451 Electric Ave., 406/837-9914, 11 A.M.–2 A.M. daily, $6–9). You can eat inside or out back in the funky garden, where live music cranks out tunes on summer weekend evenings. The bar, which

---

A GUIDE TO LOCAL BREWS

Montanans relish their local microbreweries. To help you navigate the mystery of the brews, here's a guide to the local beers you'll find.

Bayern Brewing (Missoula): Their Bayern Amber is the backbone of their brewpub, but their Dancing Trout, a filtered German wheat ale, is growing a fast following.

Big Sky Brewing (Missoula): One of the most popular brown ales in northwest Montana, Moose Drool may have gained its notoriety through merchandising its name, but it tastes darn good, too. Their other two most popular brews are Scape Goat Pale Ale, a lighter English-style ale, and Trout Slayer, a filtered wheat ale.

Blackfoot River Brewing (Helena): Look for Woollybugger Wheat, a German Hefeweisen, and Missouri River Steamboat Lager, a light, hoppy amber. Or for something more roasty and full bodied, try the Double Black Diamond Extreme Stout.

Flathead Lake Brewing (Bigfork): The young brewery with accompanying restaurant named its headliner light-bodied, hoppy ale after Flathead Lake's waves: Whitecap Pale Ale. Also, try the Wild Mile Wheat, an unfiltered summer wheat beer named after the town's famous white water.

Glacier Brewing (Polson): This brewery produces three lighter beers: the light-bodied German Kolsch Golden Grizzly Ale, the sweet and malty North Fork Amber Ale, and the Port Polson Pilsner. For a good creamy roasted chocolate flavor, pick up a Slurry Bomber Stout.

Great Northern Brewing (Whitefish): Their popular lighter beers include a Hefeweisen called Wheatfish and the light-bodied Hell Roaring Amber. If you haven't overdosed on huckleberries here, you can try them in beer with the Wild Huckleberry Wheat Lager. In winter, look for Snow Ghost, named for the snow-laden trees on top of Whitefish Mountain Resort.

Lang Creek Brewery (Marion): On the lighter end, look for the golden Dutch Skydiver Blonde, named for the local skydiving in Marion. For more richness, sip the English-style Tri-Motor Amber. To satisfy a sweet tooth, try the light-bodied seasonal Huckleberry 'N Honey.

Tamarack Brewing (Lakeside): Northwest Montana's newest brewery and restaurant puts out a light golden Bear Bottom Blonde and robust amber Yard Sale Ale – named after ski lingo used to describe a skier who crashes hard, littering the hill with skis and poles.

serves as local headquarters for the annual white-water festival, features 20 microbrews on tap. In Montana, kids can enter bars usually until 8 P.M.

Eclectic Cuisine

Known for exceptional food at modest prices, **◖ Showthyme!** (548 Electric Ave., 406/837-0707, www.showthyme.com, nightly at 5 P.M., $14–24) dishes up a broad repertoire: fresh fish, pasta, wild game, and steaks. One friend swears by the before-dinner wicked gin and tonic. Start dinner with the warm brie cheese salad or just dive straight into an entrée of Angel's chicken-stuffed green chiles smothered with red sauce. The wine list features Australian and New Zealand imports as well as West Coast vintners. For dessert, try the house specialty: a huckleberry ice cream crepe floating in huckleberry sauce. The old, cozy two-story brick bank building adjacent to the theater opens up for outside seating in summer.

French

Who knows better how to cook French delicacies than a native? **La Provence** (408 Bridge St., 406/837-2923, www.bigforklaprovence.com, 5–10 P.M. Tues.–Sat., $15–24) features gourmet Southern French and Mediterranean cuisine concocted by Marc Guizol, the owner-chef from Provence. The menu features escargots and traditional French onion soup with gruyère. Entrées sauced with wines come in fish, duck, rack of lamb, and venison or pork tenderloins. Desserts include traditional soufflés. Wines? French, of course. Sit inside surrounded by the works of local artists, or outside on the patio. For lunch and takeout, the restaurant opens the **La Petite Provence Bistro** (10 A.M.–3 P.M. Tues.–Sat., $4–9), serving gourmet sandwiches, French homemade pastries, and quiche.

Sushi

After opening in 2009, **SakeTome Sushi** (459 Electric Ave., Suite 1, 406/837-1128, www.saketomesushi.com, 11 A.M.–10 P.M. summer, 4–10 P.M. spring and fall, open

daily May–Oct.) gained a quick loyal following, making reservations a must. Located upstairs in Twin Burch Square, the restaurant includes a bar, indoor seating, and deck seating. Specialty rolls ($10–17) feature fun twists, such as The Gouge—spicy crab and mango topped with lemon peppered shiro and avocado. Nigiri and maki rolls come raw or cooked ($4–8).

COLUMBIA FALLS

Columbia Falls has never been known as a dining mecca—until recently. New restaurateurs ushered in new tastes, catapulting the cuisine beyond the fast-food enterprises along the highway.

Cafés

Coffee Traders Pines Café (1st Ave. W. and Hwy. 2, 406/892-7633, 7 A.M.–5 P.M. daily) is not just a place to grab an espresso from the local coffee roasters—Montana Coffee Traders—but also a place for breakfast (until 11 A.M.) and lunch (11 A.M.–3 P.M. daily, Sun. until 2 P.M.). The ambience still clings fondly to memories of the old local dive Pine Tree Cafe, with the pine tree still standing in the middle of the room. The menu ($5–9) features huge breakfast omelets, deli sandwiches, wraps, and salads. Given its location en route to Glacier, many folks grab an espresso with muffins, scones, or cookies for the drive and a sandwich to go for the trail. Montana Coffee Traders has two other valley cafés (328 W. Center St., Kalispell, 406/756-2326; 110 Central Ave., Whitefish, 406/862-7667).

Dining

When **◖ Three Forks Grille** (729 Nucleus Ave., 406/892-2900, 5–10 P.M. nightly) opened in 2010, it changed the face of the town's main street, introducing a two-floor restaurant whose main concern was the atmosphere and taste rather than packing in crowds. While the menu sprinkles with Italian options—an elk parmigiana meatball appetizer, shrimp risotto, and cannoli—it introduced a Montana twist

© BECKY LOMAX

Three Forks Grille in Columbia Falls is one of the Flathead's newest restaurants.

into its specialties of grilled Tuscan flat-iron steak from local free-ranging, antibiotic-free beef and Caesar salad with smoked rainbow trout. Entrées, which also include bison pot roast, run $15–23, while sandwiches and burgers range $7–9. Make reservations for weekends and summer.

When locals crave greasy barbecue, they head for **The Back Room Restaurant** (Hwy. 2, 406/892-3131, 2–9 P.M. Sun., 4–9 P.M. Mon.–Thurs., 4–10 P.M. Fri. and Sat., $7–15). The restaurant serves strictly old-time Montana feasts: gooey ribs and broasted chicken. You can order the ribs country, spare, or baby back, or if you can't decide, a gigantic combo plate. The restaurant makes their own concoction of secret spices for their sauces. Fry bread with honey, coleslaw, and homemade french fries fill the plate to overflowing. A server may call you "Hon" as she delivers you a roll of paper towels instead of napkins to handle the colossal mess. Abandon all thoughts of calories or cholesterol; dig in, and when you're done, lick your fingers.

KALISPELL

Kalispell has common national chain restaurants along Highway 93, but not in the few blocks of the downtown core. Hit **Reds, Wines, and Blues** (30 2nd St. E., 406/755-9463) for the under-40 singles scene, hopping with brews and music.

Cafés

With its bright, colorful interior displaying local art, the ◖ **Knead Café** (25 2nd Ave. W., 406/755-7510, www.theknead.com, 8 A.M.–4 P.M. Mon.–Sat., 9 A.M.–3 P.M. Sun., $6–14) can please both a vegetarian and a meat lover with its fresh and slightly different Mediterranean flavors. The restaurant serves up an eclectic collection of wraps, omelets, frittatas, pitas, and sandwiches, with beer, wine, and espresso available. Fresh bakery goodies and the art on the walls are sold here, too.

For burgers, hot dogs, shakes à la 1950s, and huge scoops of ice cream, drop in at **Norm's News** (34 Main St., 406/756-5466, 9 A.M.–5 P.M. Mon.–Sat., 11 A.M.–4 P.M. Sun., $4–8). A tradition since 1938, the soda fountain lets you munch while you browse over 2,500 magazines and newspapers. The kids go crazy with the candy collection, featuring over 400 different sugar treats. For nostalgia buffs, the jukebox and ornate back bar are just worth a look.

Pizza

For those with beer and pizza taste buds, head to **Moose's Saloon** (173 N. Main, 406/755-2337, www.moosessaloon.com, 11 A.M.–1:30 A.M. daily, $6–18), where peanut shells and sawdust cover the floor in this funky old-time bar that's been a valley staple since 1957. It will be just what you imagine a Montana bar to be—dark and loud. But the pizza is darn good, with one of the best crusts around. You'll get the kitchen sink on the combination pizza, and beer prices are cheap. If you want to forgo the atmosphere, you can order to go.

Fine Dining

North Bay Grille (139 1st Ave. W., 406/755-4441, www.nbgrille.com, opens 11:30 A.M.

FLATHEAD VALLEY

Mon.–Fri., opens 5 P.M. Sat. and Sun., bar open until 2 A.M., $10–30) fills its menu with lighter meals of upscale sandwiches, pizzas, burgers, salads, and pasta in the bar or dining room. The house dinner specialties are slow roasted prime rib and wood-fire grilled steaks. The bar serves up domestic and imported wines, and a long list of imaginative martinis and margaritas.

A chef-owned restaurant, **⟨ Capers** (121 Main St., 406/755-7687, www.capersmontana.com, opens at 5 P.M. Tues.–Sat.) is often voted a local favorite. Dinners ($14–29) feature specialty lasagnas, beef, fish, and bison, with menus changing throughout the season and using organic and naturally fed meats. Capers maintains an extensive wine list, and you can get lighter meals with brick oven pizzas.

WHITEFISH

As a resort town, Whitefish is overloaded with outstanding restaurants. Because of crowds, you'll need to make reservations to avoid long waits in midsummer or winter. In spring and fall, a few restaurants alter their hours or close for a month on a whim to go fishing; call ahead to be sure they are open.

For burgers, head to the **Bulldog Saloon** (144 Central Ave., 406/862-5601), but keep the kids out of the X-rated-decorated bathroom stalls. The downtown bar-hopping scene heats up on summer weekends with **Crush Wine Bar** (124 Central Ave., 406/730-1030) a posttheater favorite.

Cafés

For breakfast and lunch, you might have to arm wrestle a local's claim to a daily seat at **The Buffalo Cafe** (516 E. 3rd St., 406/862-2833, www.buffalocafewhitefish.com, 7 A.M.–2 P.M. daily, opens 8 A.M. Sun., $5–9; 5–9 P.M. Mon.–Sat., $8–16) to order the house Buffalo Pie, with hash browns, ham, and cheese, and topped with two poached eggs. A few blocks away, **Loula's** (300 2nd Ave., 406/862-5614, 7 A.M.–3 P.M. daily, $6–10) is the place for lemon-stuffed French toast with raspberry sauce, or portobello mushroom, roasted red

pepper, and cream cheese sandwich. Before leaving, pick up one of their trademark whole fresh-baked fruit pies to go ($18–24). **The Green Tea House** (415 2nd St. E., 406/862-5050, www.thegreenteahouse.net, 7:30 A.M.–5:30 P.M. daily, $6–9) features 60 types of teas, plus breakfasts, sandwiches, huge salads, soup, Monk Bowls with dal and curries, and options that are gluten free, dairy free, vegan, and organic. Meals to go, too.

Located a few blocks outside the downtown mayhem, **Rising Sun Bistro** (549 Wisconsin Ave., www.risingsunbistro.com, 406/862-1236, 9 A.M.–2:30 P.M. and 5–9 P.M. Tues.–Sat., 9 A.M.–2 P.M. Sun., $6–19) serves up French bistro comfort foods like tomato basil soup and Burgundian meat loaf. Their breakfast and lunches include both typical café fare like biscuits and gravy or burgers, but also specialties such as smoked salmon Benedict and salad niçoise. Daily dinner specialties are worth trying—pasta, crepes, and braised lamb shanks. Brunch is served all day on Sunday. You can dine next to the cozy fire, or in summer out in the garden. They also serve beer and wine.

Italian

A budding chain, **Mambo Italiano** (234 E. 2nd St., 406/863-9600, 5–10 P.M. daily, $10–21) transports you beyond the Flathead to Italy with its cramped noisy dining room lilting to tunes of Frank Sinatra and Andrea Bocelli. You can also enjoy a view of Big Mountain from the upstairs deck. Start with the Tootsie Roll appetizer, a ricotta-cheese-stuffed phyllo on marinara. Feast on house pasta like fettuccine alla Lulubella, a carbonara to knock your cholesterol through the roof. Order a jug of house red wine for the table—you'll be charged by how many glasses you drink (a guess on the waitstaff's part) rather than the bottle.

For pizza, Montana's homegrown chain **MacKenzie River Pizza** (9 Central Ave., 406/862-6601, www.mackenzieriverpizza. com, 11 A.M.–9 P.M. daily, until 10 P.M. on weekends, $8–20) makes a great family restaurant. It serves up traditional and eclectic (chicken fajita, Thai) pizzas with sourdough or natural-grain crusts. You'll also find giant salads, sandwiches, and pasta on the menu, and local microbrews on tap.

Asian

Although most people don't see sushi and Montana going together, the sushi at **(Wasabi Sushi Bar and Ginger Grill** (419 2nd St., 406/863-9283, www.wasabimt.com, opens at 5 P.M. daily, $9–25) is popular. Sushi rolls, sake, and grilled Asian specialties are served in a relaxed, bright atmosphere surrounded by wasabi-green walls. Large mirrors reflect the deft fingers of the sushi chefs in action as they make your rolls. While the menu also carries full teriyaki dinners, many make a feast of ordering several sushi rolls. Try the Black Widow, a peppered albacore topped with hot Sri Racha. You can get rolls to go, too.

Cajun and Creole

At **(Tupelo Grille** (17 Central Ave., 406/862-6136, www.tupelogrille.com, opens at 5:30 P.M. nightly, $16–29), the flavors come from New Orleans. Start with a duck, chicken, and andouille gumbo followed by their tasty version of shrimp and grits, where grilled shrimp doused in a spicy tasso cream sauce smothers grilled grits. If you can't decide between the Louisiana flavors, order the Cajun Creole combo plate, which piles up a platter of crawfish étouffée, shrimp Creole, and chicken and sausage jambalaya. Don't leave without your dessert: The bread pudding is scrumptious without being overly sweet.

Mexican

(Pescado Blanco (235 E. 1st St., 406/862-3290, www.pescadoblanco.com, 5–10 P.M. nightly, $15–21) has more than a cute variation on the name of Whitefish; their chefs excel at mountain Mexican cuisine. Try their popular bison enchilada. They also fly in fish twice a week for dishes such as halibut tacos with orange sauce and seared scallops with sauces appearing in the colors of the Mexican flag. Their signature margaritas are made with fresh lime and a 14 percent distilled agave wine, and they

© BECKY LOMAX

Pescado Blanco serves up mountain Mexican cuisine.

serve a full range of south-of-the-border beers and local microbrews.

Fine Dining

Whitefish also has more than its share of fine restaurants that specialize in Montana game, fish, and high-end steaks accompanied by an extensive wine list. At Whitefish Lake Golf Course, **Whitefish Lake Restaurant** (1200 Hwy. 93 N., 406/862-5285, www.golfwhitefish.com) offers historic ambience, housed in a renovated 1937 log building. During the golf season, the restaurant is open daily for lunch (summer, 11 A.M.–3 P.M., $8–12) and dinner (year-round, nightly at 5:30 P.M., $19–40). For an appetizer, try the New Zealand mussels followed by one of the restaurant's fish favorites, a halibut baked in phyllo with feta, roasted garlic, and spinach. The house specialty is roasted rack of lamb topped with a three-onion demi-glace.

The Lodge At Whitefish Lake Boat Club (1380 Wisconsin Ave., 406/863-4000 or 877/887-4026, www.lodgeatwhitefishlake. com, daily for lunch 11 A.M.–3 P.M., dinner starting at 5 P.M.) is the only restaurant overlooking Whitefish Lake. Dining is available inside or on the deck. Lunch features salads, sandwiches, and specialty pizzas ($9–15). Dinner entrées ($19–39) dress up beef, fish, pasta, and vegetarian dishes. You can go for drinks and appetizers, too, to try the sweet potato chips with blue cheese cream.

GROCERIES

The Flathead Valley has no shortage of supermarket chains and local grocers. But for

Get organic foods at Third Street Market in Whitefish.

seasonal, locally grown produce, try one of the summer **farmers markets,** which usually congregate May–September in Whitefish (Tues., north end of Central Ave.), Bigfork (Wed. and Sat., Bigfork High School), Columbia Falls (Thurs., Discovery Square), and Kalispell (Sat., Kalispell Center Mall). You can also get organic foods at several local shops, including **Third Street Market** (3rd and Spokane Ave., Whitefish, 406/862-5054) or **Withey's Health Foods** (1231 S. Main St., Kalispell, 406/755-5260).

Information and Services

SHOPPING

While Flathead Valley, thank goodness, has no Mall of America clone or factory outlet mall, it does have its share of strip malls and chain stores—most located on Highway 93 north of Kalispell. However, if you can, head to the few strikingly different shops worth browsing: art galleries, jewelry, and eclectic gift shops. Most of the one-of-a-kind locally owned stores cluster in the few blocks of downtown Whitefish, Bigfork, and Kalispell. Columbia Falls features antiques stores within a few blocks.

For classy, high quality toys—inventive, classic, and educational—stop in **Imagination Station** (221 Central Ave., Whitefish, 406/862-5668, and 132 Main St., Kalispell, 406/755-5668). They'll even ship your toys home for you, so you don't have to haul everything on the airplane. In Kalispell, visit **Sassafras** (120 Main St., 406/752-2433), an artist co-op, featuring the works of 30–40 local northwest Montana artists. Pieces range from watercolors and cards to pottery, jewelry, clothing, furniture, and sculptures. You'll find works with Glacier Park themes here, too. In Whitefish, be sure to pick up exquisite handmade chocolates at **Copperleaf Chocolate Company** (242 Central Ave., 406/862-9659) and handmade soaps at **Sage and Cedar** (214 Central Ave., 406/862-9411).

Outdoor Gear

For outdoor gear—camping, backpacking, skiing, snowboarding, and fishing clothing and equipment—several shops carry good brand-name selections and know how to fit equipment to individual people. **Rocky Mountain Outfitter** (135 Main St., Kalispell, 406/752-2446) specializes in hiking, backpacking, climbing, and skiing. Don Scharfe, the owner, is well known for first ascents on several of Glacier's peaks.

The folks at **The White Room** (130 Lupfer Ave., Whitefish, 406/862-7666) are the local telemark and backcountry ski experts, but in

MADE IN MONTANA

Looking for souvenirs to take home? Keep a lookout for the blue Made in Montana logo. Only arts, crafts, food, and other products made by Montana residents and grown or produced within the state may bear the label. More than 2,600 businesses – some producing only one item – use the distinctive label.

What products bear the Made in Montana logo? Look for foods like coffee, jams and jellies, preserves, teas, pasta, salad dressings, barbecue sauces, herbs, cheese, jerky, and cookies. Personal health care products range from soaps and shampoos to lotions and oils. Toys, games, pet goodies, furniture, and clothing also may sport the Made in Montana logo, as can arts and crafts, like photography, music, lithographs, paintings, candles, and more.

One Made in Montana company, **Montana Coffee Traders,** has been roasting beans in Flathead Valley since 1981. Their coffees celebrate Montana with the light- and medium-roasted Montana Blend and the light-roasted with a bit of vanilla and almond Glacier Blend. The Grizzly Blend promotes the protection of crucial grizzly bear habitat, and the Wild Rockies Blend promotes protection and restoration of wildlands habitat. Look for these products in local grocery stores, at four Montana Coffee Traders cafés and outlets (5810 Hwy. 93 S. and 110 Central Ave., Whitefish; junction 1st Ave. W. and Hwy. 2, Columbia Falls; 328 W. Center St., Kalispell) or order by phone (406/862-7633 or 800/345-5282) or online (www.coffeetraders.com).

For a Made in Montana product fix after you get home, check www.madeinmontanausa.com for companies that sell Made in Montana products online.

summer, the shop outfits hikers, backpackers, and climbers with gear and clothing. With two stores, **Sportsman Ski Haus** (145 Hutton Ranch Rd., Kalispell, 406/755-6484; 6475 Hwy. 93, Whitefish, 406/862-3111) carries gear and clothing for skiers, snowboarders, hikers, backpackers, anglers, hunters, campers, tennis players, bicyclists, and ice skaters. In two locations, **Stumptown Snowboards** (128 Central Ave., Whitefish, 406/862-0955; Whitefish Mountain Resort, Whitefish, 406/862-5828) are the local experts in snowboarding and skateboarding, with full equipment and clothing lines.

Maps and Books

To stock up on good topographical maps of Glacier and Flathead National Forest, you'll find the widest selection at Rocky Mountain Outfitter or Sportsman Ski Haus. Likewise, both shops carry guidebooks for hiking, fishing, and cross-country skiing in the area—a few field guides, too. You can also find guidebooks, natural history, Lewis and Clark, Montana history, and field guides for flowers, birds, and animals at **Bookworks** (244 Spokane Ave., Whitefish, 406/862-4980). Glacier Natural History Association (402 9th St. W., 406/888-5756) also has an outlet on Highway 2 in Columbia Falls.

SERVICES
Spas

Whitefish is home to two unique day spas. **Remedies Day Spa** (119 Central Ave., 406/863-9493, www.remediesdayspa.com, 10 A.M.–6 P.M. Mon.–Sat., Sun. by appointment) makes all their products for massages, soaks, and wraps from natural food ingredients found in the kitchen. The spa offers its signature kitchen fassage (massage for the face), whipped cream wrap, honey and cream hot rock foot rub, scrubs, soaks, and traditional massages ($30–140 per treatment). In an upscale quiet lakeside setting, **The Spa at Whitefish Lake** (1380 Wisconsin Ave., 406/863-4050, www. lodgeatwhitefishlake.com, 9 A.M.–7 P.M. daily, $50–195 per treatment) offers traditional spa

facials, waxing, massage, scrubs, wraps, manicures, and pedicures. Their 90-minute Stone Silence uses hot Flathead Valley river stones and aromatherapy oils, like coconilla, in a deep muscle massage.

Gyms, Pools & Water Parks

Flathead Valley houses two large physical-fitness complexes that include weights, cardio machines, indoor swimming pools, and hot tubs. To drop in for a day (adults $12, kids $5–10), call for current hours. **The Summit** (205 Sunnyview Ln., Kalispell, 406/751-4100) also has a climbing wall. **The Wave** (1250 Baker Ave., Whitefish, 406/862-2444) has a fun kids' pool with a slide and water fountain.

Two seasonal outdoor pools attract kids in summer. Drop in for $2–5 per person. The renovated **Pinewood Family Aquatic Center** (925 4th Ave. W., Columbia Falls, 406/892-3500, June–Aug., Mon.–Sat.) has a bromine 25-meter pool and kids' play pool. Kalispell opened their **Woodland Park** outdoor pool in 2004 (406/758-7812, June–Aug., daily), with slides, a current stream, and diving pools. Call for current schedules and rates.

Big Sky Waterslides (7211 Hwy. 2 E., Columbia Falls, 406/892-5025, www.big-skywp.com, Memorial Day–Labor Day, 11 A.M.–7 P.M. daily, $19–30) is a great place to take the kids to unwind after a hot day and a long drive. The park has 10 slides—both big and little—mini-golf, and bumper cars. After 4 P.M., rates drop a couple dollars per person.

Post Offices

Each major town in Flathead Valley has one post office; Kalispell has two. Hours are generally 8:30 A.M.–5:30 P.M. Monday–Friday and 10 A.M.–2 P.M. Saturday. Exceptions are noted, with locations as follows: Bigfork (265 Holt Dr., 406/837-4479), Columbia Falls (65 1st Ave. E., 406/892-7621, closes at 4:30 P.M. on weekdays), Kalispell (350 N. Meridian Rd., 406/755-6450; 248 1st Ave. W., 406/755-0187, closes at 1 P.M. on Sat.), and Whitefish (424 Baker Ave., 406/862-2151). Somers (150 Somers Rd., 406/857-3330, 8 A.M.–4:45 P.M.

Mon.–Fri., closed Sat.) and Lakeside (7196 Hwy. 93 S., 406/844-3224, 7:30–11 A.M. and noon–4 P.M. Mon.–Fri., closed Sat.) each have a post office, too.

Banks

Banks and ATMs are common in Flathead Valley, but several have branches in more than one town. Find Glacier Bank (www.glacierbank.com) in Kalispell (202 Main St., 406/756-4200), Bigfork (Old Town Center, 406/837-5980), Columbia Falls (822 Nucleus Ave., 406/892-7100), and Whitefish (319 E. 2nd St., 406/863-6300). First Interstate Bank (www.firstinterstate.com) is located in Kalispell (2 Main St., 406/756-5200; 100 Hutton Ranch Rd., 406/756-5222), Bigfork (8111 Hwy. 35, 406/837-7200), and Whitefish (306 Spokane Ave., 406/863-8888).

Cell Phones and Internet

Contrary to Glacier's sketchy cell and Internet service, Flathead Valley sees ubiquitous coverage. You may still encounter old-fashioned dial-up Internet in some motels, but most have added wireless and DSL Internet services. You can also get online in the local public county libraries on their computers for a limited amount of time in Kalispell (247 1st Ave. E., 406/758-5820), Columbia Falls (130 6th St. W., 406/892-5919), Bigfork (525 Electric Ave., 406/837-6976), and Whitefish (9 Spokane Ave., 406/862-6657). Each library has its own policies and hours (mostly Monday–Saturday, but hours vary by the day and library); call for details.

A few cafés have wireless Internet access available for patrons: **Montana Coffee Traders Cafes** (110 Central Ave., Whitefish, 406/862-7667; 1st Ave. W. and Hwy. 2, Columbia Falls, 406/892-7633; 328 W. Center St., Kalispell, 406/756-2326) and **Wild Mile Deli** (435 Bridge St., Bigfork, 406/837-3354, www.wildmiledeli.com).

INFORMATION
Newspapers and Magazines

The local valley daily news comes in the *Daily Interlake* and the weekly news in the free *Flathead Beacon,* with their daily updated online version at www.flatheadbeacon.com. You'll also find other northwestern Montana newspapers around, such as *Great Falls Tribune* and *The Missoulian.* Community weeklies, which cover everything from local events to politics, include Columbia Falls' *Hungry Horse News,* the *Whitefish Pilot,* and the *Bigfork Eagle.* For a peek into the local lifestyle, pick up a copy of the free quarterly *Flathead Living* magazine, found in the airport, hotels, stores, and resorts.

Emergencies

For medical, fire, or police emergencies in Flathead Valley, call 911. For medical emergencies in Whitefish and Columbia Falls, the **North Valley Hospital** (1600 Hospital Way, Whitefish, 406/863-3500) is closest. For emergencies in Kalispell, Bigfork, and Lakeside, the upgraded **Kalispell Regional Medical Center** (310 Sunny View Ln., Kalispell, 406/752-5111) is closest.

City police stations have jurisdictions inside city limits only; much of Flathead Valley is covered by the county sheriff's department. In an emergency, when you dial 911, you don't have to think about whether you are inside city boundaries or not; your emergency will be relayed to the appropriate jurisdiction. But just in case, here are the police and sheriff contacts you may need: Flathead County Sheriff (920 S. Main St., Kalispell, 406/758-5585), Columbia Falls Police (130 6th St. W., 406/892-3234), Kalispell Police (312 1st Ave. E., 406/758-7780), and Whitefish Police (2nd St. and Hwy. 93, 406/863-2420).

Ranger Stations

The Flathead National Forest surrounds the Flathead Valley, so you can pick up maps, current trail and camping information, forest and ski conditions, and regulations in several national forest offices and ranger stations: Flathead National Forest and Talley Lake Ranger Station (650 Wolfpack Way, Kalispell, 406/758-5200) and Swan Lake Ranger Station (200 Ranger Station Rd., Bigfork, 406/837-7500).

BACKGROUND

The Land

GEOLOGY

Glacier's mountains tell a long story—approximately 1.6 billion years of geologic history. During that eon, sediment deposition, uplifts, erosion, intrusions, and glaciation left their footprints. Sculpting Glacier and Waterton's scenery into its characteristic jagged parapets with swooping valleys, three geologic events occurred. First, sediments layered on top of each other. Then, mountains moved, and last, an ice age gouged formations.

Ever since, relentless erosion continues to shape the landscape. Wind and water chip away at peaks. Freeze-melt cycles wreak havoc on cliffs, prying off slabs of rock. Over time, weather leaves its thumbprint on the land.

Ancient Belt Sea

Approximately 1.6 billion to 800 million years ago, a shallow lake formed—the ancient Belt Sea. Covering parts of Washington, Idaho, Montana, and Canada, the Belt Sea accumulated sands washing down from adjacent highlands. Through pressure and heat, dolomites, limestone, argillites, siltites, and quartzites layered like a colorful cake, one on top of the other. In a geologic feat found in very few places in North America, Glacier retained its sedimentary rock instead of watching it

© BECKY LOMAX

ANCIENT ROCKS

Glacier contains some of the oldest exposed rock in North America.

ARGILLITES

Of Glacier's colorful rock formations, the most striking is the argillite, an iron-rich mudstone formed in layers on the floor of the shallow ancient Belt Sea 800 million–1.6 billion years ago. Its blue-green and purple-red hues leap off mountainsides and intensify under water. This clay and silt contains iron, which changes to red hematite when exposed to oxygen, thus giving Grinnell argillite its burgundy color. The Appekunney argillite did not oxidize, remaining green. Spot the red colors on Red Eagle Mountain when driving down the east side of Going-to-the-Sun Road. Find both argillites on the Grinnell Glacier Trail, the Iceberg Trail, at Red Rocks Falls, and while rafting on the Middle Fork of the Flathead.

RIPPLE ROCK AND MUD CRACKS

Raindrop impressions, water ripples, and mud cracks remain etched in stone – all evidence of ancient sea origins. Ripple rocks, found most often in red, blue, or beige layers, look like sands on a beach where waves left their marks. As the sea dried up, sediments compacted and cracked, similar to a mud puddle drying up in a driveway. Large blocks show webs of cracks filled in with other sediments – an effect looking like dull maroon or turquoise tiles. Look for slabs with ripple marks and mud cracks along the Many Glacier Valley trails.

MAGMA INTRUSIONS

Don't be fooled. Yes, Granite Park and its namesake chalet are dubbed for the igneous rock; however, no granite is in Glacier. When early prospectors found Purcell lava or pillow lava – rounded blue-gray formations – they mistakenly called it granite. This lava intruded up through sediment layers, billowing out in ropey coils and bubbles. See this lava on the Highline Trail between Granite Park Chalet and Ahern Pass.

One of the most visible magma intrusions is the diorite or Purcell sill. It appears from a distance like a 100-foot-thick horizontal black line sandwiched between thinner whitish layers. When magma boiled up between limestone layers 800 million years ago, it superheated the limestone, turning it white. You can see the diorite sill from Many Glacier Road, visible as a thick dark line on Mount Gould and Mount Wilbur. Hikers see it as black jagged teeth above Iceberg Lake or the solid line above Grinnell Glacier. The Highline Trail passes through the sill approximately one mile beyond Haystack Saddle. Look for a crystallized green sheen covering deep black. You'll notice your footing changes abruptly when you step onto the sill; instead of broken shard slabs, you'll find something more solid and volcanic.

STROMATOLITES

The Belt Sea became habitat for blue-green algae. Six species of this petite primitive life formed in the sea, doing what algae does best – removing carbon dioxide from the water and giving off oxygen. During this process, calcium carbonate formed into stromatolites, a round rock formation looking like Van Gogh's *Starry Night* swirls. You'll find stromatolites along Going-to-the-Sun Road and on the Piegan Pass Trail. The presence of these algae forms in the Belt Sea produced an oxygen-rich atmosphere that allowed other life forms to develop – yes, humans.

---

metamorphose. You can see layers at Logan Pass, where multihued sediments stripe Mount Clements.

Uplift of Mountains

Between 150 and 60 million years ago, massive tectonic movement along monstrous faults created mountains. During this uplift, a several-mile-thick Belt Sea chunk slid 50 miles east and atop much younger rock. Precambrian rocks—containing petrified preoxygen algae—shifted on top of younger Cretaceous volcanic and shale dinosaur-age rocks in a formation known as the **Lewis Overthrust Fault.** Look

Look for mud cracks in red or blue-green argillites.

for its evidence where geologists originally discovered the fault in 1890: north of Marias Pass on U.S. Highway 2. In the Rocky Mountains, Glacier has the oldest exposed sedimentary rock because of the uplift.

During the uplift, rock heated and became pliable like bread dough. Sometimes it simply folded. Find folds on Waterton Lake's east shore, above the Ptarmigan Tunnel trail, and between Josephine and Bullhead Lakes on the Swiftcurrent Trail.

Glaciation

More recently, glaciers carved the landscape. Two million years ago, the Pleistocene ice age engraved the park's topography via huge advancing and retreating glaciers. Only the tops of Glacier's highest peaks poked out as nunataks, a summit completely surrounded by ice. Glaciers—thousands of feet deep—gouged out valleys.

These ancient ice rivers bit into the landscape. When three or more glaciers gnawed away on a peak, a horn resulted, such as Mount Reynolds or Triple Divide. Sometimes two glaciers chewed ridges paper thin into arêtes (French for fish bone), such as the ragged Iceberg Wall. Large lakes filled in U-shaped valleys, the mark of glacial carving: Compare the rounded valley floor of the McDonald Valley with river carving, such as Grand Canyon's V shape. As glaciers retreated, they left large piles of debris—rocks, sand, and gravel—in the form of moraines, like a big pile of dirty laundry. Large moraines such as Howe Ridge remain from Pleistocene ice, whereas smaller rubble piles in Grinnell or Sperry Glacier basin resulted this past century.

In holes where the ice carved deeper, melting water made tarns, or small glacial lakes. The upper ends of glaciers often carved out cirques, steep-walled round basins such as Avalanche Lake basin. Lower ends of glaciers plummeted off cliffs, forming hanging valleys: Bird Woman Falls dives from a hanging valley suspended between Mount Oberlin and Mount Cannon. As you hike the Avalanche Lake trail, look for glacial striations, or large scratches, on

© BECKY LOMAX

rocks where ice abraded the surface, especially on erratics or large boulders strewn about from receding ice.

While ancient Pleistocene ice melted in Glacier about 12,000 years ago, several miniature ice ages have since shaped the land. The glaciers currently in the park are products of the last 8,000 years. During the **Little Ice Age,** 1500–1850, most glaciers grew. Park tree-ring studies show evidence of more than 150 glaciers in the early 1900s. Less than 17 percent of those remain today, the largest of which is Harrison Glacier, at 0.7 square mile. Climatologists expect the 25 glaciers remaining in 2010 to melt by within a decade. Waterton no longer has active glaciers, only snow fields. At Cameron Lake, you can look across the border to the remnants of Herbst Glacier, now too small to be classified as an active glacier.

Glaciers and Snow Fields

It's often hard to tell the difference between a glacier and a snow field. In early summer, they look the same, covered with fresh snow from winter. But they are distinctly different.

It's simple math. When more snow adds than melts annually, glaciers form. The snow transforms into icy grains through freeze-thaw cycles. Snows build up on the upper end of glaciers and push down, compressing ice crystals. Over years, the ice compacts in layers, mounting into a huge mass with a rigid surface and supple base.

Glaciers are moving ice—moving so slowly that you can't detect movement by watching them. Aided by gravity, ice presses down, forming a thin elastic barrier that carries the ice mass toward the glacier's toe, where it may calve off in chunks. Sperry Glacier moves about 12–20 feet per year, while Grinnell moves much more—30–50 feet per year. When the ice travels over convex ground features, its surface cracks, forming crevasses sometimes hundreds of feet thick. Hidden crevasses make glaciers deadly for travel.

To move, a certain amount of ice is needed—usually a surface of 25 acres and depth of 100 feet. Less than that, and the ice becomes static—a permanent snow field. Moving glaciers behave similarly to a bulldozer, gouging out troughs. Recognize them by their telltale debris bands—lines of rocks on the surface. When the ice recedes, or melts, rocks and debris are left in large moraines or as loose boulders called erratics. Contrary to the ice fields that Glacier once had, today's tiny glaciers will become snow fields by 2020.

CLIMATE

Glacier and Waterton live on a collision course for both Arctic Continental and Pacific Maritime weather. Wet weather races in from the Pacific, with accompanying moderate temperatures. Precipitation results in an annual average 29 inches of rainfall and 157 inches of snow near West Glacier. Waterton also sees more precipitation than the rest of Alberta.

Although the east side of the Continental Divide sees just as much precipitation as the west, one factor produces more extremes—wind. While winter winds often blow snow from slopes, providing forage for ungulates, they also have been known to blow trains off their tracks near East Glacier. Several east-side high passes are notorious for raging unpredictable winds causing hikers to crawl on all fours. **Chinook** winds—warm winds with speeds reaching over 90 miles per hour—happen any time of the year, but they are most obvious in winter. Native Americans called them "snow eaters" for the snow they rapidly melted. When a Chinook descends the Continental Divide's east side, it becomes warm and dry, fooling trees into thinking it's spring and catapulting their cells into spring water absorption. When temperatures plummet again, the cold freezes the water in their cells and kills the trees. This "winter kill" accounts for the number of dead silver trunks dotting east-side forests, especially visible in Two Medicine and Waterton.

Glacier is a country of weather extremes. Its maximum high hit 99°F, while its low kneeled to -36°F. Elevation makes a huge difference, too: While Lake McDonald beckons swimmers to sunny beaches, frigid winds can rage across Logan Pass. Sometimes, you can experience

PRECIPITATION AND TEMPERATURES

Taken from West Glacier.

Month	Average number rainy/snowy days	Average snowfall (inches)	Average temperature (low-high)
Jan.	17	40	12-28°F
Feb.	13	23	18-34°F
Mar.	13	15	22-41°F
Apr.	11	4	29-52°F
May	13	0.4	37-64°F
June	13	0.2	44-71°F
July	9	0	47-79°F
Aug.	9	0	46-78°F
Sept.	9	0.1	39-67°F
Oct.	11	2	32-53°F
Nov.	15	17	25-37°F
Dec.	17	38	18-30°F

four seasons in one day, so always dress in layers and carry extra clothing, no matter what the weather looks like in the morning. Rains move in fast, and snows may fall any month of the year.

Spring
While March, April, and May are appealing off-months to travel, in Glacier they are wet and cold, still clinging to winter. Snow buries the high country and much of the lowlands until late spring. May is moody, alternating between warm days and rainstorms or frequent late snows cascading avalanches in the high country.

Summer
During summer months, June habitually monsoons, but July and August usher in warmer, drier skies. Often higher elevations are substantially cooler—up to 15 degrees chillier than valley floors. While cool breezes are welcome on baking summer days, they can also bring snows in August.

Fall
Autumn begets lovely bug-free warm days and cool nights. While golds paint aspen and larch trees, temperatures bounce through extremes—from highs of 75–80°F during the day to below freezing at night. Seemingly schizophrenic, rains and snows descend for a few days, followed by clearing and warming trends.

Winter
Winter temperatures in Glacier vary depending on elevation but mostly hang in the 10–25°F

range, producing voluminous snows. Logan Pass is buried under 350–650 inches of snow per year. Temperatures can spike above freezing, with its companion rain, or below zero with an Arctic front. Because Chinooks visit Waterton more than the rest of Alberta, it is one of the warmest places in the province in winter. While the Canadian prairies suffer below-freezing temperatures, Waterton may be reveling in 30–50°F.

Daylight

Given Glacier's latitude and placement on the mountain time zone's western edge, hours of daylight fluctuate wildly during the year. In June, over 16 hours of sun leaves lots of time to play outdoors. First light fades in around 5 A.M., and dark doesn't descend until almost 11 P.M. By late August, however, dark descends at 9 P.M., with daylight shortening throughout autumn. At the winter solstice, the sun rises at 8 A.M. and sets at 4:30 P.M.

FLORA

Glacier and Waterton parks sprout rich floral diversity. Forests, prairies, and tundra burgeon with different vegetation specific to elevation, habitat, and weather. Glacier is home to 46 rare Montana plants, four of which are found only in the park. In addition, the park houses 1,150 vascular plants, 400 mosses, and 275 lichens. It harbors species at the edges of their distribution: Great Plains flowers to arctic bulbs. The Lake McDonald Valley shelters nearly 100 Pacific Coast species.

For a small park, Waterton has a corner on the rare plant market: 30 grow only within its borders, including the rarest plant, the Waterton moonwort. Waterton can also brag a total of 970 vascular plants, 190 mosses, and 220 lichens, ironically chalking up more diversity than its larger park sisters to the north—Banff and Jasper.

Grasslands

More than 100 grass species proliferate across the Glacier-Waterton prairies, which poke into valley drainages on the Continental Divide's east side and have been preserved by natural fires in the North Fork Valley. Waterton houses one of two prairie lands in the Canadian national park system and one of North America's last places where grizzly bears range into historic grassland habitat.

Aspen Parklands

Aspens dominate east-side slopes, populating the valleys of Many Glacier, Belly River, Two Medicine, St. Mary, and Waterton. Harboring elk herds in winter and broken by wildflower meadows of arrowleaf balsamroot and sticky geranium, groves of quaking aspen shake their leaves in the slightest breeze—hence their name. They mark the transition between grasslands and coniferous forests.

Montane Forests

In low to mid-elevations, dense montane forests mix poplars and firs, which vary substantially depending on moisture and winds. Cedar-hemlock forests with birch dominate wetter western valleys, while drier slopes yield limber pine, Douglas fir, white spruce, and lodgepole pine. The western larch, a conifer that loses its needles each winter, also inhabits lower-elevation forests. Below the canopy, twinflower, foamflower, and orchids find their niche along with juniper, Pacific yew, thimbleberry, and serviceberry.

Subalpine Zone

Between 5,000 and 7,000 feet in elevation, stately forests surrender to subalpine firs, dwarfed and gnarled in their struggle to survive in a short growing season, brutal winds, frigid temperatures, and heavy snows. For survival, trees develop a bent, stunted krummholz, forming a protective mat rather than growing upright. Whitebark pine and Englemann spruce also sneak into the subalpine. Between tree islands, lush mountain meadows bloom with a colorful array of columbine, bog gentian, valerian, fleabane, and beargrass.

Alpine Tundra

Nearly 25 percent of Glacier and Waterton is

© BECKY LOMAX

Fairy slippers are one of Glacier's several orchids.

alpine tundra. Above the tree line, the land appears to be barren rock. But a host of miniature plants adapt to the harsh conditions of high winds, short summers, cold temperatures, and little soil. Low-growing perennials and hairy leaves provide protection from winds and the sun's high-elevation intensity. Mats of pink moss campion, delicate spotted saxifrage, purple butterwort, and Jones columbine fling their energies into showy flowers, however tiny they may be.

Huckleberries
Of all Glacier's flora, the huckleberry draws the most attention. While several varieties grow throughout the park, from lowlands to subalpine, they all have one thing in common: a sweet berry. Look for a low-growing shrub with small green to reddish leaves. About the size of a small blueberry, huckleberries ripen into a rich dark purple-blue. Find lowland berries in late July, but mid-August–early September is known as "huck" season. Grizzly bears carboload on hucks to survive winter.

Wildflowers
Glacier's wildflowers peak late June–early August, depending on snowmelt and elevation. Early summer brings on fields of yellow glacier lilies and white spring beauties poking buds through the snowpack. In lower elevations, large white heads of cow parsnip bloom alongside roads and continue into higher elevations as summer progresses. Some years, beargrass—a tall white lily—blooms so thickly in July on subalpine slopes that the hillsides look snow covered. Paintbrush spews fields in yellow, red, fuchsia, white, salmon, and orange. Just a reminder: Picking flowers in national parks is prohibited. Use your camera instead.

Poisonous Plants
Very few plants in Glacier are poisonous to the touch. Several can be toxic if eaten, so it's best to avoid eating plants or mushrooms. Most of Glacier is inhospitable for poison ivy, oak, and sumac. But keep your eyes open for stinging nettles, which line many of the trails: Although not poisonous, they leave an obnoxious itchy

residue on contact. A few people have allergic reactions to cow parsnip: If you have sensitive skin, wear long sleeves and long pants to avoid contact with the plant.

FAUNA

Glacier and Waterton teem with wildlife: 24 fish species, 63 mammals, and 272 birds. The Crown of the Continent remains a North American bastion of an intact ecosystem, with many animals present that were here before the human impact of the past 150 years. In the late 1980s, wolves migrated from Canada, completing more of the original members of Glacier's wildlife family. Only mountain bison and woodland caribou remain extirpated.

Bears

Two bears roam Glacier's mountains: the black bear and grizzly bear. Omnivores and opportunistic feeders, bears will eat anything that is easy pickings. Spending most of their waking time eating to gain 100–150 pounds before winter, Glacier's bears feed on a diet heavy in plant matter: bulbs, roots, berries, shoots, and flowers. Ants, insects, carrion, and ground squirrels fill in proteins. Contrary to popular opinion, humans are not on their menu of favorite foods.

Because bears learn fast, they adapt quickly to new food sources, be it a pack dropped by the side of the trail or dog food left out in a campground. For this reason, Glacier imposes strict rules for handling food and garbage in picnic sites, campgrounds, and backcountry areas. All garbage cans and dumpsters are bear resistant. Bears that eat human foods and garbage find themselves moved to a new habitat, or worse, destroyed.

Because grizzly and black bears are integral to Glacier's ecosystem, the National Park Service employs several bear rangers whose jobs entail monitoring and deterring bears from trouble. For bruins who hang near roadways and front country campgrounds, the bear team uses hazing methods—loud noises, gunshots, pellet beanbags, and sometimes Karelian bear dogs—in an attempt to teach bears to stay away. Nuisance bears are transplanted to remote park drainages or destroyed if their offenses warrant. "A fed bear is a dead bear," the truism goes. A bear that dabbles in human food often aggressively seeks more.

Bears are one of the least productive mammals, giving birth once every two or three years. While black bears have a gestation of 220 days, for grizzlies spring mating season is followed by delayed implantation, where the fertilized eggs simply "hang" until winter. Pending the sow's health, the egg or eggs implant, resulting in one, two, or three cubs born during winter's deep sleep. If her health is severely threatened, she may abort the egg instead.

Bears don't actually hibernate, for their respiration and pulse remain close to normal. Instead, they enter a deep sleep in which the body temperature drops slightly. Before crawling into their dens, they scarf down mountain ash berries, rough grasses, and twigs to form an anal plug—which inhibits eating, urinating, or defecating during winter. Bears emerge in the spring ravenously hungry, beelining for avalanche chutes to rummage for snow-buried carcasses.

Megafauna

Megafauna are the big animals everyone wants to see, like bears. Glacier and Waterton harbor three elusive members of the cat family: mountain lions, bobcats, and Canadian lynx. Quiet hunters and mostly nocturnal, cats may see you while you have no idea that they linger nearby. For mountain lion, deer tops the menu, while lynx favor snowshoe hares. Both cat populations rise and fall with their prey populations. With keen eyesight and hearing, these three cats stalk their prey, the lynx with the help of large "snowshoe" feet.

Gray wolf packs inhabit fairly large ranges, 100–300 square miles, so chances of seeing a wolf are fairly rare despite their relatively high reproductive potential of 4–7 pups per year. Coyotes, foxes, wolverines, and badgers round out the large carnivore list. Although wolverines are the most elusive creatures, Glacier provides prime habitat with remote terrain, snow

© BECKY LOMAX

a bighorn sheep ram

fields, and plentiful ground squirrels. Many hikers spot them along the Highline Trail.

Ungulates crowd Glacier's high and low country. Moose browse in streambeds and lakes. Keep your eyes open in the Swiftcurrent Valley, especially around bogs and willow thickets. Elk, mule deer, and white-tailed deer live parkwide at tree line and below, while mountain goats and bighorn sheep cling to rocky alpine slopes. During late spring, goats congregate at the Goat Lick on U.S. Highway 2, looking for minerals for their depleted systems. They also are a regal staple at Logan Pass.

In Waterton, a small bison herd grazes in a paddock—a tiny remnant of what once roamed the prairies here by the thousands. Visitors may drive the viewing road and hike a short overlook trail to see the bison.

Small Mammals

Members of the weasel family—fishers, pine martens, minks, and weasels—inhabit forests and waterways. The short-tailed weasel changes color in winter: Its fur becomes white, except for the small black tip of its tail. Snowshoe hares also change to white in winter, their large namesake feet providing extra flotation on snow. In subalpine country, a chorus of eeks, screams, and squeaks bounce through rockfalls. The noisemakers are pikas—appearing like big-eared tailless mice—and the ubiquitous Columbian ground squirrel, recognized by its reddish tint. Looking like fat housecat-sized fur balls, hoary marmots splay on rocks, sunning themselves. Scampering between high alpine rocks, golden-mantled ground squirrels look like oversized chipmunks with their telltale gold stripes.

Fish

With 750 lakes and 1,500 miles of streams, Glacier provides abundant habitat for fish, both native and nonnative species. Bull trout, westslope cutthroat trout, and whitefish are among the 17 species of native fish. To promote recreational fishing, lakes were stocked with nonnative fish such as rainbow trout, arctic grayling, and kokanee salmon. Introduced species flourished, threatening native fish, whose populations are now waning. Since the 1970s, fish are no longer stocked in Glacier or Waterton.

Fish in Waterton Lakes feed on a tiny crustacean, the opossum shrimp—a relic species that inhabited the area prior to the Pleistocene ice age. As glaciers melted, the tiny shrimp returned through the Missouri-Mississippi watersheds. Spending its entire life in darkness, it lingers on the lake bottom during the day, surfacing only at night.

Birds

More than 200 species of birds means every park visitor can see wildlife. Bird checklists are available at visitors centers in both parks to assist with identification. In summer, trees teem with songbirds—cedar waxwings, thrushes, chickadees, vireos, sparrows, dark-eyed juncos, and finches. Brilliant-colored western tanagers and striking mountain bluebirds flit between treetops. Sightings of rufous and calliope hummingbirds are common.

Grouse are large-forest ground birds.

Woodpeckers, including the large, red-capped pileated woodpecker, pound at bark in search of bugs. Ground birds such as the chicken-sized grouse surprise hikers on trails, while smaller ptarmigans—whose plumage turns white in winter—blend with summer coloration into rocks. Steller's jays and Clark's nutcrackers add to the cacophony.

Because of Glacier's profuse rivers, streams, and lakes, waterfowl finds plentiful habitat. Loons, grebes, mergansers, and goldeneyes fill almost every lake, while harlequin ducks migrate to rapidly flowing streams in spring for nesting. Tundra swans use Glacier's lakes as a stopping ground during their annual migration to and from their arctic breeding grounds. American dippers, or water ouzels, nest near waterfalls: The dark bird's obvious bobbing action is a dead giveaway as to species.

Raptors

Nothing is more dramatic than sighting a golden eagle soaring along the Continental Divide. Common nesters in remote spots, goldens often return yearly to the same location. Glacier also boasts about 10 nesting pairs of bald eagles seen along waterways year-round. Above lakes, ospreys dive for fish from impressive heights, while red-tailed hawks and American kestrels hover over field mice. Listen carefully, for nights are haunted by the small pygmy owl's "whew" and the great horned owl's six deep hoots.

Snakes and Insects

For the most part, Glacier and Waterton are devoid of poisonous snakes and spiders. The climate is too harsh for rattlesnakes. However, you will find garter and bull snakes on some trails. Due to colder conditions, spiders are small, although a bite may produce swelling or an allergic reaction.

ENVIRONMENTAL ISSUES
Climate Change

The current increase in global temperatures affects Glacier Park like nowhere else. While glaciers have shrunk since 1850, ecologists predict that the park's namesakes will melt by 2020—producing not just a loss of ice, but a shift in flora and fauna. As temperatures warm, the tree line advances up in elevation, encroaching on alpine zones. Glacier's tree line was once 3,200 feet lower than today; how far it will climb is unknown.

A rising tree line will cause basins scoured clean by ice and blooming with wildflower meadows to succumb to heavy forests of spruce, fir, pines, shrubs, and bushes. Plants at the fringes of their distribution may disappear. Shifts in habitat may force wildlife to change elevation or latitude in search of food sources. Species such as the heat-intolerant **pika** may suffer extinction. Because of Glacier's easily accessed alpine areas, scientists are monitoring melt rates of Grinnell and Sperry Glaciers to help predict future impacts on the park's biodiversity.

Endangered and Threatened Species

In the 1800s, more than 100,000 **grizzly bears** roamed grasslands and foothills in the Lower 48. Today, in less than 1 percent of their historic range, fewer than 1,000 grizzlies forage for food. Greater Glacier's grizzly bears are listed as threatened on the Endangered Species List, with bear management assisting recovery.

In an effort to count the grizzly population, the U.S. Geological Survey conducted two studies 1998–2004 in Glacier and surrounding lands. Collecting scat and bear hairs via barbwire stapled to rub trees and surrounding scent lures, scientists used tweezers to bag the hairs for DNA genotyping of species, sex, and individual. The study found a healthy grizzly population, with 765 bears spread across 7.8 million acres in northwest Montana. Glacier houses the densest populations.

Grizzlies require a large range; many travel outside the park and across international boundaries. Human pressures from road and house building, agriculture and livestock, timber harvesting, and mineral, oil, and gas mining impact their habitat. Just outside Waterton,

legal Canadian hunting and predator-control programs subject bears to high mortality rates. In northwest Montana, poaching, management actions, and private landowners account for the deaths of 20–30 grizzlies per year. While bad berry crops and encroaching rural developments contribute to bears getting into trouble, inappropriate attractants—garbage, livestock grain, and bird feeders—lead to many of the deaths.

Gray wolves once ranged throughout most of North America. By 1920, predator-control programs extirpated them from Glacier and Waterton, prompting placement on the Endangered Species List. In 1986, following the natural migration of the Magic Pack from Canada, Glacier saw its first litter of pups born in over 50 years. By 2007, statewide numbers climbed to over 400, pushing the animal toward a stable enough status that the federal government delisted the wolf in Montana, and the state permitted hunting wolves in 2009 outside Glacier Park. But in 2010, a federal court reinstated protection.

Recorded sightings of the **Canada lynx** have declined substantially in the past 40 years, prompting it to be listed in 2000 as threatened. In coniferous forests, the lynx follows its chief prey, the snowshoe hare, with the cat's cyclical rising and falling populations in sync with hare numbers. Park studies have followed tracks in snow to ascertain the lynx's status.

Two indigenous trout descended from ice-age lakes that formed as glaciers retreated: **westslope cutthroat trout** and **bull trout.** Glacier provides a stronghold for these fish. Bull trout populations have declined 90 percent, forcing it to be listed as an endangered species in 1998, but pure cutthroat have yet to be placed on the list. While habitat degradation and overfishing contributed to the demise, one menace came from nonnative lake trout stocked for recreational fishing, turning them into fast cuisine. But the biggest threat comes from hybridization with other trout, like rainbows. Removing nonnative species is impractical; the park uses fishing regulations to protect pure populations.

© BECKY LOMAX

A biologist measures a grizzly bear foot during a radio collaring.

Other species not officially listed as endangered also suffer threats to survival. Of all the ungulates, **bighorn sheep** face the greatest risk. Once widely scattered across most western mountain ranges, sheep today live in fragmented pockets. Hunting, disease, agriculture, mining, competition for food, fire-suppression policies, and habitat destruction forced this grassland forager into the more rugged fringes of its historic range. Today, 400–600 bighorn sheep graze in Glacier, with an additional population in Waterton. Recent studies used GPS radio collars to track the sheep, and DNA samples revealed two genetically different populations in northern and southern Glacier. Alpine species, such as **pika** and **mountain goats,** are being monitored, for climate change poses the biggest threat to their survival.

Fire

Like snow, wind, or rain, lightning-caused fire is a natural process. It is healthy for the ecosystem, for it removes bug infestations like the pine bark beetle that produce red-needled trees, reduces deadfall and nonnative plants, releases nutrients into the soil like a good fertilizer, and maintains a natural mix of vegetation. Following years of heavy fire-suppression policy, forest fuels built up to high levels in the park. Each summer, Glacier averages 13 fires, with 5,000 acres burned; some summers, like 2003, when 150,000 acres blazed, see more. Most fires burn unevenly, creating a mosaic of charred timber amid greenery. That patchwork ultimately leads to more vegetation and wildlife diversity. In the natural process of regrowth, the burns flourish rapidly with wildflowers, birds, and wildlife.

Historical Protection

Glacier has substantial cultural and historical resources, but protecting archaeological and historic assets is difficult. At 50 years old, artifacts—even garbage dumps—are considered historic, according to federal law. To date, Glacier has identified 429 archaeological sites and Waterton 358. But many have not been cataloged. While the park does all it can to protect its cultural and historical resources, more funding is needed for adequate protection.

Non-Native Plants

Sometimes the prettiest flowers can be the most noxious. Such is the case with exotic weeds such as spotted knapweed, St. John's wort, and the oxeye daisy, introduced through horses, cars, livestock, and railroads. With their broad roots, high seed production, and chemicals that inhibit growth of native plants, these exotics infest grasslands, lessening diversity and reducing wildlife habitat. Both Parks Canada and Glacier's National Park Service curb the spread of nonnative plants through roadside mowing, herbicides, or natural means.

History

Human use of the Crown of the Continent dates back 10,000 years. Evidence of fishing in Upper Waterton Lake and driving bison across the Blakiston Valley prairies most likely belonged to the ancestors of native peoples living near Glacier and Waterton today.

Native Americans

Spanning what became the U.S.-Canadian border, the **Blackfeet,** or Nitsitapii (meaning real people), included three nomadic groups who based much of their livelihood on hunting bison in the vast prairies on the Continental Divide's east side. The most northerly group, the Sitsika, or Blackfoot, were the first to meet European traders. (To refer to the collective, Canada prefers Blackfoot, but Blackfeet is used in the United States.) The other two—the Blood (or Kainai) and Piegan (or Piikani)—made up the southern groups. For thousands of years, according to the Blackfeet, their lands ran between the Saskatchewan and Yellowstone Rivers.

During summers, Blackfeet groups convened for the Sun Dance, a ceremony held on the plains. But during the rest of the spring and summer, efforts focused individually on stocking food: hunting, digging roots, and collecting berries. As bison moved northwest to their wintering ranges, groups met again for hunts—sometimes buffalo jumps, where hunters funneled bison over a cliff. Afterward, they returned to their winter camps, sheltered in deep mountain forests.

For the Blackfeet, the Glacier Park area was known as the "Backbone of the World." Used for spiritual sanctuary, the mountains provided places for prayer and sacred ceremonies. A place to gather guidance, the mountains also yielded holy plants and roots used for their healing properties. Some of Glacier's peaks, lakes, and rivers still use Blackfeet names today: Going-to-the-Sun Mountain, Two Medicine Lake, Pitamakin Pass, and Running Eagle Falls.

On the Continental Divide's west side, the **Salish** and **Kootenai** hunted, trapped, and fished, ranging east over the mountains on annual bison hunts. Known as the Ktunaxa, the Kootenai (variously spelled Kootenay, Cootenay, or Kutenai) comprised seven bands spanning the western Rockies from southern Alberta to Missoula, Montana. The Kootenai typically used mountain passes like Marias, Cut Bank, Red Eagle, and Brown to cross through Glacier and Waterton to hunt, and the Blackfeet used the same passes for raiding parties. For the Kootenai, the Lake McDonald area was a place for sacred dances, hence its original name of Sacred Dancing Waters.

Two other native people lived in the Glacier-Waterton vicinity: the Assiniboines, or Stoney Indians, and the Gros Ventres. Both of these tribes find namesakes in the park, with a lake, a pass, and three peaks named for the Stoney. In the park's northeast corner, the Gros Ventres, which means Big Belly, left their name on the Belly River and Mokowanis drainages with Gros Ventre Falls. Little evidence remains in

© BECKY LOMAX

Great Northern Railway built chalet colonies like Granite Park a day's horseback ride apart from each other.

the park of the presence of the Flathead and Kalispel tribes.

As westward expansion brought more people, Native Americans moved within government reservation boundaries: The Sitsikas settled near Calgary. The Blood moved onto a reserve adjacent to Waterton, while the Piegans, the largest of the three Blackfeet groups, split into two, with the North Piikani settling near Pincher Creek and the South Piikani on the Continental Divide's west side in Montana. The Salish and Kootenai moved to the Flathead Reservation southwest of Glacier. Smallpox and whiskey took their toll on the tribes.

Development

In 1803, when Lewis and Clark came west, they bypassed Glacier. At Camp Disappointment, located today on the Blackfeet Reservation, they came within 25 air miles but never found Marias Pass—one of the lowest passes through the treacherous Rocky Mountains.

Soon, French, Spanish, and English fur trappers entered the Glacier-Waterton area.

Westward expansion also brought miners looking for copper and gold. But lands between the Continental Divide and the plains belonged to the Blackfeet. In 1895, the federal government negotiated a settlement with the Blackfeet to purchase the land. During the turn of the 20th century, mining boomed in Many Glacier and Rising Sun. Western Canada's first oil well spewed at Waterton, and Montana's first at Kintla Lake. Neither oil nor mining paid off, both supplanted by burgeoning tourism.

Building a Park

Pressure to find rail passages through the northern Rockies began in the mid-1800s. When Great Northern Railway finally succeeded in 1891 to lay track over the Continental Divide, the face of Glacier changed. The railroad company needed a destination for its wealthy train riders. The railroad's economic needs and preservationists spawned the idea of Glacier National Park, which became reality on May 11, 1910. The park celebrated its centennial in 2010.

William Logan—for whom Logan Pass is named—took the reins as the first superintendent of the nation's 10th park. Charged with building a headquarters, hiring rangers, constructing trails, and surveying for a road through the park's interior, Logan did little his first year but put out fires. Literally. Over 100,000 acres went up in flames. His second summer finally saw steps toward readying Glacier for visitors.

Great Northern Railway created many of the park's attractions: hotels, tent camps, chalets, roads, trails, and boats. Competing for travel time and dollars from wealthy Americans taking steamships to Europe, the railroad pitched the slogan "See America First" to lure vacationers to Glacier, which became known as "America's Switzerland."

Horse concessionaires operating from every hotel and chalet in the park merged into the Park Saddle Horse Company. By the mid-1920s, horseback provided the way to see the park. At its peak, the Park Saddle Horse Company operated more than 1,000 horses and led more than 10,000 visitors through the park each summer.

The demand for a road bisecting Glacier's interior increased. Although building the western portion began in 1919, the 52-mile project was not completed until 1932. The opening of Going-to-the-Sun Road ushered in a new era of park visitation. A fleet of 32 red buses hit Glacier's roads for touring. With increased motorized travel, camping gaining popularity, and budget motor inns added to Great Northern's property collections, while saddle trips and the chalets met their demise.

During World War II and the Depression, travel curtailment and fuel conservation plummeted visitation, forcing hotels and chalets to close. Several fell into disrepair and had to be razed. Bus tour business began to usurp rail travel, the Park Saddle Horse Company folded, private car travel increased, and the railroad's lodges lost $500,000 annually, which it offset with ridership profits. Finally, in 1954, Great Northern unloaded the remaining chalets on the National Park Service for $1. In 1957, the company sold the rest of the hotel chain to a Minneapolis hotel corporation, which subsequently sold three years later to Glacier Park, Inc., which would sell again 21 years later to Dial Corporation.

International Peace Park

In 1932, Glacier and Waterton took to front headlines as the world's first peace park. Due to the brainchild and work of Alberta and Montana chapters of Rotary International, lobbying efforts paid off, as the Canadian Parliament and U.S. Congress officially recognized the continuity between the parks. With credit to the longest undefended border in the world, they dedicated the parks together as **Waterton-Glacier International Peace Park.**

Biosphere Reserve and World Heritage Site

In 1976, UNESCO (United Nations Educational, Scientific, and Cultural Organization) designated Glacier Park as a Biosphere Reserve. Three years later, Waterton Lakes received the same recognition. As a Biosphere Reserve, the parks are recognized for their huge diversity of wildlife, plants, and habitats. In 1995, UNESCO followed the biosphere designation with declaring the parks a World Heritage Site for natural beauty and unique geological features, such as Triple Divide Peak and the continent's oldest exposed sedimentary rock.

Recreation

WALKING TRAILS

Glacier is known as a "hiker's park," and no wonder! With 732 miles of trails, everything from a short, leisurely amble to a multiday top-of-the-world Continental Divide backpack trip crams in its borders. Ranger stations and visitors centers have brochures describing hikes in their locales; the same information is also available online (www.nps.gov/glac).

No permits are needed for day hikes—only for backpacking. However, if you plan on day hiking across the Blackfeet Reservation, you will need a $10 permit, available in East Glacier, Browning, and at St. Mary Visitor Center.

Both free and pay shuttles (see *Essentials*) hit trailheads. Shuttles particularly ease hiking point-to-point routes on day trips or backpacking.

Trail Status

Conditions on Glacier's trails vary significantly depending on the season, elevation, recent severe weather, and bear closures. Swinging and plank bridges across rivers and creeks are not installed until late May–June. Some years, bridges have been installed, only to be removed a few weeks later to wait for rivers swollen with runoff to subside. Most years, higher passes are snowbound until early July, and steep snow fields often inhibit hiking on the Highline Trail until then. Large drifts across trails must be blasted to open the paths even late in July. Ptarmigan Tunnel's doors usually open mid-July–early October. To find out about trail conditions before hiking, you can stop at ranger stations and visitors centers for updates or consult Trail Status Reports (usually updated June–September only) on the park's website.

EXPLORING THE ECOSYSTEM

One of the best ways to become intimate with Glacier's wildlife, geology, birds, and cultural history is to join the regionally and nationally recognized experts from **Glacier Institute** (406/756-1211, www.glacierinstitute.org). Offered year-round, the courses blend in-the-field experiences with hands-on learning at Big Creek Camp in the North Fork or Glacier Field Camp near Apgar. You can learn to bird, bear-watch, track animals on snowshoes, photograph wildlife, find herbs and mushrooms, and identify wildflowers. College credit is available for some of the workshops and classes. Adult seminars include wilderness first aid, art, photography, science, and ecology. Youth camps for ages 7-16 emphasize outdoor science. Most single-day courses average $65; most multiday courses range $200-425, including lodging and meals.

For those looking for an intimate experience in Glacier, **Glacier National Park Associates** (406/387-4299, www.nps.gov/glac) looks for volunteers each summer for backcountry projects. Some tasks restore historic log structures, reconstruct damaged trails and backcountry campsites, and transplant seedlings from the park's native-plant nursery. Past projects have included work at Sperry Chalet and backcountry patrol cabins. Led by a backcountry ranger intern, participants usually work on one project during a three- to five-day stay in the backcountry. No special skills are required – just a desire to help.

For those itching to contribute to scientific research in Glacier, the **Crown of the Continent Research Learning Center** (406/888-7800, www.nps.gov/glac) conducts citizen science projects every summer. For several years, they have run field studies on common loons, invasive weeds, and high country species of concern, such as mountain goats, pikas, and Clark's nutcrackers. Some training is necessary but is available through the center.

Signage

All park trailheads and junctions have excellent signage. Be prepared, however, to convert kilometers to miles in your head to understand distances. Some signs show both kilometers and miles, others simply kilometers. This is, after all, the International Peace Park, and kilometers are definitely more international. If you hike in Waterton, all trail sign distances use kilometers. Just pull out your math skills: To convert kilometers to miles, multiply the kilometers listed by 0.6. (Example: Multiply 3 kilometers by 0.6 to get 1.8 miles.) To convert miles to kilometers, multiply the miles by 1.6. (Example: Multiply 2 miles by 1.6 to get 3.2 kilometers.) These calculations are simple, easy approximations you can remember for the trail. Some hikers enjoy kilometers—the number is always higher, so the accomplishment is greater! (For more accurate conversions, multiply by 0.62 to convert kilometers to miles; to convert miles to kilometers, multiply by 1.61.)

Trailheads may also display yellow **bear warnings** or orange **bear closure** signs to alert hikers to frequent bear activity. Heavily trampled areas may have a **footprint with a red slash**—universally recognized as "Don't walk here." Obey these signs: They are protecting fragile alpine meadows from abuse or protecting an area replanted with native plants.

Solo Travelers

Even though solo hiking in bear country is not recommended, some hikers venture into the backcountry alone. If you're one of them, make tons of noise while hiking and brush up on your bear skills. Solo travelers looking for trail companionship should hook up with park naturalist hikes (check *Ranger-Led Activities* for times and dates) or sign on with a commercially guided hike through Glacier Guides (406/387-5555 or 800/521-7238, www.glacier-guides.com).

Hitchhiking to Trailheads

You may see hitchhikers sticking a thumb out. In Montana, hitchhiking is legal. If hitchhiking, be cautious of where you stand on the road. Choose a spot where a car can get completely off the road to pick you up. Don't bother hitchhiking where no pullout is available; no one will stop.

BACKPACKING

Glacier National Park's backpacking is unrivaled. Sixty-six designated backcountry campgrounds spread campers out, so you never feel crowded. You can hit the popular trails—The Highline, The Belly, and Gunsight Pass—or head for something really remote, like the Nyack-Coal Loop or Waterton to Kintla. Backpacking information, permit applications, trail status reports, and backcountry campsite availability are online: www.nps.gov/glac. Call the park (406/888-7800) to speak with someone in person regarding conditions and routes. Use hiker shuttles to create easy point-to-point routes. While you can get permits and information at ranger stations (Two Medicine, Many Glacier, Polebridge) and visitors centers (Logan Pass, St. Mary), the main

Trail signs indicate bear warnings or closures due to bears.

GETTING INTO THE BACKCOUNTRY

Miles of well-marked scenic trails make Glacier rate high with backpackers.

Backcountry camping is allowed in designated locations. Each campground has 2-7 sites, with four people allowed per site. All backcountry campgrounds have pit toilets (some with great views), community cook sites, and separate tent sites. No food, garbage, toiletries, or cookware should be kept in the tent sites. A bear pole, bar, or bear-proof food storage boxes are available.

Many backcountry campsites do not allow fires; carry a lightweight stove for cooking. Take low-odor foods to avoid attracting bears, and practice Leave No Trace principles religiously.

Bring backpacking gear (tent, sleeping bag, pad, clothing, rain gear, topographical maps, compass or GPS device, first-aid kit, bug juice, sunscreen, fuel, cook gear, and stove) plus a 25-foot rope for hanging food, a small screen or strainer for sifting food particles out of gray water, a one-micron or smaller filter for purifying water (tablets and boiling can do the job, too), and a small trowel for emergency human waste disposal when a pit toilet is unavailable.

Permits are required ($5 per person per night, half price ages 8-15, kids 7 years and younger free). By mail, a limited number of sites may be reserved for $30 (plus the per-person fee when you pick up the actual permit). In person, stop by a permit office no more than 24 hours in advance to get permits at Apgar Permit Office (406/888-7859), St. Mary Visitor Center (406/732-7751), Many Glacier Ranger Station (406/732-7740), Two Medicine Ranger Station (406/226-4484), and Polebridge Ranger Station (406/888-7742). Hours generally run 8 A.M.-4:30 P.M. daily May-November. In winter, call 406/888-7800.

SUGGESTED ROUTES: 3-4 DAYS

- **Gunsight Pass Trail:** This 20-mile trail between Jackson Overlook and Lake McDonald Lodge crosses two passes and connects with Sperry Chalet. Stay at Gunsight Lake, Lake Ellen Wilson, and Sperry, but add on the spur trail to Sperry Glacier.

- **Highline Trail:** For an international hike, begin at Logan Pass and finish 30 miles later at Goat Haunt to catch the boat across Waterton Lake into Canada. Camp at Granite Park, Fifty Mountain, and Kootenai Lakes.

- **St. Mary to Two Medicine:** A 35-mile trail links prime fishing lakes along several high passes in bighorn sheep country. Camp at Old Man Lake, Morningstar Lake, and Red Eagle Lake.

SUGGESTED ROUTES: 5-10 DAYS

- **Northern Traverse:** Between Chief Mountain Customs and Kintla Lake, the 58-mile trail crosses three passes as it wanders just south of the Canadian border. Camp at Cosley Lake, Glenn's Lake, Stoney Indian Lake, Lake Francis, Boulder Pass, Upper Kintla, and Kintla Lake.

- **North Circle Tour:** Following in the footsteps of the historic horseback tours through Glacier, this 54-mile loop connects Many Glacier via Ptarmigan Tunnel with The Belly and the northern Highline. Camp at Elizabeth, Cosley, Glenn's, and Stoney Indian Lakes; Fifty Mountain; and Granite Park.

- **Continental Divide National Scenic Trail:** The trail runs 110 miles from Marias Pass to Waterton in a stunning conclusion to the 3,100-mile trail. For this route, connect front country and backcountry campgrounds.

Backpackers climb to Cobalt Lake.

© BECKY LOMAX

place to pick up permits is Apgar Backcountry Office (406/888-7859, May–Oct.).

Guides

Glacier Park allows only one backpacking concessionaire, and that's **Glacier Guides** (406/387-5555 or 800/521-7238, www.glacier-guides.com), a company that has been guiding in Glacier more than 25 years. Guide services, shuttles, food, group equipment, and permits are included for roughly $145 per person per day. Trips depart weekly for three, four, and six days. Custom trips ($170 per person per day, with four-person minimum), and one 10-day Continental Divide trip, are available. If you want the backpacking experience but don't want to carry more than a day pack, hire a Sherpa to haul up to 40 pounds of your gear ($175 per day). The company also rents packs, tents, sleeping bags, and pads. Reservations are required.

CLIMBING

Glacier's peaks and off-trail scrambles are irresistible; however, the park's crumbly sedimentary rock makes climbing risky. Loose handholds, wobbly footholds, rockfall, and unstable scree and talus slopes are hazardous. Safety while climbing is imperative. Each year, accidents and sometimes even fatalities occur from falling while climbing. Only venture off the trail for climbing if you know the terrain and inherent risks. Do not attempt climbing in Glacier alone or without experience. Most ascents are actually scrambles but still not for the inexperienced. For routes, J. Gordon Edwards's *A Climber's Guide to Glacier National Park* is the undisputed bible.

Begin all off-trail adventures by registering at a ranger station or visitors center and go prepared. Be aware of closures for bears and fragile vegetation, especially around Logan Pass. (Check with visitors centers or ranger stations for status or call 406/888-7800.) Always practice Leave No Trace principles. For emergencies, carry a cell phone along, but don't depend on its ability to work everywhere in the park. Instead, be ready to self-rescue.

No commercial guiding outfitters operate

A climber scrambles up Dragon's Tail.

climbing trips in Glacier. For those looking to hook up with climbers, **Glacier Mountaineering Society** offers volunteer-led climbs for members usually on weekends, and each summer they pack one week in July full of climbs for their Mountaineering Week. Only $25 buys an annual membership. Their website is loaded with climbing info, too: www.glaciermountaineers.com.

FISHING
Licenses
Glacier National Park does not require fishing licenses, but fishing outside the park does. Outside Glacier, anglers must possess a Montana State Fishing License. Residents pay $13–18 for two days to full season; conservation licenses are free for resident seniors. Nonresidents can purchase 2-day ($25), 10-day ($43.50), or seasonal licenses ($60), which can be purchased in sporting-goods stores and fly shops across Montana. You can also order one online from Montana Fish, Wildlife, and Parks at www.fwp.mt.gov.

On the Blackfeet Reservation, you'll need a Blackfeet tribal fishing permit (Blackfeet Fish and Game Department, 406/338-7207, www.blackfeetfishandwildlife.com, $20 per day, $30 for three days, or $65 per season). Permits for boats and float tubes are included in those rates.

Regulations
Fishing regulations vary substantially by area; anglers are required to know the rules and know their fish. You can pick up regulations when and where you buy your license. In general, the fishing season begins the third Saturday in May and ends November 30, but some lake fishing is permitted year-round. While strict daily fishing limits regulate catches in Glacier (five) and the Bob Marshall Wilderness Complex (three), many species have higher limits or no limit at all. Bull trout are a protected species and must be thrown back into the water immediately. Look for the lack of black on the dorsal fin: No black, throw it back.

Inside the park, lead is prohibited in weights, lures, and jigs; outside the park, it's recommended to use weights made of nonlead materials. To dispose of entrails in the front country, use a bear-resistant garbage container. In the backcountry, puncture the air bladder and throw entrails 200 feet out into the water away from trails and campsites.

For Glacier's regulations, stop by a ranger station or visitors center, or check the park website (www.nps.gov/glac) for a complete list. For a complete list of the State of Montana (www.fwp.mt.gov) and Blackfeet Reservation (www.blackfeetfishandwildlife.com) regulations, check the websites. For Waterton's fishing licenses and regulations, see the *Waterton* chapter.

BOATING

As of 2010, boating regulations in Glacier Park require motorized vehicles to obtain free permits. Boaters must show that their boats have been cleaned, drained, and dried to avoid bringing Aquatic Invasive Species into park lakes. Permits for up to 14 days are available at the Apgar Backcountry Permit Office, St. Mary Visitor Center, Two Medicine and Many Glacier Ranger Stations, and Polebridge Entrance Station.

Outside the park, out-of-state boats over 12 feet in length must have a home state registration and can be used in Montana up to 90 consecutive days. In-state boats must have Montana registration and decals on the boat. For a complete list of Montana boating regulations, see www.fwp.mt.gov. For boating on Blackfeet Reservation lakes, you'll need a $20 conservation permit (406/338-7207, www.blackfeetfishandwildlife.com), available in St. Mary, Browning, and East Glacier.

HUNTING

Although hunting is illegal in Glacier National Park, much of the surrounding tribal and national forest lands are prime big game and bird hunting areas. For hunting in the Bob Marshall Wilderness or in national forests, get hunting regulations, seasons, and license info from Montana Fish, Wildlife, and Parks (406/444-2535, www.fwp.mt.gov). For hunting on tribal lands, check with the Blackfeet Reservation (406/338-7207, www.blackfeetfishandwildlife.com) for regulations and licenses.

Tips for Travelers

FOREIGN TRAVELERS
Entering the United States

International travelers entering the United States must be aware that border requirements have changed. Passports or passport cards are required, even from Canada, Mexico, the Caribbean, and Bermuda. Resident aliens must possess a permanent resident card. In addition to passports, many travelers will need a visa to visit. Those visiting the United States from 36 countries in the Visa Waiver Program don't need visas but must have electronic-readable passports and limit their stay to 90 days. If you are from a country not recognized in the Visa Waiver Program, give yourself plenty of time to apply for your visa. For the list of visa waivers and visa applications, check www.state.

travel.gov. Upon entry to the United States, those from countries other than Canada or the United States must have a current I-94 form ($6 U.S. currency). Check www.cbp.gov for more info.

Entering Canada

For international travelers entering Canada, visas are not required for visitors from about 50 countries, including the United States. All others must apply for visas. Find the list of visa-exempt countries and visa requirements at www.cic.gc.ca.

Road Ports of Entry

Chief Mountain Customs (9 A.M.–6 P.M. daily May and after Labor Day, 7 A.M.–10 P.M. daily

June–Labor Day) is a seasonal east-side port of entry on Chief Mountain International Highway. A year-round port of entry on Waterton-Glacier's east side, **Piegan/Carway** (7 A.M.–11 P.M. daily) sits on U.S. Highway 89/Canada Highway 2. Because Trail Creek Customs closed more than a decade ago during flooding up the North Fork Valley, the only west-side port of entry now is **Roosville,** on U.S. Highway 93, north of Eureka. It's open 24 hours 365 days per year but is also 90 miles from West Glacier.

Goat Haunt

Even though Goat Haunt, U.S.A., is accessed only by boat or foot, the tightening of border policies has affected the small seasonal port of entry. Because of its relationship in the International Peace Park, special regulations are in effect here. For visitors in Canada traveling down Waterton Lake in private boats or touring on the MV *International,* clearing customs is not required, even though you cross the border partway down the lake. At Goat Haunt, you can get off the boat and wander around freely along the beach and walkway between the International Peace Park Pavilion and the boat dock without going through customs. However, hikers going beyond Goat Haunt must show a valid passport or passport card to go through customs, which is open 10:30 A.M. to 5 P.M. daily. Visitors from countries other than Canada and the United States must have a current I-94 or I-94W to hike beyond Goat Haunt. The forms ($6 U.S. currency) are *not* available at Goat Haunt customs but are available at Chief Mountain, Piegan/ Carway, or Roosville customs. For further information on crossing from Canada into the United States, call 406/889-3865.

For day hikers to return to Canadian soil, a customs inspection is not required; however, backpackers hiking into Canada must phone Canadian Customs and Revenue Agency (403/653-3535) upon reaching the Waterton Townsite. You can also phone them for information in advance of your trip. Those catching the Waterton boat will be given immigration forms to fill out.

Border Laws

In general, Canada and the United States have similar border laws: no plants, drugs, firearms, firewood, or live bait. Some fresh meats, poultry products, fruits, and vegetables are regulated. Pets are permitted across the border only with a certificate of rabies vaccination within 30 days prior to your crossing. Bear sprays are considered firearms in Canada; they must have a USEPA-approved label to go across the border. For clarification, call 250/887-3413. If you purchase Cuban cigars in Waterton, they are not permitted back across the U.S. border.

Money and Currency Exchange

Those popping into Waterton for a day or two may not even want to exchange money. Waterton has no bank, but the Tamarack Village (214 Mount View Rd., 403/859-2378, www.hikewaterton.com, May–mid-Oct.) does offer money-exchange services for Canadian and U.S. currency only. Most stores and businesses in Waterton accept U.S. currency, but expect Canadian currency as change. Although it's convenient to use U.S. currency, stores will vary slightly on the exchange rates honored. To receive the best exchange rates, use credit cards.

There will also be some Canadian coins floating in your change in Montana. These are sometimes treated at par; loonies, toonies, and dollars are not. For Canadians visiting the Glacier and Flathead Valley area, some businesses accept Canadian currency. They are used to converting it. If you're traveling farther south in the state where cashiers may be unfamiliar with loonies, convert into U.S. currency. Credit cards will receive the most accurate exchange rate. On Glacier's east side, you'll find no banks to exchange currency—only on the park's west side in Flathead Valley.

For both Canada and the United States, travelers checks in smaller amounts ($50 and under) work best for short trips on either side of the border; then you're not left dragging around scads of foreign currency. International travelers should exchange currency at their major port of entry (Seattle, Vancouver, Calgary).

TRAVELING WITH CHILDREN
Junior Ranger Program

Kids can earn a Junior Ranger Badge by completing self-guided activities in the *Junior Ranger Activity Guide,* available at all visitors centers. Most activities target ages 6–12 and coincide with a trip over Going-to-the-Sun Road. When kids return the completed newspaper to a visitors center, they are sworn in as Junior Rangers and receive Glacier Park badges.

Discovery Cabin

The Discovery Cabin in Apgar serves up educational kid fun during summer. Hands-on activities guided by interpretive rangers teach children about wildlife, geology, and habitats. Check with Apgar Visitor Center for directions and hours.

Hikes

For kids, short hikes work best. On Going-to-the-Sun Road, go for Avalanche Lake, Hidden Lake Overlook, and St. Mary and Virginia Falls. In Many Glacier, hike to Red Rocks Lake or hop the boat across Swiftcurrent and Josephine Lakes to hike to Grinnell Lake. In Two Medicine, take the boat uplake to hike to Twin Falls or Upper Two Medicine Lake. When hiking with children, always take snacks and water along. If toting a wee one who still needs to be carried, Glacier Outdoor Center (11957 Hwy. 2 E., West Glacier, 406/888-5454 or 800/235-6781, www.glacierraftco.com) rents kiddie packs at $20 per day.

TRAVELING WITH PETS

Pets are allowed in Glacier Park, but only in limited areas: campgrounds, parking lots, and roadsides. They are not allowed on trails, beaches, off-trail in the backcountry, nor at any park lodges or motor inns. When outside a vehicle, pets must be on a six-foot or shorter leash or be caged. In a campground, pets must be leashed or caged. Be kind enough to not leave them unattended in a car anywhere. Be considerate of wildlife and other visitors by keeping your pet under control and disposing of waste in garbage cans.

© BECKY LOMAX

Hikers with pets should head to Waterton or surrounding national forest trails, as most of Glacier's trails do not permit dogs.

In 2010, the owners of Great Northern Raft Company (800/735-7897) applied for a permit to run a dog day care in West Glacier to accommodate hikers and travelers. Call for information on location and rates. Overnight kenneling is only available at kennels in Flathead Valley. Two of the closest are in Columbia Falls—**Stage Stop Farm and Kennels** (1892 Columbia Falls Stage, 406/892-5719) and **Triple R Kennels** (636 Kelley Rd., 406/892-3695, www.triplerkennels.com)—but check the phone book for more choices in Kalispell, Whitefish, and Bigfork.

Trail Restrictions

No pets are allowed on Glacier Park trails, except by leash on the paved 2.6-mile Apgar Bike Trail. (The trail is okay for hikers, too.) Protection of fragile vegetation and preventing conflicts with wildlife are two main reasons; bears stand alone in their own class of reasons to leave poochie home. If you must hike with Fido, head to Flathead National Forest, where pets are permitted. Contrary to Glacier, Waterton does permit dogs on leashes on its trails.

SENIORS
Park Entrance

National parks (as well as lands run by the U.S. Fish and Wildlife Service, U.S. Forest Service, and Bureau of Land Management) have a great deal for seniors age 62 and older who are U.S. citizens or permanent residents: $10 buys the National Parks and Federal Recreational Lands Pass, good for life. To purchase, bring proof of age (state driver's license, birth certificate, or passport) in person to any national park entrance station. In a private vehicle, the card admits four adults within a vehicle, plus all kids under 16 are free.

Senior Discounts

The lifetime park pass also grants 50 percent discounts on fees for federally run tours, campgrounds, parking, and boat launching; however, discounts do not apply to park concessionaire services—like hotels, boat tours, and bus tours. Also, Glacier's historic hotels do not give discounts to seniors, but some private lodging establishments surrounding the park do. Ask to be sure.

ACCESSIBILITY

Visitors with special needs should pick up an *Accessible Facilities and Services* brochure. You can get these at Logan Pass, St. Mary, or Apgar visitors centers, all of which are accessible by wheelchair. Entrance stations also have them. Park information is available also by TDD: 406/888-7806.

Park Entrance

A National Parks and Federal Recreational Lands Access Pass is available free for any blind or permanently disabled U.S. citizen or permanent resident. The lifetime pass permits free access to all national parks and sites run by the U.S. Fish and Wildlife Service, U.S. Forest Service, and Bureau of Land Management. The pass admits the person who signs for the

pass, plus three other adults in the same vehicle; kids under 16 are free. This pass also grants a 50 percent discount on fees for federally run tours, campgrounds, parking, and boat launching, but discounts do not apply to concessionaire services. Passes may only be acquired in person at entrance stations with proof of medical disability or eligibility for receiving federal benefits.

Park Facilities

Five campgrounds in Glacier reserve 1–2 sites each for wheelchair needs: Apgar, Fish Creek, Rising Sun, Sprague Creek, and Two Medicine. Picnic Areas at Apgar, Rising Sun, and Sun Point also have wheelchair access. So do all lodges within the park boundaries, although they have a limited number of ADAAG (Americans with Disabilities Act Accessibility Guidelines) rooms. Other wheelchair-accessible sites include boat docks at Lake McDonald, Many Glacier, and Two Medicine, as well as evening naturalist programs in Apgar Amphitheater, Lake McDonald Lodge Auditorium, Many Glacier Hotel Auditorium, Rising Sun Campground, and Two Medicine Campground. Most parking lots offer designated parking.

Trails

Glacier and Waterton both offer wheelchair-accessible trails. In Glacier, the Apgar Bike Trail, Trail of the Cedars at Avalanche, Running Eagle Falls Nature Trail in Two Medicine, Goat Lick Overlook, Oberlin Bend Trail, the International Peace Park Pavilion at Goat Haunt, and the Many Glacier Trail from the picnic area are wheelchair accessible. Admittedly, some surfaces can be a little rough in places; just be prepared for it. In Waterton, wheelchairs can access Linnet Lake Trail, Waterton Townsite Trail, and Cameron Lake Day Use Area.

While pet dogs are not permitted on backcountry trails, aid dogs are allowed—although, due to bears, they are discouraged. If you choose to hike with an aid dog, be safe by sticking to well-traveled trails during midday.

Interpretive Services

Special programs and sign-language interpretation may be available with a two-week notice. Call 406/888-7930 to schedule.

HEALTH AND SAFETY
Bears

Safety in bear country starts from knowledge and behaving appropriately. With the exception of Alaska and Canada, Glacier beats out any other North American location for the highest density of grizzly bears, and black bears find likable habitat here, too. Regardless of bruin species, one caveat affects the safety of humans and bears: food. Proper use, storage, and handling of food and garbage keep bears from being conditioned or habituated to situations in which they may become aggressive. With strict food and garbage rules, Glacier has minimized aggressive bear encounters, attacks, and deaths—both of humans and bears.

Camp safely. Use low-odor foods, keep food and cooking gear out of sleeping sites in the backcountry, and store it inside your vehicle in

HIKING IN BEAR COUNTRY

Many of Glacier's most heavily tromped trails march smack through prime bear habitat, where a surprise encounter on the trail with a grizzly can turn one's insides to Jell-O. With a few precautions, you can eliminate scares from surprise meetings.

- **Make noise.** Glacier is one park where peace and quiet on the trail could be dangerous. To avoid surprising a bear, use your voice – sing loudly, hoot, or holler – and clap your hands. Bears tend to recognize human sounds as ones to avoid; they'll usually wander off if they hear people approaching. Make loud noise in thick brushy areas, around blind corners, near babbling streams, and against the wind. You'll often hear hikers just hooting out nonsense; it's okay. They're not crazed. It's just their signature bear noise.

- **Hike with other people.** Avoid hiking alone. Keep children near. Very few bear attacks happen to groups of four or more.

- **Avoid bear feeding areas.** Since bears must gain weight before winter, feeding is their prime directive. Often, they'll pack in 20,000 calories in a day. In early season, glacier lily bulbs attract grizzlies for their high nutritional value. By midseason, cow parsnip patches provide sustenance, in between high-protein carrion. If you stumble across an animal carcass, leave the area immediately and notify a ranger. Toward summer's end, huckleberry patches provide

high sugars. Detour widely around feeding bears.

- **Hike in broad daylight.** Avoid early mornings, late evenings, and night.

- **Never approach a bear.** Watch the body language: A bear who stands on hind legs may just be trying to get a good smell or better viewpoint. On the other hand, head swaying, teeth clacking, laid-back ears, a lowered head, and huffing or woofing are signs of agitation: Clear out slowly!

- **If you do surprise a bear, back away.** Contrary to all inclinations, do not run! Instead, back away slowly, talking quietly and turning sideways or bending your knees to appear smaller and nonthreatening. Avoid direct eye contact – a challenge in the animal kingdom. Instead, avert your eyes. Leave your pack on; it can protect you if the bear attacks.

- **Use pepper spray or play "dead."** If you surprise a bear that attacks in defense, aim pepper spray at the bear's eyes. Protect yourself and your vulnerable parts by assuming a fetal position on the ground with your hands around the back of your neck. Play "dead." Move again only when you are sure the bear has vacated the area.

- **If a bear stalks you as food, or attacks at night, fight back.** While bears stalking humans as prey is extremely rare, use any front-country campgrounds. In front-country campgrounds, you'll find detailed explanations of how to camp safely in bear country stapled to your picnic table. For information on camping in bear country, pick up a copy of *Waterton-Glacier Guide* and Glacier's *Backcountry Guide* at entrance stations, visitors centers, ranger stations, permit offices, or online: www.nps.gov/glac.

Hike safely. When taking your first hike, you'll hear jingle bells. When entering your first gift shop, you'll see them—**bear bells.**

They're everywhere. And so are the jokes, calling them "dinner bells." While making noise while hiking is the best safety assurance in bear country, bells are not the best way to do it. And many hikers hate them. To check their effectiveness, see how close you come to hikers before you hear their ringing. Sometimes, it's too close! Bear bells are best as a souvenir, not as a substitute for human noise on the trail. Human noise is best; so talk, sing, hoot, and holler. You'll feel silly at first, but after a while, you'll realize it's something everyone does here.

means at hand – pepper spray, shouting, sticks, or rocks – to tell the bear you are not an easy food source. Try to escape up something, like a building or tree.

· **Pay attention to trail signage.** Special bear signage is used at trailheads to inform hikers of concerns. Yellow **bear warning** signs indicate bears are frequenting the trail; use extra caution and make more noise than usual on these trails. Orange **bear closure** signs indicate a trail is closed, usually because one has been aggressive or is defending a carcass. Even when trailheads have no signs, hikers still need to be cautious, for Glacier is a bear's park.

· Two books are plump with accurate information on bears: Bill Schneider's *Bear Aware* and Stephen Herrero's *Bear Attacks: Their Causes and Avoidances.*

BLACK BEARS VS. GRIZZLY BEARS
While neither black nor grizzly bears are safer, it's good to know what the bear is when you see one. Even though colors are used to name the bears (*grizzly* means silver-haired), bears appear with a variety of fur hues regardless of species. A reddish-black bear can give birth to three cubs of different colors: blond, black, and brown. And grizzly bears appear in all colors of the spectrum. Don't be fooled by color; look instead for body size and shape.

Although hard to assess through binoculars, the bears are two different sizes. Grizzlies are bigger than black bears, standing on all fours at 3-4 feet tall. They weigh in at 300-600 pounds. Black bears average 12-18 inches shorter on all fours. Adult females weigh around 140 pounds, while males bulk up to 220 pounds.

In profile, the grizzly has one notable feature: a hump on its shoulders. The solid muscle mass provides the grizzly's arms with power for digging and running. Black bears lack this hump. Face profiles are also different. On the grizzly, look for a scooped or dished forehead-to-nose silhouette; the black bear's nose will appear straighter in line with its forehead. Note the ears, for the grizzly's will look a little too small for its head while a black bear's ears seem big, standing straight up. While you don't want to get close enough to check the real thing, paw prints in mud reveal a difference in claws and foot structure. Grizzly claws are four inches long, with pads in a relatively straight line, while black bear claws are 1.5 inches, with pads arced across the top of the foot.

Although both bears have mediocre vision, they are fast runners. In three seconds, a grizzly bear can cover 180 feet. And contrary to popular lore, humans are not a food source. In fact, both bears are omnivores, feeding primarily on vegetation and carrion.

As of 2010, a federal law allows people who can legally possess **firearms** under federal, state, and local laws to legally possess firearms in Glacier. However, federal law prohibits firearms in certain facilities—government offices, visitors centers, ranger stations, fee collection buildings, and maintenance facilities. Those places are marked with signs at all public entrances. Discharging firearms in the park is illegal except when presented with "imminent danger." Park officials recommend using pepper spray to deter bears rather than firearms.

Most hikers prefer to use **pepper sprays** that can deter a bear attack without injury to bear or humans. Bear sprays are not repellents like bug sprays to be sprayed on the human body, tents, or gear. Instead, you spray the capsicum derivative directly into a bear's face, aiming for the eyes and nose. While pepper sprays have repelled some attacking bears, wind and rain may reduce effectiveness, as will the product's age. Small purse-sized pepper sprays are inadequate for bears—only an eight-ounce can will do. Practice how to use it. Pepper spray is not protection: Carrying it does not lessen the need for making noise. Be aware that pepper sprays are not allowed by airlines unless checked in luggage, and only brands with USEPA labels may cross through Canadian customs.

Bears are dangerous around food, be it a carcass in the woods, a pack left on a trail, or a cooler left in a campsite. Protecting bears and protecting yourself starts with being conscious of food—including wrappers and crumbs. Gorp tidbits dropped along the trail attract wildlife, as do "biodegradable" apple cores chucked into the forest. Pick up what you drop and pack out all garbage; don't leave a Hansel and Gretel trail for bears. Bear attacks can be avoided.

Mountain Lion Encounters

These large cats rarely prey on humans, but they can—especially smaller two-legged munchkins. Making bear noise will help you avoid surprising a lion. Hiking with others and keeping kids close is also a good idea. If you do stumble upon a lion, above all, do not run. Be calm. Group together to appear big. Look at the cat with peripheral vision rather than staring straight on as you back slowly away. If the lion attacks, fight back with everything: rocks, sticks, or kicking.

Water Hazards

Contrary to popular opinion, bears are not the number one cause of death and accidents in Glacier, but rather drowning. Be extremely cautious around lakes, fast-moving streams, and waterfalls where slick moss and algae cover the rocks. Algae blooms, commonly called "rock snot," emerge in late summer, adding to the slipperiness. Waters here are swift, frigid, clogged with submerged obstacles, unforgiving, and sometimes lethal.

Giardia

Lakes and streams can carry parasites like *Giardia lamblia*. If ingested, it causes cramping, nausea, and severe diarrhea for a long period of time. It's easy to avoid giardia by boiling water (for one minute, plus one minute for each

Filter or treat water before drinking.

1,000 feet of elevation above sea level) or using a one-micron filter. Bleach also works (add two drops per quart and then let it sit for 30 minutes). Tap water in the park campgrounds and picnic areas has been treated, and you'll definitely taste the strong chlorine in the hotel water systems.

Dehydration

Many first-time hikers to Glacier are surprised to find they drink substantially more water here than at home. Glacier's winds, altitude, and lower humidity can add up to a fast case of dehydration—which often manifests first as a headache. If you are hiking, drink lots of water—more than you normally would. If you hike with children, monitor their fluid intake.

Altitude

Some visitors from sea level feel the effects of altitude—a lightheadedness, headache, or shortness of breath—in high zones like Logan Pass. Slowing down a hiking pace helps, as does drinking lots of fluids and giving the body time to acclimatize. If symptoms are more dramatic, descend in elevation as soon as possible. Altitude also increases the effects of UV radiation: You might feel cool, but your skin will still burn. To prevent sunburn, use a strong sunscreen and wear sunglasses and a hat.

Crevasses and Snow Bridges

While ice often looks solid to step on, it harbors unseen caverns beneath. Crevasses (large vertical cracks) are difficult to see, and snow bridges can collapse as a person crosses. You're safer just staying off the ice; even Glacier's tiny ice fields have caused fatalities. Also, steep slopes can run into rocks or trees; if sliding for fun, slide only where you have a safe run out.

Hypothermia

Hypothermia is insidious and subtle; it targets exhausted and physically unprepared hikers. The body's inner core loses heat, reducing mental and physical functions. Watch for uncontrolled shivering, incoherence, poor judgment, fumbling, mumbling, and slurred speech. Avoid becoming hypothermic by staying dry, donning rain gear and warm moisture-wicking layers. Leave the cotton clothing back in the car! If someone in your party is hypothermic, get him or her sheltered and into dry clothing. Give warm liquids, but be sure they're nonalcoholic and decaffeinated. If the victim cannot regain body heat, get into a sleeping bag, with you and the victim stripped for skin-to-skin contact.

Blisters

Ill-fitting shoes and incorrect socks cause most blisters. Although cotton socks feel good, they are not the best choice for hiking because they absorb water from the feet and hold it, providing a surface for friction. Synthetic or wool-blend socks wick water away from the skin. To prevent blisters, recognize "hot spots" or rubs, applying moleskin or New-Skin to the sensitive area. In a pinch, duct tape can be slapped on trouble spots. Once a blister occurs, apply special blister bandages or Second Skin, a product developed for burns that cools the blister off and cushions it. Cover Second Skin with moleskin to absorb future rubbing and hold the Second Skin in place.

Hantavirus

The hantavirus infection, which causes flulike symptoms, is contracted by inhaling the dust from deer mice urine and droppings. If you suspect you have the virus, get immediate medical attention. To protect yourself, avoid areas thick with rodents—burrows and woodpiles. Store all food in rodentproof containers. If you find rodent dust in your gear, disinfect with water and bleach (a cup and a half of bleach to one gallon of water).

Mosquitoes and Ticks

Bugs can carry diseases such as West Nile virus and Rocky Mountain spotted fever. Protect yourself by wearing long sleeves and pants as well as using bug repellents in spring and summer when mosquitoes and ticks are common. If you are bitten by a tick, remove it and disinfect the bite; see a doctor if lesions or a rash appears.

Hospitals and Emergencies

For emergencies inside the park, call 406/888-7800. For emergencies outside the park, call 911. On Glacier's west side, the nearest hospitals are in Flathead Valley. Kalispell Regional Medical Center (310 Sunny View Ln., 406/752-5111) and the North Valley Hospital (1600 Hospital Way, Whitefish, 406/863-3500) are 35 minutes from West Glacier and can be up to 90 minutes from Logan Pass depending on traffic. On Glacier's east side, Northern Rockies Medical Center (802 2nd St. E., Cut Bank, 406/873-2251) is approximately an hour from East Glacier and just under two hours from St. Mary.

ESSENTIALS

Getting There

ORIENTATION

Getting your bearings in Glacier is not difficult; the park splits along the Continental Divide into an east and west side, each with several entrances following valley drainages. Two Medicine, St. Mary, and Many Glacier dominate the east, while Lake McDonald and the North Fork cover the west. Although Highway 2 passes briefly through the park's southern tip en route between East and West Glacier, southern entrances into the park's core are all via foot or horseback trails. On the north side, Waterton Lakes National Park provides access via boat, foot, or horseback across the Canadian-U.S. border into Glacier's interior.

Only one route bisects the entire park: Going-to-the-Sun Road. If there is a rush hour in Glacier, it's on this road 11 A.M.–4 P.M. But rush hour is not restricted to weekdays; it's seven days per week mid-July–mid-August.

Most summer visitors love the park's expansive east-side views. Tiny seasonal towns fall away into miles and miles of broad prairie. On a clear day, not much obstructs a view to Ohio. By autumn, not many services remain open to take the Rocky Mountain Front's brutal winds.

The park's heavily forested west side balances remote corners of the North Fork with the busy hub of West Glacier. Mountain

© BECKY LOMAX

snows feed large rivers that drain through the Flathead Valley into Flathead Lake. Mixed with farmland, rural pockets, and resort towns, the fast-growing valley—anchored in winter by recreational skiing—is a year-round enclave for 87,000 people.

SUGGESTED ROUTES
From Western Montana

From I-90 just west of Missoula, U.S. Highway 93 North (Exit 96) leads 103 miles to Flathead Valley. This scenic route passes below the craggy Mission Mountains and along Flathead Lake, the largest freshwater lake west of the Mississippi. Drivers coming from Spokane can cut off miles by exiting I-90 at St. Regis and following the signs to Glacier Park (north on Highway 135, northwest on Highway 200, east on Highway 28). You'll pass the funky little towns of Paradise and Hot Springs, shooting back several decades, before joining Highway 93 heading north at Flathead Lake.

In Kalispell, you'll begin a confusing maze through Flathead Valley as the highway jogs and turns onto different streets. To help, follow signs to the park or West Glacier. In downtown, turn right onto U.S. Highway 2 East, which is also East Idaho Street. Travel for two miles past box stores and car dealerships. Highway 2 will turn left at LaSalle (LaSalle and Highway 2 are the same road), running north 12 miles toward Columbia Falls. At the intersection with Montana Highway 40, the highway turns right; follow it through Columbia Falls, continuing another 16 miles on Highway 2 to West Glacier. Total mileage from I-90 to West Glacier is 145 miles; driving time on the mostly two-lane highway is usually less than three and a half hours, but can be four hours or more with heavy traffic, snow, or road-construction delays. Spokane to West Glacier (271 miles) is a four-and-a-half-hour drive.

From Eastern Montana

This long but extremely scenic approach follows the Rocky Mountain Front, a highway for golden eagle migrations and the buttress for the Bob Marshall Wilderness Complex. This is also the route for those stitching together a visit to both Yellowstone National Park and Glacier. Leave I-90 in **Butte,** turning north toward Helena onto I-15 (Exit 129/227). Drive 101 miles, about one and a half hours, from I-90 to Exit 228 two miles north of Wolf Creek. Turn north here onto U.S. Highway 287.

Northward from here, high sideways winds can slow travel—gusts strong enough to rock RVs and trailers. Follow the narrow two-lane Highway 287 north 66 miles through Augusta to Choteau (pronounced SHOW-toe), the epitome of a Rocky Mountain Front town, with 1,700 residents, grain elevators, and hunting. Here, the road turns left for a bit onto U.S.

PARK ENTRANCE FEES

National parks survive in part on entrance fees. Glacier is no different. Entrance fees are collected at Two Medicine, St. Mary, Many Glacier, West Glacier, Polebridge, and Camas. When stations are unstaffed, self-pay kiosks allow for purchasing passes.

No single-day passes are sold, only seven-day passes:

	May-November	December-April
Single vehicle (admits all persons in vehicle)	$25	$15
Single person (on foot, bicycle, or motorcycle)	$12	$10

Two annual passes are also available but can only be purchased when entrance stations are staffed. Use of these non-transferable passes also requires showing photo ID, but they admit all people in a single vehicle for seven days.

• Glacier National Park Pass $35

This pass can only be purchased in person at entrance stations.

• National Park and Federal Recreation Lands Pass $80

You can buy these at entrance stations, online (www.store.usgs.gov), or by phone (888-ASK USGS, ext. 1). This pass admits a maximum of four adults in the vehicle; children under 16 are free.

In addition, lifetime passes to all national parks are available for U.S. senior citizens ($10) and U.S. citizens with permanent disabilities (free). These must be purchased in person with appropriate documentation at a park entrance station. This pass admits a maximum of four adults in the vehicle; children under 16 are free.

Glacier and U.S. park passes are *not* valid for entrance to Waterton Lakes National Park in Canada.

Glacier offers two entrance-fee-free days: September 25 for National Public Lands Day and November 11 for Veterans Day.

Highway 89, also Main Street. From Choteau, head north 72 miles to Browning. Again, narrow curves slow driving time, but you will soon see Glacier's peaks jutting up from the plains. Just before Browning, you'll join U.S. Highway 2. At Browning's west end, turn left as Highway 2 leaves town. It leads 13 miles to East Glacier. Total driving time from I-90 to East Glacier is about five hours to cover 253 miles. High winds and traffic may slow travel, but the scenery is worth the drive.

From **Great Falls,** two routes lead to East Glacier, both with spectacular views of the Rocky Mountain Front as it pops up off the plains. For easy interstate and highway driving, hop on I-15 heading north to Shelby and then U.S. Highway 2 westward to East Glacier (143 miles). Folks who want to get to Glacier quickly take this two-and-a-half-hour route.

A much more interesting approach with a few less miles, however, strikes off through small rural Rocky Mountain Front towns. From Great Falls, head 10 miles north on I-15 to catch Highway 89 north toward Browning. The route travels past Freezeout Lake, known for its snow goose migration. Connect with the Butte route in Choteau. While this 139-mile route is a few miles shorter, the narrow road makes for slower driving, taking two and three-quarter hours to get to East Glacier—longer if you stop for explorations.

From the Canadian Rockies

Many travelers link Glacier with a trip in the Canadian Rockies national parks—Jasper, Banff, Yoho, and Kootenay. The Flathead Valley connects directly to the Canadian Rockies via Highway 93, which runs north–south from Banff. To get to Glacier, travel south on Highway 93 through British Columbia toward Cranbrook. Four miles (six km) before Cranbrook, merge with Canada 3 heading 36 miles (58 km) east toward Elko. From here, you can continue east to Waterton and Glacier's east side or go south toward West Glacier.

To head to Waterton, stay on Canada 3 for 60 miles (96 km) over Crow's Nest Pass and turn south onto Highway 6 at Pincher. Drive 20 miles (32 km) to Waterton Lakes National Park, where the seasonal Chief Mountain Highway connects with Glacier Park's east side.

To head to West Glacier, drive Highway 93 south at Elko for 24 miles (39 km) toward Roosville on the Canadian-U.S. border. After crossing through customs, continue south 63 miles (101 km) on Highway 93 through Eureka to Whitefish. Drive with caution: Deer frequent the road between Eureka and Whitefish, earning it the nickname "Deer Alley." In downtown Whitefish (with 25 miles/40 km left to go), Highway 93 turns south again at the third stoplight. Drive two miles (three km) to a junction with Montana Highway 40; you'll see signs to Glacier Park. Turn left, toward Columbia Falls. En route Highway 40 becomes U.S. Highway 2. Follow the signs to Glacier Park. Expect total driving time from Banff to West Glacier to be nearly six hours.

From Calgary

From Calgary, Alberta, head south for 113 miles (181 km) on Canada Highway 2 toward Fort Macleod. (A detour to Head-Smashed-In Buffalo Jump, a World Heritage Site, is worth a couple extra hours. Information: 403/553-2731, www.head-smashed-in.com.) Just before town, the highway merges with Canada 3 for a few miles heading east.

If you are starting your Glacier adventure in Waterton Lakes National Park, turn west onto Canada 3 toward Pincher Creek (17 miles, 27 km). At Pincher, turn south onto Canada Highway 6 for 20 miles (32 km) to the park entrance. From Calgary to Waterton is 149 miles (240 km) via Pincher Creek. With speed limits in Canada being slightly slower than in the United States, the distance can be covered in two and three-quarter hours. (Posted in kilometers; 80 kph is 50 mph.)

To head straight to Glacier, continue from Fort Macleod south through Cardston to the Carway-Piegan border crossing. The 165 miles (266 km) from Calgary to the border at Carway should take about three hours. As a general rule, Canadian highway speed limits tend to be a little lower than U.S. speed limits, especially compared to Montana's rural narrow two-laners, which can hit 70 mph. From Carway, drop over the Canadian-U.S. border onto U.S. Highway 89. Drive 19 miles to St. Mary for Going-to-the-Sun Road's east entrance, 25 minutes from the border. To enter the park instead at Many Glacier, turn right at Babb 10 miles south of the border and drive 12 miles to Many Glacier Hotel and Swiftcurrent (40 minutes total).

FLATHEAD VALLEY

The closest and easiest access to Glacier National Park is Flathead Valley. If flights arrive before evening, you can catch a shuttle and be at Lake McDonald inside Glacier Park in time to catch the sunset. Because the airport has no lodging in the immediate vicinity, those coming in on late flights (or wishing to explore Flathead Valley a bit) will need to stay in Kalispell, Whitefish, or Columbia Falls. While many choose Columbia Falls for its proximity between the airport and the park, Whitefish lures others for its resort town atmosphere with shopping, nightlife, Whitefish Lake, and Whitefish Mountain Resort.

Airports

The closest airport to Glacier National Park—**Glacier Park International Airport** (www.iflyglacier.com)—services only a few airlines coming from a handful of locations: Skywest/Delta from Salt Lake City, United/Skywest from Denver, Horizon Air from Seattle, and Allegiant Air from Las Vegas. But don't ask travel agents for a flight to Glacier airport; they won't know what you're talking about. Known with the airlines as Kalispell (FCA), the airport's "international" reputation comes from a few charter flights from Canada. With only three gates, this tiny airport is easy for meeting up with groups, walking to the baggage claim just a few hundred feet from your gate, or finding the car rental desk. In the terminal, the **Kindred Spirit Gift Shop** carries local arts, crafts, and, of course, huckleberry products, and

The Glacier Grille (5 A.M.–6 P.M. daily) serves cafeteria food, espresso, beer, and wine. Inside the airport, you'll find desks for Avis, Hertz, National/Alamo, and Budget rental cars. Hotel and prearranged shuttles are right outside.

Although the airport sits within Kalispell city limits, many visitors are surprised to find the Kalispell hotels 10–15 minutes away in the opposite direction of the park. In fact, the airport sits almost equidistant between downtown Kalispell, Whitefish, and Columbia Falls. But because the airport is only 25 miles from West Glacier, you can sit on the beach at Lake McDonald the day you arrive if you want to maximize your park time.

Although Spokane, Washington, can be an alternative airport, it requires a longer drive to get to the park—about four and a half hours.

Train

For those arriving by train, station stops in West and East Glacier make for a no-brainer arrival adjacent to the park. **Amtrak's** Empire Builder service (800/USA-RAIL or 800/872-7245, www.amtrak.com) between Chicago and Seattle or Portland runs once daily each direction. Both the east- and westbound trains stop in Whitefish, West Glacier, and Essex year-round and summers in East Glacier. Between Seattle and Shelby, Montana, National Park Service guides offer educational services aboard. From Seattle, the eastbound train lands riders conveniently in West Glacier in early morning. Eastbound trains hit Whitefish at 7:26 A.M., West Glacier at 8:16 A.M., Essex at 8:55 A.M., and East Glacier at 9:54 A.M. Westbound arrivals run between 6:45 P.M. (East Glacier) and 8:56 P.M. (Whitefish). Departures are 5–10 minutes later. The train has a reputation for running late; be prepared westbound to arrive in the middle of the night. In winter, avalanches disrupt the schedule. Reservations are imperative midsummer.

Special Amtrak deals are available. Kids ages 2–15 are half price. Seniors, veterans, AAA and NARP members, military personnel, and students can also get 10–15 percent discounts: check Amtrak's website for details. High

© BECKY LOMAX

Hop Amtrak to Glacier from Whitefish Train Depot.

summer travel makes reservations highly recommended. Amtrak's federal funding frequently goes in and out of limbo, with the Glacier route high on the chopping block. Check with Amtrak for changes to schedules and service.

Bus

Bus service to Glacier is nil; no buses connect directly with East or West Glacier. Trailways's **Rimrock Stages** (800/255-7655, www.rimrocktrailways.com) runs one bus daily between Missoula and Whitefish ($39 one-way). It leaves Missoula at 8:15 A.M., arriving at 11:40 A.M. in Whitefish, where you need to grab a place to overnight until the train to West Glacier departs the next morning. Likewise with your return connection: The westbound train arrives in Whitefish in the evening, but you won't be able to catch your bus to Missoula until 11:55 A.M. the next day. On the upside, if you have to hang out, Whitefish is the place to be.

Taxis and Shuttles

Headquartered one mile north of the airport, **Flathead-Glacier Transportation** (406/892-3390 or 800/829-7039, www.fgtrans.com) provides shuttles and transportation to all east- and west-side hubs in Glacier, all towns in Flathead Valley, and Whitefish Mountain Resort. Drivers will meet any airport flights, as well as pick you up at any of the park lodges, at trailheads, or surrounding towns to transport you back to the airport. They even accommodate the early morning and late night flights. Sample one-way rates for one person from the airport are $40 to West Glacier, $55 to Lake McDonald Lodge, $130 to East Glacier, $20 to Whitefish, $20 to downtown Kalispell, and $40 to Bigfork. Each additional person costs $3. Call ahead for reservations.

Taxi companies come and go in the region, but usually Whitefish and Kalispell have taxi service. Check the phone book for current operators.

Tours

Most tours in Glacier Park originate in or adjacent to the park, rather than in Flathead Valley.

CELL PHONES

Probably one of the best inventions for emergencies, cell phones allow immediate access to help. However, in an area as mountainous as Glacier, they do not always work.

Flathead Valley has comprehensive cell phone coverage, but Glacier gets intermittent service. Dealing with a flat tire may require more than a cell phone call to AAA. Throughout much of Going-to-the-Sun Road and Glacier Park, cell-phone reception is sporadic to nonexistent. You can get service in St. Mary, East Glacier, West Glacier, Apgar, and Waterton.

Hikers and backpackers should carry a cell phone for emergencies, but do not rely on it as the sole means of rescue. High mountains and deep valleys often prevent reception. Be prepared to deal with emergencies and self-rescue.

When phones do work in Glacier, use of cell phones in the park requires etiquette:

- Turn off ringers, because phone noise catapults hikers and campers from a natural experience back into the hubbub of modern life.

- If you must make a call (and the phone does work), move away from campsites and other hikers to avoid disrupting their experience.

- In backcountry chalets, go outside and away from people.

- On trails, refrain from using phones in the presence of other hikers.

- Be considerate of other people in the backcountry and their desire to get away from it all.

However, the **Glacier Park, Inc.** (406/892-2525, www.glacierparkinc.com) six-day Great Lodges of Glacier tour includes transfers to and from Amtrak and Flathead Valley's Glacier Park International Airport.

Car Rental

Glacier Park International Airport terminal has four rental-car agencies with desks in the airport: Hertz (U.S. 406/758-2220 or 800/654-3131, www.hertz.com), National/Alamo (406/257-7144 or 800/CAR-RENT, www.nationalcar.com), Avis (406/257-2727 or 800/230-4898, www.avis.com), and Budget (406/755-7500 or 800/527-0700, www.budget. com). Kalispell and Whitefish also have rental-car agencies (find list at www.iflyglacier.com), which will deliver a car to the airport or pick you up.

RV Rental

The closest RV rentals are located near the airport, a 20-minute drive from Glacier. **J & L RV Rentals** (1805 Hwy. 2 W., Columbia Falls, 406/892-7666, www.jandlrvrentals. com) has motor homes and trailers. Although somewhat expensive (starting around $150 per day), RVing is an easy way to tour national parks with the good parts of camping but without the hassle of tents. Be aware, however, of Going-to-the-Sun Road's vehicle length restrictions (21 feet). Only the smallest RVs will be able to cross the highway. With larger RVs, you must use shuttles or bus tours to see the historic road, or rent a car.

Equipment Rental

Glacier Outdoor Center (11957 Hwy. 2 E., West Glacier, 406/888-5454 or 800/235-6781, www.glacierraftco.com) has the most comprehensive collection of rental gear. The center rents outdoor gear for rafting, bicycling, camping, backpacking, fishing, snowshoeing, and cross-country skiing—everything from sleeping bags to stoves, life jackets, rods and waders, headlamps, rain gear, tents, and coolers. Complete camping setups for rafting ($150 plus) and car camping packages ($125 plus) are available, as well as all items singly. Fishing gear ranges $5–50 plus. Reservations are recommended, and you'll need a valid ID to rent.

Other recreational rental gear—skis, kayaks, boats, bicycles—is available through specialty outdoor shops and marinas in Flathead Valley. (See *Recreation* in the *Flathead Valley* chapter.)

Food and Accommodations

Because Glacier is so close to the airport, many travelers go directly into the park on the same day. Likewise with flying out. However, for those adding Flathead Valley explorations to their itineraries, lodging varies from dirt cheap to high end, and many offer complimentary airport shuttles. No lodging exists in the immediate airport vicinity, but rather in Columbia Falls, downtown Kalispell, and Whitefish (check the *Flathead Valley* chapter for accommodations and rates). To be closest to Glacier, at 20 minutes away, head to Columbia Falls, nine miles from the airport. Lodging in "C Falls" runs the gamut from a budget motel to a golf resort. Downtown Kalispell, with its chain hotels, also is nine miles from the airport, but in the opposite direction from the park. The resort town of Whitefish sits 11 miles away, with independent motels, B&Bs, and ski and golf resorts. Both Kalispell and Whitefish are approximately a 40-minute drive from West Glacier.

Other than the cafeteria inside the airport, no restaurants are close. En route to Glacier, Columbia Falls has fast food, sandwiches, gooey ribs, and Mexican fare. Those looking for fine-dining experiences should gravitate to Whitefish or Kalispell. Check the *Flathead Valley* chapter for restaurant options.

GREAT FALLS

Straddling the mighty Missouri River, Great Falls, Montana, is an east-side gateway to Glacier. But the additional distance to Glacier and lack of easy connections with Amtrak and buses make renting a car preferable to drive the 143 miles to the park. With a flight arriving by late afternoon, you can be in East Glacier to watch the sunset that same day.

For travelers coming fairly prepared, Great Falls can work as a travel hub. But for those requiring camping equipment or RV rentals, none are available in the city itself, nor on

Glacier's east side. The nearest equipment and RV rentals are on the park's west side in West Glacier and Flathead Valley, both a convoluted detour out of the way from Great Falls.

If you have time to spend in Great Falls, two things are worth exploring. Squeeze in the **Lewis and Clark National Historic Trail Interpretive Center** (4201 Giant Springs Rd., 406/727-8733, hours and days vary by season, adults $8, kids 15 and younger free), with its historical displays, live demonstrations, and multimedia shows. Take in the **C.M. Russell Museum** (400 13th St. N., 406/727-8787, www.cmrussell.org, hours and days vary by season, adults $9, students $4), which celebrates the work of the famous Western painter Charlie Russell (1864–1926), who summered in his cabin on Glacier's Lake McDonald and is known for his early West scenes—depictions of cowboys, mountains, hunters, and horses.

Airport

Great Falls International Airport (GTF) (406/727-3404, www.gtfairport.com) receives air service from Delta/Sky West from Salt Lake City, Northwest from Minneapolis, United from Denver, Allegiant Air from Las Vegas, and Horizon Air from Seattle. Like the Kalispell airport, its international label comes from a couple charter flights from Canada. Located outside town, the airport is convenient for picking up on-site rental cars but requires hotel-provided shuttles or a taxi ride to access hotels and restaurants in town, 10 minutes away.

Train

From Great Falls, the closest westbound train depot is Shelby, 87 miles north, where **Amtrak's** Empire Builder (800/USA-RAIL or 800/872-7245, www.amtrak.com) runs from Chicago westbound once daily past Glacier. Catch a bus to Shelby, and you can ride to East Glacier, a summer only stop. National Park Service interpretive guides join the train between Shelby and Seattle. From Shelby, the train leaves daily at 5:22 P.M., arriving in East Glacier at 6:45 P.M., Essex at 7:41 P.M., West

Glacier at 8:23 P.M., and Whitefish at 8:56 P.M. On this route, Amtrak tends to run late. Not just five minutes late, but up to several hours behind schedule in winter with avalanches. Be prepared to contend with arriving in the middle of the night. Reservations are imperative midsummer.

Special Amtrak deals are available. Kids ages 2–15 are half price. Seniors, veterans, AAA and NARP members, military personnel, and students can also get 10–15 percent discounts: check Amtrak's website for details. Amtrak is frequently threatened to have its federal funding yanked. If funding is cut, the Empire Builder usually faces the axe. Check with Amtrak for any changes to schedules and service.

Bus

Trailways's **Rimrock Stages** (800/255-7655, www.rimrocktrailways.com) connect Montana locales via Butte to Great Falls, but not farther to Glacier Park nor Shelby for connecting with Amtrak. However, in 2008, **Northern Transit Interlocal** (406/470-0727, www.toolecountymt.gov) started running a 15-passenger van between Shelby and Great Falls, twice each direction on Monday and Thursday. With prior arrangement, the service will pick you up at the Great Falls Airport, or you can catch the bus at the Great Falls Transit Transfer Center (326 1st Avenue South). It stops at the Amtrak depot in Shelby. It's a free service, but they do accept donations. This same bus service also operates a Great Falls–Kalispell route twice a week. The bus passes through Browning, East Glacier, Essex, and West Glacier. Call for schedules for both services.

Taxis

Some hotels provide airport shuttle service. Otherwise, **Diamond Cab** (406/453-3241) is the only option to hop into town from the airport.

Car Rental

Great Falls has most national rental car chains. Alamo (406/727-0273 or 800/462-5266, www.

alamo.com), Hertz (406/761-6641 or 800/654-3131, www.hertz.com), Dollar (406/453-3535 or 800/800-4000, www.dollar.com), National (406/453-4386 or 800/227-7368, www.nationalcar.com), and Avis (406/761-7610 or 800/230-4898, www.avis.com) are located right in the airport terminal. The airport's website (www.gtfairport.com) lists other rental-car agencies with offices elsewhere than the airport terminal. They will either pick you up by shuttle or deliver your car to you.

Food and Accommodations

Great Falls has hotels and motels ranging from low end to moderately priced accommodations, but nothing too upscale. Most national hotel chains are downtown. For hotels offering airport shuttles, check the Great Falls Airport website (www.gtfairport.com) or the Great Falls Convention and Visitors Bureau (800/735-8535, www.greatfallscvb.visitmt.com).

For a filling meal at a reasonable price and a view overlooking the Missouri River, head for **MacKenzie River Pizza Company** (500 River Dr. S., 406/761-0085, 11 A.M.–9 P.M. daily, until 10 P.M. Fri. and Sat. nights, $7–20), Montana's creative answer to pizza chains. The restaurant serves cowboy nachos, giant salads and sandwiches, eclectic pizzas, and Montana microbrews.

CALGARY

Calgary, Alberta, is the closest metropolitan city to Glacier. If you schedule your trip in mid-July, you can take in one of the biggest rodeos in the region—the Calgary Stampede (403/269-9822 or 800/661-1767, www.calgarystampede.com). However, travel from Calgary to Glacier or Waterton can be a challenge. No train connection is available. No bus route goes all the way to Waterton, nor Glacier. For ease, most visitors traveling from Calgary rent a vehicle. With an early afternoon flight arrival, you can be walking the beach at Waterton Lake in the evening.

Airport

Calgary International Airport (YYC) (403/735-1200, www.calgaryairport.com) bustles with flights from Tokyo, London, and Frankfurt. It has restaurants, shopping, and more than 25 airlines servicing the area. Airport shuttles connect with downtown, hotels, rental-car agencies, and the Greyhound Bus Terminal. Because Calgary is still 149 miles (240 km) from Waterton, most visitors heading to the park rent a car. Others chop off part of the distance by flying via Air Canada (888/247-2262, www.aircanada.com) south to Lethbridge (www.lethbridgecountyairport.com, code YQL), where they rent a car to drive 87 miles (140 km) to Waterton.

Train

If you're traveling by **VIA Rail Canada** (800/VIA-RAIL or 800/842-7245, www.viarail.ca), you'll see lots of Canada but have a difficult time getting to Waterton and Glacier. Canadian trains hit Winnipeg and Vancouver, which are roughly the same latitude as Waterton, but in between the route jogs north, bypassing southern Alberta and southeastern British Columbia. The closest you can get to Waterton is Edmonton, 332 miles (534 km) away. Most train travelers switch to air or bus travel to Calgary and then rent a car.

Bus and Shuttle

Greyhound Canada (403/265-9111 or 800/661-8747, www.greyhound.ca, no reservations accepted) services cities in southern Alberta, but not Waterton. Bus service connects with Calgary International Airport, and daily buses run from Calgary to Pincher Creek, but no farther: In Pincher Creek, you're stuck 31 miles (50 km) from Waterton, with no car rentals available. You can hire a cab (Crystal Cabs, 403/627-4262) for around CDN$70 one-way.

Airport Shuttle Express (403/509-1570, www.airportshuttleexpress.com) runs charters from the Calgary airport to Waterton. A charter van can be economical for small groups to split the $360–380 fee and tip for the driver. Service is also available to East Glacier, Browning, and all Amtrak stations around Glacier.

Car Rental

Most major car-rental chains have desks inside the Calgary Airport terminal or within a shuttle hop down the road. Vehicles can be booked from home through American sister companies: Alamo (800/462-5266, www.alamo.com), Hertz (800/654-3131, www.hertz.com), Dollar (800/800-4000, www.dollar.com), National (800/227-7368, www.nationalcar.com), Budget (800/472-3325, www.budget.com), and Avis (800/230-4898, www.avis.com).

RV Rental

Two RV-rental companies are within three kilometers (less than two miles) from the Calgary Airport and offer transfers from the airport and airport hotels: **Canada RV Rentals** (250/814-0251 or 866/814-0253, www.canada-rv-rentals.com) and **CanaDream** (403/291-1000 or 800/461-7368, www.canadream.com). Calgary also has other large RV rental chains. Check in the phone book for listings.

RVing is a fun but somewhat pricey way (small rigs start at CDN$150 per day) to tour national parks without having to put tents up and down each day; however, be aware of Going-to-the-Sun Road's vehicle-length restrictions (21 feet). You may have to supplement your RV tour with shuttles or red bus tours to see the historic landmark, as only the smallest RVs are permitted to cross the highway.

Equipment Rental

For those needing outdoor gear, **Calgary Outdoor Centre** (2500 University Dr. NW, 403/220-5038, www.calgaryoutdoorcentre.ca) rents equipment for reasonable rates. It has gear for camping, backpacking, boating, bicycling, fishing, snowshoeing, climbing, and skiing. Per-day rates for tents start at CDN$10, backpacks CDN$9, GPS units CDN$7, stoves CDN$4, and sleeping bags CDN$6 daily. Rafts, kayaks, skis, canoes, mountain bikes, climbing gear, and car racks are also available,

as well as clothing, rain gear, and hiking boots. Call to reserve equipment ahead of time, a must during midsummer; a nonrefundable deposit by credit card is required. When you pick up your gear, try it on to be sure it fits and have the staff demonstrate how to use unfamiliar equipment. You'll also need a driver's license or photo ID to rent gear.

Food and Accommodations

The airport terminal itself houses the extremely convenient **Delta Calgary Airport Hotel** (403/250-8722 or 877/814-7706, www.deltahotels.com, CDN$235–420). Within a few miles of the airport, major chain hotels start at $110 per night. Some offer airport shuttles. For additional hotel information and reservations, check http://calgary.airporthotelguide.com or contact Tourism Calgary (403/263-8510, www.tourismcalgary.com).

Budget-minded travelers may want to head for a hostel. The **HI-Calgary City Centre Hostel** (403/670-7580, www.hihostels.ca) has dorm beds costing CDN$27–39 per night. If you are planning on staying in hostels across Canada as part of your trip, purchase a Hostelling International $35 membership, which gives 10–15 percent discounts on nightly rates.

Canadian cuisine is somewhat bland, but a few Alberta specialties merit a taste. Calgary is in the heart of cattle country; grass-fed Alberta beef graces menus in all forms. Buffalo, too. At the high end, it's amazingly tender and sweet; at the lower end, it's still decent. Expect to find the fries accompanying your burger in Canada to be different: They may have gravy on top. And contrary to many towns east of the Rocky Mountains where steak and potato fare reigns, Calgary is much more internationally cosmopolitan, with a good share of ethnic restaurants. Don't forget: Canada's 7 percent GST (Goods and Services Tax) will be added on lodging and food bills.

Getting Around

DRIVING

Driving in Glacier National Park is not easy. Narrow roads built for cars in the 1930s barely fit today's SUVs, much less RVs and trailers. With no shoulders and sharp curves, roads require reduced speeds and shifting into second gear on extended descents to avoid the fumes of burning brakes. Two roads cross the Continental Divide: Going-to-the-Sun Road bisects the park, while U.S. Highway 2 hugs Glacier's southern border. Both are two-laners; however, Going-to-the-Sun Road is the more difficult drive, climbing 1,500 feet higher on a skinnier, snakier road than Highway 2. It's also currently undergoing reconstruction. Going-to-the-Sun Road opens in summer mid-June–mid-September, while Highway 2 is open year-round. Going-to-the-Sun Road does not permit RVs and trailer-rig combos over 21 feet long.

Paved two-lane roads also lead to Two Medicine, St. Mary, Many Glacier, and Waterton. But don't have fantasies here: Just because roads are paved doesn't mean that they are smooth. Frost heaves and sinkholes pockmark them, bouncing passengers and slowing travel. Montana is also the land of dusty, potholed dirt roads: On the west side, two notorious bumpy roads lead up the North Fork Valley; on the east side, a dirt road leads into the Cut Bank Valley. In some places they are decent; in others they are as bad as they can be without requiring a four-wheel drive. Larger RVs and those with trailers will not be comfortable on some dirt roads.

Service Stations

Gas up before you go! You won't find service stations on every corner here. Gas is available in West Glacier, East Glacier, St. Mary, Babb, and Waterton, but few of the stations can mend severely broken-down vehicles. For big vehicle work, you'll need to hit Browning or Flathead Valley.

MAPS AND PLANNERS

Park maps that include both Glacier and Waterton are handed out at every entrance station and available at visitors centers, ranger stations, and online (www.nps.gov/glac). These maps are perfect for driving tours and perhaps a short walk or two. However, for those heading into the backcountry on day hikes and backpacking trips, a topographical map is more useful. Four *Trails Illustrated* maps are available: the large Glacier, including Waterton, and more detailed Many Glacier, North Fork, and Two Medicine maps. The *USGS Glacier Park* does not include Waterton. Buy these topographical maps ($10–12) through **Glacier Natural History Association** (406/888-5756, www.glacierassociation.org). For more detailed maps, USGS maps are available in the 7.5 Minute Series at Flathead Valley sporting goods store or through USGS (888/ASK-USGS or 888/275-8747, http://store.usgs.gov). For hiking Waterton, you'll find

© BECKY LOMAX

Prepare for narrow, cliffside roads in Glacier.

the best topographical map at the Waterton Lakes Visitor Information Centre (403/859-5133). You can also order it online (www. gemtrek.com). The Gem Trek Publishing map (CDN$10) shows roads, trails, and bike routes, and adds trail descriptions for easy, moderate, and strenuous hikes. It also includes the eastern end of Akamina-Kishinena Provincial Park and the Goat Haunt area of Glacier.

For hiking trails, area brochure maps (Many Glacier, Lake McDonald, Two Medicine, Logan Pass, and St. Mary) are available at ranger stations, visitors centers, hotel activity desks, and online. These do not have as much detail as topographical maps but can work in a pinch for day hikes on well-signed trails.

River floaters can find river maps in the *Three Forks of the Flathead Float Guide* for $13 at Glacier Association bookstores (406/888-5756, www.glacierassociation.org).

Yearly, the park service updates its *Glacier Vacation Planner,* a newspaper listing current campground, road, park, visitors center, border, trail, and safety concerns. Call the park for a mailed copy (406/888-7800), or the current edition is also online (www.nps.gov/glac).

For maps and information about national forests and the Bob Marshall Wilderness adjacent to the park, contact the **Hungry Horse Ranger Station** (10 Hungry Horse Dr., Hungry Horse, 406/387-3800, www.fs.fed. us/r1/flathead). For Lewis and Clark National Forest, call the Rocky Mountain Ranger Station (1102 Main Ave. NW, Choteau, 406/466-5341, www.fs.fed.us/r1/lewisclark).

SHUTTLES
Bus Shuttles

Inside Glacier, the National Park Service runs several **free shuttle** routes July 1–Labor Day. These are shuttles, not guided tours. Between Apgar and St. Mary, they stop at 17 points denoted by interpretive signs on Going-to-the-Sun Road. Get on or off at any of the stops. No tickets are needed; no reservations are taken. These extremely popular shuttles enable point-to-point hiking on some of Glacier's most spectacular trails. West-side Sun Road shuttles depart

Free park shuttles pick up riders at 17 stops on Going-to-the-Sun Road.

every 15–30 minutes, with stops at the Apgar Transit Center, Sprague Creek Campground, Lake McDonald Lodge, Avalanche Creek, The Loop, and Logan Pass. The 30-mile ride from the transit center to Logan Pass takes 90 minutes or more. Shuttles also loop through Apgar, connecting the campground, village, and transit center. East-side shuttles depart every 30 minutes from St. Mary Visitor Center. The one-hour shuttle reaches Logan Pass in 18 miles after stopping at Rising Sun, Sun Point, Sunrift Gorge, St. Mary Falls Trailhead, Gunsight Pass Trailhead, and Siyeh Bend. Both routes begin uphill service at 7 A.M., with the last departures from Logan Pass at 7 P.M. On the west side, several routes service the road; confirm your destination when you board to be sure you have the right shuttle.

Glacier Park, Inc. (406/892-2525, www.glacierparkinc.com, $10–50 one-way) runs a daily van service north–south on the park's east side early June–late September. It links East Glacier, Two Medicine, Cut Bank Creek, St. Mary, Many Glacier, Chief Mountain Customs, and Waterton. No reservations are taken, and you pay in cash when you board. Between July–Labor Day, additional shuttles run from Many Glacier to St. Mary to accommodate hikers on the Highline-Swiftcurrent and Piegan Trail. Call or check online for current schedules.

By reservation, **Sun Tours** (406/226-9220 or 800/786-9220, www.glaciersuntours.com, June–Sept.) can shuttle hikers from St. Mary or East Glacier to east-side trailheads. Costs vary with numbers of passengers, gear, time, and location.

Running shuttles year-round by reservation, **Flathead-Glacier Transportation** (406/892-3390 or 800/829-7039, www.fgtrans.com, $20–240 one-way) picks up travelers and backpackers at Glacier International Airport and transports them to Chief Mountain Customs, Many Glacier, St. Mary, Two Medicine, East Glacier, West Glacier, Polebridge, and Highway 2 trailheads. Rates are for first person; each additional person pays $3. They also run shuttles to Flathead Valley locations.

In Waterton, **Tamarack Outdoor Outfitters** (Tamarack Village Square, 214 Mount View Rd., 403/859-2378, www.hikewaterton.com, late May–early Oct., CDN$12–60) shuttles hikers to the popular Carthew-Alderson trailhead or to Chief Mountain Customs to catch GPI's east side Glacier shuttle.

Boat Shuttles

Hikers and backpackers also use tour boats as hiking shuttles to lop off foot miles. In Glacier, **Glacier Park Boat Company** (406/257-2426, www.glacierparkboats.com, June–Sept., $6–11 one-way, kids half price) carts hikers across Two Medicine Lake and in Many Glacier across Swiftcurrent and Josephine Lakes. Both add early morning Hiker Express shuttles July–August. Pay with cash at the docks; you do not need reservations for catching a return boat. If the last boat back is full, the boat company continues to run shuttles until all hikers are accommodated.

In Waterton, **Waterton Shoreline Cruises** (403/859-2362, www.watertoncruise.com, adults CDN$18–36, kids CDN$9–18) runs boat shuttles to the Crypt Lake Trailhead (late May–early October), and the tour boat to Goat Haunt, U.S.A., functions as a hiker shuttle June–mid-September for round-trip or one-way rides.

TOURS
Bus Tours

Two bus-tour companies operate in Glacier Park, both traveling the scenic Going-to-the-Sun Road. You'll get the "inside story" on the park from both of their guides.

Departing from East Glacier, Browning, St. Mary, and West Glacier, **Sun Tours** (406/226-9220 or 800/786-9220, www.glaciersuntours.com, June–Sept., adults $40–70, kids $15–20, park entrance fees not included) leads four- and seven-hour daily tours over Going-to-the-Sun Road in 25-passenger air-conditioned buses with huge windows. Interpretation is steeped in Blackfeet cultural history and park lore.

The historic **red jammer buses** with roll-back canvas tops are operated by Glacier Park,

© BECKY LOMAX

Historic red buses provide park tours.

Inc. (406/892-2525, www.glacierparkinc.com, late May–late Sept.). Daily tours (adults $30–85, kids half price, park entrance fees and meals not included) depart from all the park lodges for Going-to-the-Sun Road, Waterton, and other park environs. The company also guides the popular **Great Lodges of Glacier** tour (single $2,535, double $1,899 per person, kids 11 and younger $719), a six-day romp through four of the park's historic lodges (offered late June–mid-September). The tour begins and ends in East Glacier, but pickups are available from Glacier Park International Airport in Flathead Valley and Amtrak. Traveling by historic red jammer buses, the tour stays at Glacier Park Lodge, Prince of Wales Hotel, Many Glacier Hotel, and Lake McDonald Lodge. Rates include lodging, meals, transportation around Glacier, boat cruises, and short walks. All 15 of their tour dates sell out, so make reservations early.

Boat Tours

Five glacier-carved lakes in Waterton-Glacier International Peace Park have scenic boat tours. In Glacier, **Glacier Park Boat Company** (406/257-2426, www.glacierparkboats.com, June–Sept., $11–22, kids half price) operates daily boat tours on Lake McDonald, Two Medicine Lake, St. Mary Lake, and in Many Glacier on Swiftcurrent and Josephine Lakes. Departure times vary. Buy tickets (cash only) at the docks. In Waterton, scenic boat tours travel down Waterton Lake across the international border. **Waterton Shoreline Cruises** (403/859-2362, www.watertoncruise.com, May–early Oct., adults CDN$36, teens CDN$18, kids 4–12 CDN$12, under 4 free) departs several times daily, with a stop at Goat Haunt, U.S.A. late May–mid-September. Purchase tickets at the dock.

Hiking Tours

For day hikers and backpackers, **Glacier Guides** (406/387-5555 or 800/321-7238, www.glacierguides.com) is the only company authorized to guide hikes in the park. They lead day hikes, backpacking trips, custom hikes, and

© BECKY LOMAX

Two boats on two lakes in Many Glacier provide tours and shuttles.

chalet hikes June–mid-September. Their five-day Glacier Challenge puts together some of the park's top day hikes with catered camping ($910). Their most popular trip is the six-day Ultimate, which hikes to both historic backcountry chalets (Granite and Sperry) and includes a stay at Belton Chalet ($1,805). On each of these tours, the guides lead daily hikes 6–15 miles in length. The company also departs weekly with three-, four-, and six-day backpacking trips and offers a 10-day Continental Divide backpacking adventure ($140–145/day). You can also hire a Sherpa ($175/day) to carry your gear. Equipment, guide service, transportation in Glacier, and most meals are included.

Many tour companies—Backroads, Natural Habitat Adventures, Smithsonian Journeys, to name a few—run multiday hiking tours in Glacier, but they all subcontract with Glacier Guides for leading the hikes.

BY RV
Road Restrictions
Going-to-the-Sun Road restricts RVs and trailers. From bumper to bumper, vehicles must be 21 feet or shorter to drive the road between Avalanche Campground on the west and Sun Point on the east. A truck- or car-trailer combination must also be under 21 feet. The maximum width allowed, including mirrors, is 8 feet; maximum height is 10 feet. Despite meeting width and height requirements, camper drivers still feel pinched as they navigate the skinny lanes hemmed in by a vertical 1,000-foot wall and a three-foot-tall guardrail in construction zones.

Don't lose heart just because you travel by RV! You can still see the famed Going-to-the-Sun Road via GPI's red bus tours, Sun Tours, and free park shuttles, or rent a car in West Glacier, East Glacier, or St. Mary.

Camping
Several campgrounds inside the park accommodate larger RVs and fifth wheels. Apgar can handle the largest RVs, up to 40 feet. Fish Creek, Many Glacier, and St. Mary have sites that can fit RVs up to 35 feet. Two Medicine can accommodate RVs up to 32 feet. Only the shorter RVs can fit into sites at Rising Sun (up to 25 feet), Avalanche (up to 26 feet), and Sprague Creek (up to 21 feet, but no towed units). Large units are not recommended at Bowman Lake, Cut Bank, Kintla Lake, Logging Creek, and Quartz Creek.

Campgrounds inside the park do not have hookups, nor do campgrounds in adjacent national forests or the North Fork. (Waterton Lakes National Park, however, is an exception, for the Townsite Campground has hookups.) If hookups are essential, head outside Glacier Park to commercial campgrounds in West Glacier, East Glacier, St. Mary, Flathead Valley, outside Waterton Park, and along Highway 2.

Disposal Stations
Seven locations inside Glacier Park have disposal stations: Apgar, Fish Creek, Many Glacier, Rising Sun, St. Mary, Two Medicine, and Waterton. Many private campgrounds at West Glacier, St. Mary, and East Glacier have disposal stations. The North Fork has none. In Waterton

TRAVEL GREEN IN GLACIER

Montana may not be up to par with big cities for recycling infrastructure, but Glacier is making advances. Because the park is located at the apex of three continental watersheds, it is a prime place to practice green habits.

CUTTING EMISSIONS

- Park your car to take shuttles. Free shuttles run July–Labor Day on Going-to-the-Sun Road, and other fee shuttles link points on Glacier's east side, including Waterton.

- The historic red bus fleet converted to a bi-fuel system that allows the buses to run on propane as well as gasoline.

- Many park restaurant menus now include local products – wine, beer, meats, and veggies – to reduce long transportation.

RECYCLING

- All campgrounds, picnic areas, and visitors centers are equipped with recycling bins adjacent to bear-resistant garbage cans. Please recycle aluminum and plastic. Glacier Park, Inc., operator of most of the park lodges, provides blue containers for recycling collection in the rooms of each hotel.

- Glass is problematic in Montana, as the state has no recycling infrastructure for it yet. If you are driving, consider carrying your glass containers home with you to recycle. Glacier Park, Inc. converted their beers to kegs in their bars and to cans in stores to eliminate the waste from glass bottles. You can even buy Montana microbrews in aluminum cans. The company is also phasing out the use and sale of all plastic beverage bottles.

ECO-CONSCIOUSNESS

- The Apgar Transit Center was built with LEED principles in lighting, water, waster, construction, and landscaping. Native plants, trees, and soils from the site were reused.

- Glacier Park, Inc., operator of most of the park's historic lodges, achieved the ISO 14001 Certification for Environmental Management. Their lodges now use biodegradable products for carryout foods, CCF light bulbs in rooms, ecofriendly cleaning products, bulk purchasing, and organic BeeKind room amenities that support bee pollination. The company's commercial laundry in East Glacier reduced water consumption with the purchase of a new washer in 2009.

National Park, you'll find dump stations at the Townsite and Crandell campgrounds and commercial campgrounds outside the park.

Repairs

Should you need repair services, drive into the Flathead Valley, where your best bet is to consult RV repairs in the phone book and start calling to find who can fit you in to their repair schedule the soonest. If you cannot drive to the Flathead, **Rocky Mountain Repair** (181 Kelly Rd., Kalispell, 406/253-9694) offers mobile services and can repair many things where you are, but you'll definitely pay more for them to come to Glacier. In Waterton, **Pat's Gas Station** (224 Mount View Rd., 403/859-2266) can do minor repairs.

BY BICYCLE

Glacier is a tough place to bicycle. No shoulders, narrow roads, curves, and drivers gawking at scenery instead of the road all shove the biker into a precarious position. With that caveat said, for a cyclist nothing competes with bicycling Going-to-the-Sun Road! It's one of the country's premier bicycling routes. Other roads surrounding Glacier also make good rides, particularly the 142-mile loop linking Going-to-the-Sun Road and Highways 89, 49, and 2. Roadie racers do it in one day; tourers ride the loop in two or three days.

Bike Trails

Designated bike trails are few and far between in Waterton-Glacier. In fact, Glacier has only

Bikers relish touring Going-to-the-Sun Road.

two trails, both in the Apgar area—one paved, one dirt. No bicycles are allowed on any other backcountry trails in Glacier. In Waterton, four trails permit bicycles.

Campsites

Several of Glacier's campgrounds maintain campsites specifically for bikers and hikers: Apgar, Fish Creek, Sprague Creek, Avalanche, Rising Sun, St. Mary, Many Glacier, and Two Medicine. Held until 9 P.M., the sites are shared, holding up to eight people who pay $5 per person. If these sites are full, you must find a regular designated unoccupied tent site (impossible midsummer late at night). Hiker-biker sites have special bear-resistant food storage.

Safety

Because of narrow, shoulderless roads, bikers should have some riding ability before hitting Glacier's roads. Drainage grates, ice, and debris can throw bikes off balance quickly, adding to the challenge. Although bicyclists on Going-to-the-Sun Road are fairly commonplace, many drivers are so agog at the view that they may not be fully conscious of your presence—which

is a good reason to wear a helmet and bright colors. Skinny, shoulderless roads demand riding in single file. For added protection, be sure your bike has reflectors on both ends, and use lights in fog and at dawn, dusk, or night.

Restrictions

Because of high traffic and narrow lanes, Glacier enforces bicycling restrictions on Going-to-the-Sun Road's west side. Between June 15 and Labor Day, two sections of the road are closed 11 A.M.–4 P.M.: between Apgar Loop Road and Sprague Creek Campground; eastbound (going uphill) from Logan Creek to Logan Pass. The ride from Sprague to Logan Creek takes about 45 minutes; the climb from Logan Creek to Logan Pass usually takes about three hours.

Repairs

Bring spare tubes and brake pads, a pump, and equipment to effect minor repairs yourself. The park doesn't have bike shops to bail you out. For big repairs, head to the bike shops in Flathead Valley. (See the *Flathead Valley* chapter for suggestions.)

BY MOTORCYCLE

Motorcyclists relish riding Going-to-the-Sun Road. On sunny days, the ride is unparalleled; on inclement days, it's bone-chilling. Many motorcyclists gravitate to Montana because the state requires helmets only for those 17 years old and younger. However, since most drivers on Going-to-the-Sun Road find their attention severely divided between the scenery and the road, you may want to consider wind-in-the-hair versus protection if hit. In Waterton, helmets are required.

Motorcyclists are allowed to use the shared biker-hiker campsites ($5 per person) at the park's major campgrounds. These are first come, first served and held until 9 P.M.

If you need repairs, the Flathead Valley has several motorcycle shops. Some specialize in one brand over another, including Harley-Davidsons. Your best bet is to check under *motorcycle repair* in the phone book to pick the appropriate service for your machine.

RESOURCES

Suggested Reading

DRIVING GUIDES

Guthrie, C. W., Martha Cheney, and Diane Krage. *Glacier National Park Legends And Lore: Along Going To The Sun Road.* Helena, MT: Farcountry Press, 2002. An 88-page, mile-by-mile tour of the historic road with Native American tales from Hugh Monroe, known as Rising Wolf of the Blackfeet.

Schmidt, Thomas. *National Geographic Road Guide to Glacier and Waterton Lakes National Park.* Washington, DC: National Geographic, 2004. A handy 93-page guide to driving the park's roads. Each section is complete with a map, nature notes, landscape features, and stops.

GEOLOGY

Alt, David, and Donald W. Hyndman. *Roadside Geology of Montana.* Missoula, MT: Mountain Press, 1986. Although Glacier's roads are treated minimally here, the diagrams and descriptions are useful even to nongeologists. It is the best resource for geology on roads outside the park.

Raup, Omar B., Robert L. Earhart, James W. Whipple, and Paul E. Carrara. *Geology Along Going-to-the-Sun Road.* West Glacier, MT: Glacier Natural History Association, 1983. An easy-to-read 63-page geology guide for folks with no science background. Maps, 21 stops, and diagrams describe the geologic phenomena on the historic highway, along with great photos showing rock formations.

GRIZZLY BEARS

Chadwick, Doug. *True Griz.* San Francisco, CA: Sierra Club Books, 2003. True stories of four grizzly bears—their survival and deaths. Chadwick is a very reputable bear biologist.

Herrero, Stephen. *Bear Attacks: Their Causes and Avoidance.* Guilford, CT: The Lyons Press, 2002. Somewhat sensationalized with attention to gory detail, Herrero's book paints a picture of the myriad reasons for bear attacks while also covering safety and how to avoid attacks. Not for light sleepers who plan to go into the backcountry. Herrero is one of the leading authorities on bear research.

McMillion, Scott. *Mark of the Grizzly.* Helena, MT: Falcon Press Publishing Company, 1998. McMillion tells the stories behind 18 different grizzly bear attacks. He doesn't shy away from the gore, nor does he become preachy or judgmental, but he does examine each attack in detail to determine what we learn about bears.

Schneider, Bill. *Bear Aware.* Helena, MT: Falcon Press Publishing Co., 2004. This handy little 96-page book is packed with advice on how to hike safely in bear country. One section tackles bear myths, debunking them with facts.

WILDLIFE

Chadwick, Doug. *The Wolverine Way.* Ventura, CA: Patagonia Inc., 2010. Stories of the gluttonous creatures that epitomize wilderness gleaned from research in Glacier.

Fisher, Chris. *Birds of the Rocky Mountains.* Edmonton, AB: Lone Pine Publishing, 1997. A Lone Pine Field Guide for birds found in the Rocky Mountains—every species from raptors to waterfowl, songbirds to woodpeckers. Large drawings help with identification, and descriptions include details on size, range, habitat, nesting, and feeding. Details point out differences between similar species.

Fisher, Chris, Don Pattie, and Tamara Hartson. *Mammals of the Rocky Mountains.* Edmonton, AB: Lone Pine Publishing, 2000. A Lone Pine Field Guide for 91 species of animals found in the Rocky Mountains— a breeze to use. Each animal has details on physical description, behavior, habitat, food, denning, range, and young. Similar species are described to point out differences for identification.

Harada, Sumio, and Karen Yale. *Mountain Goats of Glacier National Park.* Helena, MT: Farcountry Press, 2008. Harada has photographed mountain goats for the past two decades in Glacier. Yale chronicles their behavior.

Wilkinson, Todd, and Michael H. Francis. *Watching Glacier's Wildlife.* Helena, MT: Riverbend Publishing, 2002. A 96-page guide to when, where, and how to see Glacier's wildlife.

HISTORY

Buchholtz, C. W. *Man in Glacier.* West Glacier, MT: Glacier Natural History Association, 1976. It's a hard book to read because of its large size with small print (it would be much better as a regular-sized paperback), but it's thick with information on Glacier's human history, from early Native Americans to park rangers.

Djuff, Ray, and Chris Morrison. *Glacier's Historic Hotels and Chalets: View with a Room.* Helena, MT: Farcountry Press, 2001. Loaded with historical photos, this quasi-coffee-table book tells the story behind each of Glacier Park's lodges and chalets, including chalets no longer existing. A great background read for anyone who falls in love with Glacier's historic lodges.

Glacier Centennial Program Committee, ed. *A View Inside Glacier National Park.* Glacier National Park, 2010. This collection of 100 stories about Glacier's 100 years celebrated the park's centennial in 2010.

Guthrie, Carol. *All Aboard for Glacier: The Great Northern Railway and Glacier National Park.* Helena, MT: Farcountry Press, 2004. For train buffs, the history of the Great Northern Railway building up Glacier as a destination for their riders.

Guthrie, C. W. *Glacier National Park: The First 100 Years.* Helena, MT: Farcountry Press, 2008. The official centennial book contains rich color and historic photos in its decade by decade waltz through Glacier's history.

Hanna, Warren L. *Montana's Many-Splendored Glacierland.* Grand Forks, ND: University of North Dakota Foundation, 1987. The fact that Hanna's book is somewhat outdated doesn't matter here; he covers historical detail that no one else does—from Marias Pass to Native Americans, dude-wranglers, and celebrity visitors. Historical photos are also included.

Holterman, Jack. *Place Names of Glacier National Park.* Helena, MT: Riverbend Publishing, 2006. A list of 663 park names—how peaks, passes, lakes, rivers, and valleys in Glacier acquired their monikers.

Lawrence, Tom. *Pictures, a Park, and a Pulitzer: Mel Ruder and the Hungry Horse News.* Helena, MT: Farcountry Press, 2000. Photos and stories from Lawrence, a Pulitzer Prize–winning journalist and editor for 32 years at the *Hungry Horse News*. Much of the history covers Glacier.

NATIVE AMERICANS

Grinnell, George Bird. *Blackfoot Lodge Tales*. Whitefish, MT: Kessinger Publishing, LLC, 2007. Grinnell, who negotiated the purchase of reservation land for the park, chronicles Blackfeet stories from his days in Glacier in the late 1800s.

Schultz, James Willard. *Blackfeet Tales of Glacier National Park*. Helena, MT: Riverbend Publishing, 1916. Original Blackfeet stories collected by Schultz in the late 1800s, including the history of Two Medicine, Cut Bank, St. Mary, Swiftcurrent, and Chief Mountain.

NATURAL HISTORY

DeSanto, Jerry. *Logan Pass: Alpine Splendor*. Guilford, CT: Globe Pequot Press, 1995. Gorgeous photos and short, easy-to-read descriptions of the Logan Pass environment, including grizzly bears, red buses, hiking, climbing, winter, wildflowers, and geology.

Kershaw, Linda, Andy MacKinnon, and Jim Pojar. *Plants of the Rocky Mountains*. Edmonton, AB: Lone Pine Publishing, 1998. A Lone Pine Field Guide for eight types of flora found in the Rocky Mountains: trees, shrubs, wildflowers, aquatics, grasses, ferns, mosses, and lichens. Although the pictures are small, the detailed descriptions of appearance, season, and habitat help in identification. Notes on each of the 1,300 species given include fun tidbits on the origin of names and Native American uses.

Kimball, Shannon Fitzpatrick, and Peter Lesica. *Wildflowers of Glacier National Park and Surrounding Areas*. Kalispell, MT: Trillium Press, 2005. One of the best regional flower guides. Flowers are categorized by color, with

big sharp photos allowing easy identification. Trees, ferns, and grasses are included, too.

Rockwell, David. *Glacier National Park: A Natural History Guide*. New York: Houghton Mifflin Company, 1995. A rather dense with detail but accurate description of Glacier Park's natural history not only on the big scale, but with personal narrative included, too. Rockwell covers geology, glaciers, flora, fauna, fires, and human impact on the ecosystem in the best in-depth natural history book available on the park.

OUTDOOR RECREATION

Arthur, Jean. *Montana Winter Trails: The Best Cross-Country Ski and Snowshoe Trails*. Guilford, CT: Globe Pequot Press, 2001. Trail descriptions include five detailed trips for Glacier and several more for Flathead Valley.

Duckworth, Carolyn, ed. *Hiker's Guide to Glacier National Park* and *Short Hikes and Strolls in Glacier National Park*. West Glacier, MT: Glacier Natural History Association, 1996. Two books covering Glacier only, not Waterton. The hiker's guide contains 110 pages describing popular trails. The short hikes is a 46-page book covering 16 favorite one- to four-mile walks.

Edwards, J. Gordon. *A Climber's Guide to Glacier Park*. Helena, MT: Falcon Press Publishing Co., 1995. The definitive guide to mountaineering in Glacier National Park. Edwards pioneered many of the routes up Glacier's peaks and is considered the park's patron saint of climbing. Routes cover technical climbs and off-trail scrambles.

Good, Stormy R. *Day Hikes Around the Flathead*. Whitefish, MT: Flathead Guidebooks LLC, 2005. A self-published book covering 85 day hikes. Both have maps, route descriptions, distances, and difficulty, with special emphasis on labeling trails as dog friendly or not. Available only through local bookstores and outdoor shops.

Meador, Mike, and Lee Stanley. *Mountain Bike Rides of the Flathead Valley.* Whitefish, MT: self-published, 2005. A 60-page roundup of the Flathead's best fat-tire rides, with maps, directions, and elevation profiles. Available only at Glacier Cyclery in Whitefish.

Molvar, Erik. *Best Easy Day Hikes in Glacier and Waterton Lakes.* Helena, MT: Falcon Press Publishing Co., 2001. A roundup of day hikes in both Glacier and Waterton. At half the size of his hiking guidebook, this focuses only on day hikes, with emphasis on well-signed, less-strenuous trails.

Molvar, Erik. *Hiking Glacier and Waterton Lakes National Parks.* Helena, MT: Falcon Press Publishing Co., 2007. The most definitive trail guide for Glacier and Waterton Parks. Molvar gives detailed trail descriptions, including maps and elevation charts, for all the popular trails inside the parks, as well as less-traveled trails. Routes cover day hikes, overnights, and extended backpacking trips. Hiker safety, campsite details, and fishing information are also included.

Molvar, Erik. *Hiking Montana's Bob Marshall Wilderness.* Helena, MT: Falcon Press Publishing Co., 2001. A detailed trail guide covering the Great Bear, Bob Marshall, and Scapegoat Wilderness Areas. Trail descriptions include maps, elevation charts, and accurate information on how to find even the more difficult to locate trailheads.

Sande, Nathan. *Instant Gratification: Selected One-Day Ski Trips in the Flathead Backcountry.* Kalispell, MT: self-published. A 66-page guide with maps and route descriptions for backcountry telemark and randonee ski trips in the Swan Mountains, Flathead Range, and Glacier Park. Available only at Rocky Mountain Outfitter in Kalispell.

Schneider, Russ. *Fishing Glacier National Park.* Helena, MT: Falcon Press Publishing Co., 2002. The most definitive fishing guide to Glacier. Schneider explains what flies to use to catch certain fish, where you'll catch arctic grayling or westslope cutthroat trout, and where you'll get skunked.

Internet Resources

GLACIER PARK
Glacier National Park
www.nps.gov/glac
The official website for Glacier National Park. It provides information on park conditions, roads, campsites, trails, history, and more. Six webcams update every few minutes. In addition to trip planning information, the site includes downloadable maps, publications, and backcountry permit applications as well as a Going-to-the-Sun Road status report updated daily.

Glacier Natural History Association
www.glacierassociation.org
The best resource for books, maps, posters, and cards on Glacier Park. A portion of the proceeds from book sales are donated back to the park.

Northern Rocky Mountain Research Center
www.nrmrc.usgs.gov
The research center works under the United States Geological Survey. The website contains current research in Glacier on grizzly bears, glaciers, climate change, bighorn sheep, and amphibians.

The Glacier Fund
www.glacierfund.org
As an official nonprofit park partner, The Glacier Fund works with the National Park Foundation to raise money to assist with wildlife research, historic preservation, trails, and education to preserve Glacier's natural and cultural history. It supports what government funds cannot cover.

Glacier Centennial
www.glaciercentennial.org
In 2010, Glacer celebrated its centennial. This site still contains history and useful information.

The Glacier Institute
www.glacierinstitute.org
An educational nonprofit park partner, The Glacier Institute presents programs for kids and adults in field settings taught by expert instructors. Field classes take place in Glacier as well as surrounding ecosystems.

Glacier National Park Associates
www.nps.gov/gla/partners/gnpa.htm
This volunteer nonprofit assists with historic preservation and trail work and is always looking for volunteers to help for a few days on projects.

National Park Service Reservation Center
http://reservations.nps.gov
Two campgrounds in Glacier—Fish Creek and St. Mary—take reservations using this service.

WATERTON PARK
Waterton Lakes National Park
www.pc.gc.ca/waterton
The official website for Waterton. It contains most of the basic park information on camping, hiking, and Parks Canada–operated services, but not the commercial services in Waterton Townsite.

Waterton Lakes National Park Information Guide
www.watertoninfo.ab.ca
Useful park information on boat tours, hiking, bicycling, dining, and lodging. Includes links for many of the commercial services in Waterton Townsite.

National Park Service Reservation Center
www.pccamping.ca
Log on to make reservations at Waterton's Townsite campground and other Canadian national parks.

Waterton Chamber of Commerce
www.watertonchamber.com
This website covers dining, lodging, recreation, visitor services, and camping for Waterton. Some services adjacent to the park are also included.

Waterton Park Information Services
www.watertonpark.com
This website details lodging, dining, services, and recreation, but also includes maps and a great history section.

FLATHEAD VALLEY
Flathead Valley Convention and Visitors Bureau
www.fcvb.org
The Flathead Valley's tourism board covers info on Kalispell, Columbia Falls, Whitefish, Bigfork, Lakeside, Flathead Lake, and ski resorts. You'll find recreation, lodging, dining, and special events.

MONTANA TRAVEL
Glacier Country
www.glaciermt.com
The official state travel website for northwest Montana. You can find lodging, dining, and activity information here, and it's easy to navigate by activity or location.

Montana Travel
www.visitmt.com
The official travel website for Montana. You'll find access to the state's activities, lodging, dining, and recreation by location or activity.

Montana Department of Transportation
www.mdt.mt.gov
Travel advisories and road conditions for Montana. Glacier's interior roads are not yet included on the website; information on Going-to-the-Sun Road is sporadic. Check the park's website for its most accurate information.

Lewis and Clark National Forest
www.fs.fed.us/r1/lewisclark/
Information on campgrounds, trails, fishing, cabin rentals, and other recreation particularly for the Bob Marshall Wilderness.

Flathead National Forest
www.fs.fed.us/r1/flathead
At the official website for Flathead National Forest, you'll find info on campgrounds, fishing, rafting, wilderness areas, cabin rentals, ski areas, trails, and other recreation. However, the recreation section is limited on specifics for trails.

Montana Fish, Wildlife, and Parks
www.fwp.state.mt.us
Up-to-date fishing and hunting information, licenses, state park, and wildlife refuge details for Montana.

CANADIAN TRAVEL
Alberta Travel Guides
www.albertatravel.ca
Heavily funded by Alberta real estate agencies, the site does have some useful travel information if you can wade through the advertising.

Travel Alberta Canada
www.travelalberta.com
The province's official portal to Alberta resorts, parks, ski areas, festivals, events, cities, outdoor recreation, and touring. It's easy to navigate by location or activity to find what you want.

Alberta Travel and Tourism Guide
www.discoveralberta.com
You can access Alberta travel information here, but it all comes in the preformatted package of the WorldWeb network, which is not as easy to navigate or understand as the Travel Alberta website.

Alberta Transportation
www.tu.gov.ab.ca
Check here for postings of Alberta's road construction, advisories, and closures.

British Columbia Transportation
www.gov.bc.ca/tran
Road reports update travel information, closures, construction, and weather for British Columbia. Webcams will give you a firsthand look.

Akamina-Kishinena Provincial Park
www.gov.bc.ca/bcparks
Information on recreation, camping, and hiking in Akamina-Kishinena Provincial Park. Maps and a photo gallery, too.

Fishing Alberta
www.fishalberta.com
Although this is a television-sponsored website rather than an official government site, it is easier to navigate to find current license info, stocked waters, and regulations.

Index

List of Maps

www.moon.com

DESTINATIONS | ACTIVITIES | BLOGS | MAPS | BOOKS

MOON.COM is ready to help plan your next trip! Filled with fresh trip ideas and strategies, author interviews, informative travel blogs, a detailed map library, and descriptions of all the Moon guidebooks, Moon.com is all you need to get out and explore the world—or even places in your own backyard. While at Moon.com, sign up for our monthly e-newsletter for updates on new releases, travel tips, and expert advice from our on-the-go Moon authors. As always, when you travel with Moon, expect an experience that is uncommon and truly unique.

MOON IS ON FACEBOOK—BECOME A FAN!
JOIN THE MOON PHOTO GROUP ON FLICKR